DEMOCRACY AND COMMUNITY

DEMOCRACY AND COMMUNITY

Democracy and Community

A STUDY OF
POLITICS IN SHEFFIELD

William Hampton

London
Oxford University Press
New York · Toronto
1970

Oxford University Press, Ely House, London W. 1

GLASGOW NEW YORK TORONTO MELBOURNE WELLINGTON
CAPE TOWN SALISBURY IBADAN NAIROBI DAR ES SALAAM LUSAKA ADDIS ABABA
BOMBAY CALCUTTA MADRAS KARACHI LAHORE DACCA
KUALA LUMPUR SINGAPORE HONG KONG TOKYO

SBN 19 215321 8

Printed in Great Britain by
The Camelot Press Ltd., London and Southampton

Contents

List of Tables

List of Diagrams

Foreword

MR. HAMPTON has written an important, interesting, and timely
book which, I am sure, will please no one completely. If part of
his theme is the difficulty of blending participation and communication in large-scale organizations, then part of his difficulty is
both that every unit of representative government contains so
many diverse interests, and that informed discussion of these
problems needs to reach so many different audiences. He has
attempted the very difficult task of writing a book that aims, on
the one hand, to be a contribution to knowledge at the highest
academic level and yet, at the same time, to provide a somewhat
rare thing, a reasonably untechnical and straightforward account
for the general reader of the factors that condition the working of
a local political system. There is something for 'political scientists',
but there is also something important and interesting for all those
involved in local politics and administration. Sheffield is the sub-
ject-matter, a large and important city in its own right, and with
many local traditions and with many social conditions significantly different from elsewhere; but if anyone reads it simply as
an account of Sheffield as I hope some will, they will also find that
many of the most basic questions of modern politics are raised.

To write a book on at least three levels at once—as a contribution to the theory of democracy, as a contribution to the debate
on local government reform, and as a contribution to local knowledge for local people—is inevitably to leave some dissatisfied.
Three different books could have been written for three different
audiences. But William Hampton happily is determined to
practise what he teaches: if the democratic element in our government demands a greater awareness about how we do use and should
use general concepts, which both define aims and give coherence
to what we are looking at, and if it also demands a greater

knowledge of how things actually work, then it is important to try to communicate theory and knowledge to the broadest possible public. Any technical vocabulary of 'political science' is best avoided, even though one must be mentally demanding: for the topics *are* difficult, complex, and important. Students of politics can readily demand that politicians and civil servants, nationally and locally, should study how to communicate more effectively with the public, but it is less easy for us to take our own golden advice.

The task is made easier, however, since the author does not confuse the scholarly attempt to be as objective as possible with a purely descriptive and often evasive neutrality. He and I at least share the belief that theory and practice are inseparable. The study of politics is only in degree more complex and less dangerous that the practice of politics. The difference of degree is significant, our priorities are different from those of the politician; we have a duty to say from our head things that are true which we might wish, from our heart, were not true. But the elements in the mixture, the interplay between fact and value, between knowing how things work and trying to know and assert how they might work better, are the same as for the politician—or for the man in the street, for that matter: it is only that the proportions in the mixture differ. The political scientist deceives himself if he thinks he has no values, explicit or implicit; but he is deceiving his readers if he does not attempt to give a true and scientifically accurate account of the variety and proportion of images, values, and interests that the public actually exhibit.

So, to my mind at least, Mr. Hampton's method in this book is admirably eclectic. It is necessary to define what we mean by democracy, and to show that some definitions are more useful and plausible than others. It is necessary to define 'community', to give this term a specific meaning that relates to the experience of ordinary people, neither just to the visions of doctrinaires nor to the vague way in which it is used with sloppy good-will in much of the contemporary discussion of local government reform by officials, publicists, and political leaders. It is necessary to show what are the attitudes to community, local political institutions, and political issues of both the local electorate and councillors: hence the interviews of *every* member of the Sheffield City Council and the especially commissioned sample survey of the electorate.

But to evaluate the results of the survey there must plainly be technical discussion of the assumptions on which it was based and of the validity of the methods—although opinions even then may properly vary as to what follows from the results. It is necessary to discover and set down statistically all the broad social factors that condition (but never determine—we would both agree) a particular politics: population, social class, educational and occupational patterns—but again no single definite conclusion can follow, only a useful narrowing of the range of possible conclusions.

So I hope that this book will appear to students of politics as being admirably old-fashioned but uniquely thorough in the depth and variety of its methods of investigation: part contemporary-history, part analysis of aggregate statistical data, part observer-participation, part structured-interview, and part a survey carefully constructed to allow the maximum of comparison with similar surveys elsewhere—above all with the national sample that the admirable and under-used Social Survey organization of the Government undertook for both the Redcliffe-Maud Commission on Local Government and the Committee on Management in Local Government. I call it 'old-fashioned' in the sense that it lets the problems determine the methods of investigation, and the problems are problems of political or public policy (although they cut right across party lines); this book does not assume for one moment that, for instance, only the measurable is real or scientific. Political scientists have lately come more and more to limit themselves to problems which can be tackled statistically or scientifically (in many senses). Something of this impetus is good. There was once far too much generalization from 'experience' or from out of the back of one's head. Generalizations need to be checked and verified scientifically. But they need to be made. We have an interpretative role to play as well as a descriptive. And what the methods of the American behavioural school have all too often missed or lacked is any sense of relevance, of studying things that are politically important even if this cannot be done solely by questionnaire or mathematical model, but also in the same kind of way, or rather in the many different ways, that the historian has to work. If the matter is important, it has to be studied as a whole and as scientifically as one can; but if it is studied purely scientifically, then only part of the problem will be illuminated—if that is the right word—for authors who see no need, or have given up all hope, of communication outside 'the profession'. There is need to remind ourselves that there is a 'British school' of political studies which has never accepted a clear-cut distinction between theory and practice and which has always been essentially 'problem-centred', as the Americans say. Mr. Hampton is plainly a member of this school, but one willing to use the new methods in conjunction with the old. I think he would be so modest, however, as not to assert too strongly that the world needs political scientists, but far more strongly that political scientists need the world.

My main hope is that this book will interest and will neither bore nor disappoint people involved in local politics. The idea of an objective study of Sheffield politics was not one that we expected would be received with universal enthusiasm by local councillors. There is a natural suspicion of 'us up here' (on a hill, as usual, and overlooking the town, to make matters worse); indeed, some political scientists can be a little optimistic to think that it can be readily accepted that we are 'just studying' local politics when we value our freedom of expression on matters of public policy quite as much as our reputation for being impartial and objective scholars. But we discovered, if not universal enthusiasm for this research work, certainly a general keen and co-operative interest. Politicians are, after all, only human: they like talking about their work to anyone who appears to have no axe to grind of the topical and partisan kind, and who is asking no favours except for such talk and, occasionally, for access to papers or minute books. They are nearly all, as the tables show, worried about the low levels of participation in local politics—usually seen simply as local elections; and so they are interested in suggestions as to how this might be remedied, and are at least open-minded to suggestions that voting as such may not be the most significant index of local democracy. And, without wishing to claim too much, rarely can one read any account of one's own profession or occupation, however bad, without being stirred to some process of reasoning critically about what it is one does, and whether the way one does it is the only possible way. (We in the universities are not, nowadays, unaware of this ourselves.) Those who wish to change nothing, read nothing and isolate themselves from argument or examination deliberately; but those who even read a little are then at least helped in focusing their own ideas. I think this book is a small contribution to civic democracy as well as to political studies.

Sometimes we are too depressed about local politics; largely because we perceive it too narrowly. Only a minority of the electorate may vote (although even here there are radical increases at ward level if people believe that the seats are marginal); but voting is only the most formal kind of participation, and direct political involvement is only one form of participation in civic affairs. If one takes membership of any voluntary organization as a criterion of some degree of participation, then, as Mr. Hampton shows from his and the Social Survey's figures, two-thirds of the Sheffield electorate claim membership of at least one organization; and 14 per cent (the same as the national figure) claim to be either officials or committee members. So there are in a town of the size of Sheffield between twenty and thirty thousand people holding some position in some voluntary organization—most of which, however spasmodically, do have some contact with the local authorities or local services. Mr. Hampton suggests that 'the frequent allegations that local citizens are completely uninterested in local affairs should be treated with some caution'. Many of his Tables are very revealing on that score. 'The number of people,' he says, 'who are well informed about local affairs, or who are interested in taking an active part in their determination, remains a minority, but a larger minority than is often assumed.' While it is true that only four out of every ten of those interviewed could name their M.P. correctly and say what party he belonged to, I share with Mr. Hampton a feeling that this is less important than, and certainly made less depressing by, the surprisingly large network of group affiliations which do exist.

These group affiliations may well be the future building-blocks of a heightened local democracy more than the electoral wards and the constituencies. Certainly one thing is clear from the analysis: that electoral boundaries do not correspond with what people perceive to be communities, nor does there seem to be any evidence to suggest that ward boundaries can create a community— in the broad sense that arbitrary lines drawn across the desert or through the jungle have, in fact, defined the boundaries of national cultures.

B

The ward and the constituency are convenient methods of electing people to form or control governments; but in no real sense are these people 'representative' of anything that is ordinarily a group or community for any other purpose than elections. Thus when local councillors and others worry about 'losing touch with the grass-roots' under schemes for local government reform involving larger areas, or fear that 'the intimacy' will be lost, they are, alas, describing a myth or an ideal rather than a practice. And they are not merely deceiving themselves but are deceived about themselves, in this respect. Mr. Hampton shows conclusively that 'The majority of councillors are not community leaders who emerge from the wards they represent; they are people interested in public affairs who seek an opportunity to represent their fellow citizens wherever it may conveniently be found.' Personally, I do not find this worrying or surprising. There is nothing that will be lost in 'community consciousness' if units are larger, so as to be more efficient, and larger units could be more effective democratically in that it will then be easier for people to comprehend who is responsible for what service. This book shows that such comprehension is low, and it is reasonable to assume that the variety of authorities and the overlapping areas of public services bewilder people. The optimum size of a unit to achieve direct democratic participation may need to be far smaller, and to vary more greatly, than the optimum size to achieve effective democratic control and communication.

Mr. Hampton's researches show, however, that there is a valid sense of community which could readily involve more participation, but on a far smaller level than the County Boroughs. Such communities can only be defined empirically, by social surveys which discover what are the local perceptions of community and by seeing what unofficial groups people do in fact form in their neighbourhoods: they vary greatly in size and shape and do not fit into any of the existing political, administrative, or legal categories. The fifth chapter, on 'Perceptions of Community', is, to my mind, the key to the importance of this book. The evidence points clearly to the fact that units of local government need to be both much larger than at present, but also much smaller. Broadly speaking, the conclusions of this study in depth of one large County Borough support the Redcliffe-Maud argument for far larger areas with a far greater integration of control of local services;

meaningful decisions can then be made in a meaningful manner
much more likely to enhance the communication factor in democracy, which is always to be seen as equally important to the direct
participation factor. But these same conclusions are a formidable
criticism of the vagueness of the Commission's report on the proposed new and small representative bodies whose function is to be
simply representative and expressive, rather than decision-making
and managerial. There is a possibility that this part of the Report, instead of being extended and thought through, could get
lost in a political compromise which would simply leave most of
the existing structure to fulfil a new and as yet ill-defined function. But these present areas are too large. 'Neighbourhood councils' must be defined in terms of genuine neighbourhoods—the
areas where people feel that they are 'at home'. If there is to be a
greater participative local democracy, it will be on the scale and
level of a 'commune' or neighbourhood council, not of a city,
seldom even of a ward.

An entirely new kind of local institution may be needed—
as Mr. Hampton suggests in his last chapter. And he plainly has
not written his last word on this. He does not believe that a 'merely
expressive' function is unimportant; such bodies are important in
the way that any pressure group representing a genuine interest
can be important; and these have been left out of the standard
accounts of local government and local politics. They will have
less to do with the existing formal structure of electoral areas
than with the kind of units which would be the relevant subject-
matter of 'community development' work—as this becomes a
way of supplementing the existing social and local government
services and of linking the role of voluntary groups with that of
the statutory and professional services. In this light the penulti-
mate chapter of this book, 'The Big Issue', is especially interesting
for its account of the role of tenants' associations in the Rent
Rebates dispute which cut across so many accepted party loyalties
and showed the inadequacy of so many established administrative
procedures. And the particular tale (in the final chapter) of the
subsequent involvement of one of our research workers (strictly
without my knowledge or permission!) in organizing a local residents' association, and the immediate political response it gained,
is far from self-indulgence on Mr. Hampton's part, but has a
moral of general significance to show the extended areas of

possibility in local government and democracy. Local councillors cannot have it both ways: if they want more participation, they must take it in what forms it comes; and in Sheffield they were sensible enough to take it.

But we need to know accurately what people want, particularly in their housing needs or their tolerance of housing that is technically sub-standard but is acceptable to them, even in terms of splendid alternatives (and the Sheffield housing record has been good and most of its planning imaginative), because of other values, such as 'community' and neighbourhood. Redoing houses, it begins to be realized, can often do more for the lives of people than total redevelopment and rehousing. But such people are rarely organized to express their viewpoints. These need to be found out. The Skeffington Committee's proposals to plan openly and to consult at every stage in planning proposals could go very far, but someone must take steps to see either that local people do come forward or that their views are ascertained, not just those of the Civic Trust and the Council for the Preservation of Rural England. And these views are more likely to be ascertained accurately by surveys than by intuition and the necessarily rather casual and fortuitous soundings of councillors. Both are needed. The decisions have to be made; politicians and administrators have to weigh the various factors in the equations; government and politics are not to be surrendered to opinion surveys; but such surveys have their place and their role. The future will need new kinds of local government services and new kinds of local government officers, some of whom, like the various inspectorates, will have to have a primary loyalty to their function rather than to the political majority on the councils. Community development officers will be needed whose functions and rights should be defined by statute or statutory instruments; and if some councils are now aware of the need for P.R.O.s or publicity officers, none seems to realize that this should be a two-way function: someone should have the duty and the professional competence to ascertain public opinion (or information from the public) on relevant local issues. These duties could never and should never take away the essential role of political representation: they should supplement, complement, and help it; but they need to be done.

Certainly Mr. Hampton's researches have shown significant

differences between what councillors perceive to be issues and what the ordinary electorate think. Take the issue of housing. The tables on pp. 207–10 show clearly that while councillors mention housing as an issue more than any other, the electorate attach a slightly greater importance to roads and traffic, which comes only sixth on the councillors' scale of importance. Talk of the sudden discovery of 'environment' as a political and social problem! It would appear that 'the misery of travel' and the 'getting to work question' loom at least as large as housing in an urban environment—even one like Sheffield in which most people live relatively close to their work. The councillors plainly get a significantly distorted impression of people's priorities through the ordinary channels. Perhaps they are only approached on critical problems, like getting a house or getting repairs done for a council tenant, but not on chronic problems, like transport or general environment. These are problems just as great; but are problems, one must add, that fall into a difficult gap of responsibility between local and national authorities, and problems which few people have tried to relate to the democratic rather than the administrative process. And one could add that comprehensive education was mentioned second as an issue by councillors (Table 8.12), but only came sixth with the electorate.

Local government does not know enough, simply by virtue of the electoral process, of what people really want. That is sufficient excuse for a study such as this. But equally, social scientists have not applied sufficiently their techniques of study to problems of public importance; the study of politics is not something remote from the political process, it must be part of it. And it is not dull or unimaginative to study one's own back-yard, particularly if this happens to be an important city, with great local traditions, with an intelligent political leadership but also with rapidly changing problems: it is only dull and unimaginative if the studies are made in a dull and unimaginative manner. Few localities do not have local histories written about them—which people politely say help to heighten civic consciousness; few major authorities should be without some study of their politics—also a part of civic consciousness. If, once again, some parts of this book seem unduly abstract and bore some politicians, and other parts seem, to some political scientists, too close to practical problems and insufficiently generalized, that is the price that Mr. Hampton has willingly paid (and which I have eagerly aided and abetted) for a blending of description and prescription which may properly lay claim to be in the very best tradition of British political studies.

BERNARD CRICK

Acknowledgements

LOCAL research incurs many debts, but brings many benefits. During the four years I spent on this study I was received with courtesy by busy people from many organizations in Sheffield and by members of the general public; many people spent hours with members of the research team; today I feel very much a part of the community I studied. My first thanks go, therefore, to the people of Sheffield who responded to the random survey, and by their anonymous help contributed a vital part of the work. My appreciation of the assistance given by the aldermen and councillors of Sheffield City Council can be more personal and I have listed the council membership in Appendix D. Every member of the council agreed to be interviewed and I am very grateful for their assistance. Many council members contributed far more than a single interview—I was never turned away—but to attempt individual acknowledgement would be invidious. I will let the following be representative of my general appreciation: Alderman Sir Ronald Ironmonger[1] and Alderman H. Hebblethwaite, leaders of the Labour and Conservative groups respectively, whose initial co-operation smoothed my way; and Mr. V. Thornes and Mr. G. E. A. Beardshaw, secretary of the Trades and Labour Council and Chief Conservative agent respectively, who constantly answered queries. The six Sheffield Members of Parliament also agreed to be interviewed, as did leaders of several local organizations; I am grateful to them all. The officers and staff of the corporation were very helpful, and I wish to thank especially Miss Mary Walton and her staff at the local history section of the Sheffield City Library.

My theoretical preoccupations in this work began from a time

---

[1] Referred to as Alderman C. R. Ironmonger in the text, which discusses the period before Sir Ronald received his knighthood in January 1970.

when I was registered as an external Ph.D. candidate at London University, but Professor Crick persuaded me both to expand my work and to incorporate it in a broader and more empirical study of Sheffield politics. I am, therefore, submitting my share of this work for the degree of Ph.D. in the University of Sheffield as a staff candidate.

The empirical research for this study was made possible by a grant from the Social Science Research Council to Professor Crick who invited me to direct the research—and I am grateful to Professor Maurice Bruce, Director of Extramural Studies, whose support enabled me to accept. I should add that Professor Crick was active in conducting a seminar at the beginning of the study, both to define our objects and to try out our ideas on some local political leaders.

Research of this kind is necessarily a team activity in which the thoughts and skills of many people blend together. James Clark and Miss Valerie Greenwood were research assistants for six months at the early stage of the compilation of background material. Mrs. Patricia Chandler and Geoffrey Green were with the project in the second year and performed the difficult task of interviewing between them every member of the Sheffield City Council. They worked on every stage of the design and analysis of this part of the research—and did much else besides, with great energy and intelligence. Miss Hazel Kendrick (now Mrs. Harris) spent a long vacation analysing aggregate data. Throughout the project Mrs. Iris Walkland made herself invaluable by her versatility and loyalty: she managed at various times to occupy herself with press cuttings, as secretary, and with editorial work on our publications—all with equal cheerfulness. The random survey was conducted by Research Services Ltd. under the very able and helpful direction of Mr. G. Levins. Each of the above will recognize his or her contribution to the following pages, but none necessarily agrees with the use I have made of it. Mrs. Susan Clarke and Miss Susan Fell gave competent secretarial assistance in a pleasant manner.

My wife, Hazel Hampton, has read every sentence of what follows, and has made a major contribution to its style. I am also sincerely grateful for her forbearance during the last few over-busy years.

After such acknowledgements it is necessary, as usual, to

emphasize that I am solely responsible for what follows—both facts
and opinions, no one else should be blamed.

Department of Extramural Studies   W. A. H.
University of Sheffield
June 1970

I

Introduction: Community and Democracy

The local administration of public services is essential; that the local organs of administration should be democratically elected bodies is not.
Management of Local Government, I, Report, p. 68

'DEMOCRACY' and 'community' are frequently invoked to support widely differing opinions. The two concepts are so interwoven that the interest is scarcely surprising, but the variety of interpretation is the cause of much confusion in the current discussion of local government. Every urban area is claimed as a natural community entitled to independence from the artifacts of government commissions, and every country area denies affinity with its neighbouring city. The ideal of a local community managing its own affairs through a popularly elected assembly is pursued despite the difficulties that arise from a great variation in size and financial resources.

The implications of our findings for local government reform are drawn together in the final chapter, but they have an interest beyond the immediate debate: most of the problems that intrigue political scientists are present in local government. It is necessary, therefore, to be selective if a study is to achieve coherence, and we are primarily concerned with the workings of local democracy in a major English city.[1]

The secondary theme is the association between community feeling and political activity. We have considered whether a concern for community affairs is transferred to an interest in local politics, and whether a reformed system of local administration could enlist the enthusiasm that is released by many voluntary

---

[1] The relationship between the American studies of local politics and studies such as this is discussed by K. Newton in 'City Politics in Britain and the United States', *Political Studies,* XVII, 2 (June 1969).

organizations. Community is treated on two levels: first, comparison between the character of Sheffield as a community and a number of other large county boroughs—a comparative study of the politics of major English cities must wait upon further research; secondly, the citizens' conception of their home area in relation to political involvement.

Generalizations about local government are difficult to sustain. There are over 1,200 local authorities in England, varying in size from districts with fewer than 5,000 population to counties and county boroughs with over a million. Information obtained from the study of one of these authorities is not easily transferable, and indeed it may be inaccurate for its own area within a short time. Nevertheless, with these limitations in mind, comparisons have been made between Sheffield and studies conducted in other areas, and with the general figures collected for government enquiries. Local studies add flesh and blood to the statistical bones of the national averages, and they can introduce a political dimension frequently avoided by official committees. The study of politics in Sheffield presents, in other words, empirical material to illustrate the abstract ideas discussed in this introductory chapter.

The City of Sheffield is large in population and financial resources, well-defined in its area, unified in its political control, and wide in its range of functions. Such an authority would appear ideally suited to fulfil the role which many theorists—including in the nineteenth century J. S. Mill and Tocqueville—advocated for local government in a pluralistic democracy. In the first place they argued that strong local authorities disperse the power of the centralized state. A system will be created where power is dispersed over many—or a plurality—of institutions, allowing none of them to become strong enough to threaten the basic liberty of the individual. Secondly, they suggested that democracy will be encouraged when the unit of government is based upon a local community. The ideal of the Greek city state—in which the idea of democracy originated—remains a powerful influence on our thinking. The citizen, we are taught to believe, may find the affairs of a modern state too large and complex for his comprehension, but he will naturally participate with his neighbours in managing local community responsibilities.

These expectations of dispersion of power and citizen involvement are obviously idealistic, but not necessarily the worse for that. Ideals give a meaning to life which is denied to the cynics and the quiescent. Ideals lead us astray, however, if they cause us to close our eyes to evidence that could disprove our policies. Many arguments in favour of the present local government system in England are presented in the terms outlined above; and many of those who argue in this way ignore the fact that local authorities in England are neither as independent as a pluralistic system would require, nor as attractive to citizen involvement as the theory would lead one to expect. The central government exercises considerable control over the policies of the local councils, and the public shows a disconcerting lack of enthusiasm for the activities of its local councillors.

Although few people have much knowledge of their local government, or show much interest in local politics, there remains a considerable reserve of local patriotism. An attachment to long-established place-names, which only serves to confuse discussions about local government reform, is one expression of such patriotism. The confusion arises because the general population, *and* many of the reformers, assume some necessary connection between the description of their home area given by the inhabitants, and the area best suited for local government purposes. It will be shown in a subsequent chapter that the descriptions that come most readily to our lips are the names of villages that have long disappeared—or counties that have long lost their relevance[2]—rather than existing local government areas. The people of Sheffield for example, regard themselves as belonging to Tinsley or Nether Edge and seldom mention the city as a whole in a description of the area in which they feel at home. This should not, however, be construed as an argument in favour of minute local authorities. There are purposes for which local community councils might be very usefully created, but they could neither accept the functions entrusted to the present major authorities, nor the extension of those functions which might be envisaged following boundary reform.

In England and Wales in recent years there have been numerous proposals for local boundary changes which would lead to larger local authorities. Many of these suggestions were clearly necessary on administrative grounds, but whenever they involved the

[2] I have discussed this point in an article entitled 'The County as a Political Unit', *Parliamentary Affairs*, XIX, 4 (Autumn 1966).

disappearance of an existing unit of local government, whether
parish, rural district, or municipal borough, there was immediate
and widespread protest. When it was possible to support this protest
with the name of a medieval town or county the outcry often
reached ludicrous proportions. During the campaign to resist the
absorption of Rutland by Leicestershire, for example, there were
allegations of 'government tyranny' and 'totalitarianism'. These
cries ignored the fact that a more effective unit of local government could have *extended* the range of local responsibility; and
that inhabitants of Rutland either lacked many important local
services, or were parasitic upon other counties. In Derbyshire
much bitterness was caused by the extension of the boundaries of
Sheffield and Derby to include contiguous built-up areas and
areas wanted for over-spill development. The extensions were
resisted for twenty years, and implemented against mass protests
culminating in a lobby of Parliament involving 600 unusually
aroused Derbyshire residents. There was strong feeling that, as
one man from Mosborough expressed it, 'villages should have
their own individuality. They shouldn't be allowed to be taken
over.'

Changes in local boundaries usually mean higher rates—in
return for wider services—so that cynics may claim that protests
are more closely related to pennies in the pound than to names on
the map, but this does not seem to be entirely correct. There is
still strong local support for what was described in 1903 as a
'system built on history and consecrated by custom',[3] which finds
expression in the attitude of one local authority to another, even
when both are controlled by the same political party. In one
mining area close to Sheffield councillors—and others interested
enough to attend an adult education class—complained about the
expansionist policy of a neighbouring small town; it was suggested
that 'they cannot understand our problems' although the two
urban districts, both Labour-controlled, were only separated by a
ridge of moorland. With the next breath came complaints of
existing local apathy, but with no suggestion that this second
complaint removed much of the urgency from the first. Indeed it
is probably true that the local electorate would object to absorption in a larger unit, particularly if a good local campaign was
launched, and it is almost certain that they would know little

[3] J. Redlich and F. W. Hirst, *Local Government in England*, Vol. II, p. 7.

about the responsibilities of the local authority they were defending. There appears, therefore, to be a contradiction between the
expressed attitudes and the observed actions of people in respect of
local self-government. In our romantic moments we look back to
a golden age of village Hampdens defending their rights, but when
we consider the day-to-day work of existing local authorities our
view becomes more prosaic.

A re-assessment of our local democracy becomes necessary as the
government adds to its social and economic responsibilities. The
scale of local responsibilities has increased and, perhaps even more
important, the government needs an expansion of local administration which it is reluctant to entrust to existing local authorities.
During the past twenty years the government produced several
reports from committees and commissions constituted to examine
aspects of local government reform, but few of these received an
enthusiastic welcome. Many of the recommendations from commissions on local government boundaries have not been implemented. One major exception, the reorganization of London's
local government, was carried through over sustained opposition
both in London and from the surrounding areas. In the House of
Commons there were angry exchanges between the government
and opposition benches amid frequent accusations of gerry-
mandering. Labour spokesmen alleged vehemently that the sole
reason for the reform was to end their party's control of the London
County Council. But this complaint fell rather flat when the
Labour Party won the subsequent elections to become the largest
group on the newly constituted Greater London Council.

In view of the complexity of the problems surrounding reorganization this lack of progress or agreement is not altogether surprising. The reformers are attempting to reconcile democracy,
efficiency, and local sentiment: it cannot be easy. The efficiency of
an administration, for example, will obviously depend upon the
function it is allocated. What, in other words, do we want it to do?
If local administration is to be concerned simply with supervising
decisions taken elsewhere, then units may be large and adjusted
only to technical considerations. Even then the size of the area
would not be easy to determine for the following reasons. First, a
return to *ad hoc* authorities for each service, each with a different
area, would mitigate against the interlocking decision-making
which is necessary if social action is to be properly planned. The

area chosen must, therefore, be a common denominator which suits no services exactly, even if devolution rather than decentralization of decision-making is the sole criterion. Secondly, the need to take account of the people affected by the services may well result in an area different in size from that obtained when purely technical factors are considered. This second point will be strengthened if it is believed that in a democracy the government should pursue—however broadly—the policy the electorate want. Institutions must then be provided to obtain the views of the public. Local authorities may be expected, in part, to fulfil this role, but if a suitable area for representative purposes differs from that most appropriate on technical grounds, then a further complication arises.

The creation of institutions appropriate to a modern industrial democracy is not an easy matter. We have to decide how far it is necessary, or indeed desirable, for representatives to carry out the wishes of the majority. This is not a straightforward decision to make. There must be an element of leadership in effective government, and there are occasions when the views of the majority may injure a minority in a manner that is inconsistent with a general understanding of democracy. The modern usage of the word democracy is itself remarkably imprecise. Since so much prestige is given to the idea of 'government by the people', it becomes incumbent upon politicians to attach the concept to the most unlikely regimes for which they are canvassing support, and the descriptive value of the adjective 'democratic' is correspondingly reduced. Democracy remains, however, the concept by which the layman understands his system of government, and a few words of explanation are desirable.

In addition to the general idea of 'government by the people', most of the electorate consider that the concept of democracy includes ideas of freedom, whether to express opposition views or more generally from the fear of government by force.[4] The idea of government by the people is, of course, no easier to handle than the word democracy itself. 'The people' cannot govern a large industrial society in any meaningful sense: the issues are too complex and the number of citizens too great. The definition is, therefore, usually limited to a view that the people should have the ultimate

---

[4] *Management of Local Government* (Maud Report), III, *The Local Government Elector*, p. 66.

sanction of dismissing a government with whose policy they disagree, and—with less assurance—that those affected by decisions
of the government should have some opportunity of making their
views known. All of which is not very exciting. It can come close
to saying that a democracy is based on the consent of the people,
and it is easy to show that in a broad sense no government *can*
exist without the consent, or at least the passive acquiescence, of
the majority of its citizens. A modern dictatorship is a group
activity, as is shown by the development of the totalitarian party;
and a modern parliamentary government is subject to a considerable degree of personal rule, as is shown by the importance of the
British prime minister. It is not possible, in other words, to interpret modern systems of government in the terms of classical Greek
views of democracy, or of Rousseau's view of democracy as the
continuing rule of the entire people.

In this study we shall not be concerned with democracy in any
pure form, for such does not, and cannot, exist. Governments,
both national and local, are made by man, and as such are only
too fallible. We shall be interested in the extent to which local
people have the opportunity to know of the decisions being taken
on their behalf, and the advantage they take of such opportunities.
We shall also be interested to discover how far those matters that
councillors consider to be important coincide with those that
concern the electorate. For if there is little rapport between what
the electorate think and what the council does, then clearly there
is a small content of popular control in our practice of local
democracy. It is a fact—unfortunate perhaps, but true—that most
people only seek to influence a decision *after* it begins to affect
them adversely. This may, in part, be due to the lack of information to which we have already referred. The complex by-laws
achieve a solid meaning only when they prevent the parking of a
car, or the construction of a pigeon-loft. We have, therefore, tried
to discover those actions of the council which cause people to complain, together with the views of the complainants on the treatment
they receive.

The mundane view of the workings of democracy which is
contained in the previous paragraph is scarcely the language of
social revolution, but even so it implies a wider view of democracy
than is taken by those who maintain that the sole right of a democratic population is to elect a government periodically. It is

c

considered here that in a democracy the people should be encouraged to take a continuing interest in matters of public concern.
We assume that people *ought* to be interested in their own government, if not for the good of their souls then at least for the good of
their social consciousness.

First, the self-confidence which accompanies some degree of
participation in the political process is of great importance in
enabling an individual to express his potentiality. We do not
intend to suggest that every citizen must be a politician. We were
reminded some years ago that politicians are not ranked with
poets or philosophers[5]—though in a democracy it is arguable that
they should be, for we certainly need men of similar calibre if not
of the same interests—but even if most of us do not choose to act
politically, we will still be the better for knowing that we might. If
'they' make all the decisions while the general population are
impotent, and feel themselves to be impotent, in matters of public
policy, then each person will be restricted, inhibited, in the full
development of his personality. Opportunities that do occur will
then be refused for fear of rejection or failure. It must be emphasized
that this becomes more than a withdrawal—or non-involvement
—in political action. Society, for people who lack confidence,
becomes dominated by those who may humiliate by their ability
in self-expression and their access to social power. The resulting
want of assurance extends into every aspect of life. In part the
answer to this debilitating lack of confidence is a concern of
education; in part the cure is dependent upon major changes in
the social structure; but in part, too, the condition itself is a
response to the lack of accessibility of government institutions.

Secondly, an increase in public interest, and awareness of public
decisions, could be advantageous to the government as well as to
those they govern. It may be contended that support for a democratic system will only be induced by participation in free institutions. The next step from apathy is often alienation rather than
acceptance, and that climate of opinion can lead to the adoption
of more violent methods of settling social disputes. It is true that a
government may encourage participation by the electorate without having any intention of encouraging freedom or individuality.
When the consent of the people is needed, then participation by
slogan and indoctrination is one method by which it may be

---

[5] W. H. Morris Jones, 'In Defence of Political Apathy', *Political Studies*, 2 (1954).

obtained. The citizen who withdraws is a threat to the system which seeks to involve him, whether that system be authoritarian or 'Western democratic'. In this study of Sheffield we are, however, deliberately parochial. We are concerned when we write of democracy with societies where men are free rather than those where they are 'forced to be free': whether such states are known by the name of democracy, republican government, or the good Greek polity, is surely not important for our purpose.

The view of democracy outlined above includes a measure both of pluralism and of popular participation. It includes, too, an insistence on the necessity for open government. The people must be informed of the decisions to be taken, and given access to information relevant to the issues being considered, otherwise democratic institutions will remain remote from any possibility of popular involvement. Good communications will not resolve real differences of opinion, but the free flow of information is a necessary condition of the rational discussion which forms the basis of democratic politics. The holders of such views as these have traditionally emphasized the importance of local government. From Tocqueville to Hayek the liberal opponents of state omnipotence have stressed that 'nowhere has democracy ever worked well without a great measure of local self-government'.[6] This view was advanced in the belief that local authorities would provide both a check on the activities of the central government, and an opportunity for local people to participate in the determination of local affairs. Unfortunately for the theory the existing local authorities are not fulfilling these high expectations.

Local authorities in England and Wales have wide responsibilities: they spend over £5,000 million each year; and they employ nearly two million people.[7] In spite of this the influence of local authorities on major public policy is no different from that exercised by other large pressure groups, and the policy pursued by a local authority is always subject to supervision by the central government either through the system of inspection or through the government's control of the purse strings. Of course major local authorities remain very important—as do other powerful pressure groups. There is a wide distinction between local services which are well administered and those which are not. There are variations

[6] F. A. Hayek, *The Road to Serfdom*, p. 174.
[7] Royal Commission on Local Government in England, 1966–9, I, *Report*, para. 33.

in the implementation of national policy which remain open
to local choice. As a recent leader of the Sheffield City Council
has suggested it is important to the local electorate to decide 'who
determines rents, rates, bus fares, types of schools, the rate of house
building, and the rate of slum clearance',[8] but these decisions are
largely concerned with the operation of policy within central
government directives. A recent example was the instruction to
local authorities to prepare plans for the introduction of comprehensive education. In areas where local councillors objected to this
policy it was possible for them to drag their feet in the preparation
of the plans, but ultimately the central government had powerful
sanctions to ensure compliance. The central government does not
treat local authorities with anywhere near the respect usually
expected by independently elected bodies, and this becomes very
clear to local councillors. Over half (55 per cent) of the councillors
from county boroughs and county councils who were interviewed
for the Committee on the Management of Local Government
thought that the central government put unnecessary limitations
on the freedom of their councils.[9]

The central government controls a major local authority like the
Sheffield City Council in several ways. First, the government
provides grants which constitute a major part of the authority's
income and may restrain the total expenditure of the council,
unless the local people are willing to increase the rate demand on
the occupiers of local property. Such action is never popular,
although it will be suggested in a later chapter that its electoral
effect may sometimes be exaggerated. The government exercises
more detailed control by insisting that its approval be sought
before any money is borrowed for capital projects, and by maintaining inspectors who visit the localities to check on the standards
in major services. Many of the Sheffield councillors interviewed
thought central control was too stringent. They instanced such
minor matters as the siting of traffic lights which needed to be
submitted to a minister before action could be taken. One
councillor complained: 'They tell us exactly how the money
should be spent even though they give a block grant.' There was
a general feeling, in line with the recommendations of the Maud

---

[8] *The Star* (Sheffield), 10 April 1968.
[9] *Management of Local Government*, II, *The Local Government Councillor*, p. 158. This
publication will hereafter be referred to in footnotes as *M.L.G.*

Committee,[10] that local authorities should be allowed far more initiative to introduce policies beneficial to their locality. The local councillors would, of course, have to answer to the electorate at a subsequent election if their policies were considered to be too extravagant or too penny-pinching.

The reasons for close central government control over local democracy are fairly clear. Local authorities are responsible for spending some one-sixth of the Gross National Product. It is not possible for any government concerned with economic planning to ignore such an important part of the country's demand for goods and services. Several Sheffield councillors drew attention to the increased control which the Labour government had introduced during the period of financial crisis. But the requirements of macro-economics may be met by global targets or restrictions. It would be entirely consistent with the needs of government planning to allocate a proportion of the nation's resources to local authorities and to allow considerable freedom in the use of these resources. Economic arguments are not, however, the only reasons for central government control over local authorities. Another reason derives from the conflict between advocating equality of provision for services throughout the country, while at the same time suggesting that more local initiative and discretion should be allowed. If local people are to increase their control over their own affairs, then obviously some local authorities will do it better than others. For many years in Wales, for example, the proportion of each age-group who went to grammar school was twice the proportion who received such education in some areas in the north of England. Local initiative, then, means that in some areas children will receive a better education than in other parts of the country, and that some local authorities will build more houses, provide more cultural facilities, repair more roads, employ more social workers, than poorer or less interested authorities. Local democracy in the sense of the right to control local policies, may conflict with the wider view of democracy which insists that people are entitled to equality of opportunity and service wherever they happen to live. But if we insist on close control to ensure that no one in Britain suffers unduly from an inefficient local council, then we are also likely to restrain the more active local authorities from pursuing some of the policies which they think would benefit the local community.

[10] *M.L.G.*, I, *Report*, pp. 78–80.

A balance between local initiative and national equality must obviously be kept, but it is not easy to define.

The functions which it is appropriate to allocate to local authorities have always been a matter of dispute. In recent years many traditional local services have been taken over by statutory bodies responsible, either directly or indirectly, to a minister of the central government. Since 1934, for example, the local obligation for the relief of poverty—a very ancient community responsibility —has been absorbed in the national welfare provisions now administered by the Ministry of Social Security. In 1936 the Ministry of Transport began to undertake responsibility for trunk roads and the importance of the national, as opposed to local, initiative in this field has continued ever since. In the post-1945 years local authorities lost their hospitals to the National Health Service and their gas and electricity undertakings to the nationalized boards. Of course some of the services administered by local authorities have expanded rapidly during these years, notably education and the provision of housing, but even here the tight control exercised from Whitehall has been a dominating influence.

The creation of new institutions intended to promote economic growth could accentuate this movement away from the local authorities. The Regional Economic Planning Councils are appointed by the minister and do not depend in any way on the local electorate for their position. It is not being suggested that economic planning can be an appropriate function of local authorities; these decisions can only be taken on the basis of a national rather than a local or sectional policy. Nevertheless any growth in the real power of the Regional Economic Planning Councils over the social and economic affairs of their region could only come in competition with local authorities. The growth of industry involves policy decisions on housing, highways, education, and welfare provision, to say nothing of town and traffic planning, that are the staple of local government. The influence local authorities have on these matters may be judged from the fact that the Regional Economic Planning Councils themselves have complained loudly that they are ignored when major decisions are taken. The Economic Development Councils for particular industries ('little Neddys') may also consider policies affecting localities where these industries are concentrated. Local authorities are not represented on these committees: the public voice is heard entirely through the muted tones of civil servants from the appropriate ministries.

The failure to utilize the structure of local government in the expansion of economic and social responsibilities would be more worrying if there was a high level of interest in its activities. If local authorities were a lively expression of local community feeling, then we might accept the varying standards that are a natural consequence of the local freedom which allows people to learn from their mistakes—or simply to have a different view of priorities from the government. But this is not the case. Fewer than half the electorate bother to vote in local elections. A quarter of the respondents to the Maud survey were unable to name a single service provided by their borough or district council, and this proportion increased to a half in respect of services provided by county councils, in spite of the fact that these include education.[11] The low level of interest in local government among the general population makes it difficult to maintain that the mass electorate is really benefiting by participating in local affairs. However sincerely we believe that everyone would gain by becoming a part of the local political community, it is quite clear that the overwhelming majority do not wish to take part in the existing structure. There is no doubt that many of the 45,000 local councillors—perhaps double that number if parish councillors are included—find great satisfaction in their voluntary work. The experience they gain may also be a useful asset in public administration and an important element in community leadership, but even if their active supporters are included they can scarcely amount to more than one or two per cent of the electorate. This is far removed from the active citizenship that nineteenth-century liberals felt to be so important.

The apathy shown by the general public towards local government may be underlined by looking at the position in Sheffield which has a record of exceptionally low polls in local elections.[12] Until ward reorganization in 1967 the local election poll in Sheffield seldom reached 30 per cent, while in some wards it fell to 10 per cent. The elector who votes is showing, of course, a minimal interest in public affairs. It is more significant of the lack of

---

[11] *M.L.G.*, III, *The Local Government Elector*, p. 8.

[12] On the other side it may be mentioned that over one-half of the *county* councillors in England and Wales elected in 1964 were returned unopposed.

enthusiasm for local government that both major parties have experienced difficulty in obtaining candidates for local office. In Sheffield in 1967, when all the eighty-one council seats were vacant, neither major party put forward a full list of candidates. When the Labour Party came to select their last twelve candidates only three people were left on the list and the ward members present considered two of these unsuitable. From the Conservative side one candidate stood because 'a mate of mine was standing . . . and we thought that it would be a jolly good lark. We thought we didn't stand a chance of getting in.' This 'pessimism' was unjustified. The election resulted in a considerable turnover of councillors —thirty-four were elected for the first time—and several of the newcomers resigned the following year. They were surprised by the result and reluctant to accept their success. Nor is this difficulty in obtaining candidates restricted to exceptional elections. In the following year one ward Labour Party, albeit in a strong Conservative area, had three selection meetings before they found a candidate.

An explanation for the relatively low proportion of the electorate who vote in Sheffield local elections is part of the general discussion of the electorate to be found in later chapters, but it may be summarized here as follows. First, the city is predominantly working-class in social composition, much more so than the national average or than many other large cities; secondly, the social groups are rigorously segregated in different areas of the city. Working-class people use their votes less frequently than their middle-class fellow citizens,[13] so that we would expect a working-class city such as Sheffield to show a low percentage poll. This tendency is accentuated by the distribution of social classes in the city which leads to the creation of wards almost certain to return councillors of the same party year after year. Marginal seats have been rare in Sheffield and the incentive to vote has been weakened through the tendency of the electorate to view the contest as a walkover. Several Sheffield people told our interviewers that they did not vote either because their party always succeeded or because it did not. This position is now changing. Boundary alterations before the 1967 elections increased the number of marginal seats. It is interesting that in the 1967 local elections

[13] This has been shown in a number of voting studies, some of which are summarized in S. M. Lipset, *Political Man*, Ch. 6.

there was a considerable increase in the poll compared with previous years—though the city remained well below the national average. This may have been due in part to the complete renewal of the council, or even to the national anti-Labour feeling that existed at the time, but as the balance of power in the council becomes marginal we may expect the overall poll to increase.

The explanation of the relatively low polls in Sheffield does little, however, to explain the lack of interest in the *activities* of the council, or the dearth of potential candidates. It is sometimes suggested that people are not interested because the city council has insufficient power, but this argument is difficult to sustain. The detailed control by the central government may deter a few potential councillors, but the majority of the electorate are unaware of the services provided by the council and are unlikely, therefore, to know the degree of power the council enjoys in administering these services. We must look elsewhere for the explanation of the general apathy which is shown towards local government.

We may be asking the wrong question. Instead of asking why people are not interested in their local authority we should consider why we expect them to show interest. The usual response will be that people are bound to be interested in matters directly affecting them, particularly when they are affected as part of a local group whose attitudes reinforce their own. The village or small town seems such an obvious extension of our family responsibilities that we speak naturally of local community feeling, and assume that this applies to political institutions. Tocqueville maintained that, 'The town . . . as the smallest division of a community . . . seems constituted by the hand of God';[14] though a few pages later, even he had to recognize that there was, in Europe, an absence of the local spirit found in America. The source of the confusion seems to lie in our use of the word community, which shares with the concept of democracy an ability to mean most things to most people. It is commonly accepted that a community implies mutual care: we speak indeed of community care and community responsibility; but when we give a name to our local community we are forced to rely upon descriptions already appropriated by local authorities. We take, in other words,

[14] Alexis de Tocqueville, *Democracy in America*, Oxford University Press, London, p. 56.

an institutional name for an administrative unit, and impute social functions to which it has no title.

The difficulty is not entirely of our own making for the concept of community is notoriously fluid.[15] One approach is concerned with boundaries and legal institutions of control—R. M. MacIver, for example, wrote:

> By a community I mean any area of common life, village, or town, or district, or country, or even wider area. To deserve the name community, the area must be somehow distinguished from further areas, the common life may have some characteristic of its own such that the frontiers of the area have some meaning.[16]

Such a definition provokes us to consider for whom such a community has meaning and in what contexts. In this book we are interested in the extent to which community feeling may affect political activity, and it is obvious that a nation state, or the city of Sheffield cannot form a community in the same sense as a small town or village. Nor does MacIver's definition correspond to the few streets considered by most people as the area within which they feel at home: both the Royal Commission survey[17] and the Sheffield survey showed that this area is thought of in much more local terms. It is the kind of area within which, when we go shopping, we expect to know some faces, or even to exchange a few words with an acquaintance. It is, in fact, a neighbourhood rather than a community, and it is within this circumscribed area that social interaction between neighbours develops—without, as we shall show in Chapter Five, any immediate political implications.

MacIver offers a structural definition which lays great stress upon geographical area and the unit of government. The area may be large or small, co-extensive with a village, or extending beyond national boundaries into extra-national communities, but it is important that there shall be a structure capable of giving expression to the commonly conceived opinions of the group. The

---

[15] For a recent discussion see René König, *The Community* (Routledge and Kegan Paul, 1968). Professor König considers a community to be 'a global society on a local basis', and rejects the use of the term to include 'mere neighbourhoods' (p. 43).

[16] R. M. MacIver, *Community: A Sociological Study*, p. 22.

[17] Royal Commission on Local Government, 1966–9, Research Study 9, *Community Attitudes Survey: England*.

geographical area is in this sense used as a determining factor of community: it is this that helps create community feeling and not, on the contrary, a sense of community that delimits geographical areas of political rule. Hobhouse, another early sociologist in this field, suggested that we should 'consider all populations living under a common rule as political communities, though they have only the bare bones of a common life'.[18]

This use of the phrase 'political community' suggests that any area designated for a local authority would serve equally well as a basis for community action. In a negative sense this may well be true. Interest in the Borough of Camden in London may not be any lower than in the replaced Boroughs of Holborn or St. Pancras; if Sheffield were to be replaced by a regional city area covering parts of south Yorkshire and north-east Derbyshire, then the poll in local elections could scarcely be much lower; but such negative conclusions are not encouraging for the reformer interested in local democracy, nor are they especially interesting to academic students of politics at the local level. The reformer will be concerned with the type and size of community which will encourage a local feeling of involvement, while the academic will be interested in the conditions affecting local political behaviour. The problem then arises, as another view of community suggests, that place of residence is often irrelevant to a sense of community or involvement in affairs. People become involved through their professional associations or trade unions, through their business organization or work, or through social contacts made at school, university, or training course. Such communities based on common interests or experience—old Etonians or engineers, Scotsmen-in-exile or anglers—do not have boundaries of the kind that can be drawn on a map, and they could not form the basis for a system of local administration. The phrase 'political community' is, therefore, likely to confuse discussions about local government reform by introducing a conflict of definitions.

The correct area for a local authority may correspond to a political community in a rather special way. Just as community in a sociological sense implies the intensification of group interaction, so the area encompassed by the 'political community' should encourage political interaction or participation by those within its sphere of responsibility. This would imply that the local authority

[18] L. T. Hobhouse, *Social Development*, pp. 41–2.

area should have both social and geographical meaning, as well as administrative suitability for the various services being provided. The local authority area certainly must be appropriate for the activities undertaken, for only if the area fits the functions will the authority appear—or indeed be—relevant to the electorate. If decisions concerning the electorate are taken elsewhere, for example in a central government department or regional authority, then it may be expected that little interest will be evinced in the local council. This suggests that 'community' and 'function' are not two conflicting principles in the discussion of local authority boundaries. Community in this sense—its political sense?—may be the interaction engendered among those affected by a particular area of political decisions. The degree of participation within this community will depend on the seeming relevance of the decisions to the electorate; the information available about the decision-making process; and the apparent opportunity to affect these decisions by local activity. The normal factors determining community—length of residence, kinship ties, and so on—will then only become relevant to the extent that they affect these political factors. This may occur, for example, if the greater knowledge of local affairs acquired by people who live in an area for a long time leads them to become more active in political life. The Maud survey found that councillors are certainly more likely to be recruited from among those who are attached to the area by friendship ties and long residence, though most of the councillors interviewed did not claim to have had much knowledge of local government before they were elected.[19]

The most frequently used criteria of socio-geographic community are concerned with the journey to work and retail shopping for durable goods.[20] These journeys define the hinterland of major centres of employment and commerce, while the shorter journeys concerned with daily shopping indicate the neighbourhood area. Mr. Derek Senior explains that:

The kind of community with which we are here concerned is not, of course, the community to which people feel they belong. That . . . is a

[19] *M.L.G.*, II, *The Local Councillor*, pp. 56–7 and 71–2.
[20] See Royal Commission on Local Government in England, 1966–9, III, *Research Appendices*, and Research Study 1, *Local Government in South-East England*, 'The Socio-Geographic Enquiry' by Patricia Ellman.

unit far too small to be relevant to the definition of areas for the running of statutory services. What we are concerned with is 'community in terms of people's actual behaviour'—the *objective* community of interest which binds together the people who participate in a self-contained complex of social and economic activities based on a single centre.[21]

Senior criticizes the recommendations of the Royal Commission for failing to pay attention to these objective criteria, but the elegance of his theory conceals the difficulties of its application. The country does not divide neatly into a number of fully formed socio-geographic entities. There are legitimate grounds for arguing about boundaries while accepting the interdependence of town and country and the need for larger planning authorities. The argument is not between supporters and opponents of 'city regions' but between different interpretations of this concept. The Royal Commission maintains that:

there is a hierarchy of socio-geographic areas, all combining town and country, whose relative size depends on the strength of their urban centres and the range of purposes these serve. It would, therefore, be necessary to decide, in the light of considerations other than those of social geography, what size and shape of socio-geographic unit would best match the needs of local government.[22]

Senior prefers large authorities as better suited to planning functions, but then introduces a second tier to accept responsibility for the personal services. The Royal Commission emphasizes the advantages of single-tier local government, and accordingly recommends rather smaller authorities than Senior's city regions as the basis for reform. It is also more concerned than Senior to maintain existing administrative boundaries.

Sheffield is a clear example of the city-region pattern. The influence of the city is felt over a large area of south Yorkshire and north-east Derbyshire. Both the Royal Commission and Senior would make Sheffield the centre of one of their major authorities, but the boundaries Senior proposes would be more extensive. He would include Doncaster, Worksop, and Chesterfield within the

---

[21] Royal Commission on Local Government in England, 1966–9, II, *Memorandum of Dissent by Mr. D. Senior*, para. 175. See also Derek Senior, 'The City Region as an Administrative Unit', *Political Quarterly*, 36, (January–March 1965), and Derek Senior (ed.), *The Regional City*.

[22] Royal Commission on Local Government in England, 1966–9, I, *Report*, para. 205.

Sheffield region, in addition to Rotherham and Barnsley.[23] The six principal towns would become centres for second-tier authorities. In fact the links between Sheffield and the peripheral towns are not very strong: the integration of Doncaster and Worksop into the Sheffield hinterland is a possibility for the future rather than a present reality.[24] To include them within a Sheffield city region would denude areas in mid-Derbyshire, north Nottinghamshire, and south Yorkshire of their natural centres. There is here the 'hierarchy of socio-geographic areas' referred to by the Royal Commission, and we believe unitary authorities to have benefits for democracy that outweigh the possibility of future planning advantages accruing from larger regional authorities.

The numerous interpretations of community cause the concept to be used on all sides of the argument about local authority boundaries. The criteria used to delimit community in economic terms may differ from those most suitable for political purposes, and will certainly be different from the small areas engendering neighbourly concern. Rural areas may recognize the importance of the economic services provided by a nearby town while regarding the extension of towns as destructive of local communities. The economic interdependence of the Sheffield area, for example, has been recognized by the co-operation of local authorities through the 'Forty-four Group',[25] which straddles three county boundaries, includes several county boroughs, and crosses the dividing line between the East Midlands and the Yorkshire and Humberside Economic Planning Regions. The advantages of such an organization are clear. It is able to discuss the future prospects of the area as a whole in order to facilitate the planning of future policies, and it can act as a powerful pressure group on the central government in Whitehall. Yet suggestions that the Forty-four Group should form the basis of a reformed major local authority met a storm of protest from the residents as well as the councillors of the smaller

[23] In a privately circulated paper Mr. Jeffrey Chapman, Senior Lecturer in Urban and Regional Studies, Sheffield Polytechnic, supported Mr. Senior, but proposed the inclusion of the Hope Valley as well.

[24] Ibid., paras., 2.18 and 2.19.

[25] The group received this name from the forty-four authorities who originally expressed an interest in joining. The membership fluctuates with changes in policy in individual councils. It is interesting to note that Sheffield, Rotherham, Barnsley, and Worksop became members, but they were not joined by either Doncaster or Chesterfield.

local authorities—even though in many cases they were defending a name on the map, rather than a particular local authority.

Nevertheless this does not mean that local government reform along these lines would be detrimental to the role of local authorities in a democracy. This role is more complex than the simple nineteenth-century liberal views would lead us to expect. Local democracy is not only a constraint upon the power of central government; nor is the encouragement of citizen participation its only justification; on the contrary, local democracy is a part of the total administration of public decision-taking. Central government and local authorities do not stand implacably opposed to one another. Systems of government must be considered as a whole. Local authorities must be justified by their place in a range of representative institutions, and not merely by their ability to slow down government action. Indeed if effective power is the ability to achieve stated objectives of policy, then the problem of British democracy is not too much power at the centre, but too little. A national economic plan, in a trading country such as Britain, is bound to be at the mercy of international events, but there are other fields where the policy of the government—*any* policy—is constantly frustrated. There are many obvious examples of this in industry, much of which resists modernization with tenacity, but the record for local government reform is certainly no better. It is twenty years since the first post-1945 local government boundaries commission was wound up by the minister, and the present progress towards changes which everyone agrees are essential is not assured.

This failure to provide a local government structure more appropriate to modern conditions is due largely to the romantic confusion mentioned earlier. The people concerned with the protection of local government still think of it in terms of village Hampdens or the glories of Athens. When the ideal of self-government is frustrated by the realities of a modern unitary state, local authorities relapse into a defensive, or on occasion bloody-minded, mood. The pity is that while those most concerned are defending an indefensible ideal, the true role of local authorities is neglected in discussions of reform. Local government should be one of the methods by which public decisions are made intelligible to the man in the street. This is where he should become involved, and be able to complain when decisions are taken which affect him. This is not to suggest that local authorities should become simply consultative bodies implementing central government decisions. In any good administrative structure decisions should be taken at the lowest level commensurate with the degree of consistency necessary in that area of policy. The government should stop worrying about the confirmation of purely local matters, such as the siting of traffic lights, and concentrate on the global allocation of resources. Local authorities should be allowed to initiate local policies they consider desirable, as long as these can be accommodated within the budget. It is, after all, the differences between one area and another in which we take pride, not the uniform provision—excellent though it may be—of a national service. But although local decision-taking remains important it should not be accepted that the extent of such decisions is the sole measure of the importance of local authorities. They are a means by which public policy can be made more open to the electorate, and in this they should act in a consultative manner. It is ridiculous—if understandable with the present local government structure—that major economic or social decisions affecting a locality can be taken without full local consultation. The effects of pit closures on local authorities in the area is only one obvious example of this type of decision. Local authorities should be far more annoyed if such decisions are taken without their participation than they are when a cherished local project— such as a swimming-pool or museum—is postponed at a time of financial stringency. The postponement can be seen as part of a national determination of priorities, but the industrial or economic decision, though taken in a national context, can affect the entire life of the locality. The realization of this fact stimulated the creation of the Forty-four Group around Sheffield.

Local authorities will need to accept reform if they are to become more important in the administration of public policy, or if they are to develop their potentiality as representative bodies readily accessible to the public. At present local authorities are neither one thing nor the other. They are not small enough—with the exception of parish councils and certain municipal boroughs— to benefit from feelings of community responsibility, and in general they are not large enough to tackle the duties which might devolve upon them as part of a national system of public administration. It has already been argued—and a subsequent chapter will provide the evidence—that our perceptions of community are founded on units that are too small, or too diffuse, to form the basis of local authority areas. At the same time it will obviously be difficult to develop any political interaction in areas which have nothing but administrative significance.

Sheffield is a city which has in many ways become isolated by its position in the centre of England. Neither truly 'North' nor really 'Midlands', it perches on a number of boundaries, bypassed by the main communications networks until the construction of the M1 motorway. It is a city where community feeling, if such exists, might be expected to influence the style of local politics rather more than in less self-contained cities. The city, as has been indicated, is also of a size that makes it a natural centre for any local government reform based upon city regions. A study of the political life of the city is of interest, therefore, both as an example of the way in which the local government system works at present, and of the possibilities for the future. This study was made at a time of unique good fortune, for the student of politics at least: a change of political control after a forty-year period (broken only by a single year) of Labour rule. Sheffield, the first major city to fall to Labour in the 1920s, was one of the last to succumb to the Conservatives in the late 1960s. The Conservatives' success was shortlived: Labour returned to power the following year; but the parties remained evenly balanced. This gives added interest— even poignancy—to the present study of Sheffield politics.

2

The Community of Sheffield

A Sheffield thwitel baar he in his hose;
Round was his face, and camuse was his nose.
GEOFFREY CHAUCER, *The Canterbury Tales*

THE definition of community, as we have already seen, is fraught with difficulties. It might, therefore, seem foolhardy, or even presumptuous, to include the concept in the title of this chapter. The intention, however, is not to consider whether Sheffield forms a community in any abstract sense, but to discuss the extent to which it is a city of shared experience. As such a discussion must be a matter of comparison, Sheffield will be compared with a number of other cities. If it is found that the people of the city are subject to influences that are less heterogeneous than those obtaining elsewhere, then it will be concluded that Sheffield is a city where the degree of shared experience is relatively high; but this does not by itself prove that the city forms a community. The influences being discussed may affect an area larger than that contained within the city boundaries, or a number of associated communities may overlap in the neighbourhood of the city. In either of these two events the local authority area would have no significance in any discussion of community in the locality.

It remains important to outline the growth and social structure of the city, even if it is accepted that such a description does not imply that Sheffield is a community in any closely defined meaning of the term. In subsequent chapters the response of the local people to their political environment will be analysed; the impression of the city given in the following pages will enable the survey results to be placed within the local, human, context. A comparison of the responses obtained in Sheffield with those obtained in other cities will also be facilitated by a description of the city.

The influences on the nature of Sheffield discussed in this chapter fall within three categories. First, there are those concerned with the growth and development of the city as a human settlement. In this matter the geographical position of the site, and the available natural resources, will be of obvious importance. It is interesting, too, to note the causes and the rate of growth which in Sheffield, during its formative years in the nineteenth century, was too rapid to be sustained solely by the natural expansion of its population. Sheffield, in common with other cities that were growing at the same time, attracted a large number of people from other areas to settle within its boundaries. It is possible, therefore, to indicate whether Sheffield is relatively a homespun or a cosmopolitan city by comparing the origin of the immigrants to various towns; the rate of movement of people into and out of the city will show the extent to which Sheffield maintained a settled population over the years.

The second group of influences to be considered are those concerned with the types of industry that predominate in Sheffield. The industries in which people work condition the life of the community within the city in a very obvious way. Indeed many towns and cities are so closely associated with particular industries that one is seldom thought of without the other. So it is with steel and engineering in Sheffield. The variation of occupational experience to which individual citizens are exposed will be affected by the degree of industrial diversification within the city, and for this reason we discuss the range of job opportunities available in Sheffield.

Finally, in this broad description of the city, the socio-economic status of the occupations followed by Sheffield people will be analysed on the basis of the Registrar-General's classifications. Social class is a well-known influence on political attitudes, so the relative importance of the socio-economic groups may be expected to affect the political style of the city.

The decennial census—supplemented in 1966 for the first time by a mid-term sample census—provides evidence on all these matters. There are, of course, other influences on the character of a city than those mentioned. The character of a city comprises all the people who live in it, and the total environment within which they make their homes. A number of these other factors are to be discussed in Chapter Five, together with an estimate of the citizen's perception of the extent of his community area; but for the present it is the character of the city that is being considered, and it is with the broad issues that we are concerned.

The cities selected for comparison with Sheffield naturally include Leeds, the other great city of Yorkshire. The close proximity of the two cities, both geographically and in size, results in a rivalry for the leadership of the county: a rivalry in which Leeds has usually prevailed. Both cities have a present population of just over half a million people.

Sheffield is a city of fairly recent creation. It was not until 1893 that the Borough sought from the Queen the title of a city, an honour which Leeds acquired in the same year. The Sheffield application, which was immediately granted, came within a period when the city was expanding very rapidly, and by the time of the 1911 census the city had become the largest in Yorkshire, and the fifth largest provincial city in Great Britain. At that time the population of Sheffield was growing at a faster rate than any other Yorkshire city, but afterwards the growth began to slow down. In common with many other large industrial cities the population of Sheffield reached a peak during the feverish activity of armament production at the time of the First World War, and then entered a period of relative stagnation. During the forty years following the 1921 census, the population of Sheffield remained stable, despite boundary extensions, and for a number of years during the inter-war economic depression the population was actually declining. Many great industrial cities showed a similar lack of growth over these years; but the population of Leeds continued to show a modest increase, until during the 1950s it became, again, the largest city in Yorkshire as well as the administrative centre for the region.

By the early decades of this century Sheffield had reached the limit of its growth as an industrial city; and commercial activities were not developing fast enough to provide a focus for further growth. Certainly there was not much room within the boundaries for further conventional housing development: the growth that did take place was accommodated in the new housing estates situated in Derbyshire and the West Riding of Yorkshire. The commercial and administrative centre of Yorkshire remained stubbornly at Leeds during all this time, which allowed for growth of a more diversified nature than proved possible in Sheffield. This

has been a matter of increasing concern to the Sheffield City
Council, but the reasons for the different patterns of growth are
very deep-seated in the rival cities. Leeds began to expand earlier
as a commercial centre, and geographically the city is much
better placed than the hilly side-track of Sheffield to become a
centre of communications.

When once a commercial centre starts to grow it will naturally
attract other similar activities and thus make its growth largely
self-generating. In this respect Sheffield has never even started.
Leeds had become a municipal entity much earlier than Sheffield,
and was incorporated in 1626, while Sheffield waited until 1843
for incorporation. Sheffield, in this respect, has much in common
with other northern towns. Many such towns grew from villages to
major centres of population in a space of time too short for the
niceties of aesthetic layout to be given much consideration. In
1904 a journalist wrote that:

It is only within the last generation that Sheffield has emerged from a
conglomeration of narrow streets and factories into a city of some display, and as yet the emergence is neither complete nor impressive.[1]

Such comments could have referred to many cities that had grown
with the industrial changes from the middle of the eighteenth
century, but in addition there are important distinctions to be
made between Sheffield and other cities that are close to it in size
and importance.

There are towns in England which can show the remains of
early British settlements from over 2,000 years ago; other towns
have maintained their importance since the Roman invasion; and
many of our greatest cities were important commercial centres in
the Middle Ages. Sheffield does not come within any of these
categories: the city of steel is essentially a child of the industrial
revolution, and especially of the nineteenth century. Sheffield
came together quickly, and it came together in response to a rapid
expansion of the demand for iron and steel products. Its growth
was not grafted on to an existing stock of commercial and industrial development, for little such development was present. In this
respect Sheffield differed very obviously from cities such as
London or Bristol, but the distinction between Sheffield and other

---

[1] Quoted in M. Walton, *Sheffield: Its Story and Its Achievements*, p. 243. I have relied
upon this interesting book for a number of passages in this chapter.

major northern cities is no less important. The populations of
Manchester and Leeds, for example, began to expand rather
earlier than did the population of Sheffield, and their expansion
was based in part on the commercial services which they provided
for surrounding industrial towns. Manchester grew as the metro-
polis of the Lancashire cotton industry, while Leeds was surrounded by a ring of textile towns including Bradford, Halifax, and
Huddersfield. These major cities developed, in other words, as the
centre of industrial complexes which looked to them for leadership. This was not the case in Sheffield where even today Rotherham is the only industrial built-up area to approach the boundaries
of the city. Sheffield at present is the largest city in the United
Kingdom which does not form the basis of a conurbation, that is,
of a continuous built-up area incorporating numerous towns and
cities. This has caused it to be entitled 'the largest village in
England', and it does retain some of the self-contained isolation
which that title implies.

Sheffield is not, then, an ancient city full of pomp and splen-
dour. Local historians can show that the site of the present city
was populated at the time of the Roman invasion, but this population was only to be found in scattered groups: there were no towns of
any importance between Buxton and Doncaster. Such settlements
as existed were based mainly upon forts established to control the
British tribes in this borderland of the Roman occupation. In the
subsequent invasions of Great Britain by Angles, Saxons, and
Danes, the area remained a border territory: the high moorlands
to the north and west providing a barrier to easy conquest. The
origin of Sheffield as a frontier village is reflected in the names of
two of the streams which run within its present boundaries: 'the
Meersbrook, whose name . . . means a frontier river' and 'the
Sheaf [whose name] is from an Old English word meaning a
"cleavage" or dividing line—a frontier'.[2] It was at the junction of
the Sheaf and the River Don in the twelfth century that the
Normans built a castle, on the site now occupied by the Castle
Hill Market and the Brightside and Carbrook Co-operative
Society's department stores—and under the protection of the
castle walls the population of Sheffield began to gather.

Sheffield is situated within a nook of the hills which form part
of the Pennine Chain. To the west of the city there is the beauty of

[2] M. Walton, op. cit., p. 14.

the Peak national park with stretches of high, unpopulated, moorland; to the north and south there are uplands; and only to the east, along the valley of the River Don, is there flat land conducive to industrial development. Scoring the surrounding hills and converging on Sheffield are the valleys of the Don, the Sheaf, the Loxley, the Rivelin, the Porter, and their tributaries. This gives to Sheffield the appearance of a corrugated basin. All streets are hills, and a circular tour of the city assumes the character of a large-scale switchback ride.

These hillside streams, which converge into the River Don at Sheffield before continuing a more placid way through Rotherham and Doncaster, have been one of the natural advantages for the growth of Sheffield industry. The other advantages are to be found in the geological structure of the surrounding area. The streams drain from the relatively impervious millstone grit of the surrounding moorlands over the coal measures on which Sheffield lies. There is, also, some iron-ore in the neighbourhood, together with other mineral resources, though these are not much exploited at the present time.

This confluence of coal, iron-ore, millstone grit to form grinding stones, falling streams to provide motive power, and a plentiful supply of timber in the hillside woods to form the charcoal needed for early smelting processes, settled the industrial future of Sheffield. The production of cutlery, tools, and other metal products has been associated with Sheffield from a very early date. There is some historical controversy over the exact origins of these industries in the area, but the mention of the 'thwitel'—general-purpose knife—in Chaucer's *Reeve's Tale* is a poetic reminder of the existence of a cutlery industry of some fame in the Middle Ages.

It is from the Middle Ages that the history of Sheffield seriously begins. In the twelfth and thirteenth centuries iron and coal began to be worked in the area. Even then the development took place in numerous villages throughout the area and Sheffield was by no means predominant. Ironworking rights, for example, were held by the monks of Kirkstead Abbey from 1161, but their site was within the boundaries of Rotherham rather than Sheffield. Other villages in the parishes of Ecclesfield and Handsworth were relatively more important in the area in medieval times than they are today when these villages are overshadowed or indeed absorbed, by the size of Sheffield: Norton, Attercliffe-cum-Darnall,

Wadsley, Dore, and Totley, are a few whose names retain local significance.

By the beginning of the seventeenth century Sheffield had emerged as the leader of the surrounding group of villages. This is clear from the details of the population of Sheffield which became available from a survey conducted on the second day in January 1615.[3] By this time the parish of Sheffield had long been divided for administrative purposes into townships comprising Sheffield itself, Ecclesall Bierlow, Brightside Bierlow, Upper Hallam, Nether Hallam, and Attercliffe-cum-Darnall, with Heeley rather ambiguously placed on the outskirts of Nether Hallam. The population of the Sheffield township in 1615 far outnumbered the other townships in the parish—the population of the whole parish was about 3,000—indicating that Sheffield had established itself as the market centre for the neighbourhood. Yet despite its growth the whole town of Sheffield remained within the township of that name. This was so even by the end of the seventeenth century, when the population of Sheffield was estimated at 5,000. None of the surrounding villages, whether in Sheffield parish or in the neighbouring parishes of Handsworth or Ecclesall, had populations of more than a few hundred at that time; but with the onset of industrialization the position began to change. As Sheffield expanded with the impetus of industrial development during the eighteenth century all the townships within the parish of Sheffield grew in importance. By 1750 there may have been 12,000 in the township of Sheffield, and 20,000 within the parish,[4] while by 1776 the estimates of a contemporary observer were 17,000 and 30,000 respectively.[5] In 1801 the first official census gave the population of the parish of Sheffield as 46,000; during the following century this figure grew ten-fold, until that day in 1911 when Leeds was overtaken.

This rapid growth in the population of the parish of Sheffield

3 This survey, ordered by Gilbert, seventh Earl of Shrewsbury, Lord of Sheffield, was intended to discover the number of citizens who could contribute to the upkeep of the poor. The officers responsible reported that out of a population of 2,007 people only 100 were able to contribute to the relief of others, while 725 were unable to live without the charity of their neighbours. The rest were, as the report put it, 'constrained to work sore, to provide them necessaries'. Quoted by M. Walton op. cit., p. 62.

4 G. I. H. Lloyd, *The Cutlery Trades*, pp. 148–9.

5 Wentworth Woodhouse Muniments, R.1. Quoted in Local History Leaflet No. 2, *Population in Sheffield, 1086–1951*, issued by the Sheffield City Library. Some of the other figures in this section are quoted from this leaflet.

between 1750 and 1850 was a part of the great expansion of
northern cities which accompanied the industrial revolution; and
it has already been suggested that Sheffield, despite the pace of
change in the area, was actually developing more slowly than other
industrial areas at the beginning of this period. At the time of the
1801 census the parishes of both Leeds and Halifax had a larger
population than Sheffield, and by 1851 these two had been joined
by Bradford. The reason for the different patterns of growth is
fairly obvious. The great expansion of the textile industries took
place at the end of the eighteenth and the beginning of the nineteenth centuries, and the textile towns naturally grew at a rapid
rate. The expansion of the iron and steel industries, upon which
Sheffield depends, belongs much more to the second half of the
nineteenth century when the demand for metal products deriving
from the growth of the ship-building and engineering industries,
the spread of the railways, and armament production, was met by
new methods of bulk steel production. The Sheffield area itself did
not compete in the bulk steel market for long. The location of the
city made it difficult to transport the products of an industry that
increasingly supplied export markets. Once the British railways
had been re-equipped with steel rails, for example, and the industry turned to overseas markets, the Sheffield rail mills were
closed.[6] The new methods of steel production depended increasingly on imported ores, which again made it more economical to
produce bulk steel in furnaces situated close to a sea-port. The
products of Sheffield industries needed to have a high value per
ton if they were to compete with other areas. This necessity was
very much in accord with the traditions of the city, so that
Sheffield continued to produce tools and other implements,
together with the special steels which these require.

The population of the township of Sheffield was practically
complete before the expansion of the steel industry in the third
quarter of the nineteenth century. During this time, a period of
very rapid growth for the borough of Sheffield, the population
increase was accommodated in the other townships within the
parish, as is shown by the figures in Table 2.1. In the townships of
Brightside and Attercliffe row upon row of small terraced houses

---

[6] John Brown's mill was closed in 1874, while Cammell's mill was moved from the
neighbouring village of Dronfield to Workington, on the Cumberland coast, in 1882.
S. Pollard, *A History of Labour in Sheffield*, Ch. 6.

Table 2.1

Population of townships in Sheffield parish, 1801, 1851, and 1901

Township	1801	1851	1901
Sheffield	31,314	83,447	90,398
Ecclesall	5,362	24,552	82,422
Brightside	4,030	12,042	73,088
Attercliffe	2,281	4,873	51,807
Nether Hallam	1,974	8,897	64,599
Heeley	(incorporated in Nether Hallam)		14,822
Upper Hallam	764	1,499	3,657
Total	45,725	135,310	380,793*

* Boundary extensions in 1900 increased the population of the County Borough to 409,070 in 1901.

Source: *Population in Sheffield, 1086–1951.*

were built by the side of the giant steel and engineering firms. Many of these houses were built 'back-to-back', and 38,000 houses of this type were in existence in Sheffield before they were prohibited by by-law in 1864.[7] This was the industrial building which moved D. H. Lawrence, writing about a village not far from Sheffield, to deplore 'the blackened brick dwellings, the black slate roofs glistening their sharp edges, the mud black with coal-dust, the pavements wet and black',[8] but in Sheffield it was not coaldust that blackened the houses, instead they were subject to the effluvium from the furnace chimneys. On the other side of the city, protected to some extent from the dust by the prevailing winds, the suburbs contained in the townships of Ecclesall and Nether Hallam expanded rapidly in the second half of the nineteenth century. These were neat little terrace-houses, with front gardens too small to grow anything but a hedge, but they provided the skilled man with a home better fitted to his rising living standards than the mean streets in the east of the city.

Sheffield in the second half of the nineteenth century was assuming its modern stature, but at the beginning of this period many areas close to the centre of the present city remained undeveloped countryside: 'In those days Sheffield Moor [today a main shopping centre] was beautified by gorse and foxgloves', a haunt of 'gipsies who were always ready for kidnapping purposes'. Eyre Street, behind the present Town Hall, was still a cornfield, and there were 'two miles of green fields between Sheffield and

[7] S. Pollard, op. cit., p. 100.
[8] D. H. Lawrence, *Lady Chatterley's Lover* (Penguin ed.), p. 158.

Heeley'. Beyond Sharrow Lane, 'the landscape seen was very fair and beautiful, the valley of the Sheaf, with Cutler Wood, remaining in all its beauty on the right bank; and the Sheaf in those days was an unspoiled, very charming stream with plenty of fish in it, and the banks edged with flowers'.[9] This description will seem

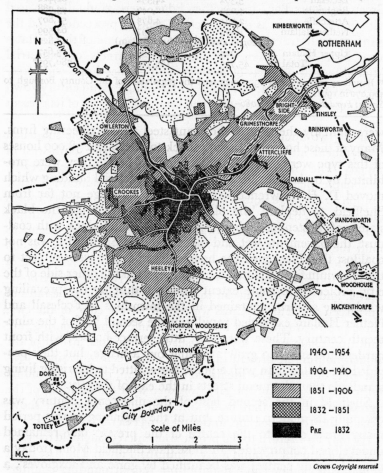

Diagram 2.1 The growth of Sheffield, 1832–1954 (after the Ordnance Survey, T. Jeffreys et al.) Reproduced from A. J. Hunt, 'The Morphology and Growth of Sheffield', in D. L. Linton (ed.), *Sheffield and its Region*.
Principal villages and hamlets are shown for 1832; for later dates extensions to the built-up area and suburban housing development only.

[9] J. H. Stainton, *The Making of Sheffield, 1865–1914*, pp. 204–5.

strange to those who know these districts of Sheffield today; it is interesting, however, to be reminded how recently the major residential areas of Sheffield were developed. The area shaded by diagonal lines on Diagram 2.1 shows how the districts already mentioned, together with others at Hillsborough, Crookes, Nether Green, Hunters Bar, and Nether Edge, were gradually covered with housing estates as the nineteenth century proceeded, and the tramcar made travel easier within the city. Some of these estates were little better than the monotonous streets of industrial Attercliffe, but in parts of Sharrow and Nether Edge wide tree-lined avenues provide a tribute to late-nineteenth-century town planning. By that time the city had attained the basis of its present shape.

In the two inter-war decades there was considerable suburban development into the countryside surrounding the south-west of the city. The villages of Fulwood, Dore, and Totley became the fashionable places to live in and they have maintained their position as the large houses in the earlier suburbs, such as Crookes and Nether Edge, have gradually been divided into multiple tenancies. After the First World War the city council began to build the estates that were to be the forerunners of the 70,000 council tenancies which are now in existence. To the south-east of the city thousands of houses were built at Wybourne, Arbour-thorne, and Manor, while in the north the widespread estates of Shiregreen and Parson Cross were built on the edge of the city. These pre-1939 estates, of both private and council housing, are shown on Diagram 2.1 by areas shaded with dots. Much of the council housing at present in existence has been built since 1945 and some of this can be identified on the map, but the rebuilding of the central areas of the city, together with the building of the high-density blocks that made Sheffield an architectural show-piece in the 1960s, belongs to the post-1954 period.

We may now return to the people who entered Sheffield over the past two centuries to build a great industrial town. The first point to note is that they came mainly from the surrounding country-side. Very few immigrants to Sheffield, even today, travel a long distance to reach the city. The hills within which the city is built have always made communications difficult with other large centres of population, and Sheffield is a considerable distance from coastal ports. The route for immigrants from the west—predominantly, of course, the Irish—is blocked by the Pennine Chain. From the east the roads in the eighteenth and nineteenth centuries were poor, and in any case did not join Sheffield to any major centres of population or immigrant port of entry. The road to the neighbouring town of Rotherham was described by Arthur Young in 1769 as 'execrably bad, very stony, and excessively full of holes',[10] so the conditions of the tracks along which the pack-horses stumbled towards the broad empty acres of Lincolnshire may easily be imagined. Sheffield products—mainly cutlery at that time—continued to be transported by trains of pack-horses until well into the eighteenth century, but by the end of the century the growth in the demand for coal, together with improvements in steel-making, made the improvement of the roads a necessity. Transport by pack-horse might have been suitable for cutlery, which is valuable relative to its weight, but it was obviously a very uneconomic way to transport coal. Nevertheless the improvement of the roads did not proceed very rapidly, even under the impetus of the turnpike Acts, and surface conditions remained bad at the beginning of the nineteenth century. Even when the canals and railways supplemented the appalling roads, the geographical position of Sheffield placed it at the end of a branch line. The main routes to the north passed through Rotherham or Doncaster.

It is not surprising, therefore, that an economic historian has concluded:

There are few indications here that Sheffield was much affected by the general increase in the geographical mobility of labour observed by contemporary writers towards the end of the eighteenth century.[11]

This conclusion was reached after a study of the places of origin of lads apprenticed to the cutlery trades in Hallamshire between 1624 and 1799, during which time 'about two-thirds of all the immigrants came from places less than twenty-one miles from Sheffield and less than one-tenth from places more than forty miles away. . . . Ireland [provided] less than half a dozen in the whole period.'[12] In the nineteenth century, when the population

[10] Quoted by A. W. Goodfellow, 'The Development of Communications', in D. L. Linton (ed.), *Sheffield and its Region*, p. 162.

[11] E. J. Buckatzsch, 'Origins of Immigrants into Sheffield 1624–1799', *Economic History Review*, II, 3 (Autumn 1950).

[12] Ibid.

of Sheffield increased from 46,000 to over 400,000, the main
catchment area for the city's expansion continued to be the surrounding agricultural areas of Yorkshire and Derbyshire. If we
add those who came from Nottinghamshire and Lincolnshire then
the list is almost complete. The city did not receive a large influx
of labour from distant parts of the British Isles. During this time
in Sheffield:

The Irish-born never amounted to more than three or four per cent,
and there were few Scotsmen or others from distant counties. . . . In
1901 . . . the whole of Scotland and Ireland . . . accounted for only 1·6
per cent of the population between them.[13]

Those immigrants who did come from some distance were mainly
skilled men for the rapidly growing steel and engineering industries. These men—like the Commonwealth immigrants who
followed them a hundred years later—settled close to their work
in the townships of Brightside and Attercliffe.

The low rate of immigration into Sheffield in the nineteenth
century was unusual for a city of its size. Hundreds of thousands of
people had crossed the Irish Sea during the previous decades to
settle in the large towns, particularly in Lancashire, Cheshire, and
in the Home Counties. Other cities were receiving many foreigners
within their boundaries. At the time of the 1911 census, for
example, Leeds included 6,500 citizens born in Russia or Poland,
while the corresponding figure for Sheffield was 750. The 1911
census listed Sheffield as one of the six cities or large towns with
the lowest rate of immigration; it also suggested that the rate of
emigration from Sheffield was relatively low.

The present city maintains a self-contained atmosphere. During
the 1950s and 1960s the immigration into Sheffield from Ireland
or from countries outside the British Isles has not been as great as
in many other areas. At the time of the 1961 census nearly 96 out
of every 100 Sheffield residents had been born in England. This
may be compared with a national average of 92 per cent, or with
93 per cent in Leeds, and only 88 per cent in the relatively poly-
glot city of Manchester. The inflow of Commonwealth immigrants
in recent years has affected Sheffield, which is one of the areas
with over 2 per cent of immigrants among the school population,

---

[13] Sidney Pollard and A. J. Hunt, 'The Growth of Population', in D. L. Linton
(ed.), op. cit., p. 178. See also *A History of Labour in Sheffield* by Sidney Pollard, Ch. 4.

but the impact has not been as great as in many other cities in the north, or in the south-east and the Midlands. At the present time (1968) there are approximately 5,000 West Indians (including children born in England) living in Sheffield, mainly in the Nether Edge area, and about the same number of Asians who have settled in Attercliffe. The 1966 sample census (Table 2.2) confirms

Table 2.2
Place of birth of residents in Sheffield, Leeds, Bradford, and England, 1966

Place of birth	England No.	%	Sheffield No.	%	Leeds No.	%	Bradford No.	%
England	40,235,130	90·4	459,190	95·3	463,720	91·9	259,420	89·3
Ireland	857,260	1·9	4,000	0·8	9,610	1·9	4,350	1·5
Other parts of the British Isles	1,635,510	3·7	7,970	1·6	12,340	2·4	5,550	1·9
Commonwealth, Colonies, and Protectorates	929,500	2·1	7,340	1·5	10,450	2·1	13,480	4·7
Foreign countries and at sea	814,670	1·8	4,040	0·8	8,510	1·7	7,510	2·6
Total	44,472,070	100·0	482,540	100·0	504,630	100·0	290,310	100·0

Note: Because of rounding the percentages for England do not add to one hundred.
Source: Sample Census 1966, Yorkshire West Riding County Report, Table 4 and Summary Tables, Table 6.

that Sheffield has a far higher proportion of its present population who were born in England than either the average for England or for the two other large West Riding cities. Sheffield also shows a much lower figure for immigration from each of the overseas sources.

It is not only immigrants to this country from overseas who fail to find their way to Sheffield: internal migration is also low. During the year before the 1961 census, for example, the total number of immigrants to Sheffield from outside the city boundaries was only 18 per 1,000 residents. The average for large urban areas was 32 immigrants per 1,000 residents. The census definition of a large urban area only includes those areas outside the conurbations whose population exceeds 100,000, but the immigration figures for Sheffield are below those of other large northern cities whether or not these form part of a conurbation. It is fortunate for Sheffield that in 1960–1, as in 1911, the emigration from the city was also exceedingly low, otherwise Sheffield would have suffered a far greater decline in population than actually occurred. The emigration rate for Sheffield in that year was 24 per 1,000 residents compared with an average of 33 per 1,000 residents in all large urban areas. During this same year Leeds, Sheffield's great rival for the leadership of Yorkshire, was enjoying a net inflow of population.

The broad outline of the growth of Sheffield may be summarized in a few generalizations. Sheffield is situated among the foothills of the Pennines, slightly away from the main communications networks, so that the city grew by absorbing people from the surrounding countryside. There has been no great movement of population into Sheffield, either from overseas or from the more distant parts of the British Isles; nor has there been a high rate of emigration from the city. The general impression remains therefore, of a city which is homogeneous in its population, relatively static in its composition, and comparatively unaffected by the outside influences that affect a major centre of commerce or communications. Generalizations such as these can only be made by comparing Sheffield with other large cities, or with a statistical average for the country as a whole. When this is done the variations between cities are often small, and there is a danger of reading too much into a trivial difference. Nevertheless these small differences become more interesting as it becomes obvious that whatever the criteria adopted Sheffield appears as a city with a relatively undisturbed population. Further information bearing on this point will be presented in Chapter Five, but now we will consider two other ways in which Sheffield emerges as a relatively homogeneous city: first the industrial structure of the city; and secondly the socio-economic status of Sheffield's inhabitants.

We have already mentioned the influence of the metal-producing and manufacturing industries upon the growth of Sheffield. The city is, of course, famous for its steel and engineering products. The very name 'Sheffield' is synonymous with the top-quality tools and cutlery made in the city. The local steel industry has naturally adapted itself to the demand from the implement manufacturers for special alloy steel, and about 60 per cent of the alloy-steel output of the United Kingdom is produced in the Sheffield and Rotherham area. This emphasis on special steel production has been accentuated by the geographical position of the city which made it unsuitable for the development of bulk steel production. The modern steel industry depends upon imported ore, and Sheffield is as far from the coast as it is possible to be in the small country of England. The major bulk steel producing plants are situated close to the coast for very sound economic reasons.

Even taking into account the importance of steel and engineering in Sheffield, the extent of the inhabitants' dependence upon these industries for their livelihood remains surprising. Following the 1961 census it is possible to present figures showing the proportion of persons in employment—or actively seeking work—both by industry and occupation. The census used twenty-four industrial classifications and twenty-seven occupational classifications, giving admirable detail but becoming rather overwhelming for the layman. Unfortunately any attempt to summarize these classifications leads to absurd over-simplication. The full details are, therefore, included in Appendix A for those wishing to make further use of the figures. The two most important facts to emerge are illustrated in Diagram 2.2, which combines a number of the

AREA	Engineering and Metals	Distribution and Services
England and Wales	1855	4838
Sheffield	4404	3887
Leeds	1557	4727
Liverpool	1177	5975
Manchester	1377	5559
Middlesbrough	2699	5490
Newcastle	1791	5907
Bristol	950	5841
Norwich	1027	5253

Diagram 2.2. Proportions per 10,000 persons employed in two broad industrial groupings
Notes: Engineering and Metals include industrial classifications V, VI, VII, VIII, and IX.

Distribution and Services include industrial classifications XIX, XX, XXI, XXII, XXIII, and XXIV.

Source: Census, 1961 (10 per cent sample): Industry tables, Table A, and Occupation, Industry, and Socio-economic Groups, County Reports, Table 4

E

census classifications into two broad groups: first, the engineering
and metal industries; and secondly, distribution and services.
Figures are included in the diagram for a number of other cities
to allow comparison with Sheffield, and for this purpose Bristol
and Norwich have been included, in addition to five northern
industrial cities, to provide a contrast from more mellow areas of
England.

First, it may be seen from Diagram 2.2 that over 44 per cent of
the Sheffield working population are employed in the five industrial classifications connected with engineering and metals. While
no one will be surprised to find that these industries are important
in Sheffield, it is interesting that no other city for which details are
given in the diagram even approaches the Sheffield position.
Middlesbrough shows about 27 per cent employed in these
industries and the other cities come a long way behind. If we turn
to the detailed figures (given in Table A.1 of Appendix A) the
position becomes even clearer. Of the cities shown Sheffield has the
largest proportion of its employed population engaged in metal
manufacture; the city is second only to Newcastle in the proportion
employed in the engineering and electrical goods industries; and
the proportion employed in manufacturing metal goods not otherwise specified is several times greater than in any other city
mentioned. This last classification includes the manufacture of
tools and cutlery, which are two of Sheffield's most famous
products. More detailed figures than those given in the Appendix
show that in Sheffield in 1961 413 persons per 10,000 employed
were engaged in the manufacture of tools and implements, and a
further 273 were engaged in cutlery manufacture. The pre-
eminence of Sheffield in the lighter trades moved one commen-
tator to suppose that:

Working in metals, whether hot or cold, comes naturally to Sheffield
people, and they may be more easily trained in such work for this
reason. Some special skills, such as hammering steel flat, seem to be
almost hereditary.[14]

As the above quotation suggests, the position shown by the
census in 1961 did not represent any departure from the figures
presented in previous census reports, although they give rather

[14] H. Townsend, 'The Sheffield Lighter Trades', in D. L. Linton (ed.), op. cit.,
p. 301.

more detail. After an examination of the 1911 census report a research team concluded:

metal-manipulating workers . . . even after making full deduction for the non-adult and non-manual workers among [them] . . . number more than one-half of the total adult male (manual) workers. These men . . . are the heart of the town. It is their work that makes Sheffield Sheffield. The 4,000 railwaymen and the 5,000 carmen in the city exist to bring them materials and machinery and carry away their manufactures; the 10,000 building operatives exist to build the factories in which they work and the houses in which they sleep; the 9,000 males supplying food, drink and tobacco exist to cater for their bodily needs.[15]

This situation continues to exist, but the dependence of the city on one group of industries becomes worrying as the leading firms in these industries reduce the number of people they employ. A city with all its employment eggs in one basket becomes extremely vulnerable at a time of industrial change. It can be seen from Diagram 2.2 that this is precisely the situation in Sheffield. Not all cities, of course, will show similar proportions of their work-force employed in the engineering and metals industries: each will have its own staple products; but none of the cities mentioned show the same dominance by one industry that exists in Sheffield. This may be confirmed by further reference to Table A1 in Appendix A. The textile and clothing group, for example, are important in Leeds and Manchester; Norwich is famous for its boot and shoe industry; Bristol has large tobacco and printing industries; but none of these industries employ a proportion of their city's working population comparable with the proportion employed by the staple industries in Sheffield: most cities have a much more diversified industrial structure.

These facts led the Sheffield City Council—in its evidence to the Hunt Committee on the Problems of Intermediate Areas—to write of an imbalance in the industrial structure of the city which 'has inevitably been reflected in a lack of industrial growth'. The city council drew attention also to the second important fact illustrated in Diagram 2.2: the relatively low proportion of Sheffield's working population who are engaged in distribution and the service industries. Most cities have around half or more of their working population employed in this group of industries,

[15] A. Freeman, *et al.*, *The Equipment of the Workers*, p. 37.

but the appropriate figure for Sheffield is only 39 per cent. This group comprises six industrial classifications and the detailed figures (given in Table A.1 of Appendix A) show that Sheffield has a relatively low proportion of its working population in *every one of these classifications*: a lower proportion in fact than any other city mentioned in the Table. Most of the other cities illustrated here are regional capitals, but this is not so in the case of Middlesbrough— now included in the County Borough of Teesside—or of Liverpool, whose position as a major port will account for the large proportion of its working population employed in the distributive and service industries. The low proportion employed in these industries in Sheffield is a confirmation of the city's failure to grow as a commercial or administrative centre, and of the common industrial experience which forms the basis of its communal life.

We may turn now to consider the status of the occupations employing the people of Sheffield. An indication of this may be obtained from the official statistics for socio-economic group which are based upon occupation. In the 1961 census a very detailed analysis was made by dividing the economically active male population into seventeen occupational groups. Such detail, though interesting, is difficult to follow, so an attempt has been made to combine the figures into three main groups: the first consists of employers, managers, and professional workers; the second of workers on own account, personal service workers, and other non-manual workers; and the third of manual workers— including foremen and supervisors—in industry and in agriculture. The figures are shown on either side of a central axis to facilitate comparisons between cities.

The larger cities quoted have a different pattern of employment from the national picture. The proportion engaged as employers, managers, or in the professions is rather lower than in England and Wales, while the proportion employed in manual occupations is rather higher. In general Sheffield agrees with this pattern, but the contrasts are even more sharply drawn. Sheffield shows a larger proportion of manual workers amongst economically active males, and a lower proportion of non-manual workers, than any other city mentioned, with the exception of Middlesbrough— another steel city. The fact that there are a relatively large number of employers, managers, and professional workers shown in the Sheffield figures compared with the other large cities—though not

AREA	Employers,Managers & Professional workers	Non–manual workers	Manual workers
England and Wales	153	208	602
Sheffield	121	174	692
Leeds	124	216	631
Liverpool	99	204	669
Manchester	96	228	657
Middlesbrough	86	147	758
Newcastle	115	216	639
Bristol	118	249	614
Norwich	104	219	652

Diagram 2.3. Socio-economic group of economically active males—per 1,000

Notes: The employers, etc., include groups 1, 2, 3, 4, 13, and 14 of the census classifications.

The non-manual workers include groups 5, 6, 7, and 12 of the classifications.

The manual workers include groups 8, 9, 10, 11, and 15 of the classifications.

The difference between the sum of the figures given here and 1,000 comprises the armed forces and indefinite (classifications 16 and 17).

Source: Census, 1961. Socio-economic Group Tables. Table 1 (10 per cent sample).

compared with the national average—is due to the continuing importance of small employers and the large number of lawyers to be found in the city.

The number of small employers is associated with Sheffield's specialization in cutlery and tool manufacture. Professor Pollard has shown that at the end of the nineteenth century:

The typical Sheffield firm was still the small family concern, existing on a narrow capital basis. . . . Most workmen were still semi-independent, working as 'in-workers' or 'out-workers', for any manufacturer who would entrust them with orders, and paying their own expenses.[16]

He writes later of the inter-war years and the picture of the light trades remains the same: 'the multitude of small firms and "little mesters" and the complex relationships of outwork and sub-contract, remained characteristic of the industry'.[17] The number

[16] S. Pollard, op. cit., p. 132.   [17] Ibid., p. 291.

of small firms is now declining, and causing the city council some concern in the process, but there are still more than one might expect. It is not possible with the statistics available to give figures for the seven towns we have been using for comparative purposes, but fairly recent figures have been made available for the Sheffield area.[18] These show that in addition to the large number of small businesses in distribution and the service industries, which is common throughout the country, there are many small establishments in the major Sheffield industries: 77 per cent of the manufacturing establishments in Sheffield employ less than 100 people.[19] Although the giant steel and engineering firms may dominate the employment position in the city, the Sheffield elector still lives in an environment with a tradition of small-scale production.

Political attitudes are affected by the number of people with whom a person works: the larger the firm, the more radical the attitude;[20] we therefore asked a sample of the Sheffield electorate how many people they worked with before asking further questions concerning their attachment to their neighbourhood and political activity. About a quarter worked in firms employing less than twenty people, and a third in firms employing over 500.[21]

The emphasis on manual occupations, which may be observed from Diagram 2.3, has caused Sheffield to be a radical city. In 1846 two Chartists were elected to the then Town Council, and by 1849 they formed the majority of the elected councillors (twenty-two out of forty-two). The Chartists did not preserve their majority long enough to control the election of aldermen, and thus secure an absolute majority, yet Sheffield still became the first major city in England to be controlled by a working-class party. In November 1926 the Labour Party obtained a majority on the city council and commenced a long era of political dominance.

[18] The figures were derived from information provided by the Ministry of Labour. They include a few firms outside the county borough boundaries, but the numbers involved are very small. All establishments with five or more employees at the beginning of 1966 are included, which means that a lot of small shops, but very few industrial establishments, are excluded. I am indebted to Dr. Martin Howe for making the raw statistics available to me. Detailed figures are shown in Appendix A, Table A.4.

[19] This proportion is derived from Table A.4. Manufacturing establishments include Standard Industrial Classifications III–XVI.

[20] See Table 7.3.

[21] Further details of the occupational characteristics of the Sheffield sample are shown in Appendix A, Table A.5.

The city has also been associated with many major events in the history of the trade union movement, and here, as one would expect, the skilled men in the major industries of the city have played an important role. The skilled craftsmen have in the past formed the heart of the British trade union movement, and an exceptionally large proportion of the Sheffield male working population fall into this category. This may be demonstrated when the manual workers' group in Diagram 2.3 is further divided by the degree of skill shown by its constituents. In Diagram 2.4 the three groups of skilled, semi-skilled, and unskilled are shown separately. The figures for the skilled workers and for the other groups have been placed on either side of a central axis to facilitate comparisons between cities. Sheffield has a larger proportion of its male labour force in skilled occupations than any other city mentioned. Forty-four per cent of the men employed in Sheffield are skilled manual workers compared with under 35 per cent so employed in England and Wales as a whole.

AREA	Skilled	Semi-skilled	Unskilled
England and Wales	349	147	106
Sheffield	440	148	105
Leeds	411	131	89
Liverpool	345	170	154
Manchester	382	164	111
Middlesbrough	414	174	170
Newcastle	386	132	121
Bristol	359	154	101
Norwich	424	127	101

Diagram 2.4. Degree of skill of manual workers—per 1,000 economically active males

Notes: The skilled include groups 8 and 9 of the classifications.
The semi-skilled include group 10 of the classifications.
The unskilled include groups 11 and 15 of the classifications.
Details of those groups are given in the notes to the census tables.
Source: Census, 1961. Socio-economic Group Tables. Table 1 (10 per cent sample).

The trade unions, therefore, are an important part of the political tradition of the city. The 'Sheffield Outrages' were the occasion of the establishment of the first Royal Commission on Trade Unions in 1867.[22] Perhaps more to their credit, the Sheffield trade unions took a leading part in the formation of the Trades Union Congress. The Secretary of the Sheffield Typographical Society, William Dronfield, was prominent in the conferences that took place throughout the 1860s, and in 1866 he called a Conference of Trades' Delegates, to be held in Sheffield in July 1866. One hundred and thirty-eight delegates attended, representing nearly 200,000 members, and Dronfield, a journeyman compositor, was appointed secretary. This conference was a fore-runner of the first annual Trades Union Congress which took place in Manchester in 1868: Dronfield was a leading delegate. More recently the Sheffield steelworkers were actively connected with a campaign to achieve some measure of 'workers' control' in the re-nationalized steel industry. A number of conferences were held and proposals were formulated that became the basis of national trade union policy, and again some measure of success may be claimed. The Act of Parliament that once again brought the steel industry under public ownership made provision for men still working at manual occupations in the industry to serve on a number of management bodies. In view of this history it is not surprising that most of the leaders of the local Labour Party have been active trade unionists. Many of them, including the present leader of the Labour Group on the city council, have been skilled craftsmen. They are following a tradition that goes back far into the nineteenth century.

Three broad components of the character of Sheffield as a city have been discussed in this chapter: the place of origin of the population; the industrial structure of the city; and the social composition of the working population as indicated by their occupational status. Sheffield emerges from a consideration of all three factors as a relatively homogeneous city. First, practically all the population have been born locally and there is very little influence from overseas or from more distant parts of the British Isles. Secondly, industry within the city is concentrated to a very high degree on the manufacture and working of metal. There is

---

[22] The Sheffield Playhouse recently produced a ballad-play by Allan Cullen which dramatized these events, and it was greeted with packed houses. It was obvious that the local interest of *The Stirrings in Sheffield on Saturday Night* attracted many people who were not regular theatre-goers.

relatively little industrial diversification compared to other cities. Thirdly, Sheffield is a working-class city—some commentators going so far as to describe it as the most proletarian city in Europe —in which manual occupations, and especially *skilled* manual occupations, form a large proportion of the job opportunities.

There has been very little change over the years in the first two of these components. Despite the recent immigration from Commonwealth countries, the numbers involved in Sheffield have not been large enough to affect the general composition of the population. The industrial structure of the city remains firmly tied to steel and engineering, and the efforts of the city council to promote industrial diversification have had little immediate effect. But although the broad dependence upon steel and engineering is unchanged there are signs that the pattern of employment is changing, and this will lead to a change in the third component. There is a movement away from manufacturing industry, and an increase in the number of those employed in other occupations. This is the tendency throughout the country, but some local details were submitted during 1967 by the Ministry of Labour to a joint meeting of city councillors and local industry. Between 1952 and 1965 the numbers employed in Sheffield in tool manufacture fell sharply, by about 17 per cent, and there was a decline in other manufacturing industry, as well as in mining. During the same period there was a considerable increase in the numbers employed in construction (51 per cent), distribution (26 per cent), and professional services (65 per cent).[23] These figures reflect, first, the technological changes that are enabling manufacturing industry to produce a larger output with a smaller labour force; and, secondly, the increasing demand for services that accompanies improved living standards. The worrying aspect for Sheffield is that the service and commercial activities of the city, even after the large *proportionate* increases quoted above, are not fully replacing the job opportunities being lost through the rationalization of the basic industries.

The social changes occurring in Sheffield are not proceeding very rapidly, and the effect on the political life of the city is correspondingly slow. The Conservatives were returned to power on the city

[23] These figures are derived from statistics given in a report of the meeting in *Sheffield Forward*, the journal of the Sheffield Trades and Labour Council, 6, 270, October 1967.

council in 1968, after almost forty years of Labour control, but this would appear to have been the result of an unprecedented swing of national opinion away from Labour. Local issues in Sheffield—for example the rent rebate scheme and boundary extensions—affected a few crucial marginal seats, but they did not appear to change the overall voting behaviour of the electorate to any significant extent: the swing against Labour in Sheffield during 1967–8 was very close to the national figure or even slightly below. The details of the closely fought elections at the end of the 1960s will be given in a later chapter; although these elections give no present proof of a long-run alteration in the basis of political support in the city, they may be prophetic of a significant change in the character of Sheffield. The traditional base of Labour support in the city may be gradually eroded by the occupational mobility resulting from changing industrial techniques. A smaller and smaller proportion of the labour force will be engaged in production and a larger proportion will be engaged on maintenance, supervision, and administration. This has been happening in the steel industry over the past few years, and the pace of change may be expected to quicken in the future. Over the next few years Sheffield may experience the kind of sea-change which was experienced nationally during the 1950s, with consumer markets rather than heavy industry providing the style of life. If this happens—and the alternative is a gradual decline in the prosperity of the city—then the political situation in Sheffield may continue to be more open as the parties adjust to a changing environment.

3

The Institutions of Local Democracy

The various tendencies towards decentralization which manifest themselves in almost all the national parties . . . result merely in the creation of a number of smaller oligarchies, each of which is no less powerful within its own sphere.

ROBERT MICHELS, *Political Parties*

IT is difficult, as we have already suggested, to write of Sheffield as a community without implying the administrative unit of that name. The city has grown by absorbing the many smaller communities that once had an independent existence in the area; these smaller communities retain an emotional significance for the inhabitants; but the local authority area provides the framework for the political activity of the city. So the present chapter is concerned with the political institutions of Sheffield, including the local political parties and other groups that seek to influence them: 'political community' in Hobhouse's definition.[1] But the people who are active in local politics also form a community in the functional meaning of that phrase: they meet each other regularly, share common interests, and denounce public apathy towards their activities with a vehemence only matched by the suspicion they sometimes evidence towards those who seek to contest their authority. Even in a city as large as Sheffield the number of people who engage in political activity is relatively small: the same individuals appear in various organizations in different capacities; and a feeling of 'belonging' is engendered in anyone who spends the time necessary to enter the public circle.

Sheffield is one of the largest county boroughs in England, and its functions are correspondingly wide. A county borough—unlike a county, where authority is divided between the county and district councils—is the sole source of local government within its area. In Sheffield the city council controls capital assets—land,

[1] See Chapter I above.

equipment, buildings, council houses, etc.—valued at over 180
million pounds. The income to the rate fund is over 30 million
pounds. The city council is the largest employer in the area,
employing 20,000 people full-time, and a further 7,000 on a part-
time basis.[2] The resources of the council are used to provide
services which include education from primary to polytechnic and
college of education level; highways and public transport; art
galleries and museums; social welfare; water supply, refuse collection, and public health; housing and town planning; and the fire
service. The police force has been a joint responsibility between
Sheffield and the county borough of Rotherham since June 1967.

The history of the Sheffield City Council begins with the incorporation of the borough in 1843. Before that date the various
services of local government in Sheffield had been provided by a
number of authorities, the most important of which were the
county magistrates, the police commissioners, the vestries, and the
highway boards. In addition the Cutlers' Company was empowered
by a statute of 1624, to make and enforce regulations in the
cutlery trade throughout the area. This fragmented authority was,
as a local historian has noted, 'ill-suited to the requirements and
ambitions of such an important town',[3] but there was considerable
opposition to proposals for reform. The Municipal Reform Act of
1835 provided an opportunity for Sheffield to obtain a charter and
to become self-governing, but the opportunity was not immediately taken. Other large industrial cities were less reticent,
Birmingham and Manchester, for example, petitioned at once for a
charter under the 1835 Act, while Leeds had been incorporated in
1626 by Charles I.

The opposition to the incorporation of Sheffield came from those
who feared that the expense, particularly if a borough police force
was added, would lead to a substantial increase in the rates. The
late 1830s were years of great distress in industrial cities, and the
opponents of incorporation could claim that the resources of the
parishes were already heavily taxed to provide poor relief, without
indulging in the vanity of a charter. In 1838 these arguments prevailed, but by 1841 the petitioners in favour of incorporation

---

[2] The figures in this paragraph are taken from the Financial Survey of Sheffield for
the year ending 31 March 1967.

[3] J. M. Furness, *Fifty Years Municipal Record, 1843–93*, p. 4. I have relied heavily on
Furness for this account of the incorporation of Sheffield.

represented a majority of the ratable value of the town. The impetus to this change of heart on the part of the larger ratepayers was given by a proposal by the Justices of the West Riding—under the 1839 County Constabulary Act—to remove the powers of the local police commissioners in Sheffield, and to place the management of the town in the hands of the county magistracy. The only way to avoid the indignity of government by a non-resident, unrepresentative body was to obtain a charter of incorporation. The charter was eventually granted on 24 August 1843, thus ending 'the country village form of government'[4] which had become inappropriate in a town with a population of over 110,000 people.

By the Royal Charter of Incorporation the borough comprised the six townships of the parish, and was divided into nine wards. The town council consisted of a mayor, fourteen aldermen, and forty-two councillors. Both the population and the area of the city have gradually expanded over the years and the membership of the council has been expanded commensurate with these changes. From the last boundary revision, which came into operation on 1 April 1967, the city is now divided into 27 wards represented by 81 councillors and 27 aldermen, making a total council membership of 108. The 27 wards are intended to achieve approximately equal electorates by the early 1970s, but at the time of the 1967 redistribution the number of electors varied from 8,600 in Mosborough Ward to 16,800 in Heeley Ward. Clearance and redevelopment will reduce the size of the electorate in Heeley over the next few years, while Mosborough is to be the site of a satellite residential development. Each ward is represented by three councillors who are elected for a three-year term of office. One councillor from each ward retires annually in rotation and is eligible to stand for re-election.

The ancient office of alderman was retained for the boroughs and county councils in the nineteenth-century reforms, but the system is now being reconsidered. The Committee on the Management of Local Government (Maud) recommended the abolition of the office and they received the support of the Association of Municipal Corporations. The Maud recommendation was made on the grounds that aldermen are unrepresentative and that the system can be used to distort the decision of the electorate as expressed

[4] Ibid, p. 4.

through the election of councillors. The opponents of the Maud Committee's recommendations, including the County Councils Association, point out that aldermen provide continuity through their longer term of office, and that they are not subject to ward pressures: they may represent the area as a whole. In Sheffield there is no evidence to support the county council's case. The twenty-seven aldermen are elected for a six-year term of office by the councillors, and half of the aldermanic bench retires every three years, although they are eligible for re-election. The councillors may elect as alderman any member of the electorate who is eligible to serve on the council, but in Sheffield it is the usual practice for aldermen to be elected from within the city council itself. The aldermen in Sheffield may be regarded simply as the most senior members of the council—in age and experience if not always in political importance—and they cannot be shown to perform any function that could not be accepted by an ordinary council member.

The political parties usually nominate their most senior councillors, but occasionally a councillor who has risen quickly to a position of influence in the council may be preferred. It is rare for an alderman to be elected without at least ten years' service as a councillor, and twenty years' service is more common, which indicates that continuity is not usually a problem on Sheffield City Council. The convention that aldermen are elected proportionate to the number of councillors elected for each party was broken by the Labour group in 1967, when they took sufficient aldermanic seats to increase their marginal majority of one to a working majority of ten. The Conservatives protested at this manœuvre, but they were at the mercy of the majority party.[5] In the following year the Conservatives had to control the council with a majority of four, and when Labour returned to power in 1969 they were still in a minority among the elected representatives. The Labour aldermen created in defiance of convention were still in office and no fresh aldermanic elections were due until 1970. Before these elections the Labour Party won a majority among the councillors and

[5] It should be noted that in some county boroughs the majority party invariably takes all the vacant aldermanic seats, though in this, and in other respects, the Sheffield attitude to aldermen is probably typical of the larger county boroughs. *M.L.G.*, V, *Local Government Administration in England and Wales*, Ch. 4. The Committee recommended that the aldermanic system be abolished. *M.L.G.*, I, *Report of the Committee*, para. 353.

proceeded to take an even larger share of the aldermen. The gentlemanly convention could not survive the pressures of close-fought political battles.

The aldermen on Sheffield City Council do not act differently from their councillor colleagues; there is no indication of greater independence resulting from their lack of direct responsibility to the electorate. The aldermen are members of their respective party groups and subject to the same degree of discipline; they enter party controversy with the same robustness as in their less exalted days; and they do not appear to exert any additional influence *as aldermen* over the affairs of the council. The aldermen are, however, the longest serving members of the Sheffield City Council, and as such hold many of the senior positions in the council. The leaders and deputy leaders of both the party groups on the council are aldermen, and so are a majority of the most influential members, but it would be wrong to construe this influence as complete domination. In both 1967–8 and 1968–9

Table 3.1
Chairmen of committees, 1967–8 and 1968–9

	1967–8 (Labour controlled)		1968–9 (Cons. controlled)	
	Chairman	Deputy Chairman	Chairman	Deputy Chairman
Aldermen	8	5	5	4
Councillors	12	15	6	7
Total No. of Cttees.	20	20	11	11

aldermen occupied more than the proportion of chairmanships which would be expected from their numbers on the council, but councillors still occupied the majority of these important positions. The situation is complicated by the fact that in both political parties the group leader and the deputy leader—all aldermen—accepted more than one office in the council. The Labour leader and deputy leader shared the chairmanships and deputy chairmanships of the important policy committee and finance committee, while the Conservative leader took the chair at both of these committees. They took these key positions by virtue of being party leaders rather than because they were aldermen. In this connection it is interesting to note that the leader and deputy leader of the Conservative group were aldermen with a relatively short period of service in the council. Their elevation had obviously been consequent upon their importance in the Conservative group. Both parties have also had councillors occupying important group positions or chairing major council committees.

The Mayor of Sheffield, given the title of Lord Mayor in 1897, has usually been elected from the membership of the council, but on two occasions a distinguished outsider has been appointed to this office. The two gentlemen concerned were the Duke of Norfolk, who held office between 1895 and 1897, and Earl Fitzwilliam who was elected Lord Mayor in 1909.[6] With these exceptions the mayoralty has been the preserve of the city councillors and aldermen. The political parties nominate their senior members for the office in rotation. The exact terms of the rotation depend on the relative strengths of the parties on the council, but once elected the Lord Mayor is expected to refrain from open political commitment during his year of office.

Membership of English local authorities is a voluntary activity. Aldermen and councillors receive financial compensation for working-time lost while on council business, but they are mostly obliged to earn their living in addition to their public responsibilities. This can impose a considerable strain on senior members of a major local authority, and the Committee on the Management of Local Government (Maud) made a number of proposals for reducing the burden of committee work. They also suggested that a management board should be constituted in local authorities to direct the work of the council, and that the members of this board should be paid a salary. These proposals proved very controversial, and there is little support among council members for the introduction of full-time professionalism into council work, but reform is in the air and most councils are considering their methods of

[6] The Duke of Norfolk was Lord of the Manor in Sheffield and lived in the neighbourhood. His period of office as mayor was notable for two events, both of which were no doubt influenced by the fact that the Earl Marshal of England was first citizen of the borough. In May 1897 the Duke of Norfolk received Queen Victoria when she came to open the new Town Hall, and in the following month the office of mayor was dignified with the title of Lord Mayor. The Duke of Norfolk subsequently became the first honorary freeman of the city, in 1899, and in 1910 he presented Norfolk Park to the corporation. The park land had been open to the public for many years before this gift, and in the seventeenth century it had been the province of numerous charcoal-burners who held licences from the Lord of the Manor: today, as a symbol of the changed social conditions, there are tall blocks of council flats in this area which is being developed into a major housing estate.

organization. The responsibilities of the Sheffield local authority are administered through a number of departments each with its own chief officer. The work of these departments is supervised by the members of the city council through a series of committees and sub-committees. These committees meet monthly in the case of the more important and less frequently for those where the work is not so heavy or continuous. Until 1968 the committee structure was closely parallel to that of the departments. A few of the committees were responsible for more than one department (for example the libraries, art galleries, and museums came under one committee), but the general pattern was one department to each committee. There were twenty full committees corresponding to twenty-four departments. In addition the police were administered as a joint force with Rotherham County Borough.

The council committees had in some instances a very large membership, with the largest of all, education, comprising twenty-eight council members and twelve co-opted non-council members. It is necessary to add that the expenditure of the Sheffield Education Committee in 1966–7 was over fourteen million pounds, so that the responsibilities, as well as the membership, of this committee were considerable. The wide responsibilities of the Education Committee led to the appointment of twenty-eight sub-committees, together with a further fifteen school governing bodies. No other committee approached this number of sub-committees, the next most prolific being the Health Committee which appointed nine sub-committees, but the total number still amounted to the substantial figure of eighty-two, plus the fifteen school governing bodies.

The proliferation of committees and sub-committees was not unusual in English local government, and the figures collected for the Maud Committee indicated that Sheffield was a fairly typical county borough in this respect. Perhaps the city was a little more addicted to sub-committees than other authorities of a similar size, but even so some of the more exotic growths of this species were not to be found in Sheffield. The Maud Committee found sub-committees devoted to a Carol Service, Cattle Grids, and Dry Rot in the Town Hall.[7] In Sheffield a series of reports on individual committees was prepared, but no full committee was superseded, and the number of sub-committees was reduced by only a dozen.

[7] *M.L.G.*, V, *Local Government Administration in England and Wales*, pp. 7 and 539–40.

F

The subject remained, therefore, a matter of dispute between the parties, for the Conservatives were committed to a much more thorough reform.

The Conservatives introduced changes in the committee structure of the council immediately upon their election victory in May 1968. The number of council committees was reduced to eleven (excluding police) in place of the existing twenty, and some were made responsible for several departments. At the same time a determined effort was made to reduce the number of sub-committees. There were only sixteen official sub-committees, though some that were subsidiary to the Education Committee were further redivided into sections, making a total of some thirty sub-divisions altogether.

The actual departments into which the council administration was divided were not affected by the changes in the committee structure, but upon taking office the Conservatives were presented with a report from consultants engaged by the previous Labour-controlled council to consider 'the organization and procedures' of the Corporation. The report[8] criticized the 'fragmented pattern of organization in both elected and official sectors', and proposed a strengthening of the policy committee (see below) together with a realignment of departments into ten groups, each with a group chief officer. The Chief Executive Officer would 'establish a Group Chief Officers' Committee to act as an overall co-ordinating mechanism' to implement the policy decisions of the council. The chief officers of departments within the groups would continue to manage activities within their own technical spheres and the group chief officer would retain responsibility for his own department.

The Conservatives accepted the main recommendations from the consultants and began the reorganization, but they were strongly opposed by the Labour group who considered that the proposals would weaken the control exercised by elected representatives.[9] Before the new structure could take full effect the Labour group resumed control of the council and rescinded the Conservative decisions.

The Labour group prepared their own plan to modernize the

[8] Report on Sheffield County Borough Council, Urwick, Orr and Partners Ltd. (1968).
[9] The opinions of the councillors are further discussed in Chapter 11.

structure of the city council. They propose to achieve a more unified organization by co-ordinating the work of committees instead of by allowing group chief officers to develop powerful departmental empires. Fourteen committees will continue to run the city services (excluding police) and these will be grouped under four co-ordinating committees. The co-ordinating committees will consist of the chairmen, deputy chairmen, and shadow chairmen of the constituent service committees and their task will be to co-ordinate policy among the services which have common ground. The departmental committees will continue to report directly to the policy or finance committees, and to the city council, in matters affecting their responsibilities. Table 3.2 gives an outline of the structure, but the reorganization is still evolving at the time of writing (1969) and further changes may be expected, especially if the Conservatives regain control.

Table 3.2
Sheffield City Council structure, 1969

Co-ordinating group	Committee	Department
None	Policy	Town Clerk and Chief Executive Officer (Printing)
	Finance	City Treasury
Culture and Recreation	Education	Education
	Libraries and arts	Libraries
		Art Galleries
		Museums
	Recreation	Recreation (including baths, laundries and cemeteries)
Health and Welfare	Children's	Children's
	Health and welfare	Public Health
		Social Care
		Weights and Measures
Planning and Housing	Town planning	Architect's
		Planning
	Property	Estate Surveyor's
		Markets and abattoir
	Housing	Housing
Engineering services	Engineering services	City Engineering (including administration, building surveyor's, cleansing, construction and maintenance, lighting, sewage disposal, and technical)
		Fire Brigade
	Public works and services	Public Works
	Transport	Transport
	Water	Water

The Sheffield City Council accepted the consultant's proposals for the constitution of three new units to help the chief executive officer with central co-ordination. The three units are concerned with the following: research into the social, economic, and industrial needs of the city; the co-ordination of activities involving more than one group of departments; and management services to establish standards of performance, improve methods, and reduce costs. These units should greatly strengthen the role of the Policy Committee, which was introduced in 1966 to improve the co-ordination of policy-making within the council. Traditionally in local government each department, under its own chief officer and committee, has enjoyed a certain degree of independence within the general confines of central government control and local rate-fund considerations. There has not been any one committee, or chief officer, who had the authority to co-ordinate *and if need be instruct* the senior officials of the council as a team. Each chief officer has been responsible to his own committee, and the Town Clerk has been at best *primus inter pares*. This picture is now changing. Many councils, including Sheffield, have introduced policy committees and appointed Chief Executive Officers in place of former Town Clerks.

The movement towards a more integrated administrative and policy-making structure will no doubt continue under the impetus of the various reports from committees concerned with local government reform, but none of the policy committees recently established have the full character of the management boards proposed by the Maud Committee. This is not surprising for the Maud proposals were opposed both by the Association of Municipal Corporations and by the County Councils Association who feared that they would remove the sense of participation enjoyed by the present elected members.[10] The policy committees, therefore, should be seen as alternatives to the management boards rather than as instalments on the way to the more thoroughgoing measures which Maud suggested.

In Sheffield the members of the council who were responsible for the creation of the Policy Committee were concerned that it should fulfil two functions. First, it should enable *one* committee to have access to *all* the chief officers, and secondly, it should enable the political party groups to obtain reports from chief officers as a

[10] Reported in *The Times*, 19 July 1968.

basis for policy decisions. The second function was considered in many ways to be more important than the first. The party groups, which will be discussed later in this chapter, have no official standing in the council—any more than have their counterparts at Westminster—and they cannot officially ask a chief officer to undertake work on their behalf. This lack of co-ordination between the party group—the true centre of power—and the chief officers prevented the party group from obtaining the information necessary to take properly backed decisions. The reports to the group had to be made by the chairman of the appropriate committee and he would naturally colour this to favour his own view. Moreover the chairman could only base his report upon information obtained from his own department. He had no authority, for example, to obtain the views of the Borough Treasurer, or other chief officer, on the wider implications of his proposals.

The Policy Committee, as constituted in Sheffield, can lead to a considerable improvement in co-ordination both between departments and between the official and political institutions of the council. Whether the committee achieves this in practice will depend largely upon the individuals who hold the key positions of power, and it is too early yet to give any firm assessment of its performance. A few general comments may be made, however, about the initial working of the committee. First, the committee has comprised the *political* leadership of the council. Both the Labour and the Conservative groups have, when in office, appointed their leader and deputy leader as chairman and deputy chairman respectively of the Policy Committee. The other members of the committee are drawn from members elected to group office. Some important committee chairmen may be excluded, and they may resent this reduction in the *feeling* of power they once obtained; but in effect the chairmen were always subject to group decisions, and they remain responsible for the day-to-day running of their departments. The difference, as one leading member of the council expressed it, is that now the council must see all the departments as part of a whole, and the departments must regard themselves as part of a commonwealth rather than as nation states. The integration of council work in this way is a very desirable objective, and the other changes in administration recently introduced should assist the Policy Committee in its work. It remains to be seen how far the recent reforms meet all the administrative needs of the council.

A second point to note about the composition of the Policy Committee is that the opposition party have been included just as they have been in all other council committees. The committee cannot, therefore, act as a true Cabinet. Some other local authorities have taken the view that a Policy Committee works best when it consists solely of members of the majority party (this would appear to be the opinion of the Labour Party nationally), but the Labour group on the Sheffield City Council considered that a more responsible opposition would result from an early involvement in policy debate. The Conservatives continued with this view when they became the party in control. The inclusion of opposition members on the Policy Committee is in line with the recommendations of the Maud Committee with respect to management boards but some councillors, particularly on the Labour benches, objected to the opposition party receiving information in the Policy Committee before the groups had discussed the issue in private. A reluctance to improve the dispersal of information is part of a much wider controversy over secrecy in council affairs; it was not intended, however, nor would it be practical, to remove all prior discussion from the confidential conclaves of the groups. When this is felt necessary the Policy Committee receives reports from the chief officers, so that the documents become the property of the council, and then further discussion is adjourned to enable the groups to consider the matter. In this way the groups receive the information they need for their deliberations, while the chief officers are not embarrassed in their responsibility to the council rather than to the political parties.

Finally, it is clear that in the first few years of its existence the Policy Committee was feeling its way. The consideration of broad policy was interspersed with many minor matters concerned more with the implementation of policy than with its determination. The distinction between policy and administration is a difficult question, and many Labour councillors hold to the view that it is impossible to separate these two aspects of council work to the extent that the Maud Committee proposed; nevertheless the Policy Committee did appear to deal with some trivial matters which should have been beneath its consideration.

Since 1919, when the Labour Party contested every council ward for the first time, the municipal elections in Sheffield have been a contest between Labour and one other major party. In all this time the council has been managed on strict party lines with regular party group meetings before the full council meeting to enable party policy to be decided. Both parties expect their members to support the decision of the group within the council chamber, and whips are appointed to supervise group management and discipline. The party that obtains the majority on the city council controls all the policy-making for the city, and appoints its members to the chairmanship and deputy chairmanship of all committees. This is not the invariable practice in county boroughs, some of which appoint a few chairmen, or more frequently deputy chairmen, from the minority party.[11] In Sheffield both parties take the view that those who have the political responsibility must also occupy the appropriate public offices. The true centre of power in Sheffield is not the council chamber, which like the House of Commons is a forum from which to appeal to the electorate, but the ruling party group which meets in private, and it is necessary to describe in some detail the constitution of the groups if the political life of the city is to be understood.

The Labour group consists of all the members of that party who serve on the city council, together with seven representatives of the political wing of the Sheffield Trades and Labour Council, which is in effect the borough Labour Party. These seven representatives have no voting rights at group meetings. The group meets once a month on the Monday before the council meeting to discuss the agenda, and once in the middle of the month for more general business. Six officers are elected by the group: leader, deputy leader, chairman, deputy chairman, whip, and deputy whip. These officers together with three other councillors elected by the group, and the chairman and secretary of the borough Labour Party, form an executive committee which meets three times a month. It is the executive committee which is the policy-making body for the Labour group, and when the party is in power they are the directing force in the affairs of the city. It is from the group executive that Labour representatives on the council's Policy Committee are chosen. The Labour group also nominates two of

---

[11] A general discussion of the effects of party politics on the operation of local authorities is contained in *M.L.G.*, V, *Local Government Administration in England and Wales*, Ch. 5. See also J. G. Bulpitt, *Party Politics in English Local Government*, and G. W. Jones, *Borough Politics*.

its members to the executive committee of the borough Labour
Party to complete the liaison between the two bodies. These
nominees have no vote at the borough Party, but other members
of the council may, of course, be present as full delegates from
constituent organizations.

The precise relationship between the Labour group on the city
council and the borough Labour Party is complex. Formally the
borough party is responsible for the formation of the policy upon
which Labour candidates seek election, while the group decide
upon the timing and priorities in the implementation of the
policy. In practice the group have, or take, more freedom than
this, and when in power can point to their constitutional position
as representatives of the electorate to justify their actions. The
borough Labour Party is also responsible for the management of a
panel of prospective council candidates, and provides a series of
evening classes each winter for intending members of the panel.[12]
Any affiliated organization may nominate eligible members for
inclusion on the panel, but acceptance is by no means automatic.
Each person nominated is interviewed by a committee of the
borough Labour Party, and many candidates for the panel are not
accepted until they undertake a more active part in local party
organization, or prepare themselves by studying local council
affairs. The Labour Party officials consider that this elaborate
procedure is necessary because in many wards the candidate
nominated by the party is assured of success at the polls. The ward
organizations of the party are free to select any candidate from the
panel who is not already committed to another ward, and a member of the panel is expected to accept nomination in any part of the
city including those where the chance of election is slim or non-
existent. The ward selection conferences are attended by a representative of the borough Labour Party to ensure that the correct
procedure is followed—no prospective candidate, for example,
may be asked to state his or her religion—but the conference
exercises a real freedom of choice. In some safe Labour wards as
many as a hundred members may attend the selection conference
and in these cases they assume the character of a primary election.
Even sitting councillors must be renominated by this procedure

---

[12] In 1969 the Labour Party forewent their classes and joined with the Conservatives
in supporting an Extramural course conducted by the author. Chief officers and leading
members of both parties were among the lecturers.

when their term of office expires and they are not always assured of success. In 1968 two councillors failed to secure renomination including the chairman of the housing management committee; the action of his ward party was prompted by a disagreement with the council's rent rebate scheme.

The Conservative group on the Sheffield City Council is organized in a manner that has a surface similarity to the Labour group organization but in fact the differences are considerable. First, it is only in recent years that the group has emerged as a specifically *Conservative* opposition to the Labour Party. For many years the group was less cohesive than its opponents with the Conservatives only the leading force in a coalition which was prone to change its approach and even its name from time to time. After the emergence of the Labour Party in 1919 the Conservatives and Liberals agreed to form a Citizens' Party to fight municipal elections, while continuing with their separate organizations for all other purposes. In this way it was hoped to avoid splitting the anti-Labour vote in the city. The Citizens' Party continued in existence throughout the 1920s, but in 1929 the Conservative Central Office in London sent a representative to Sheffield to persuade the Conservatives to contest the local elections in their own name. The result of this visit was to split both the Citizens' Party *and* the Conservative Party, for not all the Conservatives agreed to leave their Liberal allies. In the subsequent election the opposition to the Labour majority on the city council was in complete disarray and suffered the expected electoral consequences. The membership of the city council had been enlarged from sixty-eight to ninety-six before this election and most of the new seats were won by the Labour Party.

After this defeat the local Conservative Party sponsored a new party, the Progressive Party, to replace the Citizens' Party as a basis for a Conservative/Liberal coalition for local election purposes. Although a few Conservatives remained independent the Progressive Party prospered as national feeling moved against the Labour Party after the 1931 economic and political crisis. In 1932 the newly formed party won control of the Sheffield City Council. The success of the Progressives was short-lived, control returned to Labour in the following year, but the Progressive Party continued its existence. Throughout this period there were some Liberals, and a few Conservatives, who continued to contest the elections under their own name rather than accept the coalition label. Indeed the coalition became less and less representative of the Liberal Party after 1945, and the Progressive Party was re-organized in 1948 with the title of Conservative and National Liberal. The National Liberal element in the alliance consisted of a few long-established members of the city council who had first been elected in the Liberal cause. The leader of the group, Sir Harold Jackson, was himself a National Liberal—first elected to the council in 1913—and he had been a dominant influence in all the anti-Labour coalitions. It was in deference to him that the city organization kept the joint title although the Conservatives gradually became the sole political force within the group as the National Liberals retired. In 1964 Sir Harold retired and his place as leader was taken by a Conservative. The link with the previous leader was not completely lost as the deputy leader of the group had been articled as a solicitor to Sir Harold Jackson as a young man, and upon *his* retirement Sir Harold's son—another solicitor—was elected deputy leader. Both these men, however, were Conservatives.

Another obvious distinction between the Labour and Conservative organizations is the influence of the leader within the group. The leader of the Conservative group is elected annually by secret ballot, but he then *appoints* the other group officers who comprise the deputy leader, the whip (who also acts as treasurer), the assistant whip and his assistant, and the secretary. The secretary of the group is customarily the chief Conservative agent in the city who is the only non-council member of the group: he serves without voting rights. The group executive consists of the six officers, two members co-opted by the leader, and four members elected by the group at their annual meeting. The group meets monthly, on the Monday before the city council meeting, and the executive meets twice a month. The leader of the Conservative group has far greater personal power in determining his colleagues in the leadership of the group than does the leader of the Labour group, where all leading positions are open to election. This reflects a general difference in approach by the two parties nationally and the difference, though real, is not as great as the printed word would imply. The Conservative leader must take account of the views of his group in making his appointments, and the influence of the Labour leader on nominations for office may be considerable.

The third difference in the organization of the two groups to be noticed here is the separation of the Conservative group from the party outside the council. There is not a mutual exchange of delegates to each others' meetings in the way of the Labour group and borough Labour Party. In the Conservative Party in Sheffield the liaison between group and party is achieved through a Municipal Elections Committee. This committee normally meets once a quarter, and comprises representatives of the group together with the officers of constituency organizations, with the leader of the group as chairman. The Municipal Elections Committee co-ordinates and discusses municipal matters, but it has no policy-forming functions. Policy-making remains firmly with the leader and the members of the group. The Municipal Elections Committee appoints a sub-committee to consider the composition of the municipal panel, from which the wards must select their candidates. This, of course, is similar to the Labour practice and the same concern for standards is expressed by both parties.

The Conservative group, therefore, is less integrated organizationally with its parent party in the city than is the Labour group, and there is a general feeling that the Conservative members of the council feel less disciplined by their party. Nevertheless the Conservative leader may, at his sole discretion, issue whips on any matter before the city council. Members of the group are expected to observe this whip and attend accordingly. Non-observance of the whip by any member requires a written explanation to the chief whip who makes a report on the matter to the executive committee. It is interesting to note that just as the Labour group is often criticized by the left-wing within the Trades and Labour Council, so the Conservative group is criticized within the wider Conservative organization in the city. There is often an impression that the Conservative group is not sufficiently right-wing, an attitude which one senior member of the group explained as a result of the greater responsibility induced in the group by their closeness to power and the sources of information. He also considered that when in opposition a party should retain its loyalty to Sheffield, and to its city council, in relation to outside bodies: an interesting echo from Westminster of Her Majesty's Loyal Opposition!

The political party groups are undoubtedly the most important influences on the attitudes of the members of the Sheffield City

Council. The protestations of independence which some council-lors make are seldom reflected in cross-voting and only rarely in public dispute with their party leaders. This is not to suggest that public disagreement never occurs, nor that the debate *within* group meetings is not real and on occasion acrimonious, but loyalty to the party is expected and is usually received. The political parties, however, though dominant, are only one source of possible influence upon the opinions and decisions of council members who were asked a number of questions during our research to elicit the groups they considered were active in seeking to influence council opinion. The answers to these questions are, of course, subjective. One councillor may remember a communication which another forgets or completely disregards. The subjectivity of the answers does mean, however, that the council members are remembering those groups or organizations which they *perceive* as important in seeking to influence their opinions; and the answers suggest the attitude of council members to such pressure-group activity.

The council members were asked first whether they usually had letters, telephone calls, or personal visits on behalf of groups or organizations interested in particular aspects of their council work. Most of them did remember such communications, and this response was so overwhelming that only a slight variation can be noted between the parties, or between committee chairmen (including deputy-chairmen throughout) and back-bench mem-bers of the council. There is some indication in Table 3.3 that Labour back-benchers are less aware of such communications and this may reflect the different social background of the member-ship of the two groups: the Conservative councillors, for example, are more likely to be on the telephone than their Labour counter-parts, who will also in some cases be less familiar with routine office procedures for dealing with their mail. The leaders of most of the pressure groups—the tenants are an obvious exception—are also likely to come from the same social background as the Conservatives and may approach them more easily. There was no difference, however, between the chairmen—all Labour at the time of the interviews—and the Conservatives in their response to this question. The council responsibilities of the chairmen obviously overcame the other considerations already mentioned.

The council members were then asked whether they received such communications frequently, occasionally, or rarely. The

Table 3.3
Council members receiving communications from organizations

		Party affiliation		Council responsibility	
Base	Total 107*	Cons. 48	Lab. 59	Cttee. chmn. and deputies 38	Others 70
	%	%	%	%	%
Yes	89	92	86	92	87
No	10	6	14	8	11
Refused/Don't Know	1	2	0	0	1

* Excluding one Independent.
Note: The percentages in some columns may not add to one hundred
owing to rounding.
Source: Survey of Sheffield City Council.

replies were divided fairly evenly between these three categories (see Table 3.4) and again there is little variation between the parties or between chairmen and other members of the council. This seems surprising. Organizations seeking to influence the policy of the council would be expected to devote more effort towards the ruling group or towards the committee chairmen.

Table 3.4
Frequency of contact with organizations

		Party affiliation		Council responsibility	
Base	Total 107*	Cons. 48	Lab. 59	Cttee. chmn. and deputies 38	Others 70
	%	%	%	%	%
Frequently	31	33	29	29	31
Sometimes	31	29	32	32	30
Rarely	26	29	24	29	25
Never/No	10	6	14	8	11
Refused/D.K.	2	2	2	3	1

* Excluding one Independent.
Note: The percentages in some columns may not add to one hundred
owing to rounding.
Source: Survey of Sheffield City Council.

There may be a number of reasons why this does not appear to happen. First, many organizations simply circulate *every* member of the council and the subjective assessment of the frequency of such contact will depend upon the individual receiving the communications. A back-bench councillor may consider a few circulars or calls each month as frequent lobbying, while a busy chairman will consider them to be insignificant. Also, many groups wishing to influence the council seek the help of those council members who

Table 3.5
Council members' contact with groups

		Party affiliation		Council responsibility	
Base	Total 107*	Cons. 48	Lab. 59	Cttee. chmn. and deputies 38	Others 70
Mentions contact with	*No.*	*No.*	*No.*	*No.*	*No.*
Tenants' groups	28	7	21	13	15
Community associations	11	3	8	5	6
Teachers' groups	39	25	14	10	29
Other education groups	10	5	5	3	7
The Inland Waterways Protection Soc.	21	14	7	7	14
Wadsley Village Pres. Soc.	8	5	3	0	8
Other preservation soc.	12	10	2	1	11
Anglo-Rhodesian Soc.	6	6	0	0	6
Others	67	29	38	26	41
N.A. No approaches from groups	8	2	6	2	6
Refused/cannot remember/D.K.	8	5	3	2	6

* Excluding one Independent.
Note: Some council members mentioned more than one organization.
Source: Survey of Sheffield City Council.

are known to be sympathetic. In any case sympathetic councillors are more likely to remember communications than those who have no interest in the subject. When the council members were asked to specify the type of organizations that had contacted them during the previous six months, they responded by mentioning a great variety of groups. The groups mentioned most frequently are shown in Table 3.5, but the others covered a wide range of organizations including a canoe club, the West Indian Association, a mountaineering club, and the Family Planning Association.

The type of communication varied according to the organization. The teachers' groups, mainly the unions, sent round circulars which included items both on salaries and conditions of service, and on educational policy. The other educational groups were almost entirely concerned with the issue of comprehensive education. The Anglo-Rhodesian Society asked for subscriptions and attendance at meetings, while the preservation societies drew attention to the problems arising in particular areas such as Wadsley Village, Broomhall, and Dore. The Community Associations were concerned with a number of issues, for example meeting-halls and zebra crossings, but the tenants' groups were inevitably preoccupied with the rent rebate scheme. The tenants often visited the councillors in their own homes in addition to writing letters and lobbying the council meetings. The Inland Waterways Protection Society made a considerable impact upon the council members by conducting an energetic campaign against their decision to acquiesce in the British Waterways Board's plan to close the Sheffield section of the Sheffield and South Yorkshire Navigation. Every member of the council was circulated with a detailed objection to this decision, and a petition was prepared and forwarded to the Town Clerk. The city council refused to consider the petition, but the Trades and Labour Council gave their support to the protest and published an article by the Society's secretary in their monthly journal at a time when Labour controlled the city council. The Society may have been unsuccessful, but their case certainly did not go unheard; or unremembered by the council members we interviewed.

The organizations mentioned during the interviews varied between the two parties. Two-thirds of the approaches from teachers' groups were mentioned by the Conservatives, who were at that time the minority party. The Conservatives were also more aware of the preservation groups. The Labour members mentioned the tenants' associations much more frequently, which reflects the campaign these associations were conducting to secure changes in the rent rebate scheme. This campaign, which is discussed in Chapter 10, was conducted with some political sophistication, and tenants' association members lobbied the council members for the wards in which the council housing estates were situated. The councillors for these wards were, of course, predominantly Labour.

It has already been mentioned that the answers given to the questionnaire were subjective. They measured the council members' perception—or memory—of what happened rather than the actual occurrences. The object, however, is to discover which organizations influence the council members' consideration of affairs, and the subjective replies are the appropriate ones: we are not concerned with the capacity of the councillors' waste-paper baskets. Each council member was asked, therefore, whether any group or organization had volunteered information which had helped to form his or her opinion on a particular topic. They were also asked whether there was any organization whose opinions they generally took into account when forming their own opinion. As we expected these proved to be delicate questions. Many council members were reluctant to suggest that they did not exercise an independent judgement on council matters. One councillor made the point that 'in the majority of cases brought by an outside body the case is built upon a presumption of facts. . . . The tenants, for example, present cases to back their arguments, but they do not provide the whole picture.' Nevertheless nearly two-thirds of the council members recognized that organizations had given them information that had helped form their opinion on a particular council matter. Committee chairmen and their deputies were more prepared to accept this than other members of the council and the leadership groups of both parties readily entertained the idea of contact with organizations. Such contact they considered to be consistent with the positive virtue of keeping in touch with the people they represented and they were not at all

Table 3.6
Council members accepting that organizations provided information which helped to form their opinion on a particular topic

		Party affiliation		Council responsibility	
	Base	Total 107*	Cons. 48	Lab. 59	Cttee. chmn. and deputies 38	Others 70
	%	%	%	%	%
Yes	60	56	63	76	51
No	39	44	36	24	47
Refused/D.K.	1	0	1	0	1

* Excluding one Independent.
Note: The percentages in some columns may not add to one hundred owing to rounding.
Source: Survey of Sheffield City Council.

defensive about it. The views of the leadership contrasted with the views of some of the backbenchers who maintained that they made up their own minds, implying that they were above sectional interests: a rather old-fashioned, Rousseauian, approach to representation. Perhaps the leadership is simply more realistic.

The organizations providing information which helped a member of the council to form an opinion on a particular matter are naturally similar to the organizations already mentioned. The large category of 'others' again indicates that these groups are extremely varied. Perhaps the most notable feature of Table 3.7 is the *small* effect which most groups appear to have on the forma-

Table 3.7
Organizations providing information which helped council members to form an opinion

		Party affiliation		Council responsibility	
	Total	Cons.	Lab.	Cttee. chmn. and deputies	Others
Base—those answering 'yes' in Table 3.6	64	27	37	29	36
	No.	*No.*	*No.*	*No.*	*No.*
Community associations	11	5	6	5	6
Tenants' associations	19	5	14	11	8
Teachers' groups	7	4	3	2	5
Canal preservation soc.	7	4	3	3	4
Other preservation socs.	6	4	2	2	4
Others	34	12	22	15	19

Note: Some councillors mentioned more than one organization.
Source: Survey of Sheffield City Council.

tion of council members' opinions. The one real success would seem to be the notice taken of the tenants' associations by the committee chairmen and their deputies.

Although nearly two-thirds of the council members agreed that their opinions on particular issues were influenced by information received from pressure groups, less than half were prepared to state that they *generally* took account of outside organizations before forming their opinion. A really significant difference between the parties emerged in the answers to this question. The Labour respondents gave a much larger proportion of positive answers than did the Conservatives. The organizations mentioned by the

Table 3.8
Council members acknowledg-
ing one or more organizations
as a general influence on their
opinion

	Total	Cons.	Lab.
Base	107*	48	59
	%	%	%
Yes	46	37	53
No	51	62	42
Refused/D.K.	3	0	5

* Excluding one Independent.
Note: The percentages in some columns
may not add to one hundred owing
to rounding.
Source: Survey of Sheffield City
Council.

Labour people were trade unions, co-operative associations, and
other bodies affiliated to the Labour Party. Those Conservatives
who acknowledged a continuing influence on their opinion were
also likely to mention their party organization outside the council.

This difference between members of different parties continued
when they were asked if their Party group on the council generally
took account of the opinions of any other organizations. Over half

Table 3.9
Council members considering
that their party group generally took account of the opinions of another organization

	Total	Cons.	Lab.
Base	107*	48	59
	%	%	%
Yes	45	31	56
No	45	60	32
Refused/D.K.	10	8	12

* Excluding one Independent.
Note: The percentages in some columns
may not add to one hundred
owing to rounding.
Source: Survey of Sheffield City Council.

the Labour members agreed that this was so compared to less than a third of the Conservatives. The Conservatives, of course, frequently attack the Labour group on the city council for being dominated by the opinions of the Trades and Labour Council, and there is no doubt that the relationship between this body and the Labour group is different in kind from the relationship of the Conservative group to any outside body. It is interesting to note, for example, that when the members of the council were asked if the *other* group was influenced by an outside organization the Conservatives had no doubt about their answer. Over three-quarters of them replied, 'Yes, the Trades and Labour Council'. The Labour members were more hesitant. Less than half of them thought that the Conservatives were generally influenced by an outside organization and just as many confessed that they were not sure. Even those Labour members who recognized an influence on the Conservative group differed as to its nature. Half of them quoted the Chamber of Trade or the Junior Chamber of Commerce, but a variety of other organizations were mentioned.

The organizational relationship of the Labour group to the Trades and Labour Council has already been described. The relationship differs from any obtaining in the Conservative Party for two main reasons: one practical and the other ideological. First, the Labour Party is a federation of trade unions and socialist organizations, and the trade unions send delegates to borough Labour Party meetings. Secondly, the Labour Party—despite the efforts of successive Labour prime ministers—has never been unanimous in its interpretation of the proper constitutional relationship between a political party and its elected represen-tatives. There are still those who suggest that to be democratic a party leadership should be subject to control by the membership whether the leaders are in or out of office. The Labour leadership on the council, as in Westminster, deny that they are *controlled* by the party outside, but they know that such denials annoy many of their own followers. The reality of the relationship, as is usual, is much more complex than the partisan arguments would suggest. A Labour member explained that 'the Trades and Labour Council representatives sit on the executive, they have a terrific influence, but they are such an amorphous body that they do not propose a single rigid policy'. When there is a dispute over policy within the Labour Party, in other words, the conflict is present both within the group *and* within the Trades and Labour Council: the two organizations are not implacably opposed to one another. The real conflict develops when there is a majority within the two organizations for opposite sides of a dispute. This situation occasionally occurs and it is present in several of the issues discussed in later chapters. There is no completely satisfactory way of dealing with such a disagreement when one does occur, so the discussions between the two organizations continue until the issue is resolved by the usual political expedients of time or compromise.

It is not, of course, necessarily reprehensible for a party group on the city council to modify its policy in response to the opinions of outside bodies. Contact with such bodies is accepted as one of the ways in which public representatives are made aware of the wishes of their constituents, and there is a strong case for suggesting that we suffer from too little, rather than too much, contact of this kind. Eight out of ten members of the Sheffield City Council considered that their party group took account of the views of other organizations on specific issues. This proportion was far higher than the number who accepted that communications with outside bodies helped them to form their *own* opinion (Table 3.6); and it is nearly double the proportion who agreed that their group is *generally* influenced by outside organizations. There is no doubt that council members distinguish between influence and

Table 3.10
Council members considering that their party group takes account of the opinions of other organizations on specific issues

	Total	Cons.	Lab.
Base	107*	48	59
	%	%	%
Yes	81	80	83
No	13	17	10
Refused/D.K.	6	4	7

* Excluding one Independent.
Note: The percentages in some columns may not add to one hundred owing to rounding.
Source: Survey of Sheffield City Council.

control, and many of them consider that *regular* influence by one, or a few, outside organizations could slip easily from the weaker to the stronger alternative. They are anxious, therefore, to deny that any general influence exists, but they are quite ready to recognize the effect a particular organization can have on an individual issue, and there is little difference between the parties on this point. One of the Conservatives, for instance, explained that in the matter 'of car parking and traffic restrictions, the [Conservative] party formulated its own views, and then after listening to the Junior Chamber of Commerce and the Chamber of Trade, we modified our views. We also listened to them on the airport issue. Similarly after we had put forward our own plan on rent rebates we listened to the Tenants' Associations and made modifications.' But this is only one of the more detailed explanations and it does not differ in spirit from many others received from members of both parties. In all, some 200 different combinations of groups and issues were mentioned by council members and some indication of the variety may be obtained from the following examples: fishing organizations/fishing on Rivelin Valley; University/University extensions; butchers/opening hours of the abattoir; builders/effect of devaluation; British Waterways Association/closure of canal; parents' associations/education.

The ability of outside organizations to influence council members depends to a great extent on the openness with which council business is conducted. If the decisions are made privately without previous public discussions, then even those most affected will be presented with a *fait accompli* which it will be difficult to qualify. It was this feeling of ineffectiveness during their long years of opposition that must have induced the bitterness of the attacks by the Conservatives on the Trades and Labour Council. They suspected, and with some justification, that this outside body had a greater influence on council affairs than many elected representatives. Their feelings were not, however, *completely* justified. For long periods during their years of office the Labour group were a closed community: exercising a fierce version of party discipline that forbade public expressions of dissent. It was nearly as difficult for the membership of the Trades and Labour Council to penetrate the policy-making caucus as it was for other organizations to do so. The relaxation of discipline in the Labour group, and the greater emphasis on public debate which began to develop in the 1960s, gave many organizations a greater opportunity to participate in the discussions preceding policy decisions. It may be argued that local political institutions were becoming more democratic as they became more open to discussion; local politicians of both parties, and local commentators, certainly noticed a change in the style of Sheffield politics from the middle of the 1960s; but the number of people involved remained small. It is, of course, the role of the pressure groups to crystallize feeling upon a particular issue and to present an opinion to the public representatives, but not all opinions are represented by one of these stage armies. The renewed interest in ways by which the general public might be informed, or even involved, in matters of public policy may lead to improvements, but in any event we may agree with Michels in one of his rare optimistic moments:

Democracy is a treasure which no one will ever discover by deliberate search. But in continuing our search, in labouring indefatigably to discover the undiscoverable, we shall perform a work which will have fertile results in the democratic sense.[13]

Here is an issue to which we shall return in the final chapter.

[13] R. Michels, *Political Parties*, Collier Books, p. 368.

4

The Local M.P.

'Pray, what is the country?' inquired Mr. Rigby. 'The country is nothing; it is the constituency you have to deal with.' BENJAMIN DISRAELI, *Coningsby*

IN the previous chapter we considered the local political institutions in Sheffield, but one political institution remains that occupies an ambiguous position between national and local affairs: the local Member of Parliament; this chapter will be concerned with the extent to which the Sheffield M.P.s act as a local political institution. The six Members of Parliament for the city were interviewed during the summer of 1967 and were asked a series of standardized questions upon their relationship to Sheffield and to their constituents. The present chapter is largely based upon the answers to these questions together with material taken from the surveys of the local electorate and of the members of the city council. The Member of Parliament for Sheffield, Brightside, Mr. R. Winterbottom, died just before this chapter was written. The comments that follow, therefore, refer to the six Members elected at the 1966 General Election, and do not include the present Member for Brightside, Mr. Griffiths, who retained the seat for Labour at a by-election in 1968.

A local Member of Parliament is naturally expected to represent his constituents, and most Members take care to retain the support of their local party followers. Nevertheless, in these days of national 'swings', when politicians may be carried into Parliament irrespective of local considerations, the view quoted at the head of this chapter may seem somewhat old-fashioned. It should be remembered also that some Members of Parliament, quite properly, will have entered politics with an interest in national concerns: they will seek ministerial office, or specialize in economic or foreign affairs; the time they can then spend upon constituency matters will necessarily be reduced. The dual nature of the influences to which Members of Parliament are subject makes their position ambiguous in local affairs; and if, in this chapter, the emphasis is placed upon the local involvement of M.P.s, it must be remembered that this is not their only function.

Sheffield is divided into six constituencies: Attercliffe, Brightside, Hallam, Heeley, Hillsborough, and Park. The areas included in the city following the 1967 boundary extensions remain, for the time being, in their former constituencies of North-East Derbyshire and Penistone. Seven out of the eight constituencies mentioned are represented by Labour Members (1969), and the constituencies in the Sheffield area have been traditionally among the safest Labour seats in the House of Commons. In 1945 the Labour Party obtained five of the seven constituencies into which Sheffield was then divided, four of them with majorities of over 10,000. The Conservatives held the other two with rather lower majorities. In the elections of 1950 and 1951 the city's parliamentary representation remained the same. The lowest majority enjoyed by a successful candidate during these two elections, in which nationally the Labour Party lost their 1945 majority, was nearly 9,000. In five of the Sheffield constituencies the majority was over 16,000 on both occasions.

Before the 1955 General Election the city's representation was reduced from seven to six following a parliamentary boundary revision, and from then until 1964 the constituencies returned four Labour and two Conservative Members of Parliament. The majorities in every case—save one—varied from safe to overwhelming. The single exception was in the Heeley constituency, where the Conservative majority, which had been over 10,000 during the 1950s, was reduced to under 2,000 at the 1964 election. In 1966 Sir Peter Roberts, who had held the seat since its creation in 1950, retired, and the Labour Party won the seat with a majority of just under 5,000. This left Hallam as the only Conservative constituency in the city.

Of the six Members of Parliament elected, or re-elected, to represent Sheffield in 1966, not one had actually lived in the city immediately before entering the House of Commons for the first time. Two of the six, however, could claim to be local men: one lived in a nearby village, and another had a *pied-à-terre* in the city and worked in the university. One of the other four had family connections with Sheffield, but three of the six were strangers to the city when they were first nominated. These three were all sponsored by trade unions;[1] one other Member was sponsored by the Co-operative Party, affiliated to the Labour Party. The two Members most closely associated with Sheffield before their election were elected without any formal sponsorship: one of these two, of course, was a Conservative. It should not be thought, however, that the largest trade unions in the city were bringing their members from outside to occupy the safe Labour seats in Sheffield. The three Members of Parliament with official trade union sponsorship came from industries that had little connection with the basic industries of Sheffield, and one of them only became sponsored after his election to the House of Commons. The three trade unions concerned were the National Union of Railwaymen, the Union of Shop, Distributive, and Allied Workers, and the Clerical and Administrative Workers' Union. In the industrial constituencies of Sheffield the Labour Party members wanted a trade-union-sponsored candidate, but within this constraint their choice depended upon the policies and personalities of the rival applicants, and not upon the particular trade union to which he might belong. The Conservative Member for Hallam was the only Sheffield Member of Parliament whose occupation, as director of a family steel and engineering company, associated him with the industrial life of the city. The five Labour Members of Parliament included: a journalist, a university teacher, a university administrator, and two full-time trade union officials, but only the journalist was able to continue in his occupation after being elected, and he could continue only as a free-lance.

Their degree of association with the city before their election for Sheffield constituencies is no indication of the M.P.s' interpretation of their role once elected. One Member who came from outside the city moved into his constituency after his election and became the very model of a 'local' representative; on the other hand one Member who was closely associated with the city before election actually loosened his residential ties subsequently. It seems, therefore, that the way in which a Member of Parliament approaches his job is more a matter of temperament and ambition

---

[1] Mr. Winterbottom was sponsored by U.S.D.A.W., and when he died his place was taken by a nominee of the British Iron, Steel, and Kindred Trades Association, who came from South Wales.

than a result of previous interest in the locality; and those constituents who clamour for a 'local' candidate may not always get
the type of Member of Parliament that they evidently desire.

The involvement of the Sheffield Members of Parliament in
local constituency or city affairs varied enormously: two were
obviously 'local M.P.s'; two more did their constituency work
with a certain amount of enthusiasm; but the other two spent little
time in their constituency, and had no particular interest in
Sheffield as a city. The difference in approach may be indicated
from the attitudes taken to local cases raised at the M.P.'s regular
'surgery'. One Sheffield M.P. thought that the satisfaction of the
job came from dealing with constituency cases, 'and therefore,' he
added, 'I take what comes'. Another Sheffield M.P., on the
contrary, referred to a 'fleeting irritation at getting problems
which don't concern me as an M.P.' Despite these differences,
every Sheffield Member of Parliament gave his constituents an
opportunity of approaching him within the city. Five out of six
held regular surgeries at approximately monthly intervals, while
the sixth, who lived in the city, saw people by appointment at his
home, or informally at the numerous social gatherings he attended.

Constituency surgeries are a normal part of the activities of
most British Members of Parliament.[2] The intention of the surgery
is to allow any constituent to see his Member of Parliament with
the minimum amount of formality. In Sheffield an advertisement
is usually placed in the local newspaper and the sessions take place
either in the Town Hall—three out of five—or in the party offices.
Four of the Sheffield M.P.s are accompanied at their surgery by a
member of the city council, and, in view of the nature of the
problems raised, this seems a necessary precaution. Every one of
the Sheffield M.P.s stated that housing was the issue that brought
most people to the surgery, and housing, of course, is a local
authority responsibility. After housing the principal matters raised
at the surgeries were pensions and taxation problems, though the
range of matters raised was very wide and included matrimonial
disputes and quarrels with neighbours. The Members of Parliament regarded the surgeries as part of their work as public
representatives and did not consider that it was a particularly

[2] R. E. Dowse, 'The M.P. and His Surgery', *Political Studies*, XI, 3 (October 1963).
The survey reported by Dr. Dowse suggests that over three-quarters of the M.P.s at
that time held surgeries.

effective method of securing electoral support. The numbers involved were small, and the applicant might have to be disappointed in his request. The people who attended the surgeries were not, in any event, always constituents of the Member of Parliament who saw them. Four of the six M.P.s indicated that they frequently saw people from other Sheffield constituencies, one suggesting that the proportion might be as high as a third of all the cases he dealt with at his surgery. The five Labour M.P.s obviously treated this informally: if it was a constituency matter then the problem would be passed to the appropriate Member, but otherwise, as one put it, they 'happily took in each other's washing'. The relationship between the Labour Members of Parliament and the Conservative was naturally more formal, and occasionally even strained, nevertheless the cross-constituency cases still occurred quite frequently.

The cases brought to the attention of a Member of Parliament at his surgery represent only a part of the work that he does on behalf of individual constituents. Many people prefer to write to their M.P., at least in the first instance, if they wish to raise any matter with him. Five of the Sheffield M.P.s thought that they received on average between twenty and thirty letters a week from constituents and from firms or organizations within the constituency. The other M.P. put his average rather higher, at fifty each week. In addition to the letters arriving from constituency sources, each Member of Parliament receives a considerable amount of mail from other places. In most cases in Sheffield this general mail far outweighed the local correspondence, though the proportion was affected by the general interests of the individual Member of Parliament and the amount of publicity which he attracted. A public statement on a controversial issue was sure to bring letters, and they were subject on occasion to organized postal campaigns. One Sheffield M.P. reported that he had received a thousand letters concerned with abortion after Catholic priests had suggested this approach to their congregations, and on another occasion he received two hundred and fifty letters from people supporting the tenants' associations in their opposition to the rent rebate scheme. The total amount of mail which most Members of Parliament receive obviously presents a problem to them. Only three of the Sheffield M.P.s delegated any of the work arising from their mail to secretaries, and even then this delegation could only be partial. Other Sheffield M.P.s spoke of spending one or two hours a day on their correspondence, and of writing the answers by hand, sometimes during late sittings at the House of Commons, but there was surprisingly little complaint about the lack of secretarial assistance afforded to Members of Parliament. Indeed one Sheffield M.P. thought that to have an efficient secretary would take the joy out of his job: 'Reading my letters,' he said, 'is part of my education.'

The extent to which the local Members of Parliament are successful in cultivating their constituencies may be indicated in a number of ways, the most obvious being the proportion of the electorate who know the name and party allegiance of their parliamentary representative. An M.P. can scarcely claim to be making an impact in his constituency if people do not even know his name. This knowledge will be associated with the general level of education enjoyed by his constituents, and with the socio-economic status of their occupations, but the Member of Parliament can influence the awareness of the electorate by his activities or personality. In the survey undertaken in preparation for this

Table 4.1
Awareness of name and party allegiance of M.P.

(1) *By socio-economic status and education*

	Total	Socio-economic status					Education		
		1 & 2	3	4	5	6	Higher	Secondary	Lower
Base	584	60	156	139	144	83	42	75	467
	%	%	%	%	%	%	%	%	%
Correct	41	48	56	38	33	28	57	55	37
Incorrect/D.K.	59	52	44	62	68	72	43	45	63

Notes: The percentages may not add to one hundred owing to rounding. See Appendix C for definitions.
Source: Survey of Sheffield Electorate.

book four out of every ten respondents could name their Member of Parliament correctly and state the party to which he belonged (Table 4.1). Those in white-collar occupations were better informed than those in manual occupations or those who had never been employed.

The ability to recall the name and party allegiance of the local

Member of Parliament may be affected also by the voting behaviour of the elector. To vote for a candidate in an election requires the knowledge of that candidate's name, and the name of the M.P. is, therefore, more likely to be remembered by his supporters than by those who did not vote for him. In Sheffield there is only one Conservative Member of Parliament which means that Conservative voters are more likely to live in constituencies represented by Labour M.P.s than Labour voters are to live in Conservative constituencies. Liberals and supporters of other minor parties have no chance of being represented by the candidate of their choice.[3] In Table 4.2 the influence of the coincidence of party between elector and Member of Parliament may be discerned. In general the Conservative voters enjoy a higher socioeconomic status than the Labour voters, but they are less likely to live in constituencies represented by the candidates of their choice, and this is particularly true for manual workers who vote Conservative. This means that the difference between the proportion of Conservative and Labour voters who are aware of the name and party allegiance of their Member of Parliament is reduced. The

---

Table 4.2
Awareness of name and party allegiance of M.P.

(2) *By voting habits*

Base	Voting habits					
		Conservatives				
	Total 584	Total 198	S.E.S. 4 & 5 59	Other S.E.S. 140	Labour 300	Others 86
	%	%	%	%	%	%
Correct	41	43	31	48	40	37
Incorrect/D.K.	59	57	69	51	60	63

Note: The percentages may not add to one hundred owing to rounding.
Source: Survey of Sheffield Electorate.

---

range, as would be expected, is between the Conservative manual workers (31 per cent) and the Conservative voters of higher socioeconomic status (48 per cent).

Despite the influence of these other factors it remains true that a

[3] Four per cent of the sample usually voted Liberal and 4 per cent usually voted for other minor parties including the Communist Party and the National Front.

Member of Parliament will become better known in his constituency if he spends a lot of time in the area. The Members of Parliament for Brightside and Hallam constituencies, who both lived locally, were better known in their constituencies than their colleagues in other parts of the city.[4] The M.P. for Hallam compounded all the favourable influences: he was a local man, representing the Conservative Party in a largely middle-class constituency; the proportion of the electorate who knew of him

Table 4.3
Awareness of name and party allegiance of M.P.

(3) *By constituency*

		Constituency						
Base	Total 584	Atter-cliffe 98	Bright-side 84	Hallam 89	Heeley 119	Hills-borough 75	Park 73	'Non-Sheffield' 46
	%	%	%	%	%	%	%	%
Correct	41	39	46	60	35	21	40	46
Incorrect/D.K.	59	61	54	40	65	79	60	54

Note: The percentages may not add to one hundred owing to rounding.
Source: Survey of Sheffield Electorate.

was correspondingly high. The M.P. for Heeley had only recently won this marginal seat for Labour and a number of the respondents still remembered the previous M.P.'s name when approached by the interviewers.

Earlier in this chapter the point was made that Members of Parliament are approached by a large number of their constituents with a wide range of problems—not all of which come within the province of an M.P.'s duties. The information obtained from the interviews with Sheffield Members of Parliament, upon which this judgement was based, was confirmed by the response of the electorate to the survey interviewers. Six per cent of the sample had been in touch with their Member of Parliament at some time in the past—either for help, advice, or to complain about some matter that affected them. This represents a large number of

[4] The M.P. for N.E. Derbyshire who represented most of the electorate living in 'non-Sheffield' constituencies—the area recently taken into the city by boundary extensions—also lived locally.

Table 4.4
Constituents' past contact with M.P.

Base	Total 584	Socio-economic status				
		1 & 2 60	3 156	4 139	5 144	6 83
	%	%	%	%	%	%
Contact with M.P.	6	15	5	7	4	4
No contact with M.P.	94	86	94	93	97	96

Note: The percentages may not add to one hundred owing to rounding.
Source: Survey of Sheffield Electorate.

people. The electorate of Sheffield is over 300,000 and, if the sample is a correct reflection of the population, there are some 20,000 electors in Sheffield who have approached their parliamentary representative on at least one occasion in the past. It will be remembered that the Members of Parliament suggested that they received twenty or thirty *letters* a week from constituency sources—this, of course, is over a thousand a year—and in view of this information the proportion of the sample claiming contact with their M.P. does not seem exaggerated. The response from the survey becomes too small, if broken down by constituency, to enable any comparisons to be made between the six Members of Parliament; but it was noticeable that many more people had been in touch with the M.P. for Attercliffe whose postbag was larger than that of his colleagues. He is the longest serving Member of Parliament for Sheffield, which may contribute to the readiness of people to write to him, although Table 4.3 does not suggest that he is particularly well-known in his constituency.

The constituents who are most likely to have been in touch with their Member of Parliament are those employed in professional or managerial occupations. This is to be expected: letter-writing comes easily to people in these occupations, and they are used to dealing with administrative affairs. It is not possible to give any indication of the matters raised by constituents with their Members of Parliament. The largest single group (about 20 per cent) was concerned with housing and town planning, but for the rest the range is so wide that the only appropriate description is 'other'.

In addition to the work he does for his constituents in general, a

Member of Parliament must naturally retain the confidence of his local party; in Sheffield this does not appear to present difficulties. The demands made upon the Member of Parliament by his constituency party in Sheffield are slight, and unlikely to offend his conscience. Loyalty is given to the man and there are very few attempts to influence the policy he will follow. The constituency parties hold regular meetings at which policy matters are discussed, but the Member of Parliament is only occasionally present. One Sheffield M.P. told me that he *never* attended party meetings in his constituency, four others did so occasionally, and only one attended regularly. While Parliament is sitting, the Members cannot leave London to visit their constituencies for mid-week meetings, but the local parties show no interest in changing their meeting night to enable their parliamentary representative to be present. In fact two Sheffield constituency parties—to my personal knowledge—rejected suggestions from their Members of Parliament that their meeting night be changed for this purpose. In one of these constituencies a committee member claimed that the party members preferred their Member of Parliament not to attend too frequently, as this prevented them discussing business in their own way!

The constituency parties write to their Member of Parliament regularly to inform him of their activities and to forward copies of resolutions they have made upon issues of policy, but this correspondence seems to be very much for information rather than a directive for action. In one constituency a motion to support the local M.P. in his views on a certain issue was actually divided at the wish of the meeting into two separate motions: one to express confidence in the M.P. and the other to condemn the policy he was supporting. Delegates explained that they did not wish their vote on a *policy* issue to be interpreted as an attack upon the right of their M.P. to form his own opinion. More generally it may be noted, from the resolutions submitted by the Sheffield Borough Labour Party for the Annual Conference agenda, that the local Labour Party tends to be more left-wing—in the sense of following the *Tribune* line on many issues—than the Labour M.P.s for Sheffield. Indeed the Borough Labour Party is more left-wing than the constituency parties it co-ordinates, and this may be due to the greater influence of the trade union delegates at the Borough Party. In Sheffield the major trade unions are more

militant than the local Labour Parties. This situation is no longer
unheard of in British politics, but it is different from the relationship between the two wings of the national party which was
commonly thought to exist in the 1950s.[5] The policies adopted by
the Borough Labour Party seem to affect the Labour Members of
Parliament in Sheffield to a very small extent. In fact the M.P.s
appear to have very little contact with the Borough Labour Party.
One Member of Parliament was appointed to act as a liaison with
the Borough Party—he was the only one to claim regular contact
—and even he could attend meetings only infrequently because of
the demands of parliamentary attendance.

The six Sheffield Members of Parliament all had regular correspondence with the city council: the minutes of council meetings
and other formal documents were received from the Town Clerk,
though probably not read with very close attention; and matters
constantly arose which required consultation between the local
M.P. and the local authority. Four of the Members of Parliament
suggested that they dealt very often with local authority business,
while the other two considered that they dealt with such matters
only occasionally. The need for the Member of Parliament to
approach the council arose very largely from constituency cases.
Local people frequently approached their Member of Parliament
about matters—particularly housing and redevelopment—that
were more properly the concern of the city council, and the M.P.
would then write to the local authority on behalf of his constituent.
It is noticeable that several of the M.P.s preferred to write to the
officials about matters of this kind, rather than to the elected
members of the council. At the time the interviews were conducted
the Labour group controlled the Sheffield City Council and the
reluctance of the Labour Members of Parliament to approach the
chairman of the appropriate council committee with a constituent's problem seems somewhat surprising. The reasons given by
the Members of Parliament for their attitude suggested that they
believed time could be saved by a direct approach to a council
official, although in one or two instances their answers implied a

---

[5] The popular view that the trade unions represented a solid right-wing bloc
against the more left-wing constituency parties is one of the myths of post-1945 Labour
Party history. The occasions when this occurred, for example over German rearma-
ment, were widely publicized, but they give a false overall impression. See Martin
Harrison, *The Trade Unions and the Labour Party since* 1945, and R. McKenzie, *British
Political Parties*, 2nd edn., pp. 502 and 616.

lack of confidence in the ability of the committee chairmen to deal properly with the problems. It was not only on individual constituency cases that the relationship between the Sheffield Labour M.P.s and the Labour group on the city council appeared somewhat detached. One of the Labour M.P.s was appointed to act as a liaison with the Labour group, but except at times of stress—at the time of the rent rebate controversy for example—this duty appears to have been performed in a perfunctory manner.

Most of the individual members of the council, however, found it necessary—or at least advantageous—to approach the constituency Member of Parliament on occasion. Each member of the council was asked about his or her contact with the local M.P. since the council elections the previous May—a period of six to nine months depending upon the date of the interview. The answers to these questions are summarized in Table 4.5. Over three-quarters of the council members had been in contact with a local Member of Parliament during the preceding six to nine months, and over half of them had discussed at least one matter with their local M.P. which arose from a complaint by a member of the general public. It has already been suggested that the local M.P.s prefer to deal with the council officials in many of the matters that arise in their constituencies, but this does not preclude—on the evidence presented here—a great deal of cooperation and discussion about constituency problems between

Table 4.5
Contact between members of the council and local M.P.s

	Proportion who had been in contact with M.P. at least once in previous six to nine months					
	Total		Lab.		Cons.	
Subject matter:	%	*No.*	%	*No.*	%	*No.*
Local affairs	63	(68)	70	(41)	56	(27)
National affairs	69	(74)	75	(44)	63	(30)
Either local or national affairs	78	(84)	85	(50)	71	(34)
No contact with M.P.	19	(20)	15	(9)	23	(11)
Matters arising from local complaint by a member of the public	54	(57)	58	(34)	48	(23)
D.K./cannot remember	4	(4)	0	(0)	6	(3)

Source: Survey of Sheffield City Council.

public representatives at local and parliamentary level. Much of this discussion will be instigated by council members rather than by the Members of Parliament, but there are occasions when an M.P. approaches a councillor about matters affecting his ward.

The subjects discussed between local Members of Parliament and members of the Sheffield City Council have a familiar ring: they are mainly concerned with education, housing, and welfare (including pensions). Housing and pensions are the subjects upon which Members of Parliament receive most approaches for help from their constituents, and it seems that members of the council share this experience. Housing is a local authority responsibility,

Table 4.6
Subjects discussed between members of the council and local M.P.s

	Total		Lab.		Cons.	
	\multicolumn{6}{l}{Proportion who had discussed issue with M.P. at least once in previous six to nine months}
Subject:	%	*No.*	%	*No.*	%	*No.*
Provision of housing	25	(27)	29	(17)	21	(10)
Rent rebates	23	(24)	31	(18)	13	(6)
Pensions and monetary benefits	17	(18)	27	(16)	4	(2)
Education	15	(16)	14	(8)	17	(8)
Redevelopment	14	(15)	10	(6)	19	(9)
Welfare services	10	(11)	12	(7)	8	(4)
Other subjects	22	(23)	20	(12)	23	(11)
D.K./cannot remember	6	(7)	3	(2)	10	(5)

Source: Survey of Sheffield City Council

while pensions and monetary benefits are the responsibility of the government, but members of the public do not discriminate so nicely between their avenues of complaint. One in four members of the city council had discussed the provision of housing with a Member of Parliament during the previous six to nine months; almost the same proportion had discussed the rent rebate scheme; and another frequent topic was the redevelopment of the city, which involves the clearance of many houses built in the nineteenth century. Housing remains, in other words, the most important single issue in local politics, or at least it is the issue which most provokes the local electorate to approach their local representatives.

There are a number of reasons for the difference between the proportions of Labour and Conservative members of the council who had been in contact with a local Member of Parliament during this period. First, there were six Labour M.P.s concerned—including the Member for N.E. Derbyshire—but only one Conservative. An analysis of the contacts made between councillors and Members of Parliament[6] shows that more discussions occur when the councillor represents a ward within the M.P.'s constituency; the councillor is also much more likely to discuss matters with his M.P. if they are both of the same political party; both these conditions were more likely to be met on the Labour than on the Conservative side at the time the interviews took place. Secondly, it may be suggested (see Table 4.6) that the major subjects under discussion, particularly the rent rebate scheme and pensions, were more likely to cause anxiety in Labour than in Conservative wards. Very few council-house tenants lived in wards represented by Conservative councillors, and the pensioners in Labour wards were more likely to be dependent upon public funds than people of the same age in the more prosperous areas to the west of the city.

The Member of Parliament may be approached by members of the council who come within any of three groups: first, they may represent a ward within his constituency; secondly, they may live in his constituency; and, finally, they may belong to the same political party. In two Sheffield constituencies at the time of the interviews these three factors reinforced each other. In both Hallam and Brightside the majority of the councillors lived in the constituency within which their ward was situated, and only two councillors for wards attached to these constituencies held different political views from their Member of Parliament. In addition both the M.P.s were local men living in, or close to, the constituency. The result was that these two M.P.s were in contact with more local councillors, and far more frequently, than the other M.P.s for the city. The Conservative M.P. for Hallam was approached by Conservative councillors from all over the city—twenty-four of the twenty-seven Conservative councillors who had spoken to an M.P. about council matters had spoken to the M.P.

---

[6] This analysis is not reproduced in full as it is impossible to do so without identifying individual council members and M.P.s.

for Hallam—and the Labour M.P. for Brightside, who lived in the same area as many of the councillors for wards in his constituency, was in continuous contact with members of the city council. The other Members of Parliament for the city were less closely involved with the members of the local council, and it is interesting to notice that this involvement was closely related to the degree of local attachment accorded to local M.P.s earlier in this chapter. It seems that if the Member of Parliament is easily available then local councillors will take advantage of discussions with him on local or general political matters, but these matters are less likely to be raised in correspondence when the two representatives seldom see each other. The relationship remains a personal rather than a formal one, and this impression is confirmed by examining the response of the local Members of Parliament to a number of local issues. From Table 4.7 below it may be seen that local Members of Parliament are not given to discussing local issues with the city council, or even with their own party group on that body.

The relationship between the Sheffield Members of Parliament and the city council as an institution seemed, at the time our research took place, to be in a state of tension. The word 'tension' is used here in a literal sense, and not as a euphemism for suspicion or hostility. Both the M.P.s and the members of the city council are public representatives of the same electorate, and it is only natural that the overlapping of their responsibilities should lead on occasion to misunderstandings. The views of the individual Members of Parliament on this matter were cautious: one local Member of Parliament thought that the relationship between the council and his colleagues in the House should be 'detached'; another suggested that it should 'not be too close'; some of the others were more reticent, indicating only that a Member of Parliament should not interfere with matters that were the responsibility of the local authority. One of the Members of Parliament, however, emphasized that if any local issue was of 'deep concern' to his constituents, then naturally it became a concern of the parliamentary representative.

The leading members of the city council, for their part, did not welcome any intrusion by the Members of Parliament into local authority controversies. On one occasion a Labour alderman publicly rebuked a Labour Member of Parliament for expressing

an opinion on a city council decision, while in another connection
a Conservative chairman of the Housing Committee remarked
coolly: 'We are perfectly capable of handling the situation for
Sheffield without the assistance of Mr. Frank Hooley.'[7] The stric-
tures of the alderman were not generally justified; usually the
Sheffield Members of Parliament take part in local authority
controversies only if they are concerned either with the wider,
national, implications of the policy, or with the representations
made to them by their constituents. This becomes clear from the
information contained in Table 4.7. The rent rebate scheme had,

Table 4.7
Number of Members of Parliament discussing specific local issues

	Rent rebate scheme	Local airport	Housing redevel- opment	Compre- hensive educa- tion	Council closed shop
Discussed with:					
The city council party group	2	1	2	2	1
Local party organization	3	2	3	3	1
Local interest groups	3	3	3	2	2
Public: press or meetings	3	3	2	2	1
Discussed with at least one of the above	5	5	3	3	2

Source: Interviews with the six Sheffield M.P.s.

of course, created the most bitter local controversy for years, and
local Members of Parliament were approached by many of their
constituents, by tenants' associations, *and by local councillors* (see
Table 4.6 above). In these circumstances they could hardly avoid
taking an interest in the issue. The Members of Parliament were
also subject to lobbying during the controversy about a local airport. This is an issue with wider implications than those contained
within the boundaries of the city. It is understandable, therefore,
that the Chamber of Commerce should circulate the Members of
Parliament in support of their views, and that the M.P.s should
take a public interest in the subject. Half the M.P.s had also discussed housing redevelopment and comprehensive education,
which again are issues with national associations. One Member of

[7] *The Star* (Sheffield), 30 July 1968. Mr. Hooley represented the Heeley Division of
Sheffield.

Parliament stated, in fact, that when he discussed the Park Hill redevelopment it was in the context of his *general* opinions on high-density living: 'it would make no difference from my point of view if they were in Edinburgh rather than in Sheffield,' he concluded.

The attitude of the Members of Parliament towards public discussion of local issues confirms, therefore, our previous conclusion: the local M.P. is not generally expected to participate in the local political process either by active intervention in his local constituency party, or by public pronouncements on local controversies. He has a responsibility to his individual constituents, and an interest in matters of national significance, but he is not integrated into the local institutions. This may be seen by the response of the Members of Parliament to the issue of a closed shop for council employees. This is a subject upon which all the M.P.s are likely to have well-defined opinions, but it was not an issue which excited the local electorate, nor did it raise any matter of national policy. The Members of Parliament were, therefore, very little concerned with the issue. The single exception to this generalization was the Conservative M.P. who discussed it at every opportunity. Indeed, he condemned the closed shop policy of the Sheffield City Council in the House of Commons; but again he was relating this local issue to the wider political principle concerned with individual liberty.

There are some local issues on which the Sheffield Members of Parliament are asked to act as a group. Usually this will occur when either the city council or local industry needs assistance in dealing with a government department, but it can be on an issue of a more general character. The Sheffield M.P.s, for example, are always ready to defend the appellation 'Made in Sheffield' from any possible foreign competition; and both Conservative and Labour M.P.s from Sheffield supported the legislation that extended the city's boundaries in 1967. Members of Parliament from the surrounding areas—of both parties—opposed this legislation, so that an example was given of M.P.s acting on behalf of their local communities irrespective of party discipline: the whips, however, are indulgent to such constituency consciences.

On many occasions the Members of Parliament, either individually or collectively, are approached by local trade unions or employers over matters affecting local industry: the response to this is usually a parliamentary question. In 1967, however, a general concern about redundancy in several of the major industries in Sheffield caused the Confederation of Shipbuilding and Engineering Unions to convene a meeting to discuss future industrial problems. Five of the Members of Parliament, including the Conservative, attended, and agreement was reached on the formation of an *ad hoc* committee. The committee presented evidence to the Hunt Committee on Intermediate Areas and its work merged into the concern which the city council felt for the industrial future of the city and their support for the formation of the 'Forty-four Group'.[8] All the local Members of Parliament were invited to participate in the work of the group and they all supported the idea. The Member of Parliament for N.E. Derbyshire was elected chairman of the organization, and other M.P.s spoke of the first meeting as 'a truly historic occasion' and assured the local authorities of 'vocal support in the House of Commons'. They soon had the opportunity of giving this support when a few months later the North East Development Council began to advertise in the South Yorkshire area in an attempt to attract industry northwards. Both Conservative and Labour Members of Parliament challenged this action in the House of Commons, and within a month they had persuaded the Secretary of State for Economic Affairs to condemn the advertisements. But, alas for human frailty, at a subsequent meeting of the Forty-four Group only one Member of Parliament was present, which led to an attack upon the rest of the M.P.s for the area by a local urban district councillor: 'the M.P.s are not pulling their weight,' he alleged, and carried on to warn that 'we shall keep a watch on them'.

The tension between Members of Parliament and local council members was also emphasized during the rent rebate scheme controversy, though, as will be shown in a subsequent chapter, this was an issue capable of disturbing the most settled of relationships. Two local Labour M.P.s publicly condemned the scheme proposed by the Labour-controlled city council, and another Labour M.P. publicly supported the scheme. Moreover, one Labour M.P. persuaded the minister to meet a deputation from the Sheffield Trades and Labour Council, who asked the minister to delay the

[8] Forty-four local authorities were originally involved, but the number has fluctuated since.

start of 'the controversial rent rebates scheme'. A leading Labour alderman expressed surprise at this visit and was obviously hurt by the division within the Labour Party which it implied. This surprise may well have turned to astonishment when, a few months later, the same minister refused to meet an official delegation from the city council to discuss interest rates on local government housing. The city council immediately asked the local Members of Parliament for help in persuading the minister to meet them. The M.P.s raised the matter at Westminster, but no meeting was arranged for nearly nine months. During this period the Conservatives who had gained control of the city council while the minister prevaricated, continued with the requests for a meeting, and the Labour Members of Parliament continued to press the minister on their behalf.

The position of the Member of Parliament as a *local* political institution is best characterized, therefore, as ambiguous: if he attends too assiduously to local matters he risks being accused of interference by members of the city council; if, on the other hand, he concentrates on national or international concerns, he may be told that he is neglecting his constituency problems. There is no doubt that both councillors and constituents welcome opportunities to discuss local issues with their Member of Parliament, but he is expected to be discreet in his public statements. Finally, it is clear that a local M.P. is expected to act as a Westminster agent if any disagreement arises between a government department and the city council.[9] He is undoubtedly a watchdog of local interests, but he must be careful to bark at the right people.

The constituency M.P. certainly does not play a leading role in the local political system, nor is he typically a product of it. Contrary examples are to be found in areas where the M.P. achieved election after political experience in the locality he represents, but we suspect that the Sheffield situation is more usual. In these circumstances it is not possible to draw any conclusions about the effectiveness of a local Member of Parliament by looking at his home address. Non-residence in the constituency does not necessarily imply a lack of interest; and in any case we

[9] In this connection it is interesting to remember that when the Derby Order to extend the boundaries of Derby County Borough into the Derbyshire County Council area was debated in the House of Commons (H.C. Deb. 1 February 1968), Mr. George Brown was the only M.P. for a Derbyshire constituency—of either party—to support the government.

need to define the role we expect from the local Member of
Parliament. An M.P. who lives in his constituency is naturally
going to be more readily available to his constituents: he may meet
them informally and give political leadership if he is of the mind—
and the calibre—to do so; but this does not mean that he will
automatically represent his constituents more effectively than the
M.P. who becomes a minister, or who achieves a leading position
in his party. The Member of Parliament for Hillsborough, for
example, who was relatively unknown to his constituents (see
Table 4.3 above), was for a time a Minister of State at the Board of
Trade. In that capacity he had a special responsibility for industrial development in areas with similar problems to Sheffield. He
was frequently consulted by the city council, and attended meetings of the 'Forty-four Group'. If on these occasions he was wearing
his constituency hat, we may consider that his ministerial Hom-
burg was ready in his brief-case; and the difficulties the city foresaw did not remain unknown to the government department
most concerned.

The six Sheffield Members of Parliament differed in their
general approach to their profession: two were 'local M.P.s'; two
were ministers at the time of the interviews; and two shared their
endeavours between local and national concerns. The active
members of the local Conservative Party are said to insist on a
local man as their representative in Parliament, but in the Labour
Party the local man is not favoured when new candidates are
selected. There are several members of the Parliamentary Labour
Party whose home town is Sheffield, including ex-members of the
Sheffield City Council: not one of them represents a Sheffield
constituency. When a successor for Mr. Winterbottom was being
sought, two prominent Labour councillors were nominated for the
Labour candidacy, but neither was successful. The reasons for the
attitude of the Labour Party in this matter would be difficult to
elicit; those who make the decisions may not always be aware of
their motives; but there have been some hints that older members
of the city council resent those who come on to the council as a
stepping-stone to a wider political career, and there may be a
natural reaction against the bright young men who are thought to
be lacking in political experience. The prophet, in this case,
appears to be without honour in his own town.

The local electorate, for their part, do not distinguish between the Sheffield Members of Parliament on the basis of their degree of local involvement. There is no indication of a personal vote accruing to either of the two 'local M.P.s'. At the election in 1966 the movement of opinion was very similar in all the six Sheffield constituencies; and the variations that occurred were explicable in terms that were appropriate throughout the country. Local efforts, in other words, were not noticeably rewarded at the polls.

5

Perceptions of Community

England has had towns for centuries, but they have never been real towns, only clusters of village streets. Never the real urbs. *The English character has failed to develop the real* urban *side of a man, the civic side.*   D. H. LAWRENCE

THE argument of the previous chapters makes it clear that to write of Sheffield as a community is fully justified in a general sense. The city is separated from its neighbours—with the exception of Rotherham—by geographical barriers; the people of the city work together in a few major industries and most of them share a common social position: Sheffield appears as a relatively self-contained and homogeneous city. We must remember, however, that geographical location, and the drawing of a statistical profile of a city, are simply methods of comparison between one city and another. The observer is imposing his own analytical categories upon the statistical material, and in this way he may distinguish between cities and towns with different social and economic characteristics. The classification is necessary if we are to interpret the demographic and industrial statistics, but communities defined in such terms are communities imposed from without—by the observer; they are not communities developed and understood from within—by the people who live in the area.

In the following pages we are concerned with the perception of community by the ordinary citizen, and (towards the end of the chapter) with the relationship this has to the ordinary person's political knowledge and interest. We shall discover, perhaps to the disappointment of some, that a positive relationship is lacking, but this negative conclusion has some importance: local government may be reformed more easily if reformers give up chasing the will-o'-the-wisp of local authority areas based on community feeling. For our purposes community feeling must still be understood in a narrow, physical sense, simply because it would be difficult to relate any other meaning of this elusive concept to the study of local authority areas. The 'civic consciousness' of which Lawrence wrote in his essay 'Nottingham and the Mining Country', may be associated with community consciousness in its wider, functional, 'all fishermen in England' meaning; but to base representation upon interests rather than wards or constituencies would be a radical departure from constitutional traditions, and one that would have to be argued on far wider grounds than those mentioned here. We must be content to discover whether electoral boundaries could be redrawn to correspond with the electors' perception of their local community areas.

The Royal Commission on Local Government in England commissioned a special study of community perception. The study was prepared on the basis of a random sample survey conducted throughout England in the summer of 1967. At the same time a survey of the Sheffield electorate was being considered independently within the University of Sheffield as part of the research for the present study of the city. There were obvious advantages in linking our local study to the national survey. First, the use of the same questions in both surveys would allow full comparability of results: the Sheffield results could then be shown in a national context; and the national averages could be given depth by the more detailed results obtained from one city in the local study.[1] Secondly, the design of the local questionnaire could benefit from the experience gained in the national survey. Through the courtesy of Mr. Louis Moss, Director of the Government Social Survey, full advantage was taken of these possibilities in the preparation of the survey of the Sheffield electorate. The section of the local questionnaire dealing with community perception was entirely developed from the questionnaire used in the Royal Commission's survey.

We have already argued, in Chapter 1, that community is a difficult concept to define; certainly the respondents to a random survey could not be expected to agree about the meaning of such a technical word; the designers of the national survey felt the need, therefore, to develop a synonym for spatial community to use in

[1] The Royal Commission survey, published as Research Study 9, *Community Attitudes Survey: England*, conducted over 2,000 interviews, 50 of them in Sheffield; the local survey obtained nearly 600 interviews in Sheffield.

the questionnaire. The concept used was that of a 'home' area.[2] The respondents to both surveys were first asked whether there was an area around their home address in which they felt 'at home'; and they were then asked if they could give a name to the area in which they lived, and to describe its extent in some detail. As the questions specifically asked for an area *including* the home address some respondents may have been led into thinking in somewhat smaller terms than they might otherwise have done, but this would not affect the comparisons being made between Sheffield and the national results: the questions were couched in precisely the same terms for both surveys. The respondents were, in addition, very precise in their descriptions of their 'home' area, and many suggested that 'if I go outside this area I do not feel at home'. In these cases no wider area than the one described is likely to be concealed by the form of the question.

The survey results indicate that a large proportion of the Sheffield electorate feel at home in the area in which they live. Table 5.1 shows that this proportion is larger than that for England as a whole, or indeed for other large county boroughs. These results give support to the general view that Sheffield is an area in which community feeling might be expected to flourish.

The sense of belonging to an area is obviously likely to increase with the length of time spent in the vicinity, and Sheffield's relatively stable population might be the cause of the variation in response shown in Table 5.1. At the time of the 1961 census 273 out of every 1,000 Sheffield residents had lived at their existing address for over fifteen years. The corresponding proportion for England and Wales was only 198 per 1,000, and the Sheffield

---

[2] The Royal Commission performed a factor analysis and isolated three factors of involvement with the community: 'social attachment', i.e. length of residence and number of friends and relatives residing in the 'home' area; 'interest in local affairs'; and 'employment/conviviality', i.e. employment in 'home' area, and the visiting of local public houses. These three factors were all significantly correlated with two questions: whether there was a 'home' area to which the informant considered he or she belonged, and how sorry or pleased the informant would be to leave the area. The Royal Commission survey concluded that these two questions are, *'prima facie*, the best available indicators of identification with the "home" area'. Ibid., pp. 143–5. With the benefit of the work already done by the Royal Commission we were able to concentrate on their best indicators, but both surveys emphasize the individual's perception of neighbourhood rather than objective indicators of community as a system of relationships. We are mostly concerned, however, with subjective assessments when we try to relate citizens to local government units through their community involvement.

Table 5.1
Ability to conceptualize a home area

(1) *Totals*

	England (excl. London)	Large C.B. (250,000 +)	Sheffield
Base	2,199	206	584
	%	%	%
Respondents with home area	78	78	85
Respondents without home area	22	21	14

Note: The percentages may not add to one hundred owing to rounding.
Sources: Survey of Sheffield Electorate and the *Community Attitudes Survey: England*, Tables 1 and 2.

proportion also exceeded that for other large industrial cities. Simple length of residence is not enough on its own, however, to account for the greater ability of the Sheffield electorate to conceptualize a 'home' area. The proportion of the Sheffield elector-

Table 5.2
Ability to conceptualize a home area

(2) *By length of residence*

		Length of residence in 'home' area			
	Up to 5 years	Over 5 to 10 years	Over 10 to 20 years	Over 20 years	Born here
Base ⎰ England	827		435	573	364
⎱ Sheffield	139	68	100	195	82
	% %	%	%	%	%
England—respondents with home area	68		73	86	94
Sheffield—respondents with home area	70	84	91	92	91

Sources: Survey of Sheffield Electorate and the *Community Attitudes Survey: England*, Table 3.

ate who can conceive a 'home' area is greater than the two national averages irrespective of the length of time the respondents had lived in the area. The only category shown in Table 5.2 for which the Sheffield proportion is lower than the national average is for those who were born in the area. This result goes against that obtained by the national survey, where it is concluded that 'the qualitative attachment deriving from the very fact of birth in the district' promotes a sense of belonging to an area quite apart from the length of residence.[3] The difference between the national results and the response obtained in Sheffield on this point was not large enough, however, to be statistically significant.

Some support was given by the Sheffield survey to the possibility that long residence within the 'home' area is not the only factor which promotes a feeling of being at home there; previous residence in the immediate neighbourhood may also be a contributory influence. If residence in the wider locality is important in confirming a person's sense of belonging to his 'home' area, then the lack of immigration into Sheffield would provide an added reason for the greater awareness of a 'home' area shown by the inhabitants of the city. The local character of Sheffield's population—discussed in Chapter 2—is strikingly confirmed by the results obtained from the local survey. The proportion of the Sheffield electorate who are shown as having moved into the city from outside is little more than a quarter of the proportion shown for all

Table 5.3
Previous residence to existing home area

	England (excl. London)		County Boroughs		Sheffield	
Base	2,199		751		584	
	%	%	%	%	%	%
Born in area—continuous residence		17		16		14
Within L.A. area						
less than 10 mins. walk	6		n.a.		11	
more than 10 mins. walk	28	34	n.a.	56	60	71
Outside L.A. area						
less than 10 miles away	16		(10)		3	
more than 10 miles away	32	49	17	(27)	11	14
Don't know/Question Not Answered		1		(1)		1

Notes: Any apparent discrepancies in the figures are due to rounding. Figures in parentheses have been estimated by the author from the available information in the table.
n.a.—not available.
Sources: Survey of Sheffield Electorate and the *Community Attitudes Survey: England*, Tables 26 and 30 and p. 35.

[3] *Community Attitudes Survey: England*, p. 12. It must be remembered that as the surveys were conducted among the electorate it follows that anyone born in the area, with continuous residence, had lived there for over twenty years.

local authority areas. The figures available suggest that the Sheffield proportion is low even when compared with other county boroughs. In view of the local character of the population it becomes interesting to note that *11 per cent* of the Sheffield respondents had moved into the city from more than ten miles distant, but they accounted for *15 per cent* of those who denied that there was an area surrounding their address within which they felt 'at home'. Because of the small numbers involved no statistical significance may be attached to these figures, but it is intriguing to discover that the *Community Attitudes Survey: England*, found the same association between recognition of a home area and distance from previous residence—and were also unable to attach statistical significance to their results.[4]

There is no apparent correlation between recognition of a 'home' area and the socio-economic status of the respondent.[5] At first sight the lack of correlation appears surprising, but there may be conflicting factors involved. On the one hand the higher level of education, which is associated with higher socio-economic status, might be expected to make it easier for a respondent to conceptualize a 'home' area; against this must be considered the wider horizons and greater mobility associated with employment in management or the professions, that weaken the confined approach of the 'home' area. On the other hand there is no evidence that community recognition is more prevalent among the manual workers. The 'working class' respondents to the surveys were more likely than other respondents to have many years residence at their existing address; they were also more likely to have relatives living in their neighbourhood; but they were *not* more likely than respondents in other occupations to assert that they felt 'at home' in the area in which they were interviewed. In this case presumably, the conflicting influences mentioned earlier are again at work, but this time in the opposite directions.[6]

The respondents to the surveys were asked the reasons that had

[4] *Community Attitudes Survey: England*, Table 32 and accompanying text.
[5] Ibid., Table 4. The Sheffield results showed a similar lack of pattern and are not reproduced here.
[6] For a discussion of the association between socio-economic class, length of residence in the area, and the number of relatives in the 'home' area, see *Community Attitudes Survey: England*, especially the consideration of the social attachment index derived from the factor analysis.

I

caused them to move into their 'home' area to see if community
influences would show in their replies: for example, people might
wish to move closer to their relatives, or seek a home in an area
providing better amenities or facilities for neighbourhood activities. Even if such community influences were present, they were
overshadowed by the necessity of finding a house, and by the
constraint of living within reach of available employment. The
main reasons given by people for moving into their 'home' area
were concerned with accommodation or employment, and
Sheffield was not exceptional in this respect. Rather more weight
was given to accommodation, and rather less to employment in
the Sheffield results—Table 5.4—compared with the national
average, but the emphasis on the need for accommodation as a
reason for moving into the 'home' area is a familiar pattern for
large county boroughs.

The response from the areas taken into Sheffield in 1967 was
similar to the response from the remainder of the city. Sheffield
had wanted to absorb the peripheral areas of the city for many
years, but the opposition from the inhabitants and local authorities
for the areas concerned prevented any agreed extension of the
boundaries. Finally a Ministry of Housing and Local Government
Inquiry, followed by a Ministerial Order, added about 50,000

Table 5.4
Reasons for first coming to live in home area

	England (excl. London) 2,199	Sheffield Six constituencies 538	Sheffield Added in 1967 46†
Base			
	%	%	%
Born in the area	17	14	22
Accommodation reasons	38	44	43
Employment reasons	24	13	13
Better amenities/facilities than in previous area	*	16	11
All other reasons	35	30	31

* Less than 0.5%.
† This figure is the weighted sample which is based upon sixty interviews.
See Appendix C for explanation of survey procedure.
Note: Some respondents mentioned more than one reason.
Sources: Survey of Sheffield Electorate and *Community Attitudes Survey:
England*, Table 33.

people to Sheffield's existing half million inhabitants. The newcomers objected to the takeover on the grounds that long-established communities were likely to be destroyed by the new building that would be commenced by the city council, but the influx of suburban development had begun a long while before the consequent takeover by Sheffield. The proportion of the informants from the newly gained areas of Sheffield who had been born in their 'home' area was higher than that for the rest of the city, but it was only slightly above one in five. The majority of the respondents from the contiguous areas had gone to live there for precisely the same reasons that had brought people to the older areas of Sheffield, namely, housing and employment.[7] Some respondents to the Sheffield survey indicated that they had moved to the surburban areas to find better facilities or amenities, but the proportion from the recently acquired areas giving this response was rather lower than the proportion giving these reasons in the rest of the city, so it cannot be implied that the lure of a rural setting preceded the simple need for accommodation.

The national survey did not suggest that better facilities or amenities were at all important as an encouragement to moving to an area, so the Sheffield response is somewhat surprising. An examination of more detailed results than those presented here does little to explain the discrepancy. The respondents to the Sheffield survey from the older and less pleasant parts of the city were rather more likely than those in other parts of the city to give better amenities and facilities as a reason for moving to their present 'home' area. The only possible explanation is that these respondents were thinking of better facilities *within* their accommodation—such as bathrooms and inside lavatories—and that their answers represent transfers within a fairly limited area as one section of the city after another was subject to slum clearance.

The size of the 'home' area described by the respondents to the Sheffield survey did not vary greatly from one part of the city to another. The respondents from the industrial areas of Attercliffe and Brightside described somewhat smaller areas than respondents from other parts of the city, but very few respondents from any district of Sheffield described a 'home' area that was larger in

[7] See Table 5.10 for further indications that community involvement was not particularly strong among the respondents in the newly-acquired areas; not, at least, by comparison with respondents from other areas of Sheffield.

extent than a local authority ward. The proportion of the Sheffield respondents who described their 'home' area as the equivalent of the entire city was only one per cent of the total response to the survey. Nearly three-quarters of the local respondents described their 'home' area as the few streets surrounding their address, and 7 per cent considered that they were at home only in their own street—or sometimes only in that part of the street in which they lived. These results are broadly in line with those obtained by the national survey, where it is concluded that 'a feeling of "limitation" or "localisation" is more frequently present in descriptions of the "home" area given by informants . . . in very large towns and conurbations'.[8] It is only in the smaller towns that a sizeable proportion (about half) of the electorate perceive the local authority area itself as their 'home' area. In Sheffield there is a

Table 5.5
Size of home area

		Sheffield				
		Length of residence in home area				
	Large C.B. (250,000+)	Total	Up to 5 years	Over 5–10 years	Over 10–20 years	Over 20 years	Born in home area
Base (all informants with home area)	161	499	97	57	91	179	75
	%	%	%	%	%	%	%
L.A. area or larger	5	5	1	9	4	13	11
Between ward and L.A. }	31	10	6	2	2	2	19
Ward equivalent }		12	9	4	15	11	17
Smaller than the ward	64	73	81	82	76	73	52

Note: The percentages may not add to one hundred owing to rounding.
Sources: Survey of Sheffield Electorate and *Community Attitudes Survey: England*, Table 7.

tendency for the size of the 'home' area to be even smaller than that described by inhabitants of other large county boroughs, which may reflect the fact that Sheffield is one of the largest cities in England, or indicate that the city is more fragmented than comparable local authority areas. The distinct names which the respondents give to their home areas (see below) suggest that the second of these influences is present, if not decisive.

8 *Community Attitudes Survey: England*, p. 15.

The *Community Attitudes Survey: England* discovered a nation-wide tendency for those respondents with a higher educational attainment to describe their 'home' area in rather wider terms than the rest of the sample, and the Sheffield results are consistent with this pattern. There was no distinction, however, between the supporters of the two main parties in their description of their 'home' area. Presumably the longer residence of the Labour supporters cancelled out the higher educational attainment of the Conservatives. Another influence upon the size of the 'home' area described emerges from the Sheffield survey: those respondents who had lived longest in the area were more likely to describe their 'home' area in city-wide terms; and only half of those born in their 'home' area—compared to nearly three-quarters of the general sample—considered this area to be smaller than a ward in extent. It would seem that those respondents who had lived in the area a long time were more familiar with the traditional areas into which Sheffield is divided: the relative new-comers to the area were reduced to describing their 'home' area in terms of their immediate environment.

The respondents to both surveys were asked to describe a 'home' area which included their 'home' address and it was considered possible that they would also include their place of work. The respondents were asked, therefore, whether they worked within

Table 5.6
Location of employment and size of home area

					Sheffield		
					Size of home area (informants with home area)		
	England (excl. London)	All C.B.	Large C.B. (250,000 +)	Total	More than ward	Ward equiv-alent	Less than ward
Base (all employed informants)	1,313	471	127	342	51	44	195
	%	%	%	%	%	%	%
Employed inside L.A. area	66	79	89	85	84	95	85
Employed inside 'home' area	33	24	n.a.	27	39	43	23

Sources: Survey of Sheffield Electorate and *Community Attitudes Survey: England*, Tables 49 and 50.

their local authority area, and further whether their place of work was within their 'home' area. The response to these questions is contained in Table 5.6. The inhabitants of the larger local authority areas were naturally more likely to work within the area than those who lived in the more confined areas: there are wider job opportunities in a large city than in a small market town. The Sheffield proportion of 85 per cent working in their local authority area is somewhat surprising in view of the self-contained nature of the city. In the 1966 sample census only 6 per cent of the labour force of Sheffield gave a place of work outside the city, and it might have been expected that the proportion shown by our survey to be working inside the borough would have been rather larger than 85 per cent. The 1966 sample census shows, however, that in addition to the 6 per cent of the Sheffield labour force who left the city each day to reach their place of employment, there were another 4 per cent who had 'no fixed work place'; some of these nomadic employees probably travelled outside the city. The proportion of 4 per cent in this category was unusually high, but a motorway was being constructed in the vicinity of Sheffield during the late 1960s and this may have affected the pattern of employment. There are other difficulties of comparability between the census data and the present survey,[9] but the response to the Sheffield survey gives a correct impression of the actual position in the city.

The definition of 'home' area which was accepted for the surveys was dependent upon the respondents' own perception of the areas within which they feel at home. It is, therefore, a subjective definition and as such it is susceptible to a number of different interpretations. While bearing in mind these variations in size, it may be seen from Table 5.6 that about a third of the English electorate work inside their 'home' area, however they describe this concept, and that the proportion of a third falls to under a quarter in the county boroughs. The decline in the proportion who work in their 'home' area in the larger cities must be related to the tendency in these cities for the electorate to describe their 'home' area in a more localized way.

[9] The census includes all those working or actively seeking work in the economically active population; the Sheffield and English surveys did not include those too young to appear on the electoral roll, and the definition of employed respondents did not include those unemployed at the time of the interview even if they were 'actively seeking work'.

The low proportion of respondents who included their place of work in their 'home' area may, however, be looked at in a rather different way. Even among those who described their 'home' area in terms equivalent to a ward, or larger, only four in every ten were employed within the area described; for those who described their 'home' area as smaller than a ward the proportion working in the area was much lower (23 per cent). The exclusion of the place of work from the definition of the 'home' area in so many cases suggests that for many respondents the place of work is not an important consideration in the determination of the area within which they feel at home. In describing their 'home' area (see below) the respondents did not mention factories or offices: though bus routes, schools, parks, and public houses were frequent land-marks.[10]

The respondents to the Sheffield survey were asked to give a name to their 'home' area—or the area in which they lived for those who denied having an area in which they felt at home—and over 90 per cent were able to do so. The names given to the 'home' areas were derived from a village (or other name of historical significance), or housing estate, rather than a local authority area or ward, and even then, as we have already noticed, most people set their 'home' area as *a part* of this 'village': a few streets only. Only one in five gave the name of the ward in which they lived, and it may be added that only 32 of the 130 who gave this reply subsequently described their home area as equivalent to a ward in size. Even when a ward name was given it was probably remembered because it coincided with the name of an absorbed village, or of a council housing estate which had superseded the village. Village names predominate among those most frequently mentioned: some of these 'villages' still carry on a staunchly village—if scarcely rural—life, under the leadership of the prosperous business and professional people who have made their homes in them; but other areas long ago lost all traces of their village character. In Tinsley, for example, a double-decker motorway flyover has been superimposed on the grime of industrial development: the countryside seems far away.

When asked to describe their 'home' area some of the respondents

[10] On the basis of a factor analysis the national survey concluded that the factor including place of employment 'is difficult to explain as an aspect of community involvement'. *Community Attitudes Survey: England*, p. 144.

Table 5.7
Home area—description by names

	No.	%
Gave name of ward in which lived	130	22
Gave name of another ward in the city	74	13
Gave name other than a ward name	328	56
Gave no name	53	9
	585	100

Examples of most frequently given names:

Ward names:		Not ward names:		
†Manor	*Heeley	†Arbourthorne	*Norton	*Grenoside
†Netherthorpe	*Dore	*Crookes	Pitsmoor	†Shiregreen
*†Mosborough	Park	*Beighton	Stumperlowe	*Fulwood
* Handsworth	Hillsborough	†Wybourn	Meersbrook	*Norton
*†Gleadless	Firth Park	*Woodseats	Shalesmoor	*Frecheville
* Sharrow		*Greystones	*Bents Green	*Ranmoor
		*Greenhill	*Totley	*Hackenthorpe
		Graves Park	Malin Bridge	Abbeydale
		†Norfolk Park	*Tinsley	Road
		†Parson Cross	*Wadsley Bridge	NE. Derbyshire

* Village name (i.e. settlement of considerable age).
† Name of council housing estate.
Source: Survey of Sheffield Electorate.

to the Sheffield survey gave a long detailed description, full of phrases such as: 'I pass there when I go to see mother', or 'Down to the park, bus stop, or public house'. The importance of parks, shops, bus routes, and public houses as boundary marks was to be expected. A good example was given by the woman who described Tinsley as 'From here to the church at Highgate, to Sheffield Road, and the bottom of Bawtry Road as far as the Fox and Duck pub'; an area that corresponds very closely to the cluster of streets described as Tinsley on the map of Sheffield. In a more modern idiom a man described his 'home' area as 'My own road and up to the betting shop at Leppings Lane'. Most of the descriptions, however, even when sufficiently graphically expressed to indicate that they had a precise meaning for the respondent, were of very small areas; often a single street. A few of the descriptions of particular areas are given below to illustrate the meaning of 'home' areas to the Sheffield survey respondents:

'I feel at home here in the whole of *Darnall*. By the park and the shopping centre. I just go over the road to the bus to go to work.'

'From Drummond Road, up to Sheffield Lane Top, then round to Lindsay Avenue shops, and back home.' (*Parson Cross*)

'Wisewood Road—no other.'

'This street only and only as far as each corner on either side of this house.' (*Southey Green*)

'As far as Doves House at the top of the lane: down as far as Kitson's at the bottom of the lane: that's *Whitley*.'

'Down the hill to Queens Road and back again.' (*Norfolk Park*)

'As far as Barnsley, and an area of eight-ten miles. All round Grenoside, but not Sheffield.' (*South Yorkshire*)

The recognition of a 'home' area, and the manner in which it is described, are useful indicators of the extent to which a person feels involved in his immediate environment. Some people, however, may dislike an area they know well: they may feel 'at home' in a neighbourhood, but at the same time they may wish to leave 'home' and seek surroundings more congenial to their present disposition. The respondents to the surveys were asked, therefore,

Table 5.8
Attitude to leaving home area

	England (excl. London)		Sheffield	
	Inform-ants with home area	Inform-ants without home area	Inform-ants with home area	Inform-ants without home area
Base	1,710	484	499	85
	%	%	%	%
Very sorry to leave	48	14	49	13
Quite sorry to leave	26	17	18	13
Neither sorry nor pleased	17	31	22	28
Quite pleased to leave	5	14	5	13
Very pleased to leave	4	23	5	33
Don't know	*	1	0	0

* Less than 0.5%.
Note: The percentages may not add to one hundred owing to rounding.
Sources: Survey of Sheffield Electorate and *Community Attitudes Survey: England*, Table 18.

about their attitude to leaving their 'home' area. The national survey comments that the subjective assessment of an individual's reluctance to leave his or her 'home' area 'appears to possess excellent powers of discrimination between informants according to the factor of involvement . . . nearly three-quarters of those informants who had said they could conceive of an area to which they belonged, and where they felt "at home", confirmed their claim in stating that they would be "quite" or "very sorry" to leave that area'.[11] The Sheffield results were broadly in line with those obtained nationally, but some differences may be observed from Table 5.8. There were rather fewer of the Sheffield respondents, for example, who stated that they would be 'quite sorry to leave' their 'home' area; and rather more of the Sheffield respondents who recognized a 'home' area expressed neither sorrow nor pleasure at the thought of leaving. The one really large difference between the Sheffield and the national results is to be found among those respondents who cannot recognize a 'home' area: a third of the Sheffield informants in this category suggested that they would be 'very pleased to leave' the area compared with under a quarter of the national sample. It is possible that many of these respondents were living in seriously sub-standard houses and were hoping to move to more modern accommodation: the northern cities still contain more than their share of the miserable dwellings left over from the industrial greed of the nineteenth century.

The broad similarity of the Sheffield results to those obtained nationally tends to obscure a further indication of the tightly knit character of Sheffield life which is apparent from more detailed figures. The *Community Attitudes Survey: England* concludes from more detailed results that 'there is less "sorrow" at leaving the "home" area among electors living in county boroughs compared with those resident in the smaller towns and country areas'.[12] Moreover the proportion who would be very sorry to leave decreases as the size of the county boroughs grows larger: for those county boroughs with a population of over a quarter of a million only 31 per cent of the respondents who recognized a 'home' area would be 'very sorry to leave'. In Sheffield, by comparison, the proportion was 49 per cent, although the city is one of the largest county boroughs in England. The Sheffield proportion is, in fact,

[11] *Community Attitudes Survey: England*, pp. 25–6.
[12] Ibid., p. 27.

more appropriate to a small urban or rural authority than a major county borough,[13] despite the fact that Sheffield is a northern industrial city with a residue of low standard houses. If the standard of housing, or other physical factors, affects the attitude of people to leaving their 'home' area, then it obviously has less effect in Sheffield than in comparable large cities.

Within Sheffield itself there are some noticeable differences in the response obtained from different parliamentary constituencies. The 'home' areas which people are most reluctant to leave are apparently to be found in Hallam, not surprisingly since it comprises the most favoured residential suburbs. But it is not only the pleasant areas in the western part of the city that can attract the loyalty of their residents: the other constituency which people feel reluctant to leave is Brightside. The Brightside constituency contains several huge council estates built during the 1920s and 1930s, together with great steel and engineering factories surrounded by the remnants of the houses built to accommodate the labourers of the nineteenth century. The council estates, built in curving terraces of traditional, two-storey, three-bedroom houses have apparently become acceptable over the thirty or forty years of their existence; and they may provide a warning to those sociologists who visit an estate after five or ten years and proclaim that older community feelings are destroyed in the new environment: community feeling is a matter of traditional growth rather than of rationalistic planning.

It might be thought that too much is being made of the reluctance to leave Brightside, but the response of the Brightside electorate to this question was part of a pattern which showed them as the most socially cohesive group in the city. To support this generalization a number of characteristics indicating attachment to the neighbourhood have been placed together in Table 5.9. Brightside has the highest or second highest proportion of positive replies for four out of the five characteristics listed.[14] The only other constituency to show more than one first or second place is Hillsborough, an area developed in the second half of the nineteenth century, which contains great estates of the small

---

[13] Ibid., Table 19.
[14] In Chapter 4 we saw that the Member of Parliament for Brightside was the only Sheffield M.P. to live in his constituency, and he behaved in every way as a very 'local' M.P.

Table 5.9
Neighbourhood attachment characteristics of Sheffield constituencies

	Eng-land (excl. Lond.)	Shef-field	Atter-cliffe	Bright-side	Hal-lam	Heeley	Hills-borough	Park	'Non-Shef-field'
Base (all inform-ants)	2,199	584	98	84	89	119	75	73	46†
Respondents who :	%	%	%	%	%	%	%	%	%
Agree to having a home area	78	85	84	92	87	90	89	73	80
Would be very sorry to leave home area*	41	44	33	50	61	40	44	36	46
Know many or very many people in home area	68	62	68	62	61	57	68	52	76
Have lived in home area over twenty years (including those born in home area)	43	47	48	52	48	47	53	40	41
Read at least one local daily news-paper	(48)‡	92	91	96	91	92	93	90	89

* This is taken in this table as a proportion of the total sample, not only of those recognizing a 'home' area.
† This figure is the weighted sample which is based upon sixty interviews. See Appendix C for explanation of survey procedure. 'Non-Sheffield' represents the areas taken into the city in 1967 and still remaining in their previous constituencies.
‡ This percentage comprises 41 per cent who claimed to read a local evening news-paper and 7 per cent who claimed to read a local morning newspaper. There is bound to be an element of double counting in the figure given in the table as some respondents will have taken both. The Sheffield proportions for evening and morn-ing local newspapers are 80 per cent and 37 per cent respectively.
Sources : Survey of Sheffield Electorate, *Community Attitudes Survey: England*, Tables 14, 19, and 36, and *M.L.G.*, III, *The Local Government Elector*, Table 41.

terraced houses that were built after the horrors of the back-to-back courtyards were forbidden by local by-law.

The two areas with the lowest proportion of positive replies to the questions summarized in Table 5.9 were the Park constituency and 'non-Sheffield'. Respondents from Park constituency gave the lowest proportion of positive answers to four out of the five questions and the second lowest proportion for the remaining one. The reasons remain obscure. Both Park and Brightside constituen-cies contain a large number of council houses built in the inter-war years, so we are not confronting the breakdown of traditional community life as people enter the council estates.[15] If this were so,

[15] Cf. M. Young and P. Willmott, *Family and Kinship in East London*.

then why should Brightside be unaffected? The major difference between the accommodation available in the two constituencies is the post-1945 council development in Park. This consists largely of high-rise buildings, including the internationally famous blocks at Park Hill and Hyde Park. It is tempting to suggest that there is a connection between the huge size of the council complexes and the lack of community involvement, but a word of warning must be added. In 1951 a survey was conducted upon one of the estates in the Park constituency. At that time the high-rise development had not been planned, let alone inhabited, yet nearly 30 per cent of the people interviewed said that they would like to move.[16] This proportion corresponds with uncanny accuracy to the 29 per cent of the respondents from Park constituency who said they would be 'quite pleased' or 'very pleased' to move away from their 'home' area; the corresponding proportion for the Brightside constituency was only 7 per cent. There is some evidence, in Hodges and Smith, that certain parts of the estates in the Park constituency have always been regarded as 'rough': places to avoid when seeking a house. If this is so then the effect becomes cumulative as the reputation of the area causes some people to refuse accommodation on the estates while others seek transfers. Hodges and Smith report that in the early 1950s a large number of tenants were trying to exchange their houses for others elsewhere in the city, while there were few applications— not one in the year ending June 1953—for transfer to the estate.[17] The Hodges and Smith results are now over fifteen years old, and refer to only one estate out of several in the Park constituency, but a bad reputation can be difficult to overcome. If this is the reason for the low level of neighbourhood attachment shown by our respondents from Park, then it is further evidence to support the contention that community feelings are 'concerned with the interaction of the individual with other people—rather than with his relationship to his *physical* environment'.[18]

The areas shown in the table as 'non-Sheffield' are those brought within the city in 1967, but remaining in their former parliamentary constituencies: mainly North-East Derbyshire. We

[16] M. W. Hodges and C. S. Smith, 'The Sheffield Estate', *Neighbourhood and Community*, p. 90 (University of Liverpool Press, 1954).

[17] Hodges and Smith, op. cit., p. 90.

[18] *Community Attitudes Survey: England*, p. 18.

have already mentioned that the extension of the Sheffield county borough boundaries was only achieved after bitter opposition from those who claimed that active local communities would be destroyed. This viewpoint was sincerely held by many people in the areas concerned and there is no mistake about the widespread nature of the opposition;[19] but there are grounds for supposing that much of the opposition came from those who did not share the ideals of community involvement proclaimed by their leaders. The figures given in Table 5.9—and in Table 5.4—give no support to the view that the majority of the inhabitants of the acquired areas felt more involved with the affairs of their 'home' area than people in other parts of the city. Much of the opposition to the boundary extensions can probably be attributed either to a fear that council building would reduce the value of the suburban developments, or to a straightforward reluctance to pay the higher rates that would be demanded as the city improved the local authority services in the area.

So far in this chapter we have been concerned with the attitude of the electorate towards the area in which they live. We may now move on to consider the relationship between attachment to the 'home' area and the degree of interest expressed in local events and knowledge of local institutions. It was discovered in the course of the survey conducted for the Royal Commission that the best indicators of the extent to which the respondents were involved in their 'home' area are contained in their answers to two simple questions: whether there was a 'home' area to which the informant considered he or she belonged; and how sorry or pleased the informant might be to leave that area. In the analysis of the Sheffield survey the response to these two questions was combined to provide an index of neighbourhood attachment[20] which could be tested against the questions concerned with interest in local

[19] Sixty-five per cent of the respondents interviewed in the 'non-Sheffield' areas were opposed to the boundary extensions and 24 per cent were in favour. This response may be compared with 42 per cent in favour and the same proportion opposed among respondents from the rest of the city. There were many more 'don't knows' in the city compared with the surrounding areas.

[20] 'Neighbourhood attachment' was preferred as a title to avoid the ambiguities of 'community involvement' although this is the phrase used in the factor analysis on which the index is based. See Appendix C and footnote on p. 100. The index was developed by Mr. G. E. Levins of Research Services Ltd., who was responsible for the work which that organization did for both the *Community Attitudes Survey: England* and the survey of the Sheffield Electorate.

affairs and local knowledge. The index was further refined by the
response to the question concerned with the number of people the
respondent knew in the 'home' area, and gives a four-point scale
indicating the degree of neighbourhood attachment shown by the
respondents to the Sheffield survey.

First, a rather higher proportion than would be expected of the
respondents to the Sheffield survey expressed themselves as very
interested in events in the 'home' area. There is in general a
tendency for less interest to be shown in events occurring in an
area as one moves from Rural Districts, through Urban Districts
or Municipal Boroughs, to County Boroughs.[21] This decline in
interest may be observed in Table 5.10 by the fall from an overall
average of 20 per cent to a proportion of 18 per cent in large
county boroughs. The Sheffield average of 21 per cent reverses
this tendency and it is further evidence that the city is rather more
community-conscious than would be expected for a county
borough of its size. Secondly, those respondents at the higher end

Table 5.10
Interest in events of home area

			Sheffield				
			Neighbourhood attachment index				
	England	C.B.	High ←———————→ Low				
	(excl. London)	(250,000 +)	Total	1	2	3	4
Base	2,199	206	584	112	133	214	125
	%	%	%	%	%	%	%
Very interested	20	18	21	34	19	21	12
Quite interested	35	29	28	33	30	29	21
Only a little interested	27	29	28	18	29	30	30
Not at all interested	17	24	23	14	21	21	37
Don't know	1	—	—	—	—	—	—

Note: The percentages may not add to one hundred owing to rounding.
Sources: Survey of Sheffield Electorate and *Community Attitudes Survey: England*,
Table 22.

of the neighbourhood attachment index continuum are more
likely to be very interested in affairs in their 'home' area than those
respondents at the lower end. The association between neighbourhood attachment and interest in events within the area is not
surprising; it might be expected, indeed, that the association

[21] *Community Attitudes Survey: England*, p. 28.

would be even stronger, but there are other factors involved: one of which might be termed 'social awareness'.[22] Simple residence and 'love of home' are not by themselves a sufficient inducement to take an interest in local affairs; there must be other conditions present including the practice of social interaction in some other sphere, for example at work or through a voluntary organization. Those respondents employed in managerial or professional occupations, or who were members of several voluntary organizations, were more likely than their fellow citizens to show interest in the events occurring in their 'home' area.

The point that remains to be considered is the extent to which a high degree of neighbourhood attachment is associated with an awareness and interest in the *political* life of the city. This evidence will be of value in assessing the accuracy of the contention, contained in Chapter 1 above, that the concept of political community has no meaning for those interested in defining local authority boundaries. First, we may show the variation in neighbourhood attachment that exists among supporters of the different political parties in Sheffield. There is a tendency for Conservative voters to show a higher degree of neighbourhood attachment than supporters of other political parties, but the relative success[23] of the Conservatives in gaining support within categories one and two of the index is probably associated with the fact that older people (over fifty-five years of age) and long residents (over twenty years) are more likely

Table 5.11
Neighbourhood attachment by party allegiance in Sheffield

		Party allegiance				
		Total	Cons.	Lab.	Other	Never vote/ refused
Base		584	198	300	45	41
		%	%	%	%	%
Neighbourhood	High 1	19	21	19	13	17
Attachment	↑ 2	23	28	20	18	19
Index	↓ 3	37	34	39	42	29
	Low 4	21	17	22	24	37

Note: The percentages may not add to one hundred owing to rounding.
Source: Survey of Sheffield Electorate.

[22] There is a long discussion of the relationship between these factors in *Community Attitudes Survey: England*, at pp. 28 ff. and in Section G.

[23] I use this word because the Labour Party in Sheffield commands majority support within every category shown by the neighbourhood attachment index.

to vote Conservative in Sheffield than younger people. Age and length of residence have been shown to be positively associated with the factors contained within the index.[24] The Conservatives success is not connected, as might be thought, with their ability to attract support from electors with a higher socio-economic status. The socio-economic status group of the respondents is associated with only one of the factors contained within the index, and even there the association is slight.[25] The supporters of the minor political parties show a lower degree of neighbourhood attachment than supporters of the two major parties.

The proportion of the sample who were interested in taking part in local government was so small—4 per cent representing twenty-four respondents[26] that it was not possible to divide these respondents according to their position on the neighbourhood attachment index. It was possible, however, to measure a number of indicators of political awareness against the position of the respondent on the index, and the result is shown in Table 5.12. The respondents in the first category of the index were rather more

Table 5.12
Neighbourhood attachment and political awareness in Sheffield

Base		Neighbourhood attachment index			
		High ⟵		⟶ Low	
	Total	1	2	3	4
	584	112	133	214	125
	%	%	%	%	%
Aware of constituency name	44	52	36	49	37
Aware of ward name	44	42	36	50	46
Aware of name and party of at least one ward councillor	11	14	10	12	10
Aware of controlling party on city council	79	75	74	83	78

Source: Survey of Sheffield Electorate.

[24] See Table 5.2 and *Community Attitudes Survey: England*, Tables 3 and 19.
[25] See page 103 above and *Community Attitudes Survey: England*, Tables 4 and 19.
[26] In a survey for the Committee on the Management of Local Government it was found that 8 per cent of the sample expressed an interest in standing for the council. About half of these, however, expressed a preference for standing as an Independent—an option that is not really available in Sheffield—and there was a tendency for those interested in local government work to have a higher socio-economic status and a higher level of formal education than the rest of the sample. The population of Sheffield shows a lower proportion than the national average in both these categories. *M.L.G.*, III, *The Local Government Elector*, Ch. 6.

likely to know the name of their constituency than the rest of the sample. They were, in addition, more likely to know the name and party affiliation of at least one of their ward councillors, though the proportions who could answer this question were so low that no category could be said to be knowledgeable on the subject. On the other hand the respondents in the first category of the index were below average in their ability to give the name of the ruling party on the city council or of their ward: the most local political unit. In this circumstance it is pertinent to recall that when asked to give a name to their 'home' area very few people associated it with the name of a ward.[27] A high proportion in every category of the index knew which party controlled the city—the Labour Party had been in control for forty of the forty-one years preceding the survey—but those respondents in the lower categories were more likely to know than those at the higher end of the scale. And it is noticeable that the respondents in the second category of the index showed relatively little political awareness: they gave the smallest proportion of correct answers to every question summarized in Table 5.12. In short, attachment to the 'home' area is not associated with the level of political awareness exhibited by the respondent; this has profound implications for local government reformers.

We may conclude therefore that most people are able to envisage an area surrounding their home address within which they feel 'at home'. Moreover, the people who feel at home in an area are reluctant to leave it. The 'home' area was described by the respondents to the Sheffield survey in terms of a few streets, with no suggestion that the place of work or electoral boundaries affected the respondents' conception of the areas to which they belong. Also there is not a straightforward relationship between neighbourhood attachment and the degree of interest shown in the affairs of the 'home' area. This interest in events in the 'home' area is affected by other influences in addition to the way a person feels about the locality: influences, we suspect, that are connected with the experience and confidence the elector gains in his social or working life. Lastly, the survey results showed no association at all between a high position on the neighbourhood attachment index and a greater awareness of the political institutions of the city.

[27] See Table 5.7.

The distinction must again be made between a community in a social—almost anthropological—sense, and a political community. The respondents to the surveys were describing their 'home' areas in the social sense of community; they were reflecting their degree of personal attachment to a given area; an attachment that derived ultimately from 'the interaction of the individual with other people —rather than with his relationship to his *physical* environment'.[28] Community feeling in this sense is connected only very tenuously to the enhanced civic consciousness which might be expected to derive from the common social experience described for Sheffield in Chapter 2. The geographical compactness of the city, the age structure of the electorate, the homogeneity of the population, the industrial structure of the city, and other similar influences, are important in determining the political style of the city; but they affect the degree of attachment to the neighbourhood only through their effect on the relationships of people to one another. If, for example, there is a low rate of immigration into the city then obviously the inhabitants are more likely to be related to each other than in a more mobile population. In this case both neigh-bourhood attachment and civic consciousness might be enhanced, but for different reasons. This complicated interaction is shown by the results of the Sheffield survey: the respondents in Sheffield were more aware of a 'home' area than respondents elsewhere; they were slightly better informed about local government (this will be shown in a later chapter); but there was no association between the degree of neighbourhood attachment and the level of political knowledge.

If this analysis is correct then it would follow that the concept of community is much misused in discussions about local government reform. There should be a more careful distinction drawn between a person's attachment to an area, and the conditions that may enhance his civic consciousness. These two factors are not closely related—for all the slogans of Rutland or North-East Derbyshire— and it would appear, therefore, that local political affairs might be ordered within more rational boundaries without fear that such changes would reduce the interest shown in local politics. Interest in local democracy may be depressingly low, but tinkering with boundaries is unlikely to affect it adversely.

[28] *Community Attitudes Survey: England*, p. 18.

6

The Local Citizen

*In some countries the inhabitants display a certain repugnance to avail themselves
of the political privileges with which the law invests them; it would seem that
they set too high a value upon their time to spend it on the interests of the community; and they prefer to withdraw within the exact limits of a wholesome egotism,
marked out by four sunk fences and a quickset hedge.*   ALEXIS DE TOCQUEVILLE

THAT local authorities should be democratically elected bodies is
not, as the Maud Committee pointed out, a self-evident proposition. Many government services are administered by local offices
of a central ministry, or by appointed committees in localities that
may not correspond to local authority boundaries. There is very
little consistency in the allocation of functions to one or other
form of local administration; the same service at different dates, or
similar services contemporaneously, may be administered by
appointed or elected bodies with a justification that is usually
historical rather than rational. The case in favour of elected local
authorities is rehearsed in the opening chapter of the present study.
The main argument developed is the expectation that the local
citizens will find a democratically elected council more comprehen-
sible, more accessible, and more responsive to local opinion. In the
following pages, therefore, we will consider the extent to which the
Sheffield electorate has the knowledge and the inclination to use
the local representative institutions either directly or through the
medium of another organization. We will also consider the attitude
of the electors towards the affairs of the local authority and towards
the local councillors. We are considering, in other words, the
extent to which inhabitants are citizens, for the response to
initiatives in participatory democracy—of the type discussed in
Chapter Eleven—may appear depressing if we set irrelevantly
high and abstract standards. We must try instead to identify the
elements of a culture of citizenship which could be built upon—if

anyone wished. The relationship between the opinions of the electorate and of the council on matters of local importance will be considered in subsequent chapters.

A relevant measure of local political knowledge is not easy to define. One person may be active in ward affairs, and well informed about the personalities of local politics, without being aware of the arguments upon which his party's policy is based. Other people may be deeply concerned with the educational or housing policy of their local authority, without being able to remember the institutional details of ward and constituency. Perhaps only politicians and students of politics try to see things as a whole in all their inter-relations. A number of questions were included in the survey of the Sheffield electorate to test the level of knowledge of local political institutions, but it must be emphasized that a low level of institutional knowledge does not affect the validity of opinions expressed on local issues. We may understand the arguments in favour of comprehensive schools, for example, or support the introduction of a rent rebate scheme for council tenants, without the need for a detailed knowledge of the authority responsible for implementing these policies. The level of knowledge of existing institutions shown by local citizens is important, however, in considering how the electorate may express their views to the local authority.

The survey conducted for the Royal Commission on Local Government obtained 'an approximate, but fairly practical index of knowledge' by asking respondents to assign nine public services to the responsible authority: national government, local authority, or statutory body. The survey report suggests that the form of this question leads to an appearance of greater knowledge of local government affairs than has been assumed from previous research.[1] In practice, of course, it is not possible to arrive at a single index which will measure the Level of Local Political Knowledge—with capital letters; the response of the Sheffield electorate shows a considerable variation in ability to answer the different questions correctly. We must be careful not to argue from the level of knowledge on a specific matter, to a level of knowledge in general. The figures presented here, and in the other sources mentioned, should be interpreted in comparative rather than in absolute terms; we should seek to explain variations between sub-groups, or between

[1] *Community Attitudes Survey: England*, p. 85.

the level of knowledge on different topics, rather than decide that the electorate is either ignorant or well-informed about local affairs.

The survey of the Sheffield electorate found that on average the respondents could name correctly 6·4 of the authorities responsible for the nine public services mentioned to them; the equivalent figure obtained by the national survey in large county boroughs was 6·3, so that Sheffield on this occasion appears typical in its overall response. Both the Sheffield and the national survey also confirmed the slightly greater knowledge usually shown by men in matters of this kind. A number of the other generalizations commonly made about the matters affecting the level of knowledge of public affairs may, however, be qualified by an examination of the response to the Sheffield survey.

First, the relationship between socio-economic status, or education, and knowledge of social or political affairs is not straightforward at the local level. The respondents with a higher level of formal education, or with jobs that involve greater knowledge of formal procedures, might be expected to answer simple questions testing political and social awareness with greater facility than respondents without such advantages. Yet these same better-qualified respondents may be more interested in national than in local affairs; and may move from one local authority area to another more readily than respondents in more mundane occupations.[2] Thus we may find an expert in public finance who does not know the exact amount of the local rate; or mobile professionals who know more about the general principles of the welfare state than they know about the administrative details of the local authority area in which they temporarily find themselves.

In the Sheffield sample the white collar workers and skilled manual workers were better informed on some local matters than the managers and those employed in the professions, though the unskilled workers were less well informed than respondents in

[2] In the Newcastle-under-Lyme survey two questions were asked to test political knowledge: only a very small proportion could name the party in control of the county council, but a quarter could name one of their councillors. The Sheffield results, see Table 6.2, showed that four out of five respondents could name the party in control but only one in ten could name a ward councillor. Despite these differences the lack of relationship between socio-economic group or education and local political knowledge may be inferred from both surveys. Frank Bealey, J. Blondel, and W. P. McCann, *Constituency Politics*, pp. 235–6.

other occupations. It was particularly noticeable that respondents in middle-grade occupations were more likely than other respon-

---

Table 6.1
Knowledge of local political institutions in Sheffield

(a) *By socio-economic status and education*

Base	Total	Socio-economic status*					Education*		
		1 & 2	3	4	5	6	Higher	Sec.	Lower
	584	60	156	139	144	83	42	75	467
Correct response to following questions:									
Authority responsible for nine public services (Av.)	6·4	6·9	6·8	6·7	6·2	5·6	6·5	6·9	6·4
	%	%	%	%	%	%	%	%	%
Name of ward	44	43	47	50	39	39	45	56	43
Name and party of at least one ward councillor	11	23	10	12	9	8	7	16	11
Name of constituency	44	58	54	46	30	39	62	65	39
Name and party of M.P.	41	48	56	38	33	28	57	55	37

* For definitions see Appendix C.
Source: Survey of Sheffield Electorate.

---

dents to know the name of the local ward in which they lived. At constituency level, knowledge of the national political division was directly associated with socio-economic status; but respondents in socio-economic status groups one and two, while much more likely than other respondents to know the name and party of one of their local councillors, were not as successful as those in group three in naming their local Member of Parliament. The apparent contradiction may be explained by the many wards represented by Conservative councillors within Labour-held constituencies at the time of the survey. Respondents in socio-economic group three are more likely to vote Labour than those in groups one and two.[3] They are more likely than the managers and professional workers, therefore, to be represented by a Member of Parliament of their own choice, but they may not support the politics of their local councillor. It will be suggested below that the respondent's knowledge of a public representative whom he supported at the polls will be greater than his knowledge of one whom he did not support.

In the Sheffield survey the respondents with the highest level of

[3] This is shown by the figures in Table 7.2.

formal education were not the group with the greatest knowledge of local institutions. The largest proportion of correct answers was received from those respondents with a secondary education. The only questions upon which respondents with a background of higher education were better informed than their neighbours with a secondary education were those relating to their Member of Parliament. In the national survey a direct association was discovered between the level of education the respondent had enjoyed, and the number of local services he could allocate to the correct administrative authority.[4] This association was not confirmed by the survey of the Sheffield electorate and we do not have sufficient detail in either survey to press the analysis very much further. It may be, however, that the discrepancy in the results obtained from the two surveys is related to the relatively low level of mobility among the Sheffield population. Length of residence is related to the proportion of correct responses given to this question.[5]

The level of knowledge of political affairs shown by a respondent to a social survey is affected by the political party he, or she, supports. The government surveys quoted in this study did not ask questions about the political attachment of the respondents, but some information is available from the Sheffield survey. The respondents were more likely to be aware of matters concerning the party they supported than they were to remember matters affecting their opponents. In general the Labour supporters were less well informed than supporters of the Conservative party; but they did relatively better in response to the questions asking for the name of the political representatives and for the length of time the Labour party had been in control of the city council. At the time of the survey the Labour party held five out of the six parliamentary seats in Sheffield and had enjoyed a majority on the city council for forty years.[6] The Labour supporters, therefore, were more likely than the Conservatives to be represented by someone of their own party; and this advantage enabled them to come closer to the Conservative supporters in their ability to name their representative than in their ability to name their electoral district.

[4] *Community Attitudes Survey: England*, Table 89 and p. 85.

[5] Ibid. The length of residence of the Sheffield population is discussed in Chapter 2.

[6] A discussion of the voting behaviour of the Sheffield electorate, and of the elections preceding the Conservative victory in 1968, will be found in the following chapter.

Table 6.2
Knowledge of local political institutions in Sheffield

(b) *By political allegiance*

	Total	Conservative			Lab.	Others
		Total	Manual workers	Others		
Base—all respondents	584	198	59	140	300	86
Correct response to following questions:						
Authority responsible for nine public services (Av.)	6·4	6·6	6·3	6·6	6·4	6·5
	%	%	%	%	%	%
Name of ward	44	53	53	52	42	35
Name and party of at least one ward councillor	11	14	2	19	12	5
Name of constituency	44	56	44	60	37	42
Name and party of M.P.	41	43	31	48	40	37
Party with most seats on city council	79	85	83	86	75	77
Base—correct response to previous question	460	169	49	120	225	66
	%	%	%	%	%	%
Correct response to following questions:						
Approx. length of time Lab. Party in control	25	25	24*	24*	25	27
Has the Lab. Party been close to losing in that time	49	52	49	53	48	48
Have the Cons. a chance to take control in the next election	62	73	78	71	56	53

* The percentages have been depressed slightly by rounding and a technical adjustment.
Source: Survey of Sheffield Electorate.

The working-class Conservatives were, of course, even less likely than middle-class Conservatives to be represented by someone of their own party. In consequence their ability to name their representatives was considerably lower than that of either middle-class Conservatives or of Labour supporters. These were the only two questions on which the working-class Conservatives showed significantly less knowledge than Labour supporters.

More Conservatives than Labour supporters could name the party in control of the city council. The respondents who gave the correct answer were asked the three further questions that are shown at the foot of Table 6.2. A quarter of these respondents could give the approximate year in which Labour took office, and half knew that they had come close to defeat at some time. This second proportion is surprisingly low. Only six months before the survey the Conservatives came within one seat of gaining power in the 'little general election' described in the next chapter. The response to the final question shown in Table 6.2 was clearly affected by party loyalties. Nearly three-quarters of the Conservative supporters who knew that Labour were in power considered that the Conservative Party might take control after the forthcoming elections; slightly over half the Labour supporters accepted this possibility. The complacency among the Labour supporters might have been a contributory factor in the continuing failure of the Labour party to poll their full support in local elections.[7] In 1968 the Conservatives took control, and it was noticeable that the following year the Labour supporters turned out in far greater numbers to reverse this decision.

The effect of party allegiance on the ability to answer questions about political affairs is a special example of a more general influence upon a respondent's level of knowledge about various subjects. We are all more likely to seek, and to remember, information that has relevance to our own activities, and this natural tendency may be observed in the replies given to survey interviewers. The survey conducted for the Maud Committee found, for example, that men and younger people were more able than women or older people to mention spontaneously the authority responsible for nine selected local authority services. The report goes on 'to note, however, that the age difference in ability to name a service disappears in the case of old people's homes, and the sex difference disappears when the welfare clinics are mentioned'.[8] In the replies to the questions testing the respondents' attitudes to several decisions of the Sheffield City Council it was noticeable that those most directly affected had seldom failed to form an opinion, although the respondents who were not directly affected might reply 'don't know'.

A clear example is provided by the response to questions about the rates. The owner-occupiers were much better informed about

---

[7] See Table 7.8 and the surrounding text.
[8] *M.L.G.*, III, *The Local Government Elector*, p. 15.

the rates than tenants of private landlords or of the city council. The owner-occupier, of course, receives a rate demand from the city treasurer, and he is made aware of changes in the amount to be paid. Council tenants include their rates with their fortnightly rent payments and changes are less noticeable. The private tenants may pay their rates directly to the council, but many landlords of smaller properties collect the rates with the rent payments. Knowledge of the rates is, therefore, directly related to the likelihood that a separate rate payment will be made from the respondent's home.

Table 6.3
Knowledge of domestic rate in Sheffield

| | | Type of accommodation | | |
Base	Total* 584	Owner- occupier 268	Private tenant 110	Council tenant 201
	%	%	%	%
Correct rate given	5	9	3	1
Rate lower/same as in previous year	37	51	32	20
Rate higher than in previous year	26	21	24	34
Don't know	37	27	45	46

* Includes four respondents who lived in rent free accommodation.
Note: The percentages may not add to one hundred owing to rounding.
Source: Survey of Sheffield Electorate.

The correct response to the questions about rates was complicated by the introduction of a government subsidy to domestic ratepayers. The council had maintained in 1967 the same rate as the previous year, but owing to the subsidy the rate to domestic ratepayers had fallen by fivepence. In Table 6.3, therefore, the proportion of the respondents who replied that the rate had remained the same has been combined with the proportion who thought it had gone down. This combined proportion gives an indication of the number of respondents who knew the correct position, and to these may be added the very low proportion who could give the exact rate. Forty-two per cent of the respondents, therefore, were aware of the recent changes—or lack of change—in the rates. There remained over a third who did not know whether the rates had altered since the previous year; and about a quarter of the respondents who assumed that the rate had been increased.

The rates are given a great deal of prominence in local election campaigns. The parties accuse each other of placing fresh burdens on the ratepayers, and boast of their own parsimony. The figures in Table 6.3 suggest that the councillors' perception of the way to influence the electorate is deceptive. The Labour group on the Sheffield City Council in 1967 expected that the voting intentions of the electorate would be affected by their decision to maintain the rate and to pass on the five-penny subsidy to the domestic ratepayers. We may assume that those who knew of the council's decision were more likely to vote than those who did not, but even so it seems unlikely that many votes were obtained on this issue. The general level of ignorance about the rates—especially among potential supporters of the Labour party—is too great for the issue to have a wide effect on political behaviour. And the Labour councillors may be perturbed to discover that over a third of the working-class respondents to the survey could give no answer to questions about the rates, while a further third thought the rate had recently increased. The Labour expectations must have been disappointed.

In addition to the questions testing their knowledge of local affairs, the Sheffield electorate were asked a further series of questions to discover their attitude towards certain public services. The nine services were the same as those included in the questions testing knowledge of administrative responsibility. The interviewers invited the respondents to include other local services in their assessments, but only transport and highways received a measurable number of spontaneous comments. Prompt cards, such as those used by the interviewers, have obvious limitations, but they allowed full comparability to be obtained with the national survey.

The outstanding feature of Table 6.4 is the similarity of the results obtained both nationally and in Sheffield. The five services mentioned favourably most frequently are the same in both cases, although there is a little more variation in the services receiving unfavourable mentions. Housing provides one interesting divergence of views between the electorate of Sheffield and the electorate of other large county boroughs. Among the national sample more people expressed dissatisfaction with this service than gave it

Table 6.4
Attitudes towards local public services

	'quite well run'			'not very well run'		
Base	England (excl. London) 2,199	Large C.B.† 206	Sheffield 584	England (excl. London) 2,199	Large C.B.† 206	Sheffield 584
	%	%	%	%	%	%
Hospitals‡	29	43	44	11	7	5
Education and schools	30	33	29	5	3	5
Libraries	30	29	29	3	2	1
Recreational facilities	18	26	22	14	9	10
Refuse collection	31	28	19	11	14	7
Town planning	5	5	13	10	8	6
Provision of housing	10	7	11	9	12	8
Social security‡	6	8	10	3	6	8
Electricity‡	13	5	6	3	*	2
Transport	1	1	1	6	8	8
Highways/roads	*	*	*	2	2	2
Others	1	*	1	2	2	2
Mentioned at least one service	73	76	82	51	47	50

* Less than 0·5 per cent.
† County boroughs outside the conurbations with over 250,000 population; Sheffield is one of these authorities.
‡ These are not, of course, local authority services.
Sources: Survey of Sheffield Electorate, and *Community Attitudes Survey, England,* Tables 91, 94, 95, 100, 104, 105, and surrounding text.

a favourable mention. In Sheffield both the housing and town planning policies of the city council were better received than policies on these matters in other parts of the country.

The proportion of the Sheffield respondents who mentioned at least one service as being 'quite well run' was rather higher than the proportion elsewhere, while the proportion giving an unfavourable mention to at least one service was about the same. The relative satisfaction felt with local services in Sheffield becomes more significant when it is realized that both nationally and locally there is an association between an inclination to mention at least one service favourably and higher socio-economic status; Sheffield has a lower than average proportion of its population in the higher socio-economic status groups. The association between socio-economic status and the propensity to mention favourably a local service leads to the curious result that in Sheffield—a Labour-controlled city at the time of the interviews—the Conservative supporters were rather more ready than Labour supporters to give approval to some of the local council's activities. On the other hand socio-economic status was not associated with a propensity to give an unfavourable mention to a local service in Sheffield, though this was so in the national survey.[9]

The national survey report suggests that the association between socio-economic status and a favourable response to local services is due to 'a certain sensitivity in evaluating local government matters which stems from a more enhanced interest in such affairs'.[10] No doubt this assumption is in part true, but it is also true that respondents in the higher socio-economic groups live in areas *that enjoy better local authority services*. It is not surprising, therefore, that they should be more satisfied. In Sheffield, for example, many of the more pleasant municipal parks are in the western part of the city. The recreational facilities provided by the local authority naturally received a more favourable response from these areas, largely middle-class in character, than from the bleaker parts of the city.

In an attempt to draw together some of the material so far presented in this chapter, the six constituencies of Sheffield, plus the areas recently acquired from neighbouring constituencies, were placed in rank order according to the proportion of respondents to the Sheffield survey who came within certain categories. The proportion of Conservative supporters in the sample was taken as an indicator of the social composition of the constituency, and the rankings by the neighbourhood attachment index and length of residence—discussed in Chapter 5—were also included. The result of this ranking is shown in Table 6.5. Hallam, at the time of writing the only constituency represented by a Conservative Member of Parliament, contains the most exclusive residential suburbs in Sheffield. The respondents from this area were obviously attached to their neighbourhood and they were ready to comment upon local services; although they were not particularly knowledgeable about the exact spheres of responsibility for these services. On the other hand, the respondents from Park constituency confirmed, by their comparative lack of knowledge and interest about local affairs, their low degree of attachment to their neighbourhood which has already been noticed in Chapter 5. The respondents from Attercliffe were the least likely to have a favourable attitude towards any local service, and were more likely than

---

[9] *Community Attitudes Survey: England*, Table 103.   [10] Ibid., p. 92.

Table 6.5
Rank order of Sheffield constituencies by six variables

Constituency	% of Cons. supporters in sample	Favour-able attitude to at least one local service	Unfavour-able attitude to at least one local service	Know-ledge of respon-sibility for nine local services	Lived in area more than 20 years, or born there	Neigh-bourhood attach-ment index*
Hallam	1	1	1	4	4	1
Heeley	2	2	2	1	5	5
Hillsborough	3	3	6	7	1	4
Non-Sheffield†	4	5	4	2	6	3
Park	5	6	7	6	7	7
Attercliffe	6	7	3	3	3	6
Brightside	7	4	5	5	2	2

* For a description of this index see Chapter 5 and Appendix C.
† These are the areas added to the county borough by the boundary extensions of 1967.
Source: Survey of Sheffield Electorate.

respondents from other working-class areas of the city to mention at least one service unfavourably. Attercliffe is a fading area. It contains the terraced streets of nineteenth-century industrial housing, and when these are demolished in ten to fifteen years time the area will cease to be used for residential purposes. The city council are understandably reluctant to develop an area with such a short future, and the residents complain particularly about the recreational facilities provided. The respondents from Atter-cliffe, Brightside, and the areas recently taken into Sheffield, were also prone to complain about the transport department, which possibly reflects their greater reliance upon this service.

It is difficult to measure the degree of association between the rank orders contained in Table 6.5 by simple inspection. A technique has been employed, therefore, to measure this associa-tion on a scale from plus one to minus one: a score of plus one would indicate that the two rank orders were identical; a score of minus one would indicate that the two rank orders were com-pletely the reverse of one another; a score of nought would indicate that there was no relationship at all between the two rank orders. The rank order correlations contained in Table 6.6 indicate that there is a very high level of association between areas with a high pro-portion of Conservative supporters in the sample, and areas with a high proportion of respondents giving a favourable response to at

Table 6.6
Rank order correlation: Sheffield constituencies by six variables

	% of Cons. supporters in sample	Favourable attitude to at least one local service	Unfavourable attitude to at least one local service	Knowledge of responsibility for nine local services	Lived in area more than 20 years, or born there	Neighbourhood attachment index*
% of Cons. supporters, etc.	—	+0·762	+0·429	−0·048	−0·048	+0·238
Favourable attitude, etc.	+0·762	—	+0·333	+0·048	+0·238	+0·429
Unfavourable attitude, etc.	+0·429	+0·333	—	+0·524	−0·048	+0·238
Knowledge, etc.	−0·048	+0·048	+0·524	—	−0·333	+0·048
Lived in area, etc.	−0·048	+0·238	−0·048	−0·333	—	+0·238
Neighbourhood attachment, etc.	+0·238	+0·429	+0·238	+0·048	+0·238	—

* For a description of this index see Chapter 5 and Appendix C.
Note: The rank order correlation has been tested by Kendall's Tau. A short description of this method will be found in Hubert M. Blalock, *Social Statistics*, pp. 319–25.
Source: Table 6.5.

least one local service.[11] There is also a fairly high level of association between areas with a high level of knowledge about the authorities responsible for local services, and areas with a propensity to complain about the management of at least one of these services. The association between neighbourhood attachment and a favourable attitude to at least one local service is to be expected. One of the components of the index was the attitude of the respondents to leaving their home area; those respondents who were reluctant to leave the area were naturally more likely than other respondents to have a favourable attitude to some of the services the area provides. Table 6.6 confirms the low level of association between neighbourhood attachment and knowledge about the administration of local services, that was discussed in Chapter 5; and indicates, rather surprisingly, a *negative* relationship between those areas in which respondents show a high level of such knowledge, and areas with a high proportion of respondents long resident in the constituency. Presumably those respondents who have lived in an area a long while tend to be older than the more mobile residents, and older people generally show less awareness of public affairs.

We suggested at the beginning of this chapter that elected local authorities may be more responsive than appointed bodies to the complaints and opinions of the general public; but before the public can avail themselves of such democratic opportunities, they must approach the local authority with their comments or complaints. In the Sheffield survey of the electorate, therefore, the respondents were asked to name, or give the office of, the most important person in local affairs in Sheffield. The response gives a preliminary indication of the structure of authority as perceived by the general electorate. The respondents were then asked whom they would get in touch with if they wanted to make an enquiry or a complaint about a local service.

[11] A measure of association between two variables does not, of course, imply a causal relationship: the movement of both the observed variables may be the result of a third unmeasured variable. Table 6.6 does allow, however, some of the possible third variables to be considered. For example, we might hypothesize that Conservative supporters were more knowledgeable about local services and, therefore, more likely to give a favourable response to at least one of them. The association between the rank order by proportion of Conservative supporters and the rank order by knowledge is, however, practically non-existent, so that the hypothesis would not be supported in Table 6.6.

It is not easy to specify the most important person in local affairs, and the question was deliberately framed in very general terms. The Lord Mayor is the chief citizen, but in Sheffield his year of office is largely ceremonial, and may coincide with a majority of the opposing political party on the city council. On the other hand, the most important influence on policy matters within the city council rests with the leader of the majority party, but his influence will be exercised in part in the confines of the party group and away from ceremonial publicity.[12] The Town Clerk, of course, is the senior official in the local authority, and in Sheffield he carries the title of Chief Executive Officer. The respondents' answers reflected the lack of a publicized centre of authority in the

Table 6.7
The electorate's estimation of the most important person in local affairs in Sheffield

		Education*			Knowledge of responsibility for nine local services: number correctly identified		
Base	Total 584	Higher 42	Sec. 75	Lower 467	8–9 128	6–7 337	5 or less 119
	%	%	%	%	%	%	%
Lord Mayor	23	12	20	24	24	23	21
Town Clerk	5⎱	21	27	15	18	19	10
Other dept. head	12⎰						
Ald. S. Dyson	7⎱	17	13	16	19	17	10
Other cllr.	9⎰						
Others	3	2	3	3	3	3	3
Don't know	42	45	39	42	37	38	56

* For definition of education categories see Appendix C.
Note: The percentages may not add to one hundred owing to rounding.
Source: Survey of Sheffield Electorate.

city council. Forty-two per cent of the sample could give no answer to the question, and those who could reply gave a wide variety of answers. Nearly a quarter nominated the Lord Mayor as the most important person in Sheffield affairs, which would seem to indicate that the separation of the dignified from the effective

[12] The relationship between the party groups, their leaders, and the official council structure is discussed in Chapter 3.

side of public affairs, noticed by Bagehot a hundred years ago, still serves to confuse the local electorate. Seventeen per cent mentioned a council official of whom the Town Clerk (5 per cent) and the Housing Manager (4 per cent) were the most popular. Sixteen per cent named a public representative on the city council, but of these only 2 per cent gave, either by name or office, the leader of the majority party, although this would have been the most accurate answer. Alderman Sidney Dyson was the member of the city council most frequently mentioned. He had been Chairman of both the Transport and Housing Committees in the year preceding the interviews, and he had attracted publicity in the local press both during a labour dispute in the Transport Department and over the introduction of the rent rebate scheme.

The better-educated respondents were inclined to name an official as the most important person in local affairs, whereas those without much formal education mentioned the Lord Mayor more frequently. We are again reminded of Bagehot's belief that to a plain man monarchy is the only intelligible form of government. Those respondents with a low knowledge of public administration were inclined to give uninformative answers when questioned about the most important person in the city; this is scarcely surprising.

Nearly two-thirds of the respondents mentioned the council, Town Hall in general, or the appropriate department, when asked whom they would approach first with an enquiry or complaint about local services. Very few mentioned their local councillor in the first instance. The Sheffield results are similar in this respect to those obtained nationally.[13] The main influence on electors in their first approach to the council appears to be their level of education: those respondents with a higher education were more likely than other respondents to approach the appropriate department—particularly the *head* of the department; respondents with a lower level of formal education were inclined to approach their local councillor more frequently than other respondents. Even so, respondents in all educational groups

---

[13] *Community Attitudes Survey: England*, Tables 107 and 108. The Maud Committee survey also contained a section concerned with the electors' contact with local government. As the questions were framed rather differently their results are not directly comparable with those being discussed here, but they do not appear to be inconsistent with our conclusions. *M.L.G.*, III, *The Local Government Elector*, Ch. 2.

Table 6.8
Citizens' approach to authority in Sheffield

(a) *By education*

	England (excl. London)		Sheffield			
	Total	Large C.B.	Total	Education*		
				Higher	Sec.	Lower
Base	2,199	206	584	42	75	467
	%	%	%	%	%	%
Administration—general†	37	31	27	26	21	28
Administration—specific‡	30	36	37	52	47	34
Local councillor	14	10	12	5	12	13
Others	12	11	19	17	17	19
Don't know	8	11	5	0	1	6

* For definition of educational categories see Appendix C.
† General reference to 'the council' or 'the Town Hall'.
‡ Specific mention of council department or chief officer.
Notes: The large county boroughs are those outside the conurbations with over 250,000 population.
The percentages may not add to one hundred owing to rounding.
Sources: Survey of Sheffield Electorate and *Community Attitudes Survey: England,* Tables 107 and 108.

preferred to approach the administration in the first instance when they wished to make an enquiry or a complaint. Two other approaches mentioned fairly frequently were to the local Member of Parliament and to the Civic Information Service. Six per cent of the Sheffield respondents would make their first approach to authority in each of these ways compared with 3 per cent and 5 per cent respectively of the national sample.[14]

The electors turn naturally to the 'Town Hall' when they have cause for complaint or wish to make an enquiry. Most people in a county borough know where the town hall is situated, and it is easier to go there than to seek the local councillor, who may not always welcome visits to his home by members of the electorate.[15] If the first approach to authority is unsuccessful then the local elector will turn for help to his political representative, either in the council or in parliament. There is a recognition by the citizen, as the national survey report pointed out,[16] of a natural progression

14 *Community Attitudes Survey: England,* Tables 107 and 108.
15 See Chapter 8.
16 *Community Attitudes Survey: England,* p. 102.

from the administration to the elected representative. In Sheffield 64 per cent of the respondents mentioned the administration as their first line of approach; but if disappointed, either by the administration or elsewhere, then 42 per cent would approach their political representative. The Member of Parliament is often appealed to in such cases, and 32 per cent of the Sheffield respondents would approach him as either their first or their second contact, compared with 28 per cent who would approach their local councillor. The Sheffield electorate appear to place a greater emphasis upon the local Member of Parliament than is usual in these circumstances. The national sample preferred, by a narrow margin, to approach their councillor about local matters rather than their parliamentary representative.[17]

Over a quarter of the Sheffield respondents would take no further action, or would not know where to go for advice, if their initial approach was rebuffed. Some of these respondents had already suggested an approach to their local Member of Parliament, and obviously felt that there was no higher court of appeal; but others were ready to accept an officer's decision without further argument. One woman in this group replied: 'I wouldn't think of it [taking further action]. I would accept the Department's word. They are paid to know their jobs'. Other respondents spoke of their unwillingness to bother people with their individual problems if the first approach to the council was unsatisfactory. The undemanding acceptance of authority implied by such an attitude is particularly marked among those who have received only the minimum of schooling and who are employed in unskilled occupations.[18] People in these groups are often in need of advice when dealing with authority, but it is clear that they do not always receive it; nor do they always realize their need.[19]

In response to a further question, 23 per cent of the Sheffield

[17] *Community Attitudes Survey: England*, Table 112. The proportions were 26 per cent and 27 per cent respectively.

[18] The inference about the influence of schooling and occupation is drawn from the *Community Attitudes Survey: England*, Table 115. It is also interesting to note that a larger proportion (23 per cent) of the national sample than of the Sheffield sample (9 per cent) answered that they would contact no one if their first attempt was unsuccessful; but the proportion of 'don't knows' was much lower. When combined these two categories account for approximately the same proportion of both the Sheffield and the national samples.

[19] The attitudes of the councillors to their public responsibilities are discussed in Chapter 8.

Table 6.9
Citizens' approach to authority in Sheffield

(b) *Secondary contact by primary contact*

Base	Total 584	Admin. General 157	Admin. Specific 218	Local Cllr. 70	M.P. 34	Other 75	Don't know 29
				Primary contact			
Secondary contact:	%	%	%	%	%	%	%
Administration— general†	7	—	6	9	12	20	0
Administration— specific‡	15	16	19*	13	6	17	0
Local councillor	16	18	21	—	15	16	0
M.P.	26	34	26	43	—	11	0
Other	9	11	7	10	29	4	0
Don't know	19	13	11	17	21	25	100
No further contact	9	7	11	10	18	8	0

* Two-thirds of these are people appealing from a department to the *head* of the department.
† General reference to 'the council' or 'the Town Hall'.
‡ Specific mention of council department or chief officer.
Note: The percentages may not add to one hundred owing to rounding.
Source: Survey of Sheffield Electorate.

sample (26 per cent nationally) replied that they would not consider approaching a local councillor to help them at any stage of their application to the local authority. The reasons given were largely concerned with the councillor's presumed lack of competence, but many other respondents just did not know how to find their local representative. Few of the respondents refused to consider an approach to their local councillor because they did not share his political beliefs, but it is possible that many respondents were thinking of the councillor's political position when they attacked his competence to deal with their request.

When asked about their actual experience, 10 per cent of the Sheffield respondents (13 per cent nationally)[20] claimed that they had approached a councillor with an enquiry or a complaint. Although 10 per cent is a small proportion, it would represent a large number of people if related to the total electorate. It indicates that some 35,000 people have approached a Sheffield councillor

[20] *Community Attitudes Survey: England,* Table 128. In Glossop (1953) the proportion was 15 per cent. A. H. Birch, *Small Town Politics,* p. 96.

Table 6.10
Reasons for not contacting councillors

	Sheffield	England (excl. London)
Base—those who would not contact	133	568
	%	%
Reasons suggesting lack of competence on part of councillor	48	48
Reasons suggesting lack of knowledge by elector of councillor	29	21
Different political views	6	—
Other reasons	11	10
Don't know	18	28

Note: Some respondents gave more than one reason so the percentages add to more than one hundred.

Sources: Survey of Sheffield Electorate and *Community Attitudes Survey: England,* Table 116.

about a local authority matter at some time in their lives. Local councillors had been approached about similar subjects by respondents to both the national and the Sheffield surveys. Nearly a third had been concerned with housing provision, and the only other significant subjects were town planning (around one approach in ten), streets and highways, and, in Sheffield, repairs to property. More than four in every ten approaches, both nationally and locally, had been concerned with subjects so diverse as to be unclassifiable except as 'miscellaneous'. The emphasis on housing and planning permission was reflected in the difference in the response obtained from people living in varying types of accommodation. Only 3 per cent of the private tenants had approached a councillor about a local matter at any time in the past; but the proportion rose to 10 per cent of owner-occupiers, and 15 per cent of council tenants. The owner-occupiers had been concerned with a wide range of subjects, but the most frequently mentioned was planning permission (12 per cent); nearly two-thirds of the approaches to local councillors by council tenants had been concerned either with housing provision or with repairs.

We have already seen that most of the electors prefer to approach the local authority officers, or offices, rather than their councillor when they have cause to make an enquiry or a complaint. Over a third of the Sheffield sample had made such an approach at some time in the past,[21] and they had been concerned with services similar to those that had caused other members of the electorate to approach their councillors. The matters that stimulate local people are obviously those affecting their personal life: refuse collection, housing provision or repairs, the activities of the health department, the obtaining of planning permission; the important policy debates seldom cause members of the general electorate to approach the council for information, or to express their views. At the time of this study, for example, the city council were introducing comprehensive education, but only four of the respondents to the Sheffield survey had approached the Education Department about *any* matter, and three had been fully satisfied with the result. The comprehensive school proposals had been explained at a series of school meetings so that the lack of enquiries might be seen as a compliment to the good communications policy of the council, but it is more probably the result of the general tendency for the

Table 6.11
Main services about which an enquiry/complaint had been made

	England (excl. London)	Sheffield
Base—all enquiries/complaints	609	223
	%	%
Refuse collection, highways, and footpaths	26	12
Housing provision and repairs	25	41
Health and drains	10	13
Town planning	6	11
All other services	34	23

Sources: Survey of Sheffield Electorate and *Community Attitudes Survey: England,* Table 125.

elector to be moved to action only by those matters that affect him separately as an individual. The relative importance of housing and planning as a source of enquiry or complaint in Sheffield when compared with the national average may easily be explained: the city has a larger proportion of council houses within its boundaries

21 The Sheffield percentage was 36 per cent compared with 24 per cent of the national sample and 14 per cent of the national sample of large county boroughs. The figure for county boroughs does not seem consistent with any of the other figures obtained either in the national or the Sheffield surveys. *Community Attitudes Survey: England,* Table 124.

than the national average, and it has been engaged in major programmes of redevelopment in recent years. The relatively low proportion of enquiries or complaints about refuse collection and highways—and the large proportion of these that are dealt with fully and satisfactorily—may be seen as a tribute to the departments concerned.

The total number of complaints and enquiries mentioned to our interviewers was small, only 223, so that any further analysis of the

Table 6.12
Informants' evaluation of the outcome of their enquiry/complaint

	England (excl. London)	Sheffield				
		Total	Refuse coll. and highways	Housing	Health/ drains	Town planning	Others
Base—all enquiries/complaints	609	223	27	91	28	25	52
	%	%	%	%	%	%	%
Dealt with fully and satisfactorily	50	62	70	53	61	68	70
Dealt with fully but unsatisfactorily	20	16	11	24	7	4	15
Not dealt with fully or at all	24	16	15	13	25	20	15
Still being dealt with	5	6	4	11	4	8	0
Don't know	1	1	0	0	4	0	0

Note: Owing to rounding and weighting minor adjustments have been made to the raw material to produce this table. The percentages may not add to one hundred for these reasons.
Sources: Survey of Sheffield Electorate and *Community Attitudes Survey: England,* Table 126.

replies must result in sub-samples too small to give more than a hint of possibilities. Nevertheless, the informant's own assessment of the way in which his enquiry or complaint was dealt with is given in Table 6.12. In general the Sheffield respondents were better satisfied than their national counterparts: 62 per cent, compared with 50 per cent, considered that their enquiry or complaint had been dealt with fully and satisfactorily. The proportion of the Sheffield respondents who were satisfied with the outcome of their approach to the council would be even higher if it were not for the dissatisfaction felt about the outcome of approaches to the housing departments. The dissatisfaction might be explained by the number of people who apply for council accommodation and then find themselves on a waiting list for several years, but this appears to be only part of the explanation. Only a half of those who approached the council about housing repairs expressed themselves as fully satisfied with the outcome; and one-third stated that their approach had been dealt with fully, but in an unsatisfactory manner. Even so the Sheffield respondents were better satisfied than the national sample, who reported that only 38 per cent of their approaches to the council over housing repairs had been dealt with in a fully satisfactory manner.

The national survey did not explore the relationship between satisfaction with the outcome of approaches to the council and the type of local authority concerned, presumably because of the small number of occurrences involved. The Sheffield results would suggest, however, that an urban area can provide a more satisfactory service to its citizens than local authorities in rural districts. It is interesting to remember that the survey at Newcastle-under-Lyme produced a similar result,[22] and such a conclusion is supported also by some of the results discussed earlier. Respondents from urban areas, for example, were more likely than those from rural areas to mention at least one local service favourably, and less likely to mention one as being not very well run.[23] There are, of course, additional difficulties of distance and high unit costs to be met in a country area as compared with a compact town; but even so only a small proportion of the respondents from the periphery of Sheffield welcomed their inclusion in the city following the boundary changes of 1967. The city council tried to integrate them by a rapid expansion of basic services into the absorbed areas, but the probable improvement of local services did not reconcile the surburban respondents to the loss of village identity—or the higher rates—that the boundary extensions entailed.

This chapter has been concerned, so far, with the knowledge of local administration shown by the electorate, and with the approaches to authority that they make as individuals. In fact, of course, many electors approach authority through the medium of an organization. This is particularly true when they wish to

[22] Bealey, Blondel, and McCann, *Constituency Politics*, p. 245.
[23] Table 6.4 above and *Community Attitudes Survey: England*, Tables 91 and 100.

present their views on a particular local issue, and we have seen in Chapter 3 that the councillors take such representations by local organizations very seriously. The councillors themselves are likely to be drawn from the membership of local voluntary organizations,[24] and the section of the electorate who enter some form of organized public activity may be understood as the circle within which local political affairs are conducted.

Nearly two-thirds of the Sheffield electorate belong to at least one organization. The number and types of organizations they belong to are similar to the averages obtained for provincial England, and further comment may be confined to only a few of the organizations mentioned. A quarter of the Sheffield respon-

Table 6.13
Organization membership

(a) *Number of organizations*

Base	England (excl. London)	Sheffield
	2,199	584
Belonging to:	%	%
No organizations	35	35
One organization	25	24
Two or three organizations	27	27
Four or more organizations	13	13

Note: The percentages may not add to one hundred owing to rounding.
Sources: Survey of Sheffield Electorate, and *Community Attitudes Survey: England*, Table 52.

dents were members of a trade union. This high proportion, which is to be expected in a large industrial city, comprised 43 per cent of

[24] In Sheffield, 1967–8, four out of every five members of the city council had been introduced to council work through organizations. Political parties and trade unions were the organizations most frequently mentioned, as would be expected in an industrial county borough; but nearly one in five mentioned social, welfare, church, or other groups as providing their introduction to council work. Similar results are given in *M.L.G.*, II, *The Local Government Councillor*, Table 2.6. See also III, *The Local Government Elector*, p. 136, and Bealey, Blondel, and McCann, *Constituency Politics*, p. 200.

the men and 10 per cent of the women.[25] The number of women in Sheffield who claimed trade union membership was rather higher than would be found in many other cities, but this may be explained by reference to the industrial structure of the area.[26] Sheffield has a relatively low proportion of job opportunities in service and clerical occupations, and a relatively high proportion of Sheffield women work in industries where the trade unions are stronger than in the service trades. The high level of trade union membership in Sheffield may be a contributory factor in explaining the relatively low proportion who claimed membership of a political organization. The definition of a political organization did not include the political wing of the trade union movement, and many Sheffield citizens who are interested in politics may be content to remain affiliated members of the Labour Party through their trade union instead of becoming individual members. The respondents from professional or managerial occupations were far more likely than manual workers to belong to a political organization.

One last indication of the industrial character of the Sheffield electorate may be inferred from the importance of the working man's clubs in the social life of the city. Twenty per cent of the respondents to the Sheffield survey were members of a working man's club, compared with 9 per cent of the respondents to the national survey.

The women in the Sheffield sample were more inclined than the men to belong to a church organization. The distinction was similar to the one found in the Glossop survey where the proportion of women actively associated with the church was half as large again as the proportion of men.[27] The denominations favoured by those who attended church regularly differed considerably between the two surveys and it reflects the barrier that the Pennines represented to the Irish immigrants of the nineteenth century.[28] In

[25] Only 4 per cent of the women in the Maud Committee sample were members of a trade union. This national survey included London and Wales, both of which, for different reasons, have a low proportion of women trade unionists, but the proportion of 4 per cent still seems rather low. *M.L.G.*, III, *The Local Government Elector*, Table 164. *Community Attitudes Survey: England* did not publish details of trade union membership by sex.

[26] See Chapter 2 and Appendix A.

[27] Birch, *Small Town Politics*, p. 194. Further comparison becomes difficult as the questions in the two surveys were framed in different ways.

[28] See Chapter 2.

Glossop, a small town in the hills of north-west Derbyshire only twenty-four miles from Sheffield, regular church attendance was 'divided fairly equally between the Church of England, with 36 per cent, the Roman Catholic Church, with 31 per cent, and the

---

Table 6.14
Organization membership

(b) *Types of organization*

	England (excl. London)	Sheffield Total	Male	Female
Base	2,199	584	275	309
	%	%	%	%
Organizations connected with work:				
Trade union	20	25	43	10
Professional association	6	6	10	2
Club to help workmates or colleagues	7	7	13	2
Business group or club	2	*	*	*
Social or sports club at work	13	15	27	4
Any other clubs at work	3	2	4	0
Public bodies or committees	2	1	1	1
Organizations connected with politics:				
Political party or association	9	3	2	4
Any other political group	*	*	*	0
Church or other religious groups:				
Church club or group	5	5	4	6
Social club connected with church	4	4	2	5
Any other	2	3	2	4
Civic or community group:				
Tenants' or rate payers' association	3	3	5	2
Parents' association	4	2	1	2
Residents' club or community centre	2	2	2	2
Any other	1	1	1	*
Organizations connected with welfare:				
Charitable organization	4	3		
Voluntary welfare organization	1	2		
Any other	1	1		
Organizations connected with education and training:			n.a.	
Organizations for further education	3	3		
Military training group	1	1		
Youth training organization	2	1		
Nursing or first aid organization	1	1		
Any other	1	1		

Table 6.14—*continued*
Organization membership

(b) *Types of organization*

Base	England (excl. London)	Sheffield Total	Male	Female
	2,199	584	275	309
	%	%	%	%
Other groups connected with leisure activity:				
Sports team or club	9	8		
Club for games	7	7		
Dance club	2	2		
Club for hobbies or pets	2	3		
Music, drama, jazz, or art club	3	3		
Motoring association	7	4		
Any other	3	3		
Other social clubs:			n.a.	
Fraternal or ex-servicemen's club	7	2		
Women's social club	3	2		
Working man's club	9	20		
Youth club	1	2		
Club for old people	3	2		
Any other	4	3		
Anything else not covered	3	3		
No clubs or groups at all	35	35	15	53

* Less than 0·5 per cent.
Note: The percentages add to more than the proportion of the sample belonging to any organization as some people belonged to more than one.
Sources: Survey of Sheffield Electorate and *Community Attitudes Survey: England,* Table 53.

Free Churches, with 33 per cent.'[29] In Sheffield church attendance —as distinct from membership of a church organization—was divided between the Church of England, 57 per cent; the non-conformists, 20 per cent; the Roman Catholics, 15 per cent; and all other denominations, 8 per cent. The small proportion of Roman Catholics in Sheffield may be related of course, to the low level of Irish immigration into the city.

The division into denominations attempted here is based upon the proportion of the sample who claimed that they attended a place of worship; nearly two-thirds of the Sheffield respondents told the interviewers that they 'did not attend a place of worship

[29] Birch, op. cit., p. 195.

"these days"', and the proportion rose to nearly three-quarters of the respondents under thirty-five years of age. Nevertheless the comment by a local clergyman that 'the religious life of the City is ... probably weaker than many other industrial centres' is not supported by the evidence of our survey, and very little comparative evidence in support of the assertion is offered in his own work.[30] The proportion of the Sheffield sample who claimed that

Table 6.15
Attendance at a place of worship

| | England: excl. London County boroughs | | | |
	Total	All	Over 250,000 population	Sheffield
Base	2,199	751	206	584
	%	%	%	%
Proportion who claim to attend a place of worship	43	37	28	36

Sources: Survey of Sheffield Electorate and *Community Attitudes Survey: England*, Table 64.

they attended a place of worship was similar to that for other county boroughs in England, and considerably above the proportion in cities of comparable size. Sheffield has a relatively small proportion of its population employed in middle-class occupations, and there are relatively few Roman Catholics in the city; members of both these groups are more punctilious in their church attendance than other members of the electorate, and we might have expected, therefore, that religious observance in Sheffield would be relatively low. If, as the figures suggest, attendance is higher than expected, then this is consistent with the comparatively high level of community feeling that exists in the city.[31]

The management of any organization is left to an active minority. Nearly two-thirds of the Sheffield respondents claimed membership of at least one organization, and about one in five of

[30] E. R. Wickham, *Church and People in an Industrial City*, p. 13 and Ch. 5 *passim*.
[31] See Chapter 5. The association of non-manual socio-economic grades and community feeling with church attendance is shown in *Community Attitudes Survey: England*, Table 64. The Sheffield survey gave similar results.

the members claimed to be either an official or a committee member. The proportion of the total sample—14 per cent—who

Table 6.16
Officers and committee members in organizations

	England and Wales	Sheffield							
			Sex		Socio-economic status*				
		Total	Male	Female	1 & 2	3	4	5	6
Base	2,184	584	275	309	60	156	139	144	83
	%	%	%	%	%	%	%	%	%
Proportion claiming office or committee membership in at least one organization	14	14	20	9	35	15	13	8	8

* For definition see Appendix C.
Sources: Survey of Sheffield Electorate and *M.L.G.*, III, *The Local Government Elector*, Table 167.

claimed some position within an organization was identical with the proportion reported by the national survey of the electorate. The national survey report suggests that 'this figure may seem a little high and it is possible that some people may have been exaggerating their present positions in their organization,'[32] and this identical result gives an added interest to the comparison. Even allowing for some exaggeration there must be 20,000 or 30,000 people holding some position within an organization in Sheffield, though not all of these will attend to their duties very assiduously.[33] A quarter of the Sheffield respondents claiming some position within an organization claimed more than one such office. The officers and committee members were drawn disproportionately from the men and from the professional and managerial groups within the sample.

In conclusion we may suggest that the frequent allegations that people are completely uninterested in local affairs should be treated with some caution. About two-thirds of the Sheffield

[32] *M.L.G.*, III, *The Local Government Elector*, p. 119.
[33] The authors of *Community Attitudes Survey: England* presented their results in a slightly different way, but reported that 9 per cent of the sample claimed 'participation in local public service', p. 74. In her study of Banbury, Margaret Stacey counted 1,026 committee members of voluntary or church organizations out of a total population—not electorate—of less than 19,000 and she confesses that 'inevitably some associations have been overlooked'. M. Stacey, *Tradition and Change*, p. 76 and Table 16.

councillors spoke of the electorate not having sufficient knowledge to make good use of existing council services, or even to vote in an informed way at local elections.[34] The amount of knowledge required to make a full use of local authority services can be considerable, and it is not surprising that many of the electors, as well as councillors, doubt their capacity in this respect; but despite this we have shown that the response to different questions testing local knowledge may vary widely; and the questions concerned with matters close to the electors' immediate interests may elicit a reasonable proportion of correct answers. The lack of interest so often referred to by councillors and social investigators may reflect in part a lack of interest in the matters the observers consider important, and a consideration of different issues might bring a more ready response. We shall return to the relationship between the councillor and the electorate in Chapter 8.

The number of people who are well-informed about local affairs, or who are interested in taking an active part in their determination, remains a minority, but it is a larger minority than is usually assumed. The many thousands of people in Sheffield who hold a voluntary position within a local organization have already been referred to, and 4 per cent of the respondents to the survey (twenty-four individuals) expressed themselves as interested in taking an active part in local government. This proportion may be compared with the 8 per cent of the national sample who 'said they definitely or might stand for their local council in future'.[35] Although the proportions are low it is again important to remember that 4 per cent of the Sheffield electorate represents nearly 14,000 people. This figure is many times the number of electors who participate actively in local political affairs; it is almost certainly higher than the combined memberships of the local political parties; but it becomes more credible when it is related to the number of active members in voluntary organizations. It is

[34] The Sheffield results are similar to those reported in *M.L.G.*, II, *The Local Government Councillor*, pp. 230–1, except that rather more of the Sheffield councillors thought the electorate did not know enough to vote in an informed way.

[35] *M.L.G.*, III, *The Local Government Elector*, p. 133. In both Greenwich, London (1949), and in Glossop (1953), 11 per cent of the respondents to sample surveys told interviewers that they were 'very interested in politics'; in the survey at Newcastle-under-Lyme (1959), 9 per cent of those interviewed claimed that they attended political meetings. Mark Benney, A. P. Gray, and R. H. Pear, *How People Vote*, p. 47; Birch, *Small Town Politics*, p. 96; Bealey, Blondel, and McCann, *Constituency Politics*, p. 189.

also relevant to note that only one of the twenty-four had actually stood for election to the council, while a further seven had refused an invitation to stand.

The majority of those who express an interest in political activity remain, therefore, a potential rather than an active local leadership. They could be encouraged to organize their own local affairs if opportunities were made available that were less demanding than membership of the city council. They are also likely to be more interested in matters of specific local importance—the local school, the bus shelter, the replanning of *their* area—than they are in broad general policy. It follows from this argument that any future restructuring of local authority boundaries should allow people to be involved within their own small home area if interest in local government is to be encouraged. Such a policy will not be easy to establish. Many local authority services require a relatively large area before they can be administered effectively. Moreover, a policy of extreme decentralization would offend the traditional belief in representative, compendious, authorities which control the smallest details of policy within their area. There are real difficulties; but, if these difficulties can be overcome, a potential local leadership exists. The recent interest in 'grass root' councils and in community development work is an attempt to bring this potential leadership into active voluntary work within the local neighbourhood. Such attempts are consistent with the arguments of the present study; but here is a theme to which we must return in the final chapter, for it has profound implications for the future of local democracy.

7

The Local Electorate

*Among the foremost benefits of free government is that education of the intelligence
and of the sentiments which is carried down to the very lowest ranks of the
people when they are called to take a part in acts which directly affect the great
interests of their country.* JOHN STUART MILL, arguing for an extension of the
franchise in *Representative Government*

THE electorate of Sheffield have provided, in their constancy to
the Labour Party, some of the safest parliamentary seats in the
country. In 1968 five of the six constituencies in the city were
represented at Westminster by Labour members, and only one of
these, Heeley, had been considered a marginal seat at the preceding general election.[1] In the sixth constituency, Hallam, the Conservatives have enjoyed an equally safe tenure. Nor has the local
electorate proved more fickle when choosing municipal representatives than in selecting Members of Parliament. For many years
the Labour Party held approximately 70 per cent of the seats on
the Sheffield City Council,[2] and the party retained this dominant
position until the local elections of 1967 and 1968; but the
Conservatives' seats were also held with comfortable majorities,
and a marginal council election was scarcely more usual than a
close parliamentary contest.

In an industrial city surrounded by coal-fields the ascendancy of
the Labour Party comes as no surprise, but in Sheffield it is not
only the manual workers who vote Labour in large numbers. The
Labour Party has enjoyed substantial minority support from those
in non-manual occupations. The Conservative victory in the city
council elections in 1968 represented, therefore, a proud climax to

[1] In 1968 there was a 17 per cent swing against Labour in the Sheffield, Brightside
by-election, but the Labour candidate was still returned with a majority of 5,000 in a
51 per cent poll!

[2] A summary of the local election results since 1919 is contained in Appendix B.

the resurgence of support that carried this party into control of nearly all the major local authorities in the country. That successful Conservative challenge to Labour's power in 1967–8 will be analysed later in this chapter; but first the electoral behaviour of the city will be examined in more general terms.

The Labour Party's first substantial success in the Sheffield municipal elections came after the First World War. In the subsequent edition of the *Sheffield Year Book* the editor commented with pardonable exaggeration:

The elections on November 1st, 1919, the first since 1913, were the most sensational in the history of the city. In the first place fewer people troubled to go to the poll than ever before—only thirty-five per cent[3] in the fourteen wards in which there were contests. This apathy was fatal to the success of retiring councillors.

Of the sixteen retiring members two were returned unopposed, one did not seek re-election, four were re-elected, and the others were defeated. There was overlapping among the opponents of councillors, or the result would have been even worse. [*sic*]

. . . The opponents were, mostly, unknown men and women representative of Labour, Discharged Soldiers, Co-operative Societies, and National Democratic Party.[4]

The Discharged Soldiers had not been opposed by the Labour Party and the successful candidates of both those parties combined to form a group of fourteen to oppose the thirty-four councillors and sixteen aldermen who formed the ruling Coalition group, of whom the great majority were Conservatives or Liberals, though two councillors and one alderman were Lib-Labs.[5] The following year the Labour vote was maintained, but the apathy of which the editor of the *Sheffield Year Book* had complained was replaced by a substantially higher poll favouring the Conservatives and Liberals. Nevertheless the Labour Party made steady progress over the next few years until in November 1926 they took control of the city council. This control was maintained—except

---

[3] According to my calculations this should have been 34 per cent, and I have preferred this figure in Appendix B.

[4] *Sheffield Year Book, 1920*, published by the local newspaper.

[5] These men were leading members of the Sheffield Federated Trades Council, a trade union organization which did not combine with the Sheffield Trades and Labour Council (the official Labour Party organization) until 1920. See S. Pollard, *Sheffield Trades and Labour Council 1858 to 1958*, Ch. 6.

in 1932–3—until the Conservatives returned to power, this time unshared, in May 1968, only to lose it again in 1969.

The long period of one-party rule in Sheffield may be attributed in part to the social composition of the city, though, as already suggested, Labour voting has not been confined to manual workers; it was sustained by the division of the city into safe Labour and safe Conservative seats. These two aspects of Sheffield's electoral behaviour will now be considered in turn.

The survey of the electorate undertaken for the present study was conducted in November 1967. By that time the national Labour Party had already lost much of the support that carried the Labour government back into office in 1966 with a majority of nearly a hundred seats in the House of Commons. It is to be expected that the proportion of our sample shown as supporting the Labour Party will be lower than the proportion of the electorate supporting Labour candidates in the General Elections of 1964 and 1966. The proportion of the sample expressing support for either of the two major parties is likely also to be reduced because the respondents have a greater opportunity of stating a preference for a minor party in an interview than they have in the polling booth: the minor parties do not contest every seat at every election. The proportions of the sample giving support to the Labour Party (about half) and to the Conservative Party (about one-third) appear, therefore, to be a reasonable reflection of the state of public opinion at the time the survey was taken.

The survey was conducted throughout the city and included those areas recently absorbed from Derbyshire and the West Riding of Yorkshire. The newly acquired areas remained in their existing constituencies for parliamentary election purposes, and in Table 7.1, therefore, the figures obtained from the survey have been given separately for the parliamentary area, the six constituencies of the city, in order that a comparison may be made with the general election figures. Such a comparison will also be affected by the fact that three-quarters of the electorate of Sheffield vote in general elections. (The proportion who stated in the survey that they *never* vote was only one per cent.) The effect of non-voting is graphically illustrated by the local election results shown in Table 7.1. The survey was conducted mid-way between the two local elections of 1967 and 1968, in which the Conservative Party successfully challenged Labour's power in Sheffield, yet over half

Table 7.1
Proportions of the voters giving support to the two major parties
in Sheffield

Party supported	Parliamentary elections			Sheffield survey Nov. 1967		Local elections	
	1959	1964	1966	Six Constituencies	Total	1967	1968
	%	%	%	%	%	%	%
Labour Party	54	57	63	51	51	41	36
Conservative Party	44	38	34	35	34	55	57

Notes: The proportions given are calculated from the total number of
votes cast in the elections, whereas the survey is a reflection of the
entire electorate including those who do not usually vote. For a discussion of the effect on party support of the differing turn-out at parliamentary and local elections see Table 7.8 and surrounding text.
The percentages do not add to one hundred owing to minor party
intervention.

Sources: *The Times House of Commons*, 1959, 1964, and 1966, the Survey of
the Sheffield Electorate, and the *Sheffield Telegraph Year Book*.

the sample still maintained that they usually supported the Labour
Party. Many people in those two local elections were no doubt
voting in ways that were 'unusual' for them; but the major cause
of the discrepancy is the fact that only one-third of the electorate
voted in these elections. The Conservatives were better able to
maintain their support as the general poll fell and their position in
relation to the Labour Party consequently improved. A fuller
discussion of this point will be found later in the chapter.

The proletarian nature of the Sheffield population is undoubtedly the main cause of the propensity of its electorate to vote
Labour. Studies have repeatedly shown that in Great Britain
occupational status is associated with voting habits,[6] and this is
borne out in the results of the Sheffield survey. Manual workers
are far more likely than non-manual or managerial employees to
vote for the Labour Party. As Sheffield has a higher than average
proportion of manual workers the Labour Party would be
expected to do well. Table 7.2 contains other information, however, which is less consistent with national patterns of voting
behaviour.

[6] Some of the most recent evidence is summarized in Peter G. J. Pulzer, *Political
Representation and Elections in Britain*, Ch. IV. See also David Butler and Donald Stokes,
Political Change in Britain, for a discussion of this point and many others mentioned in
this chapter.

Table 7.2
Party allegiance in Sheffield

(1) *By socio-economic status and social mobility*

		Socio-economic status*				Social mobility†			
Base	Total 584	1 & 2 60	3 156	4 & 5 283	6 83	Up-ward 161	Static 179	Down-ward 136	Not known 109
	%	%	%	%	%	%	%	%	%
Usually vote Labour	51	25	37	65	49	43	57	55	50
Usually vote Conservative	34	58	44	21	42	39	31	29	39
Usually vote Liberal	4	10	5	2	2	4	4	2	3
Usually vote for another party‡	4	5	4	5	2	4	2	7	5
Never vote§	1	0	1	1	2	1	1	2	2
Refused to answer	6	3	8	6	1	10	5	5	3

* A combination of the Registrar-General's groups into a six-fold classification: (1) large employers, managers, and professional workers; (2) small employers, managers, and farmers; (3) intermediate non-manual workers; (4) skilled manual workers; (5) semi- and unskilled manual workers; (6) never employed/Q.N.A.
† These classifications are based upon a comparison of the socio-economic status of the informant and that of his or her father.
‡ The Communist Party contests seats in both parliamentary and local elections in Sheffield and recently the National Front has nominated candidates in municipal elections.
§ This figure is almost certainly an understatement.
Note: The percentages may not add to one hundred owing to rounding.
Source: Survey of Sheffield Electorate.

It is usual in national surveys for a third of the manual workers to show a preference for the Conservative Party.[7] On the other hand the Labour Party attracts the support of between 10 and 15 per cent of the business and professional classes.[8] In the Sheffield survey only 21 per cent of the manual workers supported the

[7] Pulzer, op. cit., p. 104. Robert McKenzie and Allan Silver also found that about three in every ten working-class voters voted for the Conservative Party in the survey they conducted in six urban constituencies in England in 1959: *Angels in Marble*, p. 84. In his survey in 1962 W. G. Runciman found that only 23 per cent of manual workers voted Conservative, and this lower than usual proportion was confirmed for 1963 by Butler and Stokes. W. G. Runciman, *Relative Deprivation and Social Justice*, pp. 170–1; Butler and Stokes, op. cit., p. 78. I have discussed the recent studies of working-class Conservatism at greater length in an article entitled 'Working-class Angels', *The Bulletin of the Society for the Study of Labour History*, No. 18, Spring 1969.
[8] Pulzer, ibid.

Conservatives[9] while no less than 25 per cent in the two highest categories voted Labour. In the intermediate non-manual category the Sheffield results show 37 per cent supporting the Labour Party while National Opinion Poll figures show between 25 and 30 per cent.[10] The National Opinion Poll results quoted by Dr. Pulzer were obtained in the periods of the 1964 and 1966 General Elections when the Labour Party was in the ascendancy, whereas the Sheffield survey, as already mentioned, was conducted during a period of declining Labour support; allowance for the different dates of the surveys would, therefore, tend to widen the gap between the results obtained nationally and in Sheffield. It is quite clear from the survey results that the support the Labour Party achieves in Sheffield has not come only from manual workers. It is true that a larger proportion of the manual workers vote Labour in Sheffield than the average proportion for the country as a whole, but the same variation from the national pattern may be observed among other occupational groups. The Labour Party receives a greater measure of support in Sheffield than it does nationally from each of the three main socio-economic groupings shown in Table 7.2.

The Sheffield sample was not large enough to allow breakdowns that would give further detailed information; nor, to be honest, was the interest of these results foreseen when the questionnaire was being drafted. It is not possible, therefore, to do more than suggest reasons. First, it is to be expected that any survey in a major industrial city will show a lower proportion of working-class Conservatives than a national survey which includes all rural areas. Robert McKenzie and Allan Silver cite the greater propensity of the urban working class to vote Labour as a reason for their sample from six urban constituencies containing only 29 per cent working-class Conservative voters, compared with the post-war

[9] There are always difficulties in comparing results obtained in different surveys. The respondents to the Sheffield survey were allocated to a socio-economic group according to their occupation or, in the case of non-employed housewives or retired people, according to the last job held. Other surveys classify informants according to the status of the head of household, and thus category 6 of the Sheffield survey is avoided. However, even if all the Conservative supporters in category 6 of the Sheffield survey were working class—an unlikely assumption to make—the proportion of working-class Conservatives in Sheffield would only rise to 26 per cent.

[10] Pulzer, op. cit., Fig. IV.5. The N.O.P. classification C.1. approximates to category 3 in Table 7.2.

national average of one-third.[11] We have shown, however, that the Sheffield proportion of working-class Conservatives is much lower still. One reason for the Conservatives' lack of success among the workers may be the city's industrial composition. In Chapter 2 it was emphasized that Sheffield has been predominantly a working-class city: opportunities for non-manual employment have been few compared with those in other large cities; in these circumstances the community ethos may favour the Labour Party within all occupational groupings. Those in non-manual occupations will be more likely to have friends or relatives in manual occupations, and may for this reason be more ready to vote Labour than their colleagues with completely middle-class family backgrounds. On the other hand the manual workers of Sheffield are less likely than workers in other cities to have relatives in non-manual occupations, and the lack of 'white-collar affiliations'[12] may reduce their propensity to vote Conservative.

There is another way in which the scarcity of non-manual job opportunities in Sheffield may affect voting behaviour. Several recent studies have emphasized that manual workers who describe themselves as middle class, or who aspire to middle-class status, are more likely to vote Conservative than the rest of the working-class electorate.[13] In Sheffield there are relatively few non-manual job opportunities. Middle-class aspirations are, therefore, inhibited among the manual workers, and this would reduce Conservative voting within the working class. Perhaps this argument can be summarized by suggesting that the nature of the Sheffield community, as described in Chapter 2, has in the past exerted a group pressure upon the electorate to vote for the Labour Party. The group pressure was accentuated, of course, by the uneven geographical distribution of the voting strength of the two major parties, and we will return to this later in the chapter.

If the occupational structure of Sheffield has had the suggested effect upon voting behaviour, then current changes in it—discussed

[11] McKenzie and Silver, op. cit, p. 80 n.

[12] The phrase is from John H. Goldthorpe, *et al.*, *The Affluent Worker: Political Attitudes and Behaviour*, where the association between cross-social family ties and voting behaviour is explored in Ch. 4.

[13] Runiciman, op., cit., pp. 170–1; McKenzie and Silver, op. cit., pp. 93–4. Eric A. Nordlinger obtained similar results in a survey of urban working-class men conducted in 1964: *The Working-Class Tories*, p. 163. Dr. Nordlinger discusses the difficulties arising in the use of the concept of self-assigned class at pp. 160–2.

in the conclusion to Chapter 2—could also have a considerable effect. It is not simply that there will be a larger proportion of
middle-class voters: the increase in the number of white-collar
jobs may reduce the group pressure to vote Labour both within
the middle class and among those in manual occupations. That
changes in occupational status are themselves associated with
changes in voting behaviour is shown by the figures given under
the heading of social mobility in Table 7.2: only 43 per cent of
those employed in an occupation of higher social status than their
father's voted Labour, compared to 57 per cent of those who had
retained the same status, and 55 per cent of those whose occupational status had declined compared with that of their father.[14]
The direct effect of occupational changes may be reinforced in
Sheffield, however, if the social composition of the city becomes
more fluid. The group pressure towards Labour voting would be
dissipated as the first generation of non-manual workers gradually
gives way to a second generation no longer committed to the
Labour Party by emotional ties; and the proportion voting Labour
among all social groupings in Sheffield may then decline towards
the national average. If this happens we may expect many more
marginal seats to appear in Sheffield politics.

In addition to the direct influences upon voting behaviour
arising from occupational status and family background, there are
other group pressures at the place of work. The larger factories
employ thousands of workers in conditions that favour the
strengthening of trade union influence and preclude any personal
relationship between the employee and the owner of the enterprise.
In these circumstances the group pressure to vote Labour is
intensified.[15] Table 7.3 presents data from the Sheffield survey
which confirms this relationship between size of firm and voting
behaviour.

The Sheffield survey also supports the view that trade union
members are more likely to vote Labour than non-members.
Trade union membership is, of course, associated with socio-
economic status, which in turn is associated with voting behaviour,
so that the figures may exaggerate the influence of trade union
membership upon the way a person votes. A better indication of

[14] A similar conclusion is reached by Butler and Stokes, op. cit., p. 98.
[15] Some of the data supporting this general conclusion is summarized by S. M.
Lipset, *Political Man*, pp. 248 ff.

this influence is obtained if the results are controlled for socio-economic status. In this way the association between trade union membership and voting behaviour may be examined within the

Table 7.3
Party Allegiance in Sheffield

(2) *By number of employees at place of work and trade union membership*

		No. of employees at place of work			Trade union membership			
					Total		S.E.S. 4 and 5*	
		Less than 20	20–500	More than 500	Member	Non-member	Member	Non-member
Base (all paid employees)	Total 342	79	149	112	147	195	107	176
	%	%	%	%	%	%	%	%
Usually vote Labour	54	46	55	58	69	42	n.a.	n.a.
Usually vote Conservative	30	38	30	24	16	40	15	24
Usually vote Liberal	3	4	2	4				
Usually vote for another party‡	6	5	8	4	14	19	n.a.	n.a.
Never vote§	1	3	1	1				
Refused to answer	7	6	5	10				

* See note to Table 7.2
‡ See note to Table 7.2
§ See note to Table 7.2

Notes: Two employees did not know how many were employed at their place of work. The percentages may not add to one hundred owing to rounding.
n.a.—not available.
Source: Survey of Sheffield Electorate.

working class. In the Sheffield sample 15 per cent of the manual workers (S.E.S. groups 4 and 5) who were members of a trade union supported the Conservatives, compared with 24 per cent of those who were not members. Trade union membership is associated with left voting, therefore, even when allowance is made for the influence of socio-economic status, but this association is not decisive.[16] Three-quarters of the non-trade unionists among Sheffield manual workers in our sample failed to support the Conservative Party, so their non-membership is not explainable on ideological grounds. Trade union membership is just one more source of group pressure which will reinforce a pattern of voting behaviour.

Rather more than half of the men in the Sheffield sample supported the Labour Party, and rather less than half of the women. These results are broadly similar to those obtained elsewhere, in that women are generally found to be more Conservative; but in Sheffield, of course, the dominance of the Labour Party results from a plurality of support from both men and women, whereas nationally the Conservatives usually obtain a majority of the votes cast by women. Dr. Pulzer writes that 'men have given Labour a

Table 7.4
Party allegiance in Sheffield

(3) *By Sex and Age*

		Sex		Age				
Base	Total 584	Male 275	Female 309	21–34 131	35–44 95	45–54 127	55–64 112	65 and over 118
	%	%	%	%	%	%	%	%
Usually vote Labour	51	55	48	47	60	59	48	43
Usually vote Conservative	34	31	37	31	26	27	38	47
Usually vote Liberal	4	2	5	6	3	5	2	2
Usually vote for another party‡	4	4	4	8	4	4	1	3
Never vote§	1	1	1	3	0	2	1	0
Refused to answer	6	6	6	5	5	5	11	5

‡ See note to Table 7.2
§ See note to Table 7.2
Note: The percentages may not add to one hundred owing to rounding.
Source: Survey of Sheffield Electorate.

majority at every election since the war; women only in 1945 and 1966'.[17] The interaction of sex and age on voting behaviour is complex, and it is difficult to isolate the causal factor. Dr. Pulzer

[16] This supports the conclusion reached by McKenzie and Silver, op. cit., pp. 97–9, and by Butler and Stokes, op. cit., p. 156.
[17] Pulzer, op. cit., p. 107.

draws our attention to the fact that women have a longer expect-
ancy of life than men; and the apparent Conservatism of women
may, therefore, be a reflection of the higher average age women
attain.[18] Professor McKenzie and Allan Silver have also suggested
that among the working class it is only the older women who are
more likely to vote Conservative than men of a similar age.[19]

In the Sheffield sample Conservatism is associated with age, but
the association does not take the form of a regular progression, and
among those under thirty-five years of age the Conservatives
actually have more support than among those respondents who are
between thirty-five and fifty-four. The strength of the Labour
support in the middle age groups (about six in every ten in these
age groups supported Labour compared with less than five in every
ten in the age groups below and above them) encourages the view
that voting attitudes are affected by the political environment
surrounding an individual's adolescence. The respondents in the
two age groups we are discussing would have been born between
1913 and 1932: their earliest political memories would have been
concerned with unemployment, fascism, war in alliance with the
Soviet Union, and widespread support for the Labour Party.[20]
The younger respondents to our survey would have grown up in
the political climate of reaction against the post-war Labour
government, war against communism in Korea, and of the Conservative 1950s.

The evidence from Sheffield is consistent with the view expressed
by Professor Lipset in 1959 that:

If a society should move from prolonged instability to stability, it may
well be that older people would retain the leftist ideas of their youth,
and the younger generations would adopt conservative philosophies.[21]

On the other hand Professor McKenzie and Allan Silver comment
upon the lack of a 'depression generation' in their sample of
working-class voters.[22] One reason for their conclusion might be

[18] Ibid.
[19] McKenzie and Silver, op. cit., chart 3.3, p. 87.
[20] The Labour Party secured the largest proportion of the votes cast in the General
Elections of 1945, 1950, and 1951. Those in their teens or twenties at this time would,
therefore, have had a greater possibility of growing up in a family where the parents
voted Labour than children of earlier generations.
[21] Lipset, op. cit., p. 267.
[22] McKenzie and Silver, op. cit., p. 90.

that McKenzie and Silver were assuming that political socializa-
tion takes place at a higher age than is in fact the case. They
examine the age group whose members were between seventeen
and twenty-six years of age during the 1930s, and find that there is
no greater propensity for this group than older age groups to
support the Labour Party. The figures from the McKenzie and
Silver survey show, however, that the two age groups below the
one they quote have a lower proportion of Conservative voters
than older age groups.[23] These two lower age groups comprise
respondents who were born between 1913 and 1935, and they
correspond almost exactly to the two age groups that show the
lowest proportions of Conservative supporters in the Sheffield
sample. It may be, therefore, that political views are fixed several
years before the age that McKenzie and Silver considered; or that
the effect of events of the inter-war period on the political climate
of the 1940s influenced those who became politically aware in that
decade. The McKenzie and Silver survey was conducted in 1958;
nine years later the Sheffield survey was able to interview an age
group younger than those we have been discussing, and it was
found that the proportion of Conservative supporters had returned
to a level almost identical with that of respondents twenty years
older. The evidence from the Sheffield sample, therefore, is consistent with the concept of political generations.[24]

Although the social composition of the Sheffield electorate
provides the most persuasive argument for the long period of
Labour control in the city, the continuous nature of this control
was encouraged by the geographical distribution of the various
social groups. The growth of Sheffield has already been outlined
and it is now necessary only to draw attention to the electoral
consequences of the pattern discussed in Chapter 2. The city

[23] McKenzie and Silver, op. cit., p. 88.
[24] Butler and Stokes provide further evidence supporting this concept by examining
the Labour share of support for the two main parties from new electors, 1935–66,
op. cit., pp. 53–5 and 59. They go on to project a gain in Labour strength as the older
generation favouring the Conservatives dies. The political effect of 'such projections',
they warn, 'must be understood to be *ceteris paribus*', and could be countered by a
movement towards the Conservatives, or away from Labour, within younger generations, op. cit., pp. 263–74. Our evidence, supported by opinion polls among those who
will vote for the first time at the General Election of 1970/1, suggests that Labour is *not*
receiving the same support from this generation that it received from their fathers.
There is a marked increase both in support for minor parties and in those 'not interested
in politics', which makes the prediction of electoral trends difficult.

lies in the foothills of the Pennine Chain, with the River Don collecting its tributaries together and flowing eastwards through the city towards Rotherham and Doncaster. The great industrial development of the Sheffield area took place in the Don Valley, and the workers in the heavy industries settled in widespread estates of mean terraced houses in the surrounding area. In the south and west—away from the smoke and dust, and close to the glorious hills of north-east Derbyshire—there were developed the residential areas of Hallam and Ecclesall, where the managers and professional people built substantial houses and tended their gardens.

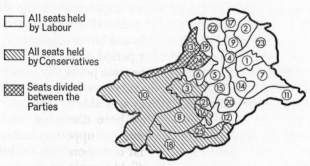

Diagram 7.1. Sheffield City Council
Party representation by wards, 1966–7

KEY TO ABOVE DIAGRAM AND TO DIAGRAMS ON PAGES 178 AND 180

List of Wards

1. Attercliffe	12. Heeley	23. Tinsley
2. Brightside	13. Hillsborough	24. Walkley
3. Broomhill	14. Manor	25. Woodseats
4. Burngreave	15. Moor	26. Beauchief
5. Cathedral	16. Nether Edge	27. Birley
6. Crookesmoor	17. Nethershire	28. Castle
7. Darnall	18. Norton	29. Dore
8. Ecclesall	19. Owlerton	30. Gleadless
9. Firth Park	20. Park	31. Intake
10. Hallam	21. Sharrow	32. Mosborough
11. Handsworth	22. Southey Green	33. Netherthorpe

Note: There were twenty-five wards in Sheffield until the boundary extensions of 1967 when the number was increased to twenty-seven. Not all the ward names were retained following the 1967 changes so that the total number of names given in the key is thirty-three. Naturally all names do not occur on all three maps to which this key refers.

Sheffield is divided by the layout of its housing, therefore, into two distinct areas. Some other cities have grown outwards from the centre as the middle class—and presumably the more Conservative-minded voters—have moved out into the suburbs. If local government wards in these cities are cut like slices of cake then they will include some working-class areas in the centre, and some middle-class areas on the outskirts. The result will be a balanced electorate with some possibility of electoral change. In Sheffield this has proved impossible until very recently. Before 1967 a line could be drawn on the map (see Diagram 7.1) from Hillsborough in the north to Gleadless in the south with the Labour areas to the east, and the Conservative areas to the west. The marginal seats—such as they were—straddled this line like a disputed no-man's-land; but if the battles were occasionally fierce, the victories were few. Only three wards changed hands on five or more occasions in the council elections held between 1945 and 1966. These 'marginal' wards were Sharrow (ten changes), Heeley (seven changes), and Hillsborough (five changes). In nearly every ward a councillor, once elected for either the Conservative or Labour interest, could expect to remain until he chose to retire—and some remained a very long time indeed: in the middle of the 1960s one member had achieved over fifty-five years' service on the council

Table 7.5
Sheffield County Borough elections,
1945–66

Ward elections	No. 524*	% 100
Of which		
Uncontested	38	7·2
Lab. straight fight with Communist	34	6·5
Seat changed hands	39	7·4
No change	485	92·6

* There was no election in Firth Park Ward in 1947.
Source: Sheffield Telegraph Year Books.

and there were six others who had served around forty years. The stability of the party representation on the Sheffield City Council between 1945 and 1966 is strikingly illustrated in Table 7.5 which shows that nearly twice as many wards were uncontested by one of the two major parties than changed hands following an election. Local election campaigns in Sheffield were a matter of form: the results a matter of course.

During these years the turn-out in Sheffield local elections was abnormally low. It was rare for more than one in every three electors to go to the polls, and in some years this figure dropped to one in four, or even to one in five. In several wards, for example Manor, Attercliffe, and Southey Green, there were occasions when only one out of every ten electors cared enough to vote. Sheffield's record in this respect was much worse than that of other large cities where usually two out of five electors vote in local elections.[25]

It is not easy to distinguish voters from non-voters for the purpose of analysis. Members of the electorate are reluctant to confess to an interviewer that they have neglected their duty as citizens; consequently when the replies are compared with the actual voting figures they reveal considerable overclaiming. In Glossop in 1953, for example, 49 per cent of the electorate went to the polls, but in a subsequent survey 62 per cent claimed to have voted.[26] In Newcastle-under-Lyme in 1958, 38 per cent actually voted, 'though

Table 7.6

Voting claims following the 1967 local elections in Sheffield

Base	Total	Voting habits			
		Conservative			Labour
		Total	Manual workers	Others	
	584	198	59	140	300
	%	%	%	%	%
Respondent claimed to have voted	61	74	73	74	56
Reasons given for not voting:					
Couldn't be bothered	8	4	5	4	10
Not able to vote (ill, away)	9	8	5	9	10
Purposely decided not to vote	12	7	5	7	13
Other reason	6	6	5	5	5
Can't remember reason	4	3	5	1	4

Notes: Only two respondents denied knowledge of the election, and only four stated that they did not vote because they did not know the candidates.
The percentages may not add to one hundred owing to rounding.

Source: Survey of Sheffield Electorate.

[25] Detailed figures may be found in the Registrar-General's *Statistical Review of England and Wales*, published annually.
[26] Birch, *Small Town Politics*, p. 98.

N

nearly twice as many said they had done so'.[27] In view of these previous experiences it was realized that no reliance could be placed upon the answer to the straight question, 'Did you vote in the last election?'; the Sheffield survey, therefore, sought to test the question rather than the respondents. In order to reduce the social pressure upon the respondents, the question was phrased in a negative manner and in very leading terms.[28] Despite this attempt to reassure the respondents that non-voting was acceptable to the interviewer, 61 per cent of the sample spontaneously claimed to have voted, although the actual turn-out had been only 33 per cent. In Table 7.6 the reasons given by those who said they had not voted have been grouped under main headings. It must be emphasized that these replies are not representative of all those who did not vote, but only of those who admitted to that omission six months later.

More Conservative than Labour supporters claimed to have voted, and it is interesting to note that there was no significant difference in this respect between working-class Conservatives and those from other occupational groups. It has often been suggested that middle-class electors are more likely than working-class electors to use their vote,[29] and the evidence from the various wards in Sheffield—presented later in this chapter—supports this contention: the fact that no differences emerged when the Conservative claims were distinguished by social grouping suggests that the working-class Conservatives had adopted the attitude— viz., that one *should* vote—of their middle-class fellow-voters. The results suggest, therefore, that the attitude of an elector to the voting process is influenced more by ideology than by social class.[30] The Conservatives, as McKenzie and Silver contend, may

[27] Bealey, Blondel, and McCann. *Constituency Politics*, p. 229.

[28] Question 21, Sheffield survey: 'At the last local elections in Sheffield, in May this year, nearly three-quarters of the people did not vote, for one reason or another. Can I ask you—if you did not vote at that election—what was your reason?' 'Any other reasons?' In analysing the answers to this and other questions, the voting habits of the Sheffield respondents were not obtained from their answers to Q. 21, but from those to a subsequent question, 'When you *do* vote, which party do you usually vote for?'

[29] Lipset, op. cit., pp. 182 ff., contains a summary of the evidence on non-voting and a list of references. Bealey, Blondel, and McCann, op. cit., pp. 229 ff., draw a similar conclusion from voting claims in Newcastle-under-Lyme.

[30] This conclusion would support the view of McKenzie and Silver, op. cit., pp. 121 ff., but not all our evidence supports their further suggestion that working-class Conservatives are more knowledgeable about politics than other manual workers; cf. Ch. 6.

be more optimistic about the effectiveness of taking part in the electoral process.

It was noticeable in the Sheffield survey that the reason given by a lot of respondents for not voting was a conviction that it did not matter which party obtained a majority. Others were dissatisfied with the Labour Party generally, and some of these spoke bitterly about the rent rebate scheme introduced by the Labour-controlled city council. Others were not so rational in their expression of a political point of view through their voting behaviour: one woman stated that she usually voted, but had stayed away at the 1967 election as a protest; she and her husband were dissatisfied with things over the past year, she complained that the cost of everything was going up. This respondent then went on to inform the interviewer that she usually voted *Conservative*: both the government and the city council during her year of discontent were, of course, controlled by the Labour Party! The one Scottish Nationalist in the sample stated emphatically that he was 'not interested in the English M.P. or the councillors'.

Besides those respondents who considered that 'it made no difference who got in'—a sentiment expressed most graphically by the young man who claimed that 'they only get in to shout and make a noise'—there were many others who did not vote because they regarded the result of the election in their ward as a foregone conclusion. Some respondents said that their man 'would get in anyway'; others replied that their party 'never gets in anyway'; the resulting action was the same for both groups: they did not vote. These replies illustrate that the effectiveness of an individual vote is consciously considered by many voters, and this view can be fully substantiated by a detailed analysis of the election results in Sheffield since 1945.

Such an examination indicates that there are two major factors, in addition to the nationwide political temperature, which affect the size of the poll; these are the two already indicated by the voting claims of the Sheffield sample. First, more people vote in the safe Conservative seats than in Labour seats. Presumably the Conservative voters feel it more of a social duty to vote, even when their individual vote can have little effect, than do their Labour opponents; although, as already suggested, it is difficult to relate this to any simple causal factor such as social class. It must be remembered, also, that the Labour Party controlled the city

Table 7.7
Average poll in contested wards in
Sheffield since 1945

Sheffield	% 34
Marginal seats*	43
Conservative seats	39
Labour seats	29†
Lab. straight fight with Communist	19

* Marginal seats are defined as those in the
three wards in which seats have changed
hands more than five times in the period
covered.
† If the seats where Labour had a straight
fight with the Communists are excluded
then the average poll in Labour seats
increases to 30 per cent.
Source: Sheffield Telegraph Year Books.

council throughout the period referred to in Table 7.7. Abstentions
on policy grounds were more likely, therefore, to affect the Labour
vote than the Conservative. It is more difficult for a political party
to satisfy its supporters when in office than in opposition; and the
local elections gave the Conservatives a chance to register a
protest against the Labour-controlled city council.

Secondly, more people will vote if there is a chance, even a
small one, that the seat will change hands.[31] The marginal seats in
Sheffield return a higher average percentage poll than the safe
seats of either political party. In part this is due to the complacency, or hopelessness, of the electorate in the safe wards, but
there is also the effect of a substantial majority on the local party
organization. Parties do not fight hard in safe seats, neither in their
own, nor in those of their opponents. It will be remembered from
Table 7.5 that many of the safest seats were not even contested.[32]

[31] Michael Steed drew attention to the influence of marginality on voting behaviour
in his appendix to *The British General Election of 1966* by D. E. Butler and Anthony
King. The figures given in L. J. Sharpe (ed.), *Voting in Cities*, also confirm the link
between marginality and high polls, though Torquay is quoted as an exception on
p. 228. The evidence from Newcastle-under-Lyme shows no consistent relationship
between marginality and turn-out, Bealey, Blondel, and McCann, op. cit., p. 224.

[32] If they were, then presumably the poll would be even lower than in the other safe
seats, thus depressing the average still further. The lowest polls of all were those where
the Labour councillor was challenged by a Communist only: in these wards Labour
often had over a thousand majority in a 10 per cent poll.

And a party will on occasion run a 'dummy' candidate, without conducting any campaign, in other seats they cannot expect to win. Such a 'dummy' candidate compels the holders of the seat to devote some of their forces to retaining it, while the opposition campaigns in a more hopeful marginal ward.

In addition to the two general considerations mentioned above there was a further factor affecting the size of the poll in Sheffield from the late 1950s onwards: the redevelopment of the central area. As the houses demolished were mainly in the nineteenth-century working-class areas the Labour vote suffered most. Between the compiling of the electoral register in October and the elections in the following May thousands of electors moved to other areas of the city. These people were difficult for the political parties to trace, and there was no postal vote allowed unless they had moved outside the city altogether. The fact that entire areas were cleared at one time disrupted the party organization as the ward officials left, and it took time to build an organization in the newly developed areas. A few of the respondents to the Sheffield survey gave as a reason for not voting the fact that they had not received any literature about the election. Some specifically mentioned the lack of a poll card—these are issued by the Returning Officer in general elections but not in local elections—assuming that without a card they were not entitled to vote; and it would seem that confusion over the conditions to be fulfilled still prevent a number of electors from going to the polls.[33] The wards affected most by redevelopment in the period referred to were Crookesmoor, Cathedral, Moor, and Burngreave—all of these wards returned very low polls during the 1960s.

This discussion of the turn-out at Sheffield local elections has concentrated on political influences: marginality, belief in efficacy of voting, party organization, and attitudes to party policy at any given time; this is not to suggest that apathy pure and simple is unimportant. There are many—probably far more than the 8 per cent who confess to it—who just 'can't be bothered to vote'; but one factor that does not appear to be important is the degree of attachment felt by the electorate towards their neighbourhood. The four wards constituting Brightside—the constituency with the highest all-round score on neighbourhood attachment character-

---

[33] Two members of the Sheffield sample—one aged 26 and the other 36—thought that they were not entitled to vote as they were not householders.

istics[34]—are among those which customarily return the lowest polls; but they include two where the contests are often between the Labour and Communist parties only.

One woman in the Sheffield sample replied that she had not voted in the local elections because 'it was only a small one, and we only go to the big ones'. In this she obviously typified many other electors, for the poll in local elections is only a fraction of the number who vote in general elections. Usually a general election is held some months before or after the local elections of a particular year so that it is difficult to make comparisons between the two: changes in voting behaviour might reflect changes in opinion between the two dates; or voting behaviour may change as a consequence of different attitudes to the two types of election.[35] In 1966, however, the local elections were held within a month of the general election so that movements of opinion between the two dates may be assumed to be minimal. Public opinion polls suggest, moreover, that such movement as there was continued to favour Labour. In Table 7.8 the percentage poll for each of the six Sheffield constituencies in the general election of 1966 is given, together with the percentage poll at the subsequent local elections in the wards that constituted them. The vote obtained by each of the two major parties at the local election is then expressed as a percentage of the vote that party obtained at the general election. It is clear that the Labour vote fell much more than the Conservative.

The Labour Party were less successful than the Conservatives in retaining their general election vote in the local elections in each of the Sheffield constituencies. The differences between the constituencies were compatible with the general conclusions concerning turn-out: the middle-class residential area of Hallam has a more conscientious local electorate, whichever way they vote, than the working-class areas of Attercliffe or Park; and the area with the closest consistency between local and national polls—together with the highest total turn-out in both general and local elections

---

[34] See Table 5.9 and the surrounding text.

[35] Differential turn-out is discussed in relation to parliamentary by-elections by Anthony King in 'Why all governments lose by-elections', *New Society*, 21 March 1968; and by Nigel Lawson in 'A new theory of by-elections', *The Spectator*, 8 November 1968. See also Jorgen Rasmussen, 'The disutility of the swing concept in British psephology', *Parliamentary Affairs*, 18 (1964–5), and H. B. Berrington, 'The General Election of 1964' (with discussion), *Journal of the Royal Statistical Society*, 128 (1965).

Table 7.8

Turn-out in the general election and in the local elections in Sheffield, 1966

Constituency	General election turn-out	Local election turn-out	Local election turn-out as a proportion of general election turn-out		
			Total	Labour	Conservative
	%	%	%	%	%
Attercliffe	68	16	24	21	27
Brightside	66	19	29	—	—
Hallam	75	28	37	27	48
Heeley	79	33	42	30	50
Hillsborough	70	22	32	26	35
Park	65	17	26	(21)	(29)
Sheffield	71	22	31	(24)	(42)

Note: The Conservatives in 1966 did not contest three out of the four wards comprising the Brightside constituency, nor did they contest one ward out of the four comprising the Park constituency. The percentages in brackets, therefore, are estimates, and in the case of Brightside even an estimate was not feasible with the limited evidence available.

Source: Sheffield Telegraph Year Book, 1966–7 and Butler and King, *The British General Election of 1966.*

—was Heeley, the only marginal area in the city. The political consequences are clear: the Conservative Party is more successful in persuading its supporters to vote in local elections than is the Labour Party;[36] the Conservative Party, therefore, will do better in local elections than in parliamentary elections for this reason alone, and it will be unwise to draw conclusions about a future parliamentary election from voting in a local contest.

For several decades before 1967 the Labour Party majority on Sheffield City Council was normally impregnable. About 70 per cent of the council were Labour Party members, and as only one-quarter of the council came forward for re-election each year[37] the electorate could not change the controlling group at any single election. In 1967, however, such an opportunity for change was presented. In April of that year the boundaries of Sheffield were

[36] This conclusion is directly contrary to the experience reported from Newcastle-under-Lyme, Bealey, Blondel, and McCann, op. cit., pp. 222–4.

[37] The membership of an English county borough council comprises three councillors for each ward, and one alderman to every three councillors. One-third of the councillors—or one-quarter of the council—retire each year, and one-half of the aldermen are elected by the councillors every three years.

extended to include certain contiguous areas from Derbyshire and the West Riding of Yorkshire. These additions increased the population of the city by approximately 47,000—from about half a million—and were made the occasion for a complete reorganization of the ward boundaries. The extensive redevelopment of the older areas of the city had in any case made such a reorganization desirable, and after the reallocation of polling districts no ward retained the same boundaries as before 1967. In addition two new wards were created from the areas taken in from Derbyshire. It was decided, therefore, that the entire council—including aldermen—should retire and each ward elect three councillors in May 1967.

The timing of this exceptional election was not favourable to Labour. The fortunes of that party nationally had been in decline since the very first months of their overwhelming victory in 1966. The financial crisis of July 1966 and the consequent restrictions on home production had disappointed expectations of the more rapid growth rate which formed the basis of Labour's social programme. The Prices and Incomes policy of the government remained unpopular, and the new powers taken to enforce the policy with penal sanctions were bitterly opposed by the trade unions. The year 1967 was the year in which Labour lost control of most of the industrial cities that had been the traditional base of the party's strength in local elections. The time was propitious for the Conservatives in Sheffield, and they went into the 1967 campaign with the unaccustomed feeling that they could take control of the city council.

The manifesto that the Conservatives produced in preparation for the campaign contained a comprehensive programme for the city: they attacked the policies of the Labour council which they maintained had stunted the industrial development of the area; and they promised to create the conditions for balanced employment by encouraging the growth of new industries. In reply the Labour Party naturally claimed that the policies they were already pursuing would have these desirable results. The industrial future of the city was undoubtedly the most important matter discussed during the campaign, but it was too complicated an issue to have any emotional impact upon the mass electorate. In any case both political parties agreed about the need to secure greater industrial diversification in the city, the disagreement arose about the best method of promoting it; and, of course, each party maintained that they would put more effort into the task. There were, however, a number of other local issues that had aroused strong feelings.

The attitude of the electorate to four of the most controversial decisions of the Labour council was obtained from their replies to the Sheffield survey conducted mid-way between the local elections of 1967 and 1968. The first point to note from the summary of the survey results contained in Table 7.9 is that on three out of the four issues the Labour council's decision was adherents by a majority of those who expressed a clear opinion.[38] The one exception was the council's decision *not* to proceed with the development of an airport close to the city. Half the sample were opposed to this decision while only a third expressed themselves in favour. The support for the airport was found among adherents of both major parties, and it was spread fairly evenly throughout the various occupational groupings in the city. The manual workers, hardly less than the managers who might be expected to use an airport more frequently, were in favour of Sheffield developing this new communications centre.

On two of the other issues the division of opinion was on more straightforward party lines, though even in these cases about a quarter of the Conservative supporters in the sample supported the Labour council's decision. The first of these issues, comprehensive schools, was extremely complex. The Labour council had decided to introduce comprehensive schools throughout the city and consequently to discontinue the eleven-plus examination to select pupils for different types of secondary education. The leadership of the Conservative Party in the council supported the principle of comprehensive schools, but opposed the Labour scheme on a number of points. It is not clear, therefore, whether the 52 per cent of Conservative supporters who were opposed to the decision of the Labour council were opposed to comprehensive schools as such or only indicating their support for the proposed Conservative amendments. On the other issue the Conservatives showed much less ambiguity: 57 per cent were opposed to the Labour group's decision to implement a closed shop for manual workers employed by the council.

[38] A fuller discussion of the four issues mentioned here will be found in Chapters 9 and 10.

Table 7.9
Summary of attitude of electorate to four issues in Sheffield elections 1967–8

	Total 584			Labour supporters 300			Conservative supporters 198		
Issue	Support Labour council decision	Oppose Labour council decision	Neither support nor oppose	Support Labour council decision	Oppose Labour council decision	Neither support nor oppose	Support Labour council decision	Oppose Labour council decision	Neither support nor oppose
	%	%	%	%	%	%	%	%	%
Rent rebate scheme for council-house tenants	50	41	7	42	48	8	61	32	6
Comprehensive schools	47	29	16	57	16	18	28	52	15
Closed shop for council employees	39	38	18	49	26	18	23	57	18
Local airport	34	50	13	36	47	13	32	54	12

Note: The percentages will not add to one hundred as some respondents are in a 'don't know' category.
The percentage who 'don't know' varies from 2 per cent on the rent rebate scheme issue to 8 per cent on the comprehensive schools issue. Fuller details of those issues will be found in Chapters 9 and 10.
Source: Survey of Sheffield Electorate.

In the issues already mentioned it is difficult to imagine that the division of opinion had a great influence on voting behaviour. Perhaps a quarter of a party's supporters opposed its policy on a particular issue, but this was balanced by an equal number of dissenters on the other side; even on the airport issue where 47 per cent of the Labour supporters opposed the council's decision, it is difficult to believe that many votes were gained or lost on this issue alone. The decision to introduce a rent rebate scheme for council tenants was entirely different in this respect: it most certainly lost the Labour Party a lot of votes in the local elections of 1967 and 1968. In several wards the anger of the council-house tenants over this scheme almost certainly caused the Labour Party to lose normally safe seats. It will be noted from Table 7.9 that 48 per cent of Labour supporters opposed the introduction of the rent rebate scheme. The main opposition was centred on the council estates which usually provided the Labour Party with overwhelming majorities. Seventy per cent of the council-house tenants in the Sheffield sample usually supported the Labour Party, compared with 18 per cent who usually voted Conservative; but 68 per cent of the council house tenants in our sample were opposed to the rent rebate scheme. A large proportion of the Conservatives, on the other hand, supported the scheme, though it is interesting to notice that this largely reflected the different socio-economic status of the supporters of the two parties. When the opinions of the working-class Conservatives were examined it was found that only 44 per cent supported the rent rebate scheme, compared with 47 per cent who were opposed. These proportions are similar to those found among Labour Party voters. Even those Conservatives who supported the rent rebate scheme were unlikely to express their support by voting Labour, for their own party was officially committed to the introduction of a similar scheme.[39]

In 1967 many of the council-house tenants, faced with a united front from the two major parties on the principle of a rent rebate scheme, either stayed at home or voted for the Communist candidates who were opposed to the scheme. In most of the wards in which they stood the Communists increased their vote from the previous year three- or four-fold. In one ward, consisting entirely of council houses, the Communists secured 963 votes; in several wards the increased vote going to the Communist would have been

[39] For the differences between the parties on this issue see Chapter 10.

sufficient to enable the Labour candidate to win a seat that went
to the Conservatives.

When the result of the council elections was declared in 1967 the
Labour Party had retained control in Sheffield by the narrowest
possible margin: a majority of one. Labour obtained 41 seats, the
Conservatives 39 seats, and one Independent was returned.[40] The
bare results do not indicate just how close the contest had been.
Seven out of the twenty-seven wards returned councillors of more
than one political persuasion, even though all three councillors
had been elected at the same time. In one ward, Walkley, only one

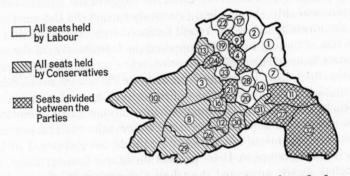

Diagram 7.2. *Sheffield City Council. Party representation by wards, 1967–8*
Notes: One Independent candidate was elected as councillor for Mosborough
          Ward (32) in 1967–8.
          A general key to these diagrams will be found on p. 165.

vote separated the three successful candidates, two of whom were
Labour, and the third Conservative. The Labour Party naturally
claimed that the length of the ballot paper, and the changes in
ward boundaries, had confused the electorate, but there is no
evidence that these factors had any significant effect in assisting
one party rather than another. Minor parties who placed only one
candidate in a ward may have gained from the 'wealth of votes' in
the electors' possession, but the results in the following year suggest
that votes obtained by minor parties are better attributed to
political influences, and particularly the introduction of the rent
rebate scheme, than to any general confusion arising from the use

[40] He was the local vicar in one of the Derbyshire areas taken into Sheffield, and he
had led a vigorous campaign against their inclusion. Resentment at the extension of
the boundaries undoubtedly affected the voting behaviour of the electorate in the two
newly created wards where 65 per cent of our sample opposed the changes.

of a multi-vote ballot.[41] To continue the military metaphor, the Conservatives had crossed the no-man's-land on Sheffield's electoral map, and had established bridgeheads in wards deep in Labour territory.

The excitement created by this 'little general election'—as the newspapers termed it—encouraged a very high turn-out by Sheffield local election standards. About a third of the electorate voted in 1967 compared with 22 per cent the previous year: it was the highest local poll in Sheffield for twelve years. In part this reflected a national tendency for more people to vote in the local elections of 1967 in order to express their opposition to the Labour government, but the detailed figures again support the view that the electorate are affected in their decision to vote by the likelihood of a seat changing hands.[42] The affect of marginality on the poll appears to be so strong that it overcomes other possible influences on the turn-out. The boundary between Gleadless and Intake wards, for example, divided a housing estate, and was widely criticized for splitting the natural communities of the area in a most unnatural manner. It was suggested that the electorate of these two wards would be confused by the electoral districts within which they were placed. If this was so then it was certainly not reflected in the turn-out: over half the electorate of Gleadless voted—the highest turn-out of any ward—and the poll in Intake was well above the average for the city. This area had been widely regarded before the election as the most marginal in Sheffield, and the political factors obviously had more effect than the failure to relate the ward boundaries to local communities.[43]

The Labour group, through their majority of one among the councillors, were enabled to secure the election of eighteen of the twenty-seven aldermen and thus to increase their overall majority on the council to ten;[44] but despite this manipulation of the alder-

[41] I have discussed this point in 'The Electoral Response to a Multi-vote Ballot', *Political Studies*, XVI, 2 (June 1968).

[42] Ibid.

[43] The Conservatives won all six seats in the two wards by comfortable majorities, so that in 1968 this area was no longer considered the most marginal in the city. The expected consequence followed: the turn-out in Gleadless and Intake—and in the similar case of Hillsborough—fell while the poll in other, more marginal, areas increased. The average turn-out in Sheffield in 1968 was almost identical to that of 1967.

[44] This use of the aldermanic system to boost a narrow majority is discussed on pp. 52–3 above.

manic elections the control of the Labour Party remained vulnerable to a renewed Conservative attack in May 1968. In that election only one-third of the council seats became vacant, but the opportunities in the wards that had returned a divided representation in the previous year were favourable to the Conservative Party. In addition the single Independent resigned after one year on the council, following his transfer to another diocese, and two seats were vacant owing to resignations by Conservative councillors. The political atmosphere surrounding the 1968 elections was similar to that of 1967: the Labour government had lost even more popular support during the intervening year; and the local issues outlined earlier in this chapter had continued to provide lively popular controversy. The council-house tenants in particular had campaigned actively throughout the year against the rent rebate scheme, and three tenants' association candidates were nominated in the council elections of 1968, as well as eleven Communists who were opposed to the rent rebate scheme.

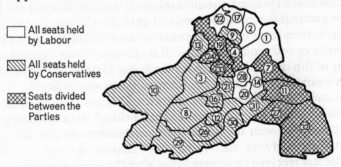

Diagram 7.3 *Sheffield City Council. Party representation by wards, 1968–9*
Note: A general key to these diagrams will be found on p. 165.

The result of the election was a triumph for the Conservatives: they held all the seats they had won in 1967, and gained seven more from the Labour Party, plus the seat vacated by the Independent. The Conservatives had pushed their advantage even further into traditionally Labour areas: four more wards—Owlerton, Netherthorpe, Darnall, and Mosborough[45] returned their first non-Labour councillors for generations; and in the whole of the Heeley parliamentary constituency—which returned a Labour Member of Parliament in 1966—there remained not a single Labour councillor.

[45] Mosborough was a safe Labour area before its incorporation into Sheffield.

As in 1967 the voting in a number of wards was extremely close: five seats were won with majorities of less than one hundred, and in two of these cases the majority was less than ten votes. Moreover the smaller parties continued to poll hundreds of votes in areas adversely affected by the rent rebate scheme. One tenants' candidate received over 600 votes and another over 500; the Communists, though not receiving quite the volume of support they had gained in 1967, polled many more votes than in previous years. In two wards, Owlerton and Netherthorpe, the Conservatives won seats from the Labour Party by majorities that were far lower than the number of votes received by the Communist candidate.

The results in Owlerton and Netherthorpe wards were decisive in determining the control of the city council. Forty-seven Conservative councillors were returned compared with Labour's thirty-four; the aldermen remained unchanged, leaving the effective Conservative majority on the city council at just four seats. The Conservatives were in a stronger position than this narrow overall majority would suggest. If their majority of thirteen among councillors could be retained until the aldermanic elections of 1970, then some of the aldermen elected to bolster the Labour majority in 1967 could be replaced by Conservatives. As only one-third of the councillors were now coming forward for re-election each year, the task facing the Labour Party was difficult.

In 1969 the Labour Party regained enough of their lost support to resume control of the council. They held all the seats they were defending and won five from the Conservatives to give them an overall majority of six. In several Labour strongholds their candidates received large majorities after the previous year's shock results. In Walkley ward the Labour candidate defeated a sitting Conservative councillor by eighteen votes, with an Independent obtaining over 700 after a campaign against a redevelopment scheme.[46] But Labour's victory was far from secure; they controlled the council by virtue of the majority of aldermen they had taken in 1967, and they remained in a minority among elected councillors. In the elections of May 1970, however, the Labour Party won sufficient council seats to enable them to control the election of aldermen and further strengthen their majority.

The Conservative success in 1968 may be attributed to three

---

[46] See Ch. 11 for a discussion of this campaign.

circumstances: first, the redrawing of the city boundaries that caused the entire council to come forward for re-election in 1967; secondly, the unpopularity of the Labour government in 1967 and 1968; and, finally, the local opposition to the introduction of a rent rebate scheme for council tenants. But long-term changes in the economic and social composition of Sheffield had been dissipating the traditional basis of Labour support for several years.

First, we have stressed the alterations in the job opportunities available. The demand for manpower in the traditional, heavily unionized industries of Sheffield is declining, and there is some growth in the number employed in professional and service occupations. In metal manufacture and other metal-using industries, for example, the number of employees declined by 5,000 between June 1962 and June 1967; in the same period the number of professional and scientific workers increased by 5,000.[47] The reduction in group pressure to support the Labour Party, arising from such occupational changes, is accentuated by the second social change: the crowded working-class districts are being redeveloped, and people are moving into new housing estates in areas in which there is a greater concatenation of social classes than has been usual in housing development in Sheffield. In these circumstances the Labour Party will find it more difficult to secure the unquestioning loyalty it enjoyed in the past. As the community life of Sheffield, described in Chapter 2, becomes less homogeneous, the electorate will be subject to increasing cross-pressure both at work and at home; and once the hegemony of the Labour Party is broken the electorate may become more volatile in their voting habits.[48] In this more fluid political situation we may expect the ideological struggle between the parties to become more intense. The electorate will need to be convinced rather than exhorted, and policies may become more important as the Sheffield elector is wooed afresh after several decades of monogamous fidelity.

---

[47] *Sheffield Forward*, Nov. 1968. The figures were obtained from the Department of Employment and Productivity. Some service industries declined during this period, notably distribution, construction, and transport, so that the labour force of Sheffield showed an overall decline of 7,300 between 1962 and 1967. This gave urgency to the demands for industrial diversification being made by the city council and other organizations within the city.

[48] cf. Frank Parkin, 'Working-class Conservatives: a Theory of Political Deviance', *British Journal of Sociology*, Sept. 1967, and Butler and Stokes, op. cit., pp. 121–2.

8

The Representatives

It is no doubt of importance to the welfare of nations that they should be governed by men of talents and virtue: but it is perhaps still more important that the interests of those men should not differ from the interests of the community at large.

ALEXIS DE TOCQUEVILLE

THE local councillor[1] does not usually perform his public duties in the spotlight of publicity; nor are councillors, as a group, regarded with any particular respect by the general public. The individual councillor may be treated with some deference, especially if he achieves a year of office as mayor, but he will practise his political skills against a chorus deploring the low calibre of local political representatives. Such sentiments are not new: George Jones has quoted from *The Times* of 1880 to show that they existed before the creation of the present local authorities;[2] but the criticisms of local councillors undoubtedly increased as the local aristocracy, whether of birth or wealth, was replaced on the councils by men and women of more humble origins.[3] The present councillors are criticized for being too old, too uneducated, and too unversed in business affairs, to control the major expenditures of modern local authorities.[4]

To assess the calibre of a body of people as amorphous as local

[1] In this chapter councillors will be taken to include aldermen unless the context clearly requires otherwise. A discussion of the respective roles of aldermen and councillors on Sheffield City Council will be found in Chapter 3.

[2] G. W. Jones, *Borough Politics*, p. 150.

[3] J. M. Lee, *Social Leaders and Public Persons*, has discussed this change over the past eighty years in his study of Cheshire County Council. See also Birch, *Small Town Politics*, Ch. 3.

[4] The terms of reference of the Committee on the Management of Local Government implied that action was necessary to improve, or at least to maintain, the calibre of local councillors. The matter is discussed in their Report at pp. 142–4, but their only recommendation is that people aged 70 or over should be disqualified from standing for election to a local authority. Understandably, the Committee did not attempt to measure quality.

councillors is very difficult. Ability is not reserved to people of one age-group, sex, degree of education, or type of occupation; and much will depend upon the time and enthusiasm devoted to council duties. For example, the assumption of power by the Labour Party in Sheffield in 1926, under the leadership of a railwayman, did not imply a decline in the vigour of council policy; and J. M. Lee has commented upon the 'pathetic performance' of one of the social leaders of Cheshire who, as chairman of the county council, appeared before a parliamentary committee.[5] L. J. Sharpe and Dr. Jones have contested both the assumption that councils are composed largely of housewives and retired people, and the implied conclusion that these groups are necessarily less effective than other local councillors in fulfilling their responsibilities.[6] With these warnings that we should not make individual assessments of merit from generalized demographic description fresh in our minds we may, in this chapter, examine the membership of the Sheffield City Council for the municipal year 1967–8. We shall be able to determine how representative the councillors were of the adult population of the city, and we shall then proceed to discuss the extent to which their views coincide with those of the general electorate. We shall not presume to judge whether the members of the council corresponded to Tocqueville's 'men of talents and virtue'; such judgements are best left to their constituents.

The exceptional turnover of members of the Sheffield City Council in 1967 means that the profile of the 1967–8 council presented in the following pages is not an adequate reflection of earlier councils. As we have seen in the previous chapter, every member of the city council had to renew his, or her, mandate from the electorate in 1967, and more Conservatives were returned than at any election for a generation. Thirty of the eighty-one councillors elected, and two of the twenty-seven aldermen, had not served on the retiring city council. Every member of the newly elected city council was interviewed between January and April 1968.[7]

---

[5] Lee, op. cit., pp. 111–12. See also *M.L.G.*, V, *Local Government Administration in England and Wales*, p. 41

[6] L. J. Sharpe, 'Elected Representatives in Local Government', *British Journal of Sociology*, 13, 3 (1962); G. W. Jones, op. cit. Ch. 7.

[7] As the interviews represented a complete census of the membership of the city council, the results are not subject to any sampling error, or error arising from non-response, but they are not necessarily typical of Sheffield councillors in other years.

They were questioned about their backgrounds and about their attitude to their council work, and invited to give their views on local issues. The councillors, as distinct from aldermen, were also asked to describe their relationship with their ward electorate. Some of the questions were taken from those asked by the Government Social Survey[8] in preparing evidence for the Committee on the Management of Local Government; other questions had been part of our own survey of the Sheffield electorate a few months earlier. It is possible, therefore, to compare the results of the interviews both with those obtained from the sample of council members in England and Wales,[9] and with the response from the Sheffield electorate.

Table 8.1 shows just how far the councillors we interviewed represented a break from the continuity that previously had been a feature of council membership in Sheffield. Nearly half of the council had served for three years or less by May 1967, and for the Conservative group the proportion was over two-thirds. There had been a large intake of new councillors after a few elections in the past, in 1926 and 1946 for example, but in these years the newcomers were supporters of the Labour Party. Once elected to the council the Sheffield councillor has tended to stay a long while. It has been usual for a fifth of the council members to have served for twenty-one years or more; a further third to have served between ten and twenty years; and for just under a half to have served for nine years or less. The proportion of really long-serving councillors in Sheffield appears to be larger than in other county boroughs: only eleven per cent of the national sample had served for twenty-one years or more.

With the exception of the years 1926 and 1967 the average length of service of members of the Sheffield City Councils shown in Table 8.1 has been twelve years.[10] The Labour and opposition groups have not differed much in this respect; the range for both

---

[8] By courtesy of the Director, Mr. Louis Moss.

[9] As the national survey of councillors was conducted three years before the Sheffield survey any comparisons must be treated cautiously. The Labour Party was in the ascendant in 1964, but by 1967 the Conservatives had made enormous gains in the local elections. A national sample of councillors in 1967–8 would have contained, therefore, many more Conservatives than one taken in 1964.

[10] The average length of service of 12·5 years for membership of the 1966–7 council is identical with that found in Wolverhampton in 1962–3. G. W. Jones, op. cit., p. 381. Tenure on the Newcastle-under-Lyme council is discussed in Bealey, Blondel, and McCann, *Constituency Politics*, pp. 306–10.

Table 8.1
Length of service on Sheffield City Council—selected years

Year	Up to 3 years			4–9 years			10–20 years			21 years or more			Average	Members of city council		
	Cons. %	Lab. %	Total %	Cons. %	Lab. %	Total %	Cons. %	Lab. %	Total %	Cons. %	Lab. %	Total %	Years	Cons. No.	Lab. No.	Total No.
1926	27	53	41	23	37	31	30		16	20	5	12	8	30	38	68
1936	20	16	18	39	37	38	20	45	34	20	2	10	11	44	56	100
1946	22	40	33	19	14	16	35	29	31	24	17	20	11½	37	63	100
1956	24	14	17	21	30	27	31	37	35	24	20	21	12½	29	71	100
1966	36	26	29	14	19	18	29	32	31	21	22	22	12½	28	72	100
1967	69	29	47	10	24	18	12	24	19	8	24	17	8½	49	59	108
All C.B. 1964 (sample: 439)			27			26			35			11	—			—

Note: To save space 'Cons.' is used as an abbreviation for the opposition to the ruling Labour group. The opposition may consist at various dates of Conservatives, Liberals, National Liberals, Progressives, Citizens, or a combination of these groups.

Sources: Sheffield Telegraph Year Books and M.L.G., II, The Local Government Councillor, Table 1.35.

groups falls within ten to fourteen years; but there is a slight tendency for the opposition councillors to stay even longer than the members of the Labour group. This tendency would not be expected from the socio-economic composition of the two groups. The national survey found a high turnover rate among councillors in professional and business employments, and the opposition in Sheffield contained a high proportion of councillors from these occupations.[11] It may be that the safe seats in Sheffield during these years[12] led to a high degree of self-selection. If a candidate wished to avoid election, then the wards to contest were quite clear; there was not, until 1967, much chance of election 'by accident' in Sheffield with the consequent need for resignation or failure to seek re-election. Following the 1967 Conservative land-slide in Sheffield several of their victorious candidates left the council after only a short period of office.

In 1967–8 ninety-one (84 per cent) of the 108 members of the Sheffield City Council were men; this high proportion was similar to the national average. Twelve out of the seventeen women on the city council were members of the Labour Party,[13] and they have not been content, as might be expected in the industrial north, to accept a back-bench role in the Labour group; several have held important positions and Dame Grace Tebbutt was leader of the party in the city council for four years before her retirement in 1966.

The Sheffield City Council contained an unusually large num-ber of young people at the time of the interviews, but this was due entirely to the influx of young Conservatives. Four of the Conser-vative councillors were under twenty-five years of age; a quarter were under thirty-five; and over half were under forty-five. The Conservative group was, in fact, much younger than the general electorate. In the Labour group, by contrast, only one councillor was under thirty-five years of age, and nearly two-thirds were over fifty-five. The Labour leaders were worried about their failure to retain young people on the council, and—in recent years at least—

---

[11] *M.L.G.*, II, *The Local Government Councillor*, p. 244. It is interesting that the analysis by J. Blondel showed a higher turnover rate among Labour councillors in Newcastle-under-Lyme. Bealey, Blondel, and McCann, op. cit. p. 306.

[12] For details see previous chapter.

[13] The majority of women councillors were found to be members of the Labour Party in a number of other cities recently studied. G. W. Jones, op. cit. pp. 112 and 124; L. J. Sharpe, op. cit., p. 200; and L. J. Sharpe (ed.), *Voting in Cities*, p. 141.

Table 8.2
The Sheffield councillor—1967–8

	Councillors					Electorate: Sheffield
	England and Wales (1964) Total	C.B.	Sheffield Total	Cons.	Lab.	
Base	3,970	439	108	48	59	584
	%	%	%	%	%	%
Sex: Male	88	n.a.	84	90	80	47
Female	12	n.a.	16	10	20	53
Age: Up to 34	4	6	13	25	2	22
35–44	15	20	20	31	12	16
45–54	26	26	21	21	22	22
55–64	31	29	28	10	42	19
65 and over	23	19	16	10	20	20
Question not answered	1	*	2	2	2	*
Education: Lower	44	56	39	10	63	80
Secondary	38	31	44	65	29	13
Higher	15	11	17	25	8	7
Question not answered	3	2	0	0	0	0
Socio-economic status						
1. Large employers/prof.	17	20	34	63	10	7
2. Small employers/farmers	34	15	7	8	7	3
3. Non-manual	22	31	31	21	39	27
4. Skilled manual	13	21	16	6	24	24
5. Semi and unskilled	6	8	11	2	19	25
6. Never employed/Q.N.A.	8	5	1	0	2	14
Net Income: Nil	(10)	(9)	8	4	10	19
Up to £540			5	0	8	30
Over £540–1,000	(39)	(48)	28	10	42	24
Over £1,000–1,300			15	4	22	8
Over £1,300–1,550	(29)	(27)	12	15	10	4
Over £1,550–2,100			9	15	5	3
Over £2,100–2,600	(13)	(10)	2	4	0	*
Over £2,600			21	46	2	1
Question not answered	9	6	1	2	0	11

Notes: The national survey was conducted in November and December 1964; the Survey of Sheffield City Council in January to April 1968; and the Survey of the Sheffield electorate in November 1967.

n.a.: not available.   * Less than 0·5 per cent.

Definitions:

Education: Lower—finished full-time education at secondary modern or elementary school; Secondary—finished full-time education at grammar, technical, or equivalent schools; Higher—full-time education past the secondary level.

Socio-economic status: Large employers and professional workers—Registrar-General's socio-economic groups 1, 3, and 4; Small employers and farmers—S.E.G. 2, 13, 14; Intermediate non-manual workers—S.E.G. 5, 6, 7, 12; Skilled manual workers—S.E.G. 8, 9; Semi- and unskilled workers—10, 11, 15; Never employed/Q.N.A.—S.E.G. 16 and all others.

Net Income: Net income after tax and other deductions. The national categories were not precisely the same as the Sheffield categories, and comparisons must take account of the change in the value of money between 1964 and 1968.

Sources: Survey of Sheffield Electorate; Survey of Sheffield City Council; *M.L.G.*, II, *The Local Government Councillor*, Tables 1.1, 1.2, 1.9, 1.11 and 1.16.

promotion within the Labour group has come quickly for promising young Labour councillors. One or two had to resign subsequently when their employers objected to the amount of time they were spending on council business; three left to become Members of Parliament while still in their early thirties.

The councillors interviewed in Sheffield had a good educational background compared with the sample interviewed for the Maud Committee. The Conservative group, however, provided most of the councillors with higher educational qualifications: nine out of ten Conservatives had remained at school for a secondary education, and a quarter of them had gone on to a university or other college of higher education. Nearly two-thirds of the Labour group, by contrast, had left school at the elementary or secondary modern stage. Even so the proportion of Labour councillors who had left school at an early age was still lower than that found among the Sheffield electorate: 80 per cent of whom completed their schooling at elementary or secondary modern schools.

Nearly three-quarters of the Sheffield city councillors in 1967–8 were employed—or had last been employed—in white-collar occupations (socio-economic status groups one, two, and three). This proportion was similar to the national averages obtained for the Maud Committee. The reliance upon councillors from white-collar occupations was noticeable in both political groups; but while the Conservatives came mainly from business or the professions, the Labour councillors came from junior non-manual occupations. It is surprising to discover that even in an industrial city like Sheffield a minority of the Labour councillors came from manual occupations.[14]

In order to judge whether the occupational character of Sheffield councillors had changed over the past forty years, the descriptions given on the ballot papers have been analysed for selected years. The categories contained in Table 8.3 are not comparable with those contained in Table 8.2, but they allow a fuller description. The proportion of manual workers among Labour councillors has

[14] Blondel noticed that manual workers were at a disadvantage, even in the Labour Party, in seeking election to Newcastle-under-Lyme Borough Council, but he found that over half the Labour councillors were manual workers. Bealey, Blondel, and McCann, op. cit., pp. 304–6. The occupational status of councillors in a number of major cities is discussed in L. J. Sharpe, 'Elected Representatives in Local Government', *British Journal of Sociology*, 13, 3 (1962); L. J. Sharpe (ed.), *Voting in Cities*, pp. 310–16 and *passim*; and G. W. Jones, op. cit., *passim*.

remained fairly steady for the past thirty years, while the proportion of Labour councillors coming from white-collar occupations has increased. A gradual decline in the proportion of Conservative councillors coming from business or commercial occupations has been matched by an increase in the proportion coming from the professions and other white-collar occupations. The Labour group are now much less reliant upon full-time agents and trade union

Table 8.3
Occupations of members of Sheffield City Council—selected years

	Business and commercial			Professional			Other white collar			Manual		
	Cons.	Lab.	Total	Cons.	Lab.	Total	Cons.	Lab.	Total	Cons.	Lab.	Total
Year	%	%	%	%	%	%	%	%	%	%	%	%
1926	48	3	23	4	3	7	0	5	3	0	40	23
1936	55	1	25	31	7	17	0	16	9	0	32	18
1946	56	5	23	22	3	11	8	18	14	0	29	18
1956	41	7	18	28	6	13	14	18	16	0	28	19
1966	39	7	16	43	11	20	11	24	20	0	28	20
1967	40	3	19	36	7	20	10	22	17	4	29	18

	Full-time T.U. or Political Agent			Retired			Married women			Others or not stated*		
	Cons.	Lab.	Total	Cons.	Lab.	Total	Cons.	Lab.	Total	Cons.	Lab.	Total
Year	%	%	%	%	%	%	%	%	%	%	%	%
1926	0	18	10	12	5	7	4	3	3	32	24	25
1936	2	23	14	7	9	9	5	11	8	0	0	0
1946	3	29	19	6	8	7	6	10	8	0	0	0
1956	7	17	14	10	9	9	0	13	9	0	3	2
1966	4	11	9	0	7	5	4	11	9	0	1	1
1967	2	8	6	2	12	7	6	18	13	0	0	0

* In 1926 the occupations of the aldermen were not stated. In that year also one councillor gave his occupation as that of a 'gentleman'.

Notes: To save space 'Cons.' is used as an abbreviation for the opposition to the ruling Labour group. The opposition may consist at various dates of Conservatives, Liberals, National Liberals, Progressives, Citizens, or a combination of these groups.
The actual membership of the council from which these percentages are derived is contained in Table 8.1.

Source: Sheffield Telegraph Year Books.

officers, partly because the trade unions have become less willing to release their full-time officers for council work. Apart from the changes mentioned, the occupational composition of the Sheffield

City Council has been changed very little in the past thirty years.[15]

The net income the councillors enjoy is obviously related to their occupation, and those shown in Table 8.2 to have no income are the married women without paid employment. Half the Labour councillors who had an income received less than £1,000 net per annum, while nearly half the Conservative councillors received over £2,600.

The proportion of Sheffield councillors who are without paid occupations has changed little during recent years. Of these the proportion of retired people on the council has declined slightly and the proportion of married women (or housewives) has increased slightly, but together these groups still account for about one in five of the Sheffield councillors. The proportion of Sheffield councillors who have retired from their employment tends to be rather lower than the average for other councils in England and Wales. The survey conducted for the Maud Committee found that 20 per cent of all councillors had retired from full-time work and even for county boroughs the average was 16 per cent. The proportion of housewives in the Maud sample of county borough councillors was 8 per cent, which is similar to the Sheffield proportion before the 1967 elections.[16]

The profile of the Sheffield City Council sketched in the preceding paragraphs shows that the average level of education among councillors is higher than that found in the population at large; the proportion of retired people is not excessive; and the managerial and professional classes are over-represented, rather than

---

[15] Dr. Jones also comments upon the stability in many of the occupations represented on Wolverhampton Borough Council. The proportion of shopkeepers had remained about the same since 1888, and the proportion of manual workers since 1919. G. W. Jones, op. cit., p. 369. In Birmingham the proportion of businessmen has declined since 1945, but they still constitute one-third of the city council. White-collar workers are taking an increasing share of the council seats. D. S. Morris and K. Newton, 'Profile of a Local Political Elite: Businessmen on Birmingham Council, 1920–66,' University of Birmingham, Faculty of Commerce and Social Science, Discussion Papers, Series F. No. 6 (May 1969).

[16] *M.L.G.*, II, *The Local Government Councillor*, Table 1.6. The proportion of women and retired people on the Sheffield City Council is similar to that found in several other county boroughs that have been investigated in recent years, though the proportion in Torquay is much higher. L. J. Sharpe, 'Elected Representatives in Local Government', *British Journal of Sociology*, 13, 3 (1962); G. W. Jones, op. cit., p. 369; L. J. Sharpe (ed.), *Voting in Cities*, pp. 141 and 225; and D. C. Miller, 'Industry and Community Power Structure: A Comparative Study of an American and an English City', *American Sociological Review*, 23 (1958), p. 14. The electoral performance of women as city council candidates is discussed by Peter Fletcher in *Voting in Cities* at pp. 317–19.

under-represented, when compared with the rest of the electorate. The housewives include university graduates and they can scarcely be said to weaken the composition of the council. Why then do the worries about the calibre of local councillors persist? Perhaps the major reason is that councillors are expected to fulfil a dual function. Through the committee system they control the administration of the local authority, and in addition they are expected to present the grievances of their ward constituents. This dual function implies two different approaches by the councillor to his, or her public duties, and very few councillors combine them successfully. Nor is it necessary that they should do so. We want councillors of sufficient calibre to head the major committees, but we also need other councillors who will share the same background as the people they represent;[16] in Sheffield both groups are present. In all probability the average councillor today differs very little from his predecessors in his capacity for public responsibility; it is the scale of these responsibilities that has increased and caused the public concern about the calibre of councillors; but, as Tocqueville reminded us, democracy does not imply government exclusively by an aristocracy of talent any more than by an aristocracy of wealth or position.

When the Sheffield councillors were asked what had given them most satisfaction during their period of office one Conservative replied: 'There are only eighty-one councillors in Sheffield and I am one of them'; but most councillors gave replies that related either to areas of council policy, or—another Conservative—to 'helping people who don't know how to set about helping themselves'. When asked to state a preference between these two aspects of council work the Sheffield councillors responded in a manner similar to those interviewed in the national survey. The Conservative councillors were more inclined than the Labour councillors to prefer the broad policy aspects of their work, but this is due in part to the different socio-economic composition of the two groups. Councillors in managerial, professional, or white-collar occupations are more likely than manual workers to prefer making policy

---

[16] These two types of councillors cannot be directly associated with occupation; able committee chairmen come from all occupations, and so do ward-based back-benchers. The development of what he described as a 'ministerialist party' and a 'country party' among county councillors in Cheshire is contained in Lee, op. cit., Part III; see also L. J. Sharpe, 'Leadership and Representation in Local Government', *Political Quarterly*, 37, 2 (1966).

Table 8.4
Aspect of council work preferred by councillors

		England and Wales		Sheffield	
		All councils	C.B.	Total	Cons.	Lab.
Base		1,235	134	108	48	59
		%	%	%	%	%
Broad policy decisions		43	46	43	52	36
Problems of particular individuals		34	34	31	29	31
Both/No preference		19	18	25	19	31
D.K./Q.N.A.		4	2	2	0	3

Note: The percentages may not add to one hundred owing to rounding.
Sources: Survey of Sheffield City Council, and *M.L.G.*, II, *The Local Government Councillor*, Table 4.2.

to dealing with the problems of particular individuals, although this distinction is not complete. Women councillors, whatever their background, generally prefer dealing with the problems of individuals to policy making,[17] but the Sheffield results contain some interesting exceptions. *All* the Conservative women councillors in Sheffield in 1967–8 preferred dealing with the problems of particular individuals, but only half the Labour women councillors expressed this preference. The obvious reason is that the Labour group controlled the council at the time of the interviews, and it is easier to develop an interest in policy making if one gets the opportunity to implement decisions. Several Conservative councillors spoke of the frustration of being in permanent opposition; one of them commented: 'when we really cared [about a policy] we had to sell it to the Labour group as their own idea'.

The influence of opportunity in deciding a councillor's attitude to the two broad aspects of council work is clearly seen from the replies given by the Labour councillors in Sheffield. The background of many of these councillors would suggest that they would prefer to deal with the problems of particular individuals, but many of them held important positions in committees concerned with the making of broad policy. The result of this cross-pressure was that nearly a third of the Labour group could not decide between these two aspects of council work.

The occupation of office was also responsible no doubt for the

[17] *M.L.G.*, II, *The Local Government Councillor*, Tables 4.3 and 4.4.

large proportion of Labour councillors who saw their main job to
be the governing of the city rather than the representation of their
ward. Over half of the Labour councillors expressed this opinion
compared with one-third of the Conservatives. Other councillors
sought refuge from a difficult question by replying 'both', and only
a quarter (15 per cent of the Labour councillors and 36 per cent of
the Conservatives) thought their main job was to represent the
ward. In this case, of course, councillors do not include aldermen,
who have no ward to represent.

The Labour councillors in Sheffield served on many more
council committees and sub-committees than their Conservative
counterparts: only 19 per cent of the Labour group served on less

Table 8.5
Committee and sub-committee membership of Sheffield councillors

		Political group		Status on council	
Base	Total 108	Cons. 48	Lab. 59	Ald. 27	Cllr. 81
	%	%	%	%	%
Committees and sub-committees:					
5 and under	31	44	19	22	33
6–10	44	33	54	59	40
Over 10	25	23	27	19	27

Source: Survey of Sheffield City Council.

than five compared with 44 per cent of the Conservative group. It
is necessary, of course, for the ruling group to maintain a majority
on the committees of the council, and this pressure is reinforced by
the socio-economic status composition of the Labour group. The
national survey found that manual workers were, on average,
members of more committees than councillors from other socio-
economic groups.[18] The aldermen on Sheffield City Council were
less likely than the councillors to be members either of only a few,
or of a large number, of committees. The relatively small proportion of aldermen who were members of more than ten committees
becomes more surprising when it is remembered that two-thirds of
them were members of the Labour group. The Sheffield aldermen
differed from the national sample in this respect,[19] but the results

[18] *M.L.G.*, II, *The Local Government Councillor*, Table 3.6.
[19] Ibid., Table 3.5. Forty-four per cent of the aldermen in the national sample
belonged to nine or more committees compared with 19 per cent of the councillors.

are compatible with the suggestion in Chapter 3 that aldermen as such do not play a special role on Sheffield City Council.

The council members were asked how much time they spent on their public activities. They were not asked to keep detailed diaries and consequently the figures shown in Table 8.6 are based upon subjective estimates that may contain considerable errors. Nevertheless it is noticeable that the response from the Sheffield councillors is rather lower than that obtained from other county boroughs in England and Wales.

The Labour councillors in Sheffield spent more time than the Conservatives both on committee work connected with the council and on individual electors' problems. There were two reasons for this distinction between the political parties. First, the Labour councillors were members of the ruling group and they provided all the committee chairmen, who naturally spent more time on committee work than other councillors. Secondly, the Labour group included a high proportion of manual workers, who tend to spend more time on their council duties than councillors from other socio-economic groups. The national survey showed that this difference between councillors from different occupational

Table 8.6
Time spent by council members
(*per average working month*)

	England and Wales		Sheffield		
	Total	C.B.	Total	Cons.	Lab.
Base	3,970	439	108	48	59
	hrs.	hrs.	hrs.	hrs.	hrs.
Council and committee meetings*	29·2	47·0	40·1	33·4	45·6
Electors' problems	7·5	11·3	11·7	10·7	12·7

* Including preparation for meetings, party groups, personal contacts, and travelling time.
Note: Councillors spend other time on public duties in addition to that shown in this table, e.g. on school governing bodies, attending conferences, speaking at local functions.
Sources: Survey of Sheffield City Council and *M.L.G.*, II, *The Local Government Councillor*, Table 3.1.

backgrounds was present in both the aspects of council work shown in Table 8.6. Nevertheless the relationship between socio-economic status and time spent on council work was not as clear-cut in

Sheffield as the national averages would suggest. The Labour councillors from managerial and professional occupations held many of the committee chairs, and the Conservatives were led mainly by councillors from the professions. The councillors in these leading positions within the council and their party naturally spent a lot of time on council work, and the difference in this respect between councillors from different backgrounds was consequently reduced.

The national survey showed that although the total number of hours spent each month on public duties varied considerably, the distribution of this time was very similar for different types of councillors.[20] Those councillors who spent least time on committee work also spent least time on the problems of individual electors, and busy councillors were busy at both aspects of their work. In Sheffield there was no regular relationship between the amount of time spent by a councillor on committee work and the amount spent on the problems of individual electors.[21] It follows, therefore, that a reduction in the amount of committee work expected from a councillor would not necessarily result in more time being spent in pastoral work in the wards—although this was implicit in the Maud Committee recommendations.[22] The amount of time spent with electors is determined more by the councillor's attitude to his role than by the time left over after committee work.

The national survey found that councillors from the higher socio-economic groups spent least time on the individual problems of electors, and this conclusion was fully supported by the response from the Conservative councillors in Sheffield. The Labour councillors, however, could not be so easily distinguished in this manner. The interest shown by Labour councillors from managerial and professional occupations in the problems of individual electors in Sheffield indicated that the degree of importance placed upon the different aspects of a councillor's work was not entirely a consequence of occupational experience. It was also a matter of ideology. The Labour councillors, of all occupational backgrounds, retained a belief that one of their major functions was to represent their individual ward members. The

[20] *M.L.G.*, II, *The Local Government Councillor*, p. 95.
[21] A scatter diagram showed a completely random relationship between the two variables.
[22] *M.L.G.*, I, *Report of the Committee*, p. 44.

Conservative councillors were inclined to approach their council work as executives: controlling, or when in opposition containing, the policy of the local authority. This difference in approach was illustrated by one Conservative councillor who was known by the author to work hard in committee for policies that would benefit the less fortunate among the Sheffield electorate. In the four weeks before the survey she had not discussed council matters with a single member of the public in the ward she represented. This councillor preferred dealing with the problems of particular individuals, but she dealt with these as an executive rather than on a personal basis.

In the present study we are particularly interested in the relationship between the councillors and the electorate. We do not share the view of one committee chairman who told the Maud Committee investigators that: 'the real trouble with local government is that it is far too close to the electorate'.[23] On the contrary we are impressed by the high proportion of councillors who complain that the local electorate are not interested in their work. This attitude was much more prevalent among the Sheffield councillors than among the national sample. In addition nearly a fifth of the Sheffield councillors gave replies that could not be related to the triple categorization adopted for the national survey. The Sheffield councillors drew attention to the distinction many of

Table 8.7
Councillors' view of the attitude of the general public to the work of the council

	England and Wales		Sheffield		
Base	Total 1,235	C.B. 134	Total 108	Cons. 48	Lab. 59
	%	%	%	%	%
Public attitude is:					
Favourable	53	44	15	4	24
Unfavourable	5	3	6	6	5
Not interested	39	47	62	77	51
Other	—	—	18	12	20
D.K./Q.N.A.	3	6	2	2	2

Note: The percentages may not add to one hundred owing to rounding.
Sources: Survey of Sheffield City Council and *M.L.G.*, II, *The Local Government Councillor*, Table 8.1.

[23] *M.L.G.*, V, *Local Government Administration in England and Wales*, p. 40.

the electorate make between 'the council' and individual council members, and to the occasional, but intense, interest aroused when an elector faces a personal problem. The councillors also mentioned the influence of an elector's political opinion upon his attitude towards the council. A Conservative alderman replied: 'it all depends on the end of the city, at the Labour end the present council can do no wrong, and at the other end they can do nothing right'. This opinion, as the rent rebate controversy made clear, was an exaggeration; but there is no doubt that the replies of *the councillors* were affected by their political beliefs. Only two (4 per cent) of the Conservative councillors thought the public attitude was favourable to the city council, while over three-quarters of the Conservatives thought people were not interested. The proportions of the Labour group giving comparable replies were a quarter and a half respectively. The national survey did not consider the political affiliations of the councillors interviewed and this makes it difficult to interpret their results. If a council is composed entirely of supporters of one political viewpoint, for example, then their overall view of the electorate's attitude to the council will be more favourable than if the council membership is divided between the supporters of two or more rival parties. This may explain the relatively favourable impression that rural district councillors receive of their electorate even though they have relatively little contact with them.[24]

Councillors in urban areas are approached by their constituents more frequently than councillors in rural areas,[25] and the response from the Sheffield councillors showed that the electorate in the city make considerable use of their representatives. A third of the Sheffield councillors had been approached by fifty or more of their electors in the four weeks before the interviews. The average number of contacts during this period was forty-five per councillor, which may be compared with an average of thirty-six per councillor in other county boroughs in England and Wales. The Labour councillors were in contact with their electors far more frequently than the Conservative councillors, and this is consistent with the different attitudes the two groups adopt towards the role of the councillor.

The frequency with which a member of the council encounters

---

[24] *M.L.G.*, II, *The Local Government Councillor*, p. 216, and Table 8.1.
[25] Ibid., Tables 8.10 and 8.11.

Table 8.8

Councillors' contacts with electors—four-week period

	England and Wales		Sheffield		
	Total	C.B.	Total*	Cons.	Lab.
Base	1,235	134	107	48	59
	%	%	%	%	%
No contacts	10	5	6	10	2
1–4 contacts	20	11	5	6	3
5–8 contacts	18	12	7	12	3
9–12 contacts	9	10	15	21	10
13–19 contacts	} 40	} 31	10	10	10
20–49 contacts			23	23	24
50 and over contacts		27	34	17	47
Question not answered	3	4	0	0	0
Average number of contacts in 4 weeks	26	36	45	35	53

* Excluding one independent.

Note: The percentages may not add to one hundred owing to
  rounding.

Sources: Survey of Sheffield City Council and *M.L.G.*, II,
  The Local Government Councillor, Table 8.11 and p. 227.

the electors is affected by their attitude as well as by that of the
councillor. The middle-class electors, who form a larger proportion of the electorate in Conservative than in Labour wards, are
more likely than working-class electors to approach an officer of
the council instead of their ward representative.[26] In addition a
number of Conservative councillors had arrived on the council
only a few months before the interviews. The longer-serving
councillors were in far more frequent contact with the electorate
than these 'new boys', which suggests that a councillor becomes
known in his ward *after* his election rather than before.

The most frequently used method of communication between
councillors and members of the electorate was the telephone.
Councillors from both parties received telephone calls from
members of the public fairly frequently, and a quarter of the
councillors had received twenty or more such calls about council
matters in the four weeks before the interviews. Letter writing was
much less popular: over half the councillors received less than one
letter a week from their constituents. One Labour councillor
explained: 'the pattern now is for people to phone and for me to

[26] See Chapter 6.

Table 8.9
Methods of contact between electors and councillors in Sheffield

No. of contacts in four week period:	Elector visited councillor's home			Councillor visited elector's home			Telephone conversation			Councillor received letter from elector			Other ways		
	Total 108	Cons. 48	Lab. 59	Total 108	Cons. 48	Lab. 59	Total 108	Cons. 48	Lab. 59	Total 108	Cons. 48	Lab. 59	Total 108	Cons. 48	Lab. 59
	%	%	%	%	%	%	%	%	%	%	%	%	%	%	%
None	43	65	25	31	35	29	19	27	14	19	25	15	31	35	29
1 or 2	17	17	17	19	27	12	15	19	12	22	31	15	9	19	2
3 or 4	11	8	14	17	21	14	8	10	7	14	12	15	7	12	3
5–9	12	6	17	15	10	19	16	15	17	22	21	24	8	6	10
10–19	11	0	20	11	2	19	15	12	17	12	6	17	19	17	22
20 or over	6	4	7	6	4	8	26	17	34	8	2	14	20	2	31
Don't know	1	0	0	1	0	0	1	0	0	2	2	0	4	2	3

Note: The percentages may not add to one hundred owing to rounding.
Source: Survey of Sheffield City Council.

go round to see them if it is necessary. This is a changing pattern for they used to call personally at my house'. Personal visiting is still an important method of communication for many councillors. Over two-thirds of the members of the Sheffield City Council had visited a constituent within the four weeks before the interviews, and over half had received such a visit. In some cases several visits both by constituents and by councillors were made each week.

The Conservative councillors were far less ready than the Labour councillors to visit or to receive constituents at their homes. In most cases the Conservative councillors had received no visits from members of the public in the four weeks before the interviews, and four out of five had received less than three such visits. Many of the Labour councillors, on the other hand, spoke of their home being always open to visiting constituents. In part this reflects a cultural difference between people from middle-class and working-class backgrounds. The working-class elector, or councillor, accepts personal visits far more easily than his middle-class neighbour. This point may be illustrated by a few of the comments made in the course of the interviews. One Conservative councillor told the interviewer: 'I do not encourage people to call at my home'; and a middle-class member of the Labour group made no visits to the homes of the electors, preferring to send an officer to deal with any complaints. Another Labour councillor, a retired manual worker, took the different view that 'personal contact is the greatest service one can render'; he made seventy or eighty visits per month to the homes of his constituents. Several of the younger Conservative councillors also realized that personal visits were expected in the working-class areas of their wards, and they canvassed throughout the year to maintain contact with their electors.[27]

In Sheffield in 1967–8 a third of the councillors lived in the ward they represented. Most of these councillors were members of the Labour group. Many of the Conservative councillors were newly elected for areas that were not traditionally Conservative in their representation; they lived in the residential suburbs, and sometimes knew little of the areas they had contested. The middle-class Labour councillors were also unlikely to live in the ward they

---

[27] Professor Bealey suggests that the councillors in Newcastle-under-Lyme were diffident about encouraging members of the public to approach them. He explains: '... the expectant voter is often disappointed. Thus the councillor may offend rather than please, losing votes rather than gaining them, by being too zealous in the services of his constituents.' Bealey, Blondel and McCann, op. cit., pp. 379–80.

represented, and the relatively low proportion of Sheffield councillors who have their home in their ward is due almost certainly
to the sharp dichotomy of the city into middle-class and working-
class areas.[28] The proportion of Sheffield councillors who live in
the ward they represent is in fact much lower than the proportions
found among councillors in other areas where comparable studies
have been made. In Newcastle-under-Lyme, at the time of the
Keele University study, 56 per cent of the councillors lived in the
wards they represented, and in Wolverhampton Dr. Jones found
that the proportion was 44 per cent. In an unpublished study of
forty-one local authorities in the Leeds area of the West Riding of
Yorkshire, Dr. Dilys Hill showed that usually at least two-thirds of
the councillors lived in the ward they represented. The proportion
was below this figure in only two of the thirty-five urban district
councils and non-county borough councils that she studied. In the
six county boroughs in her area the appropriate proportions were
at least two-thirds in Dewsbury, Halifax, Huddersfield, and
Wakefield; one-half in Leeds; and one-third in Bradford.[29]

Table 8.10
Attachment of councillors* to ward they represent in Sheffield

	No. of cllrs.	Proportion living in ward represented	Proportion of cllrs.' friends living in ward represented					
			All	Most	Half	Few	None	D.K.
	No.	%	%	%	%	%	%	%
Conservative	39	18	0	12	15	52	19	2
Labour	41	46	3	12	20	44	20	0
All councillors†	81	33	2	13	18	47	19	1
Cllrs. living in ward represented†	27	100	7	40	19	26	7	0

* Aldermen are not allocated to a particular ward so this Table relates to councillors only.
† Including one independent.
Note: The percentages may not add to one hundred owing to rounding.
Source: Survey of Sheffield City Council.

[28] The political effects of this division are shown by the maps in Chapter 7.

[29] Bealey, Blondel, and McCann, op. cit., p. 360; G. W. Jones, op. cit., pp. 95–100.
Dilys M. Hill, 'Democracy in Local Government: A Study in Participation and Communication', unpublished Ph.D. thesis, Leeds, 1966. In Newcastle-under-Lyme the
Labour councillors were more likely than the Conservatives to live in the wards they
represented, but in Wolverhampton the opposite was the case. Dr. Jones suggests that
in Wolverhampton the lack of party organization within the Conservative group led
the wards to select local candidates.

As a low proportion of Sheffield councillors lived in the ward they represented, it was not surprising to discover that very few of the electors knew where their councillors lived. Only 15 per cent of the Sheffield sample of the electorate claimed to have this knowledge, compared with 36 per cent of the national sample. The claims of the respondents in answer to this question were not checked, and both figures are likely 'to be somewhat inflated over the actual level of true awareness'.[30] The Sheffield respondents also told the interviewers that if they wished to contact their local councillor they would first go to the Town Hall rather than to his home.[31]

The simple division of councillors into those who live in the ward they represent and those who do not can exaggerate the importance of residence in determining the attachment a councillor feels for the ward he represents. The councillor who was so meticulous about visiting the homes of his constituents, for example, did not live in the ward he represented so conscientiously. The Sheffield councillors were asked, therefore, to estimate the proportion of their Sheffield friends who lived in the ward they represented. The response to this question is included in Table 8.10. Although the distinction between the parties is still present it is not as stark as the residence factor would suggest. Councillors from both political parties tended to draw their friends from all over the city. Two-thirds of the councillors have only a small proportion, or none, of their friends living in the ward they represent, and it is interesting to note that two of the councillors who have no friends in the ward they represent actually live in the ward.

The analysis of the place of residence of Sheffield councillors, and of the distribution of their friends throughout the city, suggests that councillors do not find their social relaxation among their ward constituents. The majority of the councillors are not community leaders who emerge from the wards they represent; they are people interested in public affairs who seek an opportunity to represent their fellow citizens wherever it may conveniently be

[30] *Community Attitudes Survey: England*, p. 108.

[31] The preference for the Town Hall approach was more pronounced in Sheffield than the national survey results would have suggested. The figures are as follows. Town Hall: Sheffield 39 per cent (large county boroughs 32 per cent); councillor's home: Sheffield 25 per cent (29 per cent). Electors also mentioned a number of other methods of approach. *Community Attitudes Survey: England*, Table 117.

found. The potential councillors make their friendships with people who share their interests, and it is in this way that they are encouraged to seek election to the city council. About half the councillors we interviewed were already friendly with people associated with the council before their own election.

The formal relationship which existed between many of the Sheffield councillors we interviewed and the people they represented was emphasized by their descriptions of the ways in which they got to know about the needs and attitudes of members of the public. In Table 8.11 the proportions of the councillors selecting each of several possible methods are given and they may be compared with the national results. The emphasis on one *main* method is somewhat artificial; most of the councillors use a variety of methods and, as one alderman complained, 'one cannot compare cheese with apple tart'; nevertheless the interviews do not suggest that the replies to this question are misleading. A very low proportion of Sheffield councillors, compared with the national sample, rely upon informal personal contacts for their main

Table 8.11
Main way in which councillors keep in touch with the public

	In local authority area				In ward (Sheffield—Cllrs. only*)		
	England and Wales		Sheffield	Cllrs.			
	All councils	C.B.	Total	only*	Total	Cons.	Lab.
Base	1,235	134	108	81	81	39	41
	%	%	%	%	%	%	%
Informal personal contacts	67	60	30	25	33	28	39
Formal approaches/letters	8	8	17	16	16	19	13
Meeting people through vol. orgs.	6	4	4	2	1	0	2
Political parties	3	5	13	15	12	8	17
Special org. set up for purpose	3	8	3	4	22	31	15
Local press	1	1	19	23	0	0	0
Election campaign/canvassing	2	4	2	1	10	14	7
Reports from council depts.	2	2	4	2	0	0	0
Other ways	3	3	7	9	4	0	6
Not answered	5	5	2	1	0	0	0

* As aldermen are not allocated to a particular ward these columns refer to ward councillors only.
Note: The percentages may not add to one hundred owing to rounding.
Sources: Survey of Sheffield City Council and *M.L.G.*, II, *The Local Government Councillor*, Table 8.9.

source of information about public attitudes and needs. To compensate for this there is a greater reliance upon more formal channels of communication including the political party organization, the local press, and letters or visits received from the general public.

The local press devotes a considerable amount of space to local government matters and nearly all the councillors are regular readers of at least one local newspaper. One in every five of the councillors, in fact, gave the local press as their principal source of information about the general public within the local authority area. There is a morning and an evening newspaper published in the city[32] and a number of weekly newspapers serve the surrounding areas. The relationship between the city council and the local press is relatively good. The Labour councillors occasionally complain that the press favours the Conservatives, but in recent years the leadership of both parties has respected the needs of the municipal correspondents. The chairmen of committees hold press conferences immediately after the committee meetings, and both the morning and the evening newspapers carry informed articles about most of the important issues coming before the council. This is not to say that the local press is sycophantic; the local editors run campaigns which may offend the majority party, and local politicians complain of misrepresentation as frequently in Sheffield as elsewhere; but there is not the mistrust, or downright indifference, that has been commented upon in Wolverhampton and in the local authorities surrounding Leeds.[33] Some councillors resented Mr. Michael Finley's (former editor of the *Morning Telegraph*) policy on comprehensive schools but the whole city had cause to be grateful for the persistence with which his predecessor exposed the misconduct within the local police force in the early 1960s.[34]

The Sheffield councillors (excluding aldermen) were also asked to distinguish their main source of information about the needs and attitudes of their ward electorate. At ward level informal personal contacts became more important, particularly for the Labour councillors, but house-to-house canvassing and ward 'surgeries' at which an elector could meet his councillor also became significant.

[32] Both are under the same ownership, though they are very different in style and occasionally in policy.

[33] G. W. Jones, op. cit., pp. 73–4; Dilys M. Hill, op. cit., Chapter 6.

[34] *Sheffield Police Appeal Inquiry*, H.M.S.O., Cmnd. 2176 (Nov. 1963).

The Conservatives stressed these party activities, presumably because so few of them had the opportunity of meeting their ward electorate as neighbours. Ward 'surgeries' do not appear to be very widespread in other local authority areas in Yorkshire. Dr. Dilys Hill reports that they had been tried in fifteen of the areas she studied, but 'all had died from lack of demand'.[35] Two-thirds of her councillors lived in the ward they represented compared with one-third in Sheffield. It is interesting to remember that the only Sheffield Member of Parliament without a regular surgery at the time we interviewed them was the late Mr. Winterbottom, who lived in his constituency, and who pursued a vigorous and highly personal 'open door' policy.[36]

For the past few pages we have been concerned with the ways in which the councillors keep in touch with the views of their electors, but how close are these views to those of the councillors themselves? The assessment by the councillors of the relative importance of various local authority matters can be compared with the assessments made by the respondents to the survey of the electorate. Both the councillors and the electors were asked to pick out from a list presented to them by the interviewer the most important issue with which the city council had been concerned in the previous year or two. They were then asked to name the second most important and the third most important.[37] The councillors chose the provision of housing and the rent rebate scheme most frequently as the most important issue; usually they followed this by naming one of the educational issues, or housing if they had not placed it first; and their third preference was distributed fairly evenly between several of the issues. The electors agreed with the councillors by choosing the two housing issues most frequently as the most important issues, but in making their second and third choices they often overlooked education and emphasized redevelopment or roads and traffic.

---

[35] Dilys M. Hill, op. cit., p. 284.

[36] See Chapter 4.

[37] The use of a prompt list meant that the respondents were encouraged to choose from within that list even though they were invited to name services not mentioned if they so wished. The list method was used in order to obtain a comparative assessment by councillors and public of certain major local authority services together with the local issues already chosen for detailed study. The major services on the list were taken from the categories found to be most significant by the Maud Committee surveys, but as the response to these surveys was unprompted the results are not strictly comparable with those obtained in Sheffield.

In Table 8.12 the first, second, and third choices have been combined to give the proportions of councillors and electors placing the issue among the three most important, and this enables us to obtain a rough order of prominence. The councillors were in no

Table 8.12
The importance of local issues in Sheffield

(a) *Relative assessment by councillors and electors*

	Proportion placing issue 1st, 2nd, or 3rd in importance						
	Total		Cons. supporters		Lab. supporters		Others
	Cllrs.	Electors	Cllrs.	Electors	Cllrs.	Electors	Electors
Base	108	584	48	198	59	300	86
	%	%	%	%	%	%	%
Issue:							
Provision of housing	62	49	46	55	76	45	52
Comprehensive education	52	25	35	22	66	26	29
Rent rebate scheme	43	37	54	30	34	43	31
Provision of education	35	27	38	29	34	24	31
Redevelopment	32	42	31	38	34	44	49
Roads and Traffic	19	53	31	56	10	53	50
Recreation and social facilities	15	13	2	11	25	14	12
Utility services	11	21	15	26	8	18	21
Closed shop for council employees	11	4	23	4	2	5	5
Local airport	7	16	17	21	0	13	12
Local radio station	1	6	2	6	0	6	3

Sources: Survey of Sheffield City Council and Survey of Sheffield Electorate.

doubt that housing and education were the most important subjects with which they had been concerned. The four issues connected with these two subjects came at the top of the list, though not in the same order, for both Conservative and Labour councillors. The choice for fifth place was redevelopment which is associated with the provision of housing. The councillors emphasized the importance of controversial issues upon which they were *attacking* their political opponents. Thus the Labour councillors gave prominence to comprehensive education while the Conservatives stressed the rent rebate scheme for council tenants and gave some importance to the closed shop for council employees introduced by the Labour administration. Neither the Conservative nor the Labour electors agreed with the importance placed upon these issues by their respective councillors.[38]

The Conservative and Labour supporters among the electorate did not differ very much from each other about the most important local issues of the previous year or two. The four issues most frequently mentioned were roads and traffic; the provision of housing; redevelopment; and the rent rebate scheme. Redevelopment was stressed more by the electors than by the councillors; but the most significant difference between the electors and their representatives concerned roads and traffic. Over half the electors mentioned this issue compared with one in five of the councillors. The Labour councillors in particular appeared to underestimate the relative importance of roads and traffic when their response is measured against the interest shown in these matters by the electorate. The misery of getting to work through congested streets is obviously not confined to the conurbations.

The councillors and the electorate were asked in which area they thought the council had done most to help people or to improve things during the previous year. All groups mentioned the provision of housing most frequently.[39] The Labour councillors mentioned the rent rebate scheme and comprehensive education more often than the Conservative councillors, while the Conservatives preferred to mention the utility services or roads and traffic. The rent rebate scheme and comprehensive education had been introduced by the Labour controlled city council, so naturally the Labour councillors considered that these policies had benefited the city in the previous year.

About three-quarters of the electorate, whichever party they supported, selected housing, redevelopment, or roads and traffic

[38] Dr. Gregory has argued that councillors continually anticipate reactions to their policies that are not forthcoming from the local electorate. Roy Gregory, 'Local Elections and the "Rule of Anticipated Reactions",' *Political Studies*, XVII, pp. 30–47 (March 1969).

[39] Without the aid of a prompt card the national sample of county borough councillors chose town planning, housing, and education most frequently when asked a similar question. The national sample of the county borough electorate chose housing most frequently, but the significant feature of their response was 'that over half the informants either could not say what the council had done, did not know which activity had done most, or thought the council had done nothing to help people or improve things in the last year'. *M.L.G.*, II, *The Local Government Councillor*, Table 3.26; and III, *The Local Government Elector*, Table 146 and p. 107.

Table 8.13
The importance of local issues in Sheffield

(b) *Areas in which council has assisted most in 1967*

	Total		Cons. supporters		Lab. supporters		Others
	Cllrs.	Electors	Cllrs.	Electors	Cllrs.	Electors	Electors
Base	108	584	48	198	59	300	86
Issue:	%	%	%	%	%	%	%
Provision of housing	38	36	38	37	38	35	36
Rent rebate scheme	10	6	5	6	14	7	3
Redevelopment	9	22	9	21	8	22	22
Provision of education	9	3	7	3	8	3	3
Comprehensive education	8	4	4	3	12	5	2
Roads and traffic	8	15	11	18	5	12	14
Utility services	5	4	8	4	2	4	2
Local radio station	2	2	4	2	0	2	1
Recreational and social facilities	1	3	0	1	2	4	1
Closed shop for council employees	0	*	0	0	0	1	0
Local airport	0	0	0	0	0	0	0
Other/D.K./Q.N.A.	11	7	12	8	10	6	13

Proportion selecting each issue

* Less than 0·5 per cent.
Note: The percentages may not add to one hundred owing to rounding.
Sources: Survey of Sheffield City Council and Survey of Sheffield Electorate.

as the areas in which the council had assisted them most during the previous year. Very few mentioned the rent rebate scheme or education although these had provided the big political controversies in Sheffield during 1967. The provision of a local airport was not mentioned by anyone, which was understandable as the council had decided against continuing with its development.

The violent controversy about the rent rebate scheme for council house tenants caused many councillors, and members of the electorate, to regard this as the most important issue for the succeeding year when they were asked to look into the future. There were, however, some differences between the councillors' and the electors' assessment of the relative importance of other issues. The Conservative councillors were far more concerned about the future provision of housing than were their supporters among the electorate. The Labour councillors on the other hand mentioned housing less frequently than their supporters. One prominent

Labour alderman had made a public statement indicating that the housing shortage in Sheffield would be overcome within a few years, and the Labour councillors obviously considered that their existing policies were proving successful. But the most significant difference between the response from the electors and from their elected representatives again concerned roads and traffic. A quarter of the electors interviewed considered that this would be the most important issue in the year ahead, and the proportion rose to nearly one-third of the Conservative supporters.[40] Only a few of the councillors mentioned this issue. One-third of the

Table 8.14
The importance of local issues in Sheffield

(c) *Issue estimated to be most important in coming year*

		Proportion selecting each issue				
	Total		Cons. supporters		Lab. supporters	Others
	Cllrs.	Electors	Cllrs.	Electors	Cllrs. Electors	Electors
Base	108	584	48	198	59 300	86
	%	%	%	%	% %	%
Issue:						
Rent rebate scheme	24	22	26	16	22 26	21
Provision of housing	14	12	20	8	9 13	15
Provision of education	6	4	11	7	3 3	1
Roads and traffic	6	24	8	31	4 22	19
Comprehensive education	6	7	1	8	9 6	10
Redevelopment	4	7	2	8	6 8	3
Utility services	3	2	4	2	3 2	3
Recreational and social facilities	3	4	0	4	5 4	7
Closed shop for council employees	0	1	0	1	0 1	1
Local airport	0	5	0	7	0 4	5
Local radio station	0	1	0	1	0 1	0
Others/D.K./ Q.N.A.	34	8	27	6	39 9	8

Note: The percentages may not add to one hundred owing to rounding.
Sources: Survey of Sheffield City Council and Survey of Sheffield Electorate.

[40] A survey conducted in Glasgow in May 1964, found that a relatively high proportion of the electorate thought the corporation should spend more on the 'city streets'— even if the rates had to be increased. Ian Budge, 'Electors' Attitudes towards Local Government: A Survey of a Glasgow Constituency', *Political Studies*, XIII, 3, p. 390 (1965).

councillors considered that issues other than these mentioned on the card would predominate in the forthcoming year. They suggested the major development scheme at Mosborough, industrial re-organization within the city, and administrative changes within the council itself.

The councillors have difficulty in discovering the issues in which the electorate is interested. It is one of the functions of the public representative to inform, and indeed to educate, the electorate in matters of civic concern, and in fulfilling this function the average Sheffield councillor speaks or writes to about a dozen electors each week, but the initiative comes mainly from the latter. The councillors see his constituents when a 'crisis'—the need for a house, an overflow in the bathroom, dustbins unemptied—impels them to approach a public representative. He gets, therefore, a distorted view of the priorities given to various issues by members of the public. A few councillors spend time throughout the year knocking on the doors of people who would otherwise remain unknown to them, but the majority do not find it necessary or convenient to spend their severely limited time in extensive nursing of their wards. Indeed the Sheffield councillor usually regards himself, or herself, as a representative of the city rather than of a particular ward, and this view is encouraged by the centralized lists of candidates maintained by the political parties. (These are described in Chapter 3.) The councillor who emerged as a community leader in the ward he, or she, subsequently represented is comparatively rare on Sheffield City Council. Once again it is clear that local community feeling is not related to the present representative institutions.

Many of the Sheffield councillors, in fact, seemed estranged from the people they were representing; they spoke almost bitterly of the lack of interest shown in council activities; and six out of ten councillors thought the public did not know enough to vote in an informed way in local elections. The degree of knowledge possessed by the electors about local affairs has already been discussed in Chapter 6, but we may add that the lack of confidence which the councillors expressed in the general public was not entirely justified by the attitude of the electorate in response to our survey. In most cases the electors agreed with the councillors about the relative importance to be attached to each issue, and where they differed the comparison was not unfavourable to the electors. It was the councillors, for example, rather than the electors, who placed the greater stress upon the dramatic, but short-term, controversies over comprehensive education and the rent rebate scheme. The electors were more concerned about the long-term issues of redevelopment, the conception of a local airport, and traffic management. Indeed roads and traffic could become the central local issue over the next few years and councillors should be aware of the importance the electorate place upon this problem.

In the passage at the head of this chapter, Tocqueville maintained that public representatives should not have interests that differed from those of the community at large. This ideal is difficult—Michels believed impossible—to attain, and at times it appears to be inconsistent with the need for leadership in public affairs. There is a need for councillors from a variety of social backgrounds, and with alternative views of their function on the council; but leadership in society, in the future as in the past, will continue to be provided by those who exercise it in their daily affairs whether as managers, skilled craftsmen, or in a professional capacity. The councillors in Sheffield for the municipal year 1967–8 were of a higher socio-economic status, and better qualified educationally, than the people they represented, and so were the sample interviewed in the national survey. The public concern about the calibre of local councillors can only be justified, therefore, by referring to *individuals* rather than to *categories* of councillors. It is not true that there are too few businessmen, or too many housewives, on our local councils; but the councils *are* failing to attract or to retain specific individuals who would become valuable public representatives. These individuals may be young ambitious professional men, or active trade unionists; they will have in common an interest in local authority work that is frustrated by their failure to reconcile the amount of time required for council service and their regular occupation. This is why the Committee on the Management of Local Government recommended that employers should 'accept that the release of their staff for work as members of local authorities is in the public interest',[41] but they also recognized that release would not always be possible. If this recommendation were to become more than a pious hope then it could do more than any other single change to improve the calibre of council members. The 'local councils' proposed by the Royal

[41] *M.L.G.*, I, *Report of the Committee*, p. 148.

Commission on Local Government could also provide an opportunity for those with a limited amount of time available for public service.[42] But the problem of providing an adequate correspondence between the views of the electors and the decisions of their representatives will remain. Periodic elections are too blunt an instrument to register opinions on individual topics, and the councillors should not assume too readily that they embody the commonweal. In recent years the increasing responsibilities undertaken by local authorities have suggested additional institutional opportunities for the general public to participate in local administration. In the final chapter we shall consider some of these and give examples from recent experience in Sheffield.

[42] See Ch. 11.

9

Pressure Group Politics in Sheffield

*Thus if the general will is to be clearly expressed, it is imperative that there
should be no sectional associations in the state. . . . But if there are sectional
associations, it is wise to multiply their number and to prevent inequality among
them. . . .*　　　　　　　　　　　　　　　　　　　　　　J.-J. ROUSSEAU

THE classical liberal theory of representative democracy affirms
that the Member of Parliament or local councillor is the com-
municating link between the governed and the governors. The
elected representative is expected not only to present the complaints of his constituents, and to remedy the injustices that they
suffer, but also to embrace their opinions. Such a simple view had
little relevance to mass democracy. The public representative who
has thousands of constituents cannot know, let alone agree with,
the views of all of them. Their views are organized by the political
parties, or by the profusion of groups dedicated to a particular
cause or interest; and these bodies have come between the elector
and the elected representative, presenting the views of the organized few as the voice of the inarticulate majority.

The organization of group opinion in this manner is not to be
condemned in a Rousseauian purity of definition. The ordinary citizen, while concerned with the affairs of his immediate environment,
cannot easily comprehend the wider political issues, nor formulate
his views for presentation to those in positions of authority. There
is a need for parties and pressure groups, and we should not be
perturbed at their number. We may be concerned, as Rousseau
suggested, at the difference in the relative strength of various
groups and we may doubt whether they do in fact represent what
they purport to. Or we may worry about the lack of organization
among some people affected very strongly by the decisions of the
government; but that is a different matter.

Political parties are more complex than the other organizations representing public opinion. A party has as its objective the achievement of general political office, and for this reason it must provide a policy that covers all the principal areas of public responsibility. The policies in each of these areas should be consistent one with the other, but inevitably compromises are necessary to achieve cohesion within a group large enough to challenge for power. Some pressure groups are related closely to particular parties: the trade unions, for example, are an integral part of the Labour Party, and industrial and commercial groups have an affinity with the Conservative Party; but the majority of pressure groups try to influence both parties—and follow a strategy, in the American phrase, of supporting their friends.

The Trades Union Congress, the British Medical Association, the Confederation of British Industry, the National Farmers' Union, and other major interest groups, frequently by-pass Parliament completely, and represent their members directly at the appropriate level of the administration—even the highest. Ministers and senior civil servants commonly consult appropriate interest groups about the general content of impending legislation or subordinate legislation—though not about the precise wording of the Bill, finding it politically useful to try to gauge their reaction to legislation and administratively useful to gather opinions about its feasibility.[1] But although the activities of the major interest groups have been accepted in Whitehall, they are much less developed at the level of local government. Indeed in the smaller authorities pressure group activity is practically non-existent; even in the larger authorities the pressure groups will be concerned almost exclusively with council members. The 'local officials are not in the position of civil servants, meeting professional members of organized pressure groups in a structured, face-to-face situation'.[2]

In one sense, of course, the local councillors represent the local interest groups; they will be members of trade unions, church organizations, chambers of commerce, and other groups, to a much larger extent than the electorate.[3] They will express the

[1] A convenient appraisal of the available material on this topic is contained in S. A. Walkland, *The Legislative Process in Great Britain*.

[2] Dilys M. Hill, 'Democracy in Local Government: A Study in Participation and Communication', unpublished Ph.D. thesis, Leeds 1966, p. 104.

[3] The group memberships of the electors are discussed in Chapter 6 and those of the councillors in Chapter 8. The attitude of the council members in Sheffield to pressure group activity is detailed in Chapter 3.

views of the local shopkeepers if parking restrictions threaten free access to the High Street shops, and the views of owner-occupiers if the rates increase too rapidly. There are some controls on this process: teachers, for example, may not serve on their employing authority, and council tenants who are members of the local authority may not vote on housing matters; but, in general, influence in English local government has been exercised directly by the council member.[4] This approach has gradually been supplanted, especially in the larger towns, by more formal pressure group activity, but this fact has found little recognition in textbooks on British government.[5]

In Sheffield we discovered that most of the councillors received communications from organizations outside the council, and the majority accepted that these communications helped them to form their opinions on particular topics. Some two hundred different combinations of groups and issues were mentioned to our interviewers by the council members.

Only a few of the groups that hopefully send their information sheets and protest letters to members of the city council achieve a sustained influence on policy making. The most important of these are the industrial and commercial organizations. The trade union movement through the Trades and Labour Council[6] is closely associated with the local Labour Party, and hence with the Labour group on the city council. The Sheffield Chamber of Commerce and the Chamber of Trade are regularly consulted by the Conservative group on the Sheffield City Council. Dr. Dilys Hill has reported that a similar situation exists in two other large Yorkshire county boroughs—Bradford and Leeds—where the Chamber of Commerce has achieved the 'right to be consulted' on matters such as parking restrictions and the development of a local airport.[7]

[4] Dr. Jones has given a good picture of this process at work in Wolverhampton. G. W. Jones, *Borough Politics*, Chs. 14 and 15.

[5] See, for example, the view of Professor Birch that 'this aspect of local democracy does not appear to flourish in England'. This judgement is based upon research conducted in the small town of Glossop in the early 1950s, and it is misleading as a guide to English local politics in the 1970s. A. H. Birch, *The British System of Government*, p. 241.

[6] The Trades and Labour Council receives delegates both from trade union branches and from Labour Party organizations. In many other areas two separate organizations exist side by side: a trades council and a borough or city Labour party. The relationship of the two branches of the Labour movement in Sheffield is discussed below and in Chapter 3.

[7] Dilys M. Hill, op. cit., pp. 298–9. The position in Newcastle-under-Lyme is referred to in Bealey, Blondel, and McCann, *Constituency Politics*, pp. 380–1.

The other group of influential organizations is the education lobby. Approximately half of all local government expenditure is devoted to education and a major authority will employ thousands of professionally qualified teachers. In Sheffield the teachers are organized through the usual trade union and professional associations. They are represented on the education committee of the city council by a co-opted member,[8] but this does not exhaust their influence. There is a consultative committee upon which representatives from all the teachers' organizations meet with the chairman, deputy chairman, and senior opposition spokesman from the education committee, together with the Chief Education Officer and members of his staff. This committee meets periodically and discusses many aspects of educational policy before the education committee or the party groups consider them formally. There are also active parents' associations. These include a local branch of the Confederation for the Advancement of State Education, the Sheffield Parents' Association, and the Association for Better Consultation. The educational groups circulate regular and lengthy memoranda to members of the Education Committee, and occasionally to all councillors; their leaders lobby educationalists on the city council both formally and on social occasions.

The economic and educational groups have a continuous existence, but there are other associations that emerge very rapidly in opposition to a specific council policy. When the controversy is concluded they disappear. The best examples of these volatile groups are the tenants' associations formed to oppose council house rent increases, and residents' associations formed to contest a development plan for their area. Associations formed for these purposes can attract hundreds of members in a matter of weeks, and have a considerable impact on local politics, before lapsing into insignificance. Such associations seldom continue as a long-term influence on matters affecting the local residents: they are essentially defensive organizations. In part this is due to the difficulties they encounter in penetrating the decision-making process in the manner of the industrial, commercial, and educational groups. The councillors are unwilling to surrender their representative role to the officers of a local tenants' association, being, with the best will in the world, professionally jealous and

[8] In 1969 the council decided to include two teachers' representatives on the Education Committee. At the time of writing this was awaiting the Minister's approval.

suspicious of spontaneous leadership, while community associations sponsored by the council often lack the independence necessary for success. It must also be accepted, as one Sheffield councillor commented rather sadly, that 'disasters seem to call forth more response than rejoicings!'[9]

In Sheffield there have been several controversies about city policy in the past few years that enable illustrations to be given of local pressure group activity. The development of a local airport was supported very strongly by local industrial and commercial interests; the closed shop for council employees was first advocated by the Trades and Labour Council; and the introduction of comprehensive education provoked disagreement among the educational specialists even though the general public appeared at first unmoved. The discussion around these three issues will be outlined in the following pages, and we shall then consider, in the following chapter, the council tenants' reaction to the introduction of a rent rebate scheme.

THE LOCAL AIRPORT

In 1920 Sheffield City Council obtained powers by Act of Parliament[10] to acquire a local airfield for development into a municipal airport. In May 1969, the Labour group on the city council, resuming control after a break of one year, reversed a Conservative decision to reserve land for this purpose at Todwick. In the intervening period of nearly half a century the controversy was seldom dormant for very long; every few years fresh proposals were made for a local airport, and on every occasion the city council, after considering the matter for some time, decided against any immediate action.

In the 1960s the fear was constantly expressed that Sheffield would suffer economically if businessmen were unable to land their company aircraft within easy reach of the city. In the nineteenth century Sheffield had been by-passed by the major railway networks, and the city was warned not to allow itself to 'become an aerial backwater'[11] in the twentieth century. The analogy drawn with the failure to develop the railways was not misplaced. In

---

[9] *Morning Telegraph*, 20 June 1969. (The *Sheffield Telegraph* became the *Morning Telegraph* on 15 September 1965.)

[10] Sheffield Corporation Act 1920. 10 and 11 Geo. V, c. xcii.

[11] The phrase was used by Sir Miles Thomas, then chairman of B.O.A.C., speaking in Sheffield in 1954.

both cases the hills upon which Sheffield is built made the development of communications difficult, and the flatter parts of the region attracted the first railway lines and airports. In 1961 the Lord Mayor claimed that 'the council have looked all over Sheffield and surrounds for a suitable site, but there is not even a place to fly model planes'.[12] By the 1960s, however, there were three airports within a fifty-mile radius of Sheffield: Ringway, near Manchester; Yeadon, near Leeds; and Castle Donington, in the East Midlands. The consultants engaged at various times found it difficult to estimate the commercial viability of a further airport closer to the city. Their reports were cautious, and they recommended at most the development of a small airport for business use at Todwick.[13] If a further regional or international airport was needed in Yorkshire then the consultants, and other planners, preferred the Thorne Waste site which is east of Doncaster.

In these circumstances, where no clear policy emerged from years of discussion, there were three possible lines of approach, and all three were represented among the councillors from both political parties. There were those who favoured the construction of a municipal airport at a site, usually Todwick, near Sheffield. They believed this to be necessary for the industrial and commercial prosperity of the city, and expected an increasing amount of freight, as well as business executives, to travel by air in the future. These views were expressed by the Chamber of Commerce; the local Conservative Member of Parliament; the majority of the Conservative group on the city council; the local newspapers, particularly the *Morning Telegraph*; the Sheffield Aero Club;[14] Mr. Richard Winterbottom, then Labour Member of Parliament for Brightside; and a minority of the Labour group on the city council. This minority included Alderman Ironmonger who publicly supported the plans for an airport until the Labour group's decision to abandon the scheme. Before he became Leader in May 1966, he was chairman of the Air Facilities Sub-Committee of Sheffield City Council.

[12] *Sheffield Telegraph*, 20 January 1961.

[13] The two most important reports to appear during the 1960s were 'A Regional Airport for Yorkshire and the North East', Yorkshire Airport Development Association, 1964; and 'The Commercial Prospects for an Airport for the City of Sheffield', Alan Stratford and Associates, 1967. Todwick is eight miles to the east of Sheffield.

[14] The Sheffield Flying Club, a predecessor of the Aero Club, joined with other groups in 1929 to urge the city council to buy a site for an airport at Coal Aston. The site, 286 acres, was bought for £40,500, but subsequently used for housing purposes.

The opponents of the airport stressed the commercial difficulties that the project would face. They saw it as a facility that would benefit only a few business executives, and saw no reason why it should be provided at the ratepayers' expense. These arguments were mainly used by the Labour members of the city council, led by Alderman Dyson, but one Conservative councillor told our interviewer: 'Undoubtedly it would have lost the city money, and arguments that businessmen would benefit the city by getting to appointments in Europe in half-an-hour less time than by Castle Donington did not impress me.' The Sheffield Airport Objectors Committee was opposed to the airport on amenity grounds, as were many of the rural district and parish councils in the vicinity. Sir Roger Stevens, chairman of the Yorkshire and Humberside Economic Planning Council, joined with the other chairmen of Economic Planning Councils in the north of England in preferring further development at Ringway before another airport was built in Yorkshire. If another airport became necessary then Sir Roger and the West Riding County Council accepted the preference of the consultants for the Thorne Waste site. The extensions to the motorway network that reached Sheffield during the late 1960s reinforced the arguments of those who were opposed to a municipal airport. Castle Donington and Yeadon were both within an hour's drive, and the trans-Pennine motorway on completion would provide similarly fast access to Ringway. It was soon pointed out that it took an hour to travel from central London to London airport.

There was a third group who were of the opinion that Sheffield should abandon any pretensions to a conventional airport, and concentrate upon providing facilities for helicopters, and—thinking ahead to the 1970s—V.T.O.L.[15] aircraft. Sometimes these opinions were advanced by those who despaired of a decision on the wider issue, but a few people were convinced that they represented the best solution to Sheffield's need for air communications. One Labour councillor told our interviewer early in 1968 that 'the proposed idea for a local airport is an obsolete idea. One must think to the future, and here one should be thinking of putting airports on the coast, so that planes will make a noise only over the sea. Feeder systems should be built to these airports from the centre of the city.'

[15] Vertical take-off and landing.

The developments which this councillor foresaw were still in the future. The city council built a small heliport in the early 1960s, but it was little used. In one year it was reported that only twelve helicopters had landed in the twelve-month period. But by March 1969, it was announced that the Ministry of Technology were hoping that 100-seater jump-jets would be providing fast inter-city travel by the middle of the 1970s. Professor T. E. H. Williams of Southampton University was studying possible sites in eight cities including Sheffield. The supporters of a local airport were enthusiastic in their welcome of this new sign of interest in Sheffield's transport problems. As the *Morning Telegraph* remarked drily: 'The city is not used to being considered as a place of any importance; it is even less used to any sympathetic consideration of its communications.'[16] Mr. John Osborn, Conservative Member of Parliament for Hallam, pressed the Minister of Technology for more information;[17] and the Conservative Leader on the city council, Alderman Hebblethwaite, explained the advantages of combining a small executive landing strip with a V.T.O.L. pad at Todwick. When Labour finally squashed that idea within twelve hours of regaining office in May 1969, Alderman Ironmonger softened the blow by remarking that while Todwick 'would always be an executive airstrip and a perpetual burden on the backs of the ratepayers, there may be greater scope for V.T.O.L. aircraft. At least it is worth investigating.'[18] The fifty-year-old controversy had taken yet another twist.

The Sheffield Chamber of Commerce has consistently pressed the city council to build an airport. The reason for its interest was succinctly expressed by its secretary in 1964 when he said: 'Fixed-wing aircraft landing near Sheffield would be a boon to the city, its businessmen, and its industries.'[19] To support this claim the Chamber of Commerce circulated a questionnaire to nearly 900 members to provide evidence of the potential demand for an

[16] *Morning Telegraph*, editorial, 24 March 1969.
[17] Mr. Osborn wished to know whether the report from Southampton University covered the possibility of S.T.O.L. (short take-off and landing) as well as V.T.O.L. The answer was no. Mr. Osborn was concerned at the possible noise nuisance of V.T.O.L., and he instigated a seminar on Inter-city Transport, under the auspices of the Parliamentary and Scientific Committee, which considered tracked hovercraft and advanced passenger trains as well as V.T.O.L. and S.T.O.L. H.C. [781] 1131 (16.4.69) and private correspondence with the author.
[18] *Morning Telegraph*, 29 May 1969.
[19] *Sheffield Telegraph*, 14 January 1964.

executive airstrip. The president claimed that they had successfully brought forward by five years the construction of the
Sheffield–Leeds spur of the M1 motorway, and they hoped for
similar success with their plea for another and equally important
means of transport—the aeroplane.[20] The results of the survey,
together with supporting evidence were forwarded to the Town
Clerk. Of the 894 members of the Chamber, 235 completed the
questionnaire. Seventeen companies operated their own light aircraft and would use local facilities if provided. In addition, a
further 84 companies made extensive use of air travel. The Chamber estimated that approximately 2,400 movements annually were
initiated by these Sheffield companies, and that this level of
traffic would justify the provision of a local airstrip.[21]

The results of the Chamber of Commerce survey became available at the same time as the report from the Yorkshire Airport
Development Association which had been supported by subscriptions from Sheffield industry. The report did not support the
development of a regional airport at Sheffield which would 'simply
be duplicating the service at Ringway, Manchester'. The head of the
study team also considered that 'the travelling people of Sheffield
[were] quite satisfied with the present air service. . . . We consider a town within 45–60 minutes drive from an airport to be
adequately provided for'.[22] The Sheffield supporters of a local
airport were very disappointed with this report. Indeed one
industrialist whose firm had subscribed to the Yorkshire Airport
Development Association announced: 'After reading this report
I intend to write and ask for our money back'.[23]

The pressure from the Sheffield supporters of a local airport had
some success in influencing the final report from the Yorkshire
Airport Development Association. At a meeting of the Association
in May 1964, the original report was adopted, but it was also
agreed, on the proposition of the secretary of the Sheffield Chamber of Commerce, to include Sheffield among the places qualifying
for an executive airstrip.[24] The airport supporters enjoyed a few
months of near unanimous agreement within the city. Both party

[20] *The Star* (Sheffield), 25 March 1964.
[21] 'Report to the Town Clerk of Sheffield in support of a request for airstrip facilities
for the city of Sheffield,' The Sheffield Chamber of Commerce, 1964.
[22] *Sheffield Telegraph*, 18 March 1964.
[23] Ibid.
[24] *The Star* (Sheffield), 14 May 1964.

groups on the city council supported the development of local facilities for fixed-wing aircraft, and a newly formed company announced its intention to operate regular passenger services from the city.[25]

During 1965 and 1966 the opposition gradually reappeared. It was realized that the working of coal seams lying under Todwick would cause subsidence along the line of the main runway. The city council would have to compensate the National Coal Board if this coal was to be left unused.[26] The extensions to the MI brought the motorway closer to Sheffield—reducing the time needed to travel from Sheffield to the airport at Castle Donington —and the city council delayed a decision while they commissioned a series of consultants' reports on the airport proposals. In 1965 the Master Cutler, who was also chairman of Westland Aircraft Ltd., attacked the 'monstrous incompetence'[27] of the city council in not providing an airstrip for the city. Alderman Ironmonger made a confident reply, but it soon became clear that support for the airport was on the wane, for in November 1965, the Managing Director of British Midland Airways stated that Sheffield Corporation would have a very hard job in front of them to make an airport pay its way. He suggested that 'patience and pepper-corn rents would be needed to give the proposed airport a chance of success'.[28] Other local authorities in the area remained lukewarm or even hostile to the airport scheme, and the residents of Todwick formed an Action Committee to oppose the use of a site in their village.

By the end of 1966, when Alan Stratford and Associates presented their interim report, the supporters of the airport were on the defensive. Alderman Ironmonger admitted that he had been embarrassed when the report was published, and agreed that 'it is not entirely favourable, particularly if you are anti-airport before you read it'.[29] Alderman Dyson considered that no local authority could commit itself to the development of an airport on the basis of the interim report, and he expressed himself strongly to this effect in the council chamber.[30] In April 1967, the Policy Committee of

[25] *The Star* (Sheffield), 26 November 1964.
[26] 'Report on Proposed Development of Sheffield (Todwick) Airport', Sir Frederick Snow and Partners, 1967, p. 3.
[27] *The Star* (Sheffield), 27 October 1965.
[28] *Morning Telegraph*, 11 November 1965.
[29] *Morning Telegraph*, 8 September 1966.
[30] Ibid.

the city council recommended that the Todwick plan be dropped. The Chamber of Commerce and the Conservative group on the city council still proposed that the land be bought in case it should be needed in the future, but although the Conservatives adopted this policy during their year of office in 1968, the Labour group rejected it when they returned to power in 1969.

Within a few months of the 1967 decision to drop the Todwick plan we interviewed every member of the Sheffield City Council and a random sample of the electorate. We asked for their views on the decision and the evenly balanced argument that we have already described is reflected in the response we obtained. There was not a clear majority for or against the decision either among the councillors or among the electors. The balance was held by the one in eight who sat on the fence, neither agreeing nor disagreeing with the decision. In both political parties about a quarter of the councillors disagreed with their official party line on this issue, and among the electors opinions were even more divided. The Labour supporters among the electorate, in fact, were more inclined to disagree with their party's decision than to agree with it, although there was not a majority for either point of view. Plainly there was sufficient public opinion to support, or not to obstruct, firm leadership in either direction.

The Sheffield Chamber of Commerce conducted its campaign for a municipal airport both through its members and friends in the Conservative group on the city council, and by statements in

Table 9.1
Attitudes towards Sheffield City Council's decision not to support a local airport

	Total		Cons. supporters		Lab. supporters	
	Cllrs.	Electors	Cllrs.	Electors	Cllrs.	Electors
Base	108	584	48	198	59	300
	%	%	%	%	%	%
Very strongly agree	31	20	10	18	49	21
Quite strongly agree	14	14	17	14	10	15
Neither agree nor disagree	12	13	8	12	15	13
Quite strongly disagree	16	14	21	10	12	15
Very strongly disagree	27	36	44	44	14	32
Don't know	0	3	0	3	0	3

Note: The percentages may not add to one hundred owing to rounding.
Sources: Survey of Sheffield Electorate and Survey of Sheffield City Council.

its own name. It could not rely exclusively upon its influence in the Conservative group because the Labour party controlled the city council for most of the time. In its campaign the Chamber of Commerce was greatly aided by the *Morning Telegraph* which constantly equated a local airport with the future prosperity of the city. For a short while, in the first optimistic years of the Labour majority at Westminster, the Labour group on Sheffield City Council was also persuaded that the airport would be a symbol of a modern city.

The advocates of a local airport finally failed in their objective because the business and commercial support which the Chamber of Commerce claimed to represent did not appear. In their answers to the 1964 questionnaire some members of the Chamber of Commerce were willing to declare that their companies would benefit by the use of airstrip facilities in Sheffield;[31] but they were relying on a subsidy from the ratepayers to finance the almost certain commercial losses. As early as 1962 Councillor Roy Hattersley (later a minister in the Labour government) made it clear that the city council was willing to make land available if a group of people came forward with proposals to develop and maintain an airstrip that would impose no burden on the rates.[32] No such group was forthcoming. The small airline companies that were formed to operate regular services from Todwick were hesitant about the commercial success of the venture. One company withdrew their application for a licence after five weeks on the grounds that Sheffield was already well provided with fast trains to London. The local evening paper commented: 'it is as well that the company discovered this rather obvious fact before committing itself. . . .'[33] The various consultants engaged by the city council, or by other planning bodies, could never discover the potential demand that the Chamber of Commerce foresaw. The crucial report by Alan Stratford and Associates concluded: 'Making the most favourable estimates of airline potential . . . it appears unlikely that the scale of business would compensate the city or the operators adequately for their investment'.[34] Inevitably, and with some reluctance, the Labour group on the city council came to

[31] Sheffield Chamber of Commerce, op. cit.
[32] *Sheffield Telegraph*, 7 June 1962.
[33] *The Star* (Sheffield), 16 December 1966.
[34] Alan Stratford and Associates, op. cit., p. 50.

believe that the views of the Chamber of Commerce were not supported by the commercial judgement of its members: and the decision was taken.

THE CLOSED SHOP FOR COUNCIL EMPLOYEES

In April 1964, the Sheffield Trades and Labour Council resolved to seek an interview with the Labour group on the city council. They wished to press the claim for making membership of a trade union a condition of employment in the corporations' departments. The request for the imposition of a 'closed shop'[35] had originally been made in 1962, but its implementation had been delayed while discussions took place on the exact form it should take. The Trades and Labour Council had asked for a closed shop among manual workers only as they felt unable to speak for the staff associations and the teachers. Within the Labour group, however, there were some councillors who felt that the 8,000 non-manual employees of the corporation should not be excluded from the policy; and there were others who were not in favour of making union membership a condition of employment for any group of workers.

The Trades and Labour Council argued that all the employees of the council benefited from the negotiations conducted by the trade unions on their behalf, and that they should all contribute towards the cost of providing the negotiators. Mr. Vernon Thornes, the secretary of the Trades and Labour Council, said in response to a newspaper interview, that the law provided that taxes for central and local government services had to be paid, and the view of his council was that, equally, costs of union services should be paid for by everyone.[36] The trade unions contended that in the balance of power between employer and employee, the

[35] In 1946 a Trades Union Congress resolution made a distinction between a 'union shop', where each worker chose the trade union he wished to join, and a 'closed shop', where a worker was restricted to joining one particular union. The first of these the T.U.C. considered desirable but they did not endorse the second. The Sheffield Trades and Labour Council always claimed that they wished to enforce a 'union shop' where the employee joined 'the appropriate trade union'—the appropriate union being the one which had been a signatory to the agreements covering the work of the employee. The Trades and Labour Council definition in effect did not give much choice to most of the council's employees. The term 'closed shop' was used throughout this controversy and it will be used here.

[36] *The Star* (Sheffield), 26 August 1966. The Trades and Labour Council's policy is explained in their official journal, *Sheffield Forward*, December 1964, and September 1966.

balance remained heavily weighted in favour of the employer. It was not right, therefore, to argue that the closed shop was an attack on the freedom of the individual. Liberty was always subject to restrictions for social ends, and the trade unions had a social right to protect themselves.

The opponents of the closed shop included the Conservative group on the city council; Mr. Osborn, Member of Parliament for Hallam; the local newspapers; the teachers' and other white-collar trade unions; and a minority in the Labour group. They all maintained that they were in favour of council employees belonging to trade unions, but they abhorred compulsion; the trade unions should do their own recruiting.

Despite continual pressure from the Trades and Labour Council progress was slow; but on 12 January 1965, the Labour group on the city council decided to adopt a closed shop policy for corporation departments.[37] At this point it appeared that the policy was only to be applied to the 14,300 manual workers, but a month later the Labour group made it clear that trade union membership would be a condition of employment for all council employees. This all-or-nothing ruling placed the Trades and Labour Council in a difficult position. The trade unions could not really quarrel with the principle of applying the closed shop policy to all employees, but they must have realized that the opposition to such a policy would endanger their own more limited objective.

The opposition was soon apparent. The chairman of the local branch of the National and Local Government Officers (N.A.L.G.O.) said that although N.A.L.G.O. wanted people to join trade unions, they were not in favour of a closed shop. However, as the corporation had not yet made a decision the branch had not decided to take any action. The secretary of the Sheffield branch of the National Union of Teachers (N.U.T.) stated that his members would be prepared to resign rather than submit to such a measure. 'If they persist,' he added, 'we shall fight them

[37] In 1959 the Wolverhampton Trades Council made a similar application to the borough council, but they were unsuccessful. The Wolverhampton Labour group, who were in control at that time, took the advice of the Labour Party head office that it was illegal to enforce trade union membership as a condition of employment. This advice probably owed as much to political caution as to legal opinion. G. W. Jones, op. cit., p. 309.

tooth and nail.'[38] The N.U.T. was supported by the Sheffield branch of the National Association of Schoolmasters (N.A.S.), whose secretary recalled that successful joint action by teachers had defeated a similar proposal at Durham in 1950.[39]

The discussions between the Labour group and the trade unions continued into the summer of 1965 until the corporation bus drivers, accusing the teachers of deliberately dragging out the negotiations, persuaded the Trades and Labour Council to support a strike unless the closed shop was introduced in all council departments. Upon a plea from their president, Councillor William Owen, the strike action was subsequently delayed for one month to allow the teachers to give their reply.

In July 1965, therefore, the city council were faced with the possibility of a strike by the manual workers, particularly in the transport department, if they did not introduce a closed shop; and the certainty of mass resignations from their clerical and teaching staffs if they made union membership a condition of employment. The Labour group proposed a compromise: they agreed in principle to the closed shop, but it would only become operative for any group of employees upon application from the appropriate trade union. This meant that the Transport and General Workers' Union would be able to implement a closed shop in the transport department, while N.A.L.G.O. and the teachers' unions could retain the *status quo*. There would also be a 'conscience clause' to excuse any employee who objected to joining a trade union on religious grounds. A trade union deciding to implement the closed shop would be responsible for getting people to join, and for operating the conscience clause. In the last resort appeals would go to the Establishments Committee of the city council.

The city council accepted the closed shop policy on 4 August 1965. In opposing it on behalf of the Conservative group, Alderman Holmes said that he deplored recommendations brought about by outside influences.[40] In subsequent months there were many similar attacks upon the Trades and Labour Council. The Conservatives claimed that the Labour group on the city council

---

[38] *Sheffield Telegraph*, 10 February 1965. Only a few years later a local N.A.L.G.O. branch meeting voted in favour of a closed shop policy. The 'white collar unions' were becoming more militant. *Morning Telegraph*, 24 July 1969.

[39] *The Star* (Sheffield), 13 February 1965.

[40] *Sheffield Telegraph*, 5 August 1965.

were subject to control by an organization that was not account-
able to the electorate. The Labour party naturally rejected these
accusations. Mr. Thornes sought to explain the bifurcation of the
Trades and Labour Council in the following way: the Labour
councillors were elected on a manifesto presented by the political
wing of the Trades and Labour Council, which was in effect the
Borough Labour Party, but the closed shop had not appeared in
this manifesto; it was the industrial wing of his council that had
made the application for the closed shop, and as such it was in the
nature of a normal unions-to-employer application. Lengthy
negotiations had been necessary to persuade the Labour group to
accept the policy.[41] The Trades and Labour Council had no
power to dictate to the city council.[42] The Conservatives were
sceptical about this explanation, but it was supported by members
of the Labour group. Some months later several influential Labour
councillors told our interviewers that they would not have taken
the initiative in implementing a closed shop. They took the
decision, they told us, in response to industrial negotiations, in the
same way that any other large employer might have taken a
similar decision if faced with such a demand backed by a threat of
industrial action.

The official decision by the city council did not conclude the
controversy. Two months later the Trades and Labour Council
was complaining that the decision had not been implemented in
some departments. The chairman of the Establishments Committee replied that only eleven of the twenty-eight eligible trade
unions had in fact applied to implement the closed shop policy,
but the corporation later agreed to inform manual workers of the
policy of the council by placing a leaflet in their wage packets. By
November 1965, twenty trade unions had applied. Mr. Thornes
continued to be concerned about the difficulties of implementing
the policy. At the end of October 1965, he said: 'I should think the
responsibility for carrying out council policy rests with council
officers—in this case the Town Clerk working with the establishments officer. It is impossible for the unions to check on who is in
or out of a union in some departments. Only the employer can do
that.'[43]

[41] *The Star* (Sheffield), 26 August 1966.   [42] *The Star* (Sheffield), 12 May 1966.
[43] *The Star* (Sheffield), 28 October 1965. Other details in this paragraph are taken
from *The Star*, 15 October and 27 October 1965 and *Morning Telegraph*, 9 November
1965.

The difficulty to which Mr. Thornes referred meant that there always appeared to be an element of chance (the Conservatives suggested discrimination) in whether or not a non-unionist was reported to the Establishments Committee, and this added to the bitterness such cases aroused. In April 1966, three non-union members were recommended for dismissal by the Establishments Committee and this decision was ratified, over intense Conservative opposition, at the May meeting of the city council. One of the men concerned, Mr. Platts, had been employed by the council for twenty years. He said: 'My main reasons for refusing to join are political. I object to the principle of the block vote, the political levy, and that Frank Cousins is a member of the government. I am not anti-union. It is just this union I am against. If there was an alternative I would join it.'[44] This statement hit at two weak points of the closed shop policy. First, although the unions claimed that they were operating a 'union shop' rather than a 'closed shop', Mr. Platts had no alternative to joining the Transport and General Workers' Union, which negotiated his conditions of employment. Secondly, the conscience clause only applied to those who refused to join a union on religious grounds. The case was extensively discussed during the 1966 local election campaign; polling day was on 12 May, and the Conservatives maintained their violent opposition to the dismissals over the ensuing months. In July the Conservative Member of Parliament for Hallam tried unsuccessfully to get the Minister of Housing and Local Government to intervene,[45] and the July meeting of the city council ended in uproar as the matter was discussed yet again. The local newspaper reported that 'all dignity seemed to depart from the chamber for a considerable time'.[46]

While the political row concerning the dismissal of Mr. Platts continued, another case became public. The National Union of General and Municipal Workers reported three part-time workers to the Education Committee for failing to join the union. One of the women, a widow, maintained that she only earned twenty-nine shillings a week and could not afford the weekly subscription. At the same time the first employee to benefit from the conscience clause won his appeal. He said: 'I believe unions are troublemakers seeking power for their own ends. It is a subtle form of

[44] *Morning Telegraph*, 10 May 1966.   [45] H. C. [732] 366–7 (19 July 1966).
[46] *The Star* (Sheffield), 7 July 1966.

communism . . . I prayed about the matter and left it in God's hands'.[47]

At the beginning of August 1966, Alderman Ironmonger, leader of the Labour group declared: 'We are not in full control of the situation. We have set down conditions of employment, and it is up to us [i.e. the city council] and no one else to apply them. Under the present arrangements we cannot avoid accusations that we are parties to victimization . . . I don't want a monthly court . . . and we are very concerned about the image this has created.'[48] The local evening newspaper congratulated Alderman Ironmonger on proving 'himself a man with the kind of stature required to be a real leader of the city council',[49] but the President of the Trades and Labour Council warned that there could be trouble if the Labour group sought to amend the policy.[50] He elaborated on the official trade union view in a long article in the September issue of *Sheffield Forward*, in which he accused the Conservatives of inflating one or two individual cases into a political attack upon the trade unions and the Labour-controlled city council. He gave examples of the many industries in which the closed shop was regularly enforced, and claimed that other local authorities in the area were enforcing similar conditions of employment. He reiterated that 'compulsory trade union membership is [no more] an interference with personal liberty and the right of the individual to choose for himself . . . than the same loss we all suffer in order to live together in an orderly fashion in a civilized society. Combining with fellow workers enables the individual to widen the collective liberties of all members.'[51] In the last paragraph of his article, however, he stated that the trade unions were always prepared to discuss the application of the closed shop policy with the leader of the city council and the chairman of the Establishments Committee.

The city council suspended the monthly meetings of the Establishments Committee that interviewed non-unionists immediately after the statement by Alderman Ironmonger in August 1966, but fresh negotiations about the application of the closed shop policy did not begin until October. During the following weeks there were several meetings between the Trades and Labour Council

---

[47] *The Star* (Sheffield), 22 July 1966.
[48] *Morning Telegraph*, 2 August 1966.
[49] *The Star* (Sheffield), 2 August 1966.
[50] Ibid.
[51] *Sheffield Forward*, September 1966.

and the Labour group, and in March 1967, a revised policy was presented to the city council. The revisions excluded existing part-time employees—less than eight hours per week—from the requirement to join a trade union, and made several improvements in the machinery through which the unions could ensure that the policy was being implemented. The Conservatives again tried unsuccessfully to reject the policy, and promised to withdraw it when they were returned to office.

When the Conservatives were elected to power in May 1968, they did not immediately fulfil their pledge to end the closed shop. They were compelled to take action the following January, however, when the National Union of General and Municipal Workers tried to get four school meals supervisors dismissed for refusing to join a union. The women were not dismissed and the closed shop policy was rescinded. The trade unions threatened strike action and prepared for a major struggle, but before this occurred the Labour Party regained control of the city council— in May 1969—and reintroduced their former policy.

We interviewed the councillors, and a sample of the electorate, a few months after the introduction of the revised policy in 1967. Half the councillors were opposed to the closed shop, and it is unlikely, therefore, that the council would have introduced such a policy as the result of a free vote without further trade union pressure. The opposition consisted mainly of Conservative councillors, but a few Labour councillors were opposed to the policy, and two Conservatives agreed with it. The electorate were evenly divided, with one in five of the supporters of each party expressing no opinion. About a quarter of the Conservative supporters among the electorate agreed with the policy and a similar proportion of the Labour supporters disagreed.

The Trades and Labour Council concentrated its campaign for the introduction of a closed shop almost entirely on the members of the Labour group on the city council. The reasons are obvious: the unions were dealing with a city council controlled by councillors sympathetic to their aims; and the issue was primarily between employer and employee. The Chamber of Commerce, on the other hand, in its campaign for support for a local airport, needed to win wide public interest in order to influence councillors with whom it was not in political sympathy. Of course, the trade unions needed to defend their policy from the criticism of the

Conservatives, who raised the general political principles inherent in the closed shop policy, but even if the Conservatives had retained office the trade unions would have been more concerned with industrial negotiations than with general publicity. The editor of the local newspaper, who had himself opposed the closed

Table 9.2
Attitudes towards Sheffield City Council's decision to introduce a closed shop

	Total		Cons. supporters		Lab. supporters	
	Cllrs.	Electors	Cllrs.	Electors	Cllrs.	Electors
Base	108	584	48	198	59	300
	%	%	%	%	%	%
Very strongly agree	34	22	2	12	61	28
Quite strongly agree	10	17	2	11	17	21
Neither agree nor disagree	6	18	2	18	8	18
Quite strongly disagree	8	10	6	12	10	8
Very strongly disagree	42	28	90	45	3	18
Don't know	0	5	0	4	0	5

Note: The percentages may not add to one hundred owing to rounding.
Sources: Survey of Sheffield Electorate and Survey of Sheffield City Council.

shop policy, warned the Conservatives that if they sought to reverse this policy then they would 'run the danger of confusing party principles with the matter of ordinary industrial management. . . . The closed shop, once conceded to such unions as want it, is not an easily reversed position'.[52] The editor spoke from experience: his newspapers were produced within a closed shop industry.

COMPREHENSIVE SCHOOLS

During the 1950s there was growing criticism of the tripartite system of education based on the eleven-plus examination on the grounds that it was educationally unsound and socially divisive. The Labour Party, and some educationalists of all political beliefs, wanted 'to reorganise the state secondary schools on comprehensive lines, in order to end the segregation by the eleven-plus examination'.[53] Those who opposed any change of policy believed

[52] *Morning Telegraph*, 5 February 1969.
[53] *Signposts for the Sixties*, p. 29. This Labour Party policy statement was accepted by their sixtieth annual conference, October 1961. The policy had been developed in the discussion documents issued by the Labour Party in the mid-1950s.

that the system embodied in the Education Act of 1944 enabled each child to receive the education for which he, or she, was best suited. They were also concerned to preserve the excellent educational standards achieved by many state grammar schools.

In Sheffield until about 1957 there was no inclination on the part either of the officials in the Education Department or of the Education Committee to modify the tripartite system. The criticisms of the eleven-plus examination were discounted. For instance in 1956 the Sheffield Education Department reported to the committee: 'There can be little doubt that, whilst the so-called "eleven-plus examination" is something which the normal pupil in the last year of junior school can and does take in his stride, some are affected by the undue publicity given to the anxieties with which adults have tended to surround it and by the pressures which arise from such anxieties'.[54]

Accordingly the Department concentrated on developing secondary modern schools, with sufficient increase in the places available in the selective schools to ensure that 'there was a sufficiency of places in grammar, technical and intermediate schools for those who showed that they had the ability and aptitude to profit from an academic secondary course'.[55] The Education Committee was at that time faced with the problem of accommodating in the secondary schools the increased number of children born at the end of the Second World War. In the period 1955–7 the secondary school population in Sheffield increased by 3,895 (25 per cent), of whom 3,610 were accommodated in secondary modern schools. In the following two years there was a further increase of 3,588 secondary pupils.[56] Under this pressure the size of classes in secondary modern schools began to increase,[57] and a number of new schools were planned.

One of the schools commenced in 1957 (opened in 1960) became a comprehensive school, but the other schools opened in this period were secondary modern. The leading members of the Labour group on the city council were still not convinced by the arguments in favour of a completely comprehensive system. As late as 1962 Alderman Ballard, chairman of the Education Committee,

[54] 'Report to the Education Committee on eleven-plus selection', October 1956, quoted in *Sheffield Education Committee Report, 1955–7*, p. 22.

[55] *Sheffield Education Committee Report, 1957–9*, p. 25.

[56] *Sheffield Education Committee Report, 1955–7*, p. 11, and *1957–9*, p. 13.

[57] *Sheffield Education Committee Report, 1955–7*, p. 16.

believed there would always have to be some form of selection at eleven-plus; nevertheless, Sheffield would evolve a system of comprehensive education. The important thing, he concluded, was that selection at eleven should not be irrevocable.[58] Myers Grove Secondary Comprehensive School was, in reality, a compromise arising from the dispute within the Labour group, rather than the harbinger of a new policy. The original intake to the school was based on parental choice. Parents of children at primary schools within the area could, if they wished, withdraw their children from the eleven-plus examination and allow them to proceed to the comprehensive school. The parents of about half the children in the area took this course, and their children were joined at Myers Grove by those who took the eleven-plus and failed. Parents were being given, as Alderman Ballard expressed it, an 'opportunity to minimize the ordeal of the eleven-plus examination'.[59] Selection, however, remained, and most of the children capable of passing the eleven-plus continued to sit the examination. The intake to Myers Grove, therefore, was far from comprehensive, and from September 1961, a stream from among those who had been success-ful in the eleven-plus examination was admitted to the school. Despite the difficulties of running a comprehensive school in a continuing selective environment, Myers Grove proved a success, and its example influenced the subsequent introduction of full comprehensive education in the city.

The opposition to comprehensive schools within the Sheffield Labour Party came mainly from the older members. When the Labour Party gained control of the city council in 1926, one of the first things they did was to establish municipal grammar schools to meet the need of the working class for social and educational advancement. As a result many of the older members of the council resisted the further development into comprehensive education as a threat to their previous achievements. This group were influential in the Education Committee, which at that time enjoyed a measure of delegated authority without being responsible in the ordinary way to the city council.

The movement in favour of comprehensive education was led in Sheffield by a group of young teachers who had joined the Labour Party in the 1950s. They were supported by the Sheffield Trades

---

[58] *Sheffield Telegraph*, 28 March 1962.
[59] *Sheffield Forward*, May 1960.

and Labour Council. By 1960 an informal group consisting of influential members of the Trades and Labour Council, young graduates from the Labour group on the city council, and influential local teachers, were meeting to discuss ways of stimulating the change to comprehensive schools. Early in 1961 Councillor Peter Horton, a teacher in the West Riding, wrote two important articles in the official journal of the Trades and Labour Council. 'A wind of change,' he wrote, 'is beginning to blow in education in this country. I hope that one effect will be to modify the tripartite system of secondary education in this city, for I believe it to be outdated, unfair, undemocratic, and wasteful of talent.'[60] He outlined a development plan for comprehensive education in the city, and the battle within the Labour Party was fairly joined. To continue the campaign a branch of the Socialist Educational Association was formed at a meeting held at the Grand Hotel, Sheffield, on 15 July 1961. The committee consisted of Mr. Flannery, subsequently President of the Sheffield Teachers' Association, and a member of the political executive of the Trades and Labour Council; Mr. Walker, Mr. Buchanan, and Mr. (later Councillor) Albaya; and Councillor Price, subsequently Member of Parliament for Perry Bar, Birmingham. Councillor Horton became secretary of the new association which was affiliated to the Borough Labour Party.[61] Councillor Price became vice-chairman of the Education Committee in 1963, and Councillor Horton became vice-chairman in 1966, and chairman in 1967.

By 1961 national opinion was moving firmly towards comprehensive education. Labour councils in some parts of the country were building comprehensive schools, and the new policy was causing fierce controversy in several cities. In Sheffield the opening of Myers Grove Comprehensive School was received calmly, and even when the Labour group announced its plans to introduce full comprehensive education in the northern part of the city there was little public discussion. In 1964 the municipal correspondent of the *Sheffield Telegraph* wrote a long article[62] in which he sought to provoke a debate about the comprehensive reorganization, but no correspondence ensued. This lack of response was the more surprising as he had deliberately mentioned the future effect of the

[60] *Sheffield Forward*, January and March 1961.
[61] Details from *Sheffield Forward*, September 1961.
[62] *Sheffield Telegraph*, 18 June 1964.

reorganization on the King Edward VII School, a former direct grant school of national status.

Within the Sheffield Labour Party the lobby in favour of comprehensive education was successful by 1962, when the Education Committee decided to move as quickly as possible towards the abolition of selection at eleven-plus. Teachers form an able and active minority within the Labour Party, and their influence was very strong on this issue; they were, of course, pressing for the implementation of Labour Party national policy, which assisted their campaign. General support within the Labour Party for comprehensive education was shown by a well attended one-day conference organized by the Sheffield Trades and Labour Council at the Memorial Hall, Sheffield, on 18 March 1962. The conference was addressed by Mr. W. S. Hill, the headmaster of Myers Grove Comprehensive School, and an exhibition of work from the school was on view. The implementation of the policy for comprehensive schools was made easier when the Education Committee lost its special status and became a normal statutory committee.

The city council decided to implement the reorganization area by area, starting in the northern part of the city where several new schools could readily be combined with existing schools to form large comprehensives. The eastern region, which included the massive Park Hill council housing complex and several older estates, came next; and finally the schools in the south and west of the city would become comprehensive. By starting in the north of the city, the Education Committee introduced reorganization into a predominantly working-class area where parents were less involved with the changes. There were few grammar schools in the area, and most of the children left school at, or soon after, the minimum leaving age of fifteen. Strenuous opposition could be expected when the middle-class areas in the south and west were affected, but by then the changeover would be a reality in most of the city.

Alderman Mrs. (later Dame Grace) Tebbutt, then leader of the Labour group on the city council, announced the plans for the northern part of the city in March 1963. At the same time it was announced that Alderman Ballard, then chairman of the Education Committee, would consult representatives of the teachers to explain the scheme in greater detail. It seems that the Labour group had accepted the plans from the Sheffield Director of

Education, and announced them, without consulting the representatives of the teachers. The teachers objected very strongly to the method by which the plan had been adopted, and for a time relations between them and the city council were strained. Some of the teachers, especially in the grammar schools, were critical also of the principles of comprehensive education, though in this they received no support from the leadership of the N.U.T. The Labour group read the warning signs, and from that time on great care was taken to carry the teachers' support for every stage of the programme. The elaborate consultative procedure, referred to at the beginning of this section, originated in this period.

By 1963–4 the Labour Party had adopted comprehensive education as one of the main planks in its municipal election platform. The Conservative group were more equivocal. Its leader continued to oppose the plans on the grounds that the socialists were trying to kill the grammar schools, but several of the younger members of the group, including Sir Harold Jackson's son, Peter, were willing to accept the comprehensive principle while criticizing details of its application. Alderman Peter Jackson became chairman of the Education Committee during the Conservative year of office, 1968–9, and his attitude was opposed by many Conservative supporters.

The opinions of the parents were not organized until as late as January 1965, when the Sheffield Parents' Association (S.P.A.) was constituted. This organization was based largely upon the parents of children attending the King Edward VII Grammar School, who wished to maintain the school outside the comprehensive system. The S.P.A. had only just been formed when the Education Committee began discussions with the teachers on the form comprehensive education should take in the south and west of the city. The S.P.A. admitted that they had not expected things to move so quickly, and their chairman wrote to Alderman Ballard, and to the Minister of Education, pointing out that 'the Education Act of 1944 requires that, so far as is possible without unreasonable public expenditure, pupils are to be educated in accordance with the wishes of their parents. Would you agree,' he asked, 'that this requires the local authority to consult parents before entering into extensive schemes of reorganization?'[63]

The S.P.A. organized a public meeting on 25 February 1965,

[63] *The Star* (Sheffield), 5 February 1965.

at which 200 people heard fierce attacks on the plans of the city council. One of the speakers claimed that setting up comprehensive education in neighbourhood schools could result in the disastrous creation of social and even racial ghettoes.[64] He added that comprehensive schools would be best if they were allowed to 'grow fat on the dead grammar schools. They need our children as a sort of educational fertiliser for their own schools.'[65]

In March 1965, the S.P.A. started to organize a petition against comprehensive education with a target of 45,000 signatures. Alderman Ballard announced that such a petition would not alter the city's plan for a change-over to the comprehensive school system;[66] but the association were not deterred. The S.P.A. initiative brought forward a counter-petition in favour of comprehensive schools. The organizers, a group of seventy Sheffield parents and teachers, had a target of 50,000 signatures to outbid the S.P.A.[67] They recognized that 'governments take notice of pressure groups unless there is a counter move. The worst effect of the S.P.A. petition would be that the Minister would modify the Sheffield scheme.'[68] An earlier attempt to organize parental support for comprehensive schools had received little publicity. It originated within the University of Sheffield and two of the leaders were Mr. Frank Hooley, Assistant Registrar and later Labour Member of Parliament for Heeley, Sheffield, and Dr. Peter Mann, then chairman of the local Association of University Teachers. They brought new life to the nearly moribund local branch of the Confederation for the Advancement of State Education (C.A.S.E.) which achieved a permanent existence and took part in the later stages of the debate.

By the end of March 1965, the Education Committee had passed the plan for comprehensive education throughout the city, and the public debate appeared to be over. The proposals had never aroused the passion shown in some other parts of the country, and the most important stages of the controversy had taken place within the confines of the party organizations; the party leaders themselves were conscious of their failure to arouse public

[64] The social separation of Sheffield into two homogeneous segments, described in Chapter 7, made this point more valid than it would be in many other cities.

[65] *Sheffield Telegraph*, 26 February 1965.

[66] *The Star* (Sheffield), 17 March 1965.

[67] Both groups found it easier to announce targets than to collect signatures.

[68] *The Star* (Sheffield), 31 March 1965.

interest in the issue. At the end of 1965 the Department of Education and Science asked all local authorities to submit their proposals for comprehensive education to the minister. The Sheffield proposals were submitted in August 1966, and approved.

The whole question was re-opened during 1967 when it was announced, following the Plowden Report on Primary Education,[69] that the plans for comprehensive education in Sheffield were to be modified. Children were to attend primary school until the age of eight, transfer to a middle school until the age of twelve, and then proceed to a comprehensive school. The number of comprehensive schools was to be increased from twenty to thirty-five, but not all of them would contain sixth forms. This plan was attacked from every angle. The teachers criticized it on educational grounds, and there were suggestions that the division between comprehensive schools with and without sixth forms would be as sharp as that between grammar and secondary modern schools. The situation was further confused in February 1968, when the Department of Education and Science announced that the raising of the school leaving age had been postponed: they asked the Sheffield Education Committee to review its plans in view of this decision and to include proposals for all levels of schooling. Work on this revision was well advanced when the control of the city council passed to the Conservatives in 1968. The constant changing of educational plans caused a new parents' organization, the Association for Better Consultation (A.B.C.) to be formed at the end of 1968. They intended to be more critical than C.A.S.E. of council policy.

In their election manifesto the Conservatives had formulated detailed amendments to the Labour group's proposals, but their scheme was still based on broad comprehensive lines. The attitude of the group was, of course, largely determined by the views of the leadership, who were favourably disposed towards comprehensive education, but they were not as detached from the other members of the group as Table 9.3 would suggest. The interviews upon which Table 9.3 is based were conducted at the end of 1967 (electors), and at the beginning of 1968 (councillors), so that the decision referred to is the one taken by the Labour-controlled city council. It was the Labour scheme to which the

[69] *Report on Children and their Primary Schools*, Central Advisory Council on Education (England), H.M.S.O., 1967.

Table 9.3
Attitudes towards Sheffield City Council's decision to introduce comprehensive schools

Base	Total		Cons. supporters		Lab. supporters	
	Cllrs. 108	Electors 584	Cllrs. 48	Electors 198	Cllrs. 59	Electors 300
	%	%	%	%	%	%
Very strongly agree	44	25	4	17	76	30
Quite strongly agree	17	22	10	11	22	27
Neither agree nor disagree	5	16	10	15	0	18
Quite strongly disagree	14	10	31	18	0	7
Very strongly disagree	20	19	42	34	2	9
Don't know	1	8	2	7	0	9

Note: The percentages may not add to one hundred owing to rounding.
Sources: Survey of Sheffield Electorate and Survey of Sheffield City Council.

Conservatives were objecting, but just over half the group were in favour of some degree of comprehensive education.[70] The majority of the electorate who expressed an opinion were in agreement with the decision taken to introduce comprehensive schools, but, understandably, about a quarter of the respondents either refused to commit themselves or did not know how to answer. By the time of the interviews education plans existed in confusing profusion.

When the Conservatives did gain control they decided to keep to the time-table already agreed with the D.E.S. They reserved the right to amend the plan, but they did not wish to enter a battle with a Labour government—thus perpetuating the indecision about the city's educational plans; nor did they wish to reintroduce the very unpopular eleven-plus examination. The amendments they proposed were important; one would have allowed 'high flyers' to transfer as early as possible to schools with a sixth form;[71] but these did not satisfy many of their own supporters. The S.P.A. renewed their efforts to prevent the grammar schools—particularly King Edward VII School—from being incorporated in the new system, and members of the Conservative group on the city council publicly opposed their leaders. A group of 'disillusioned Conservative voters' from all parts of the city placed a large display advertisement in the

[70] This emerged in response to a later question.
[71] *The Star* (Sheffield), 19 June 1968.

Morning Telegraph.[72] They accused the Conservative group of adopting the Socialist plan which in opposition they had described as a 'hotch-potch', and the advertisers questioned the future value of voting Conservative.

The Conservative group were in a difficult political position. The party was divided on the merits of the comprehensive principle in education, and many of their strongest supporters among the electorate were opposed to the integration of the grammar schools into the comprehensive system. On the other hand the Labour voters were strongly in favour, and so were the Liberals and those who supported other smaller parties. If the Conservatives continued with the Labour scheme they risked losing votes in their own strongholds, but if they reintroduced the eleven-plus examination they would forfeit their chances in the key marginal seats at the forthcoming local elections.[73] Political expediency, therefore, supported the leadership in continuing with the plans for comprehensive education, but constant amendments were being announced in response to pressure from such groups as the S.P.A. These amendments were never introduced, for the Labour Party regained power in May 1969. The last child from a Sheffield school took the eleven-plus examination in February 1968.

The three issues discussed in this chapter provide examples of groups outside the city council trying to persuade the councillors to adopt a policy that might otherwise have been neglected or ignored. In each case the pressure was exerted upon the councillors not the officers, and many of the people concerned were intimately involved with one or other of the party groups. In the case of the airport, the Chamber of Commerce was associated with the party in opposition, and they failed in their objective; the closed shop was advocated by the trade unions who could dominate the Borough Labour Party if they exercised their affiliated voting power; the policy for comprehensive schools was supported by a group of young teachers who were also members of the Labour Party.

Both the trade unions and the socialist teachers were successful, but it should not be concluded that they succeeded simply because

[72] *Morning Telegraph*, 14 October 1968.
[73] In the May 1969 elections there was a noticeable drop in the Conservative poll throughout the city, while the Labour vote remained fairly constant from 1968.

they belonged to the majority party, nor that the Chamber of Commerce failed because it did not. There was a conflict within the political parties, as well as between them, over all these issues, with the exception of the Conservative group's opposition to the closed shop. The conflict within the party groups frequently became public. Two leading Labour aldermen disagreed in the council chamber over the merits of the airport scheme; articles by city councillors published in *Sheffield Forward* were critical of the existing policies of the Labour group both on education and on the closed shop; the Conservative leaders were abused by their followers both within and without the city council over their policy towards comprehensive education. The closed politics that at one time were typical of Sheffield, and of many other cities, have obviously become more open as younger councillors have replaced the older leadership.

Public opinion outside the political parties and their close associates was less well organized. Public opposition to the airport, for example, was virtually non-existent in Sheffield, and the protests from the surrounding villages appeared very late. Alderman Ironmonger was amazed that so little had been done by Todwick residents until 1966: 'I know,' he said, 'I should not like it if one [an airport] were being built at the bottom of my garden.'[74] Later he appealed for more reaction from the public to the proposals, so that the council could know what the electorate thought about the possibility of an airport at Todwick.[75] The opponents of the closed shop relied upon the Conservative party, and the publicity provided by the local press, to explain their point of view. The few individuals concerned received some support from the people with whom they worked,[76] but no pressure group appeared to oppose the decision of the Labour group.

The introduction of comprehensive education is the issue which provoked the greatest number of pressure groups. There were already in existence several teachers' organizations, and they were ready to defend the trade union interests of their members

[74] *Morning Telegraph*, 6 January 1966.
[75] *Morning Telegraph*, 1 February 1967.
[76] Employees of the Transport Department signed a round robin to show their willingness to work with Mr. Platts. *The Star* (Sheffield), 12 May 1966; see also *Morning Telegraph*, 20 August 1966. The teachers' unions would not agree to their members making inquiries about the trade union membership of school meals supervisors. *The Star* (Sheffield), 6 February 1969.

as well as to express views on educational principles. Indeed one
of the consequences of the events described in this chapter was the
introduction of closer liaison between the teachers' organizations,
the Education Department, and the Education Committee. The
parents' associations came later, and at first gained little public
interest. During the Conservative year of office, however, both
those for and against comprehensives harried the council un-
mercifully. The immediate controversy appeared to be settled
with the return of the Labour Party to power in 1969, but the
pressure groups created to contest this issue have remained in
existence. The Labour group in 1969 retained places on reformed
school management bodies for the representatives of the parents
elected by parent-teacher associations or by general assemblies of
parents. There has developed, therefore, the possibility of considerable consultation about educational policy between the
Education Committee and pressure groups representing both
teachers and parents. The principle of comprehensive education
was really accepted by the city council before the pressure groups
were effectively organized, but their influence will be felt as the
policy is implemented.

Pressure group activity in local politics is certainly of a different
character from the quiet consultations that take place in Whitehall.
But so is the general nature of local political life different from the
firmness of cabinet government. National pressure groups often
have to accept the big decisions while they seek to influence the
details of administration; in local government the policy decisions
are taken by political groups that are closer to their electorate.
The local electorate may frequently be indifferent, but once
aroused it can put pressure upon local councillors in a way that is
not really possible in the more remote atmosphere of national
politics. It is worth while in local politics, also, to influence the
most humble back-bench councillor who, unlike his parliamentary
counterpart, is not presented with a cabinet decision as a *fait
accompli*. The important policy decisions are taken by the full
party group.

Local pressure groups may be concerned more with principles,
therefore, than with administrative details. During the comprehensive schools issue, for example, the teachers and parents were
concerned with the broad generalizations, while the party groups
argued about detailed plans. In national terms these roles would

have been reversed, with the House of Commons debating the principle on Second Reading, while the pressure groups lobbied the civil servants on administrative procedures. There is some indication at the local level that this contrast might not be as clear-cut in the future as it has been in the past. Local authorities are becoming more keen, and are being officially encouraged, to involve the general public in matters of administration. Examples of this are to be found in the arrangements for consultation envisaged for the Sheffield education service, and in the consultation that has now become a statutory requirement during the process of town planning.[77] The Seebohm Committee recommended that similar principles be extended to the administration of the personal social services.[78] But these changes are still in their early stages, and some councillors remain unconvinced that more consultation is necessary. Meanwhile the public are roused, as the Sheffield councillor reminded us, by 'disasters' rather than by opportunities to participate, and we may consider, in the next chapter, the most explosive decision to be taken by Sheffield City Council in recent years.

[77] Town and Country Planning Act, 1968.
[78] Report of the Committee on Local Authority and Allied Personal Social Services (Cmnd. 3703).

IO

The Big Issue

There are some cottages lately built for working classes which are of a very good construction. These houses are built back-to-back but are so well arranged that they have good ventilation. The dungsteads and privies for the houses, both of front and rear, are in a roomy back court and are as little nuisance to sight and smell as such objects can be.

Report on Sheffield for the Royal Commission on Health of Towns, 1842

LOCAL authorities receive about two-fifths of their income from central government grants. In addition, they require the sanction of the Minister of Housing and Local Government before they can raise a loan to finance each item of capital expenditure. These financial controls enable the government to exert considerable influence over the policy pursued by the local authority, and in no area of policy is this more true than in housing. The number of houses built, the location of the sites, and the type of dwellings provided are all affected by changes in the basis upon which government grants are allocated. At one time the grants paid for high-rise buildings were higher than those for conventional housing, and at another time grants were increased for housing intended to replace the nineteenth-century slums. Local authorities were compelled by financial necessity to adapt their housing policy in response to these changes in the grant. They were also under pressure from successive housing ministers to introduce differential rent schemes so that the government grants could be used to reduce the rents of those tenants who most needed help.

On some occasions, therefore, local councillors are under pressure both from their constituents and from the central government; these conflicting pressures can produce major disputes between local representatives and their customary supporters. The rent rebate scheme for council house tenants introduced by the Sheffield City Council in 1967 provided an example of just such a dispute.

The immediate reason for the introduction of an income-related rent scheme[1] in Sheffield was the increasing burden of interest charges on the housing revenue account. The government's policy of financial stringency had been accompanied by increased interest rates which at times reached eight per cent. Local authorities are compelled by law to spread their capital costs for housing over a period of sixty years, and even the grants provided by the central government could not prevent the high interest charges from creating financial difficulties for those authorities that intended to continue building.

The decision to introduce a rent rebate scheme was opposed by many people who suggested that the central government should protect local authorities from the effects of increasing interest rates. They believed that the object was to squeeze a higher total amount of rent from the council house tenants, rather than to redistribute the grants more equitably; and they were confirmed in this belief when it was noticed that the first scheme proposed contained no provision for the continuation of a rate contribution to the housing revenue account.

Opposition also arose from the nature of the scheme itself. In a rent rebate scheme the rents are first fixed at a standard level, and any rebate is then granted on an individual basis after subsequent consideration. The Sheffield council house tenants were aware, therefore, of the rent increases that would apply to houses of certain types, but the individual rebates remained problematical until the applications had been considered. The immediate rent increase was naturally more real to many tenants than the promised rebate. There was also a deep emotional objection to the declaration of income that would be necessary when applying for a rebate. Sheffield, in common with other northern industrial cities, had suffered from mass unemployment in the depression years between the two world wars. The memory of the 'means test' administered as a condition of assistance to the long-term unemployed had left a bitterness not easily erased even thirty years afterwards.

The tenants' associations formed to oppose the rent rebate

---

[1] Under a full differential rent scheme the rent of every tenant is related to his income, and consequently all tenants have to make a declaration of the income they receive. Under a rent rebate scheme only those tenants claiming a rebate from a standard rent need to declare their income.

scheme differed from the pressure groups discussed in the previous chapter in a number of ways. First, they were based upon the limited area of a housing estate; their leaders came from the neighbourhood, and were frequently inexperienced in public affairs. Secondly, they were mass organizations. Thousands of tenants joined the associations to combat a scheme which, they felt, represented an attack upon their homes and their families. The feelings aroused by such an emotional issue were naturally more passionate than those encountered in normal political activity. The traditional mass meetings were followed by the less acceptable mass lobbying of city councillors at their homes, and ultimately by a short-lived rent strike.

The rent rebate scheme was also a clear example of a local issue affecting the electoral prospects of political parties. The electorate was divided fairly evenly on the issue: the owner-occupiers were in favour of the scheme, and the council tenants were opposed; but the council estates formed the Labour Party's safest wards, and the loss of support that the party suffered caused them to lose control of the city council for only the second time since 1926.[2] The political divisions within the Labour Party over this issue went very deep: the Labour group itself decided to introduce the policy of rent rebates by a very narrow majority; and the subsequent dispute within both the group and the wider Labour movement caused much personal bitterness.

The pressure upon local authorities to introduce differential rents for their subsidized housing began with the Housing Subsidies Act, 1956.[3] The government had come to believe that private builders should provide for most of the general need for housing, while local authorities devoted their resources to programmes for slum clearance. Two million permanent new houses had been built in the previous ten years, and it was thought that the emergency housing shortage had been met. There still remained the problem of slum clearance which since 1939 had been largely at a standstill. It was estimated that there were over one million slum dwellings in Britain which had to be cleared, and most of the worst slums were in the industrial cities. In Sheffield

---

[2] The electoral consequences of the introduction of the rent rebate scheme are discussed in Chapter 7.

[3] 4 & 5 Eliz. II, c. 33. A committee under the chairmanship of Mr. Henry Brooke had previously reviewed various methods of fixing council house rents. Their report, published in November 1953, included a description of differential rent schemes.

itself there remained many back-to-back houses of the type described so favourably in the quotation at the head of this chapter; a hundred and twenty-five years of occupation had not improved the amenities provided in those squalid streets.

The Act of 1956 reduced the subsidy for housing provided for general need, and the government intended to end the subsidy altogether within a few years. Housing subsidies had risen to £47 million, and the Chancellor of the Exchequer, in his post-election budget in 1955, had called for economies by local authorities in both capital and revenue expenditure. A policy of restricted borrowing by local authorities from the Public Works Loan Board was announced, and during the year the rate of interest charged by the Board was raised four times. Houses built to rehouse people from slum clearance areas, however, continued to attract subsidies at the existing level. The government considered that unless discrimination was exercised in applying these subsidies to rent relief there was bound to be a misuse of public funds. The Minister of Housing and Local Government, Mr. Duncan Sandys, in a statement to the House of Commons in 1955, said: 'There is no doubt that, in general, council house rents are today being subsidised to a greater extent than the financial circumstances of the individual tenants require. . . . Provided, therefore, that they [the local authorities] subsidise only those tenants who require subsidising, and only to the extent of their need, local authorities should be well able to continue building the new houses they require with appreciably less Exchequer assistance than hitherto.'[4] He went on to explain that local authorities needed an incentive to introduce differential rent schemes. 'At present,' he said, '. . . no matter how much they increase their revenue from rents, they still have a statutory obligation to pay into the Housing Revenue Account a fixed contribution from the rates.'[5] The Bill proposed in 1955 abolished this obligation so that local authorities could use their increased revenue to reduce the rate subsidy. In May 1956, the Ministry issued a circular giving local authorities who were thinking of introducing differential rent schemes a guide based on details of five schemes already in operation.[6]

[4] H. C. Deb. [545] 377 (27 October 1955).
[5] H. C. Deb. [545] 378 (27 October 1955).
[6] Ministry of Housing and Local Government Circular, 29/56.

Local authorities throughout the country introduced differential rent schemes during the late 1950s, usually after intense opposition from their tenants.[7] In Sheffield the Conservative-Liberal group on the city council consistently urged that rents should be fixed in relation to the age, locality, and amenities of the dwellings, and that these standard rents should be reduced for certain tenants by using a formula based on need. The Labour group, who were in control, opposed these proposals. Their view was expressed by Councillor Roy Hattersley, then Deputy Chairman of the Housing Committee,[8] who in announcing rent increases in August 1960, said that these were based on the principle that rents should be determined by the value of the property, not by the income of the tenant. Any other system, he continued, would result in a worsening of the relationship between tenants, and between tenants and the Housing Department. It would 'also impose inexcusable indignities on the tenants.'[9] Two years later Councillor Hattersley, by then Chairman of the Housing Committee, spoke of differential rents and similar schemes as 'arbitrary, complicated and humiliating'.[10] This reference was made during a speech announcing the intention of the council to introduce concessionary rents for retirement pensioners. The Conservatives maintained that concessionary rents were a rebate scheme and that the Labour group were, therefore, moving away from their previous policy. Councillor Hattersley, however, distinguished the giving of rebates to particular groups from the individual assessment implied in a rebate scheme.

The difficulties of operating an indiscriminate rebate scheme for retirement pensioners led the Labour group step by step towards an income-related scheme. Two-thirds of the pensioners received national assistance which included the payment of rent; in their case the increased subsidy was effectively by-passing the pensioners and going to the National Assistance Board. The remaining third of the pensioners were either too proud to apply for National Assistance, or they did not need its help. The council, therefore,

---

[7] Dr. Jones shows how the majority of the Wolverhampton Borough Council were in favour of a rebate scheme in 1959, but Labour group discipline ensured that it was defeated in open council. G. W. Jones, *Borough Politics*, pp. 185 and 315.

[8] Later Member of Parliament for Sparkbrook, Birmingham, and a minister in the Labour government.

[9] *Sheffield Telegraph*, 4 August 1960.

[10] *The Star* (Sheffield), 7 November 1962.

was subsidizing either pride, or the better-off pensioners. Although sympathy could be felt for those pensioners whose self-respect would be compromised by applying for National Assistance, the rebate scheme still appeared illogical. In the summer of 1964 the Labour group proposed that rebates should be discontinued for those pensioners receiving National Assistance, and the following year (October 1965) the Housing Management Committee proposed an income limit for pensioners receiving concessionary rents. By this time Mr. Hattersley had entered Parliament.

Throughout this period the Conservative group on the city council continued to suggest that council house rent increases should be accompanied by differential rents. In January 1964, they presented a fully developed rent rebate scheme to the council that contained many of the principles later found in the scheme introduced to the Labour group by Alderman Dyson. Rents were to be related to the gross ratable value of the house, and the contribution from the rate fund to the housing revenue account was to be discontinued. Rebates would be available for tenants whose rents exceeded one-seventh of their gross income. The first two pounds of a wife's earnings would be ignored, together with certain pensions, but National Assistance benefits would be included. A surcharge of seven shillings and sixpence per week would be payable for each adult occupier in addition to the tenant and his wife.[11] The city council rejected the Conservative proposals at their meeting in February 1964. In opposing the scheme Alderman Ironmonger denied that there was a need to worry about housing finance, and maintained that the purpose of the Conservative scheme was simply to abolish the rate subsidy to the housing revenue account.[12] Councillor Hattersley drew attention to the absence of any form of allowance for dependent relatives, which, he suggested, penalized the tenant on a low income who had a large family.[13] It was noticeable that many of the Labour criticisms were no longer about the principles of rent rebates, but about the finance and particular nature of the Conservative scheme.

Later in 1964 a Labour government replaced the Conservatives

[11] Details of this scheme were distributed to every member of the city council. They were summarized in *The Star* (Sheffield), 30 January 1964.

[12] *Sheffield Telegraph*, 6 February 1964.

[13] Ibid.

at Westminster. The policy of the Ministry of Housing and
Local Government was, therefore, determined by the political
friends of the Labour group in Sheffield. The national policy on
council house rents, however, remained unchanged, and the
city council continued to receive circulars advocating differential
rents or rent rebate schemes.[14] The economic position of the
country and the consistently high interest rates made it imperative, in the government's view, that the local authorities should
concentrate the available subsidies on those tenants who most
needed help. At first the official policy of the Labour group in
Sheffield continued to be opposed to rents related to income. They
believed that local authority housing was a social and community
service, and that deficits in the housing revenue account should be
met by the community at large from a rate fund contribution,
rather than by large rent increases. The deficits continued to
grow, however, and periodic rent increases became unavoidable.
In the mid-1960s council house rents were becoming too high for
many prospective tenants, while the rate contribution rose to
the equivalent of a sixpenny rate. The city council felt the need to
reconsider their policy, and the reconsideration became more
urgent when the government proposed to reduce the grants payable towards the additional costs of high-rise buildings and the
development of difficult sites.[15] The housing policy of Sheffield
was committed to both of these expensive forms of provision.
The first speech by Alderman Dyson after his appointment as
chairman of the Housing Management Committee was devoted
to an attack on the government's proposals, and the Sheffield
Members of Parliament were asked to challenge 'anomalies'
in the Bill at the Committee Stage 'rather than have it left to
the whims of Dame Evelyn Sharp and the Minister'.[16]

Alderman Dyson had previously startled many of his colleagues

---

[14] *The Housing Programme 1965–70*, Cmnd. 2838 (November 1965) and 'Rent Rebate
Schemes', Ministry of Housing and Local Government, Circular 46/67 (June 1967).
The National Executive Committee of the Labour Party had expressed support for
some rent rebate schemes as early as 1956, but at that time they opposed the ending
of a rate contribution towards housing costs. Labour Party Research Department,
Information Paper No. 56 (July 1967). This information paper contains an 'illustra-
tive' rent rebate scheme.

[15] The Housing Subsidies Bill received a second reading on 15 December 1965.
Owing to the intervention of a General Election the Bill did not become law. A revised
Bill was enacted as the Housing Subsidies Act 1967 (1967 Ch. 29).

[16] *Sheffield Telegraph*, 3 February 1966.

by attacking the housing policies pursued by the council. As early as November 1964, he had suggested that the Housing Department's annual report tried to cover up the real problem of rent arrears. He maintained that ordinary working people could not afford the higher rents being charged for council houses, and he warned that the council would have to take a new attitude to management and control. The problem of arrears, he believed, was caused by people who desperately needed accommodation accepting a house they could not pay for.[17] During the following year (1965) there were several reports that the council was having difficulty in letting flats. Alderman Hebblethwaite, the Conservative leader, believed that 75 per cent of the people who moved from slum clearance areas could not afford to rent a new corporation house.[18] It was reported that while the waiting period on the general list for a lower rental pre-war house was as long as twelve years, applicants could move into a council house within twelve months if they were willing to accept the first accommodation offered.

In February 1966, Alderman Dyson was appointed chairman of the Housing Management Committee with a mandate to consider the rapid growth of the city's housing finances and the rents payable by council tenants. The City Treasurer was asked to prepare a memorandum to assist the reappraisal of policy and this was published as an eighty-page booklet in November 1966.[19] At first the general public were unaware that a major revision of policy was being considered, but in August 1966, every council tenant received a questionnaire asking for personal details of income and family dependants. The information was needed to provide statistics upon which a rebate scheme could be based and no names or signatures were required; the forms were destroyed immediately after they had been processed. The local Communist Party, and members of the Sheffield branch of the British National Party urged tenants to ignore the survey, and small groups of demonstrators lobbied councillors as they entered meetings in the Town Hall. They carried banners protesting about differential rents, but little interest was aroused. Over 62,000 questionnaires were circulated and 56 per cent were

[17] *The Star* (Sheffield), 5 November 1964.
[18] *The Star* (Sheffield), 11 August 1965.
[19] *Housing Finance in Sheffield.*

returned properly completed. The tenants who expected to benefit from a change in the method of rent assessment, for example the old age pensioners, were naturally more ready to return the survey forms than more prosperous tenants. The information received had to be adjusted, therefore, to ensure that the total picture drawn from the survey did not contain any avoidable bias.[20]

The booklet, *Housing Finance in Sheffield*, outlined the nature of the housing revenue account, assessed the existing financial situation, and estimated the changes that would take place over the succeeding four years. The deficit in the current year— 1966–7—was expected to reach £191,000, *after* allowing for a standard rate fund contribution of £558,000. In subsequent years both the deficit and the standard rate fund contribution were expected to increase until in 1970–1 it was estimated that they would be £607,000 and £809,000 respectively.[21] The expected deficiencies could be met either by increasing the rents or by making a larger contribution from the general rate fund.[22] If existing policies were continued then rents would need to increase immediately by at least 8 per cent—equivalent to a flat rate increase of two shillings and ninepence—with further increases in subsequent years. If all the deficits were met from the general rate fund then the contribution would double, from the equivalent of a sixpenny rate to more than one shilling, during the following five years, and the government would view such a development with disfavour.

[20] The tenants who responded to the survey were frequently referred to as a 'sample' of the total. In fact, of course, no *sample* was taken. The questionnaires were circulated to every tenant and the completed forms represented the *response rate* to a total census. The report from the City Treasurer ignores this distinction and claims that the response rate of 58 per cent (2 per cent of the forms were returned improperly completed and could not be processed) was 'an adequate sample upon which a workable rent structure could be based'. (*Housing Finance in Sheffield*, p. 45.) A self-selecting effective 'sample' of 56 per cent is in fact a poor basis for policy making, as the adjustments to avoid bias indicated. Better results could have been obtained by a smaller— say 10 per cent—random sample if the response rate had thereby been increased. The amateurism of some official surveys in local government could be an increasing problem if the Skeffington proposals on consultation in planning are acted upon. Sometimes it seems as if it is more important to have held a survey than to have made it relevant or accurate. Professional local research units are plainly needed, but councillors will also need to learn how to use them. A research unit was established in Sheffield in the autumn of 1969 (see Ch. 3).

[21] *Housing Finance in Sheffield*, Tables I and II.

[22] There is a statutory requirement on local authorities to balance their Housing Revenue account annually. Deficits cannot be allowed to accumulate.

The City Treasurer drew attention to two disadvantages of the existing rent structure. First, tenants in lower income groups might pay such a high proportion of their incomes in rent that they might suffer actual hardship; and some future tenants from slum clearance areas might face financial difficulties when transferred to property with higher rents. Secondly, subsidies were being given to all tenants whether or not they were in real need. This was contrary to the purpose of subsidies as announced by successive Housing Ministers. The City Treasurer concluded that these disadvantages could only be overcome by 'the adoption of some form of rebate scheme.'[23] He suggested that all those tenants who could afford it should pay the current rental value of their dwelling, which should be fixed at one and a third times the gross ratable value. Tenants unable to pay these rents would be able to claim a rebate 'and only then would their financial circumstances be investigated'.[24] He presented a choice of four possible rebate schemes for consideration by the city council, and suggested a surcharge of seven shillings and sixpence per week for each adult occupier in addition to the tenant and his wife.

Immediately the City Treasurer's report became available the public controversy over rent rebates began in earnest. Alderman Dyson accepted the analysis and proposed a version of the rebate scheme that brought in sufficient rent income to end the necessity for any rate subsidy to the housing revenue account.[25] The Conservative group also welcomed the City Treasurer's report which, they claimed, embodied principles they had been advocating for many years.[26] The Labour group met on the Monday following the publication of the report, adjourned until the following Monday, and adjourned again until the Monday after that. Finally it agreed to an amended version of the scheme proposed by Alderman Dyson. The amendments gave greater benefits to tenants on low incomes and reintroduced a rate subsidy of £300,000 per annum. The length of the debate within the Labour group indicated the closely balanced support for both sides of the argument. The crucial majorities were less than ten in a group of

[23] *Housing Finance in Sheffield*, p. 64.
[24] Ibid.
[25] *Morning Telegraph*, 12 November 1966.
[26] Ibid.

seventy-two members.[27] The opponents of the rent rebate scheme within the Labour group included several senior members, but they were met by a formidable, and judging from the issues discussed in the previous chapter somewhat unusual, alliance between the leader, deputy leader, and chairman of the group. These three, Aldermen Ironmonger, Lewis, and Dyson, held the key chairmanships of the city council Policy, Finance, and Housing Management Committees. Opposition to the scheme was further weakened when the representatives of the Trades and Labour Council announced in the Labour group that they supported the principle of rent rebates. The decision within the Trades and Labour Council political executive had also been taken by a very narrow majority, but it gave vital support to the leadership of the group when their policy was in its formative stages. The amended policy was accepted by the city council at their meeting on 4 January 1967, against the opposition of the Conservatives who deprecated the amendments to the original proposals in the City Treasurer's report.

The rent rebate scheme was to become operative in July 1967, and soon after the decision of the city council the tenants began to organize in opposition. In January 1967, the Arbourthorne Tenants' Association was formed on one of the older, pre-war, housing estates. Several women on the estate, including Mrs. Mary Macdonald who was to become a leading figure among the tenants, invited councillors to a public meeting. A number of topics were discussed, but it was obvious that the main concern of the women was the rent rebate policy, and they proceeded to circulate a petition calling on the city council to rescind the scheme. The Communist Party was actively encouraging the tenants to form associations to oppose rent rebates, but in these first few months of 1967 the distribution of leaflets had little effect. In the Arbourthorne Tenants' Association the main influence was a group of left-wing Labour Party members. By March the association had between four and five hundred members, and they enlarged their committee to twenty-six, including many active trade unionists. Two members of the Trades and Labour Council, Mr. Len Youle and Mr. Nick

[27] See Peter Harvey's article, *Morning Telegraph*, 6 January 1967, which he rather optimistically entitled 'Crisis over—what now?'

Howard,[28] also sat on the Arbourthorne Tenants' Committee, although neither lived in the area.

Mr. Youle, a veteran of the Labour movement in Sheffield, was leading the opposition to the rent rebate scheme within the Trades and Labour Council. The delegates to this body were incensed at the decision of their political executive to support the scheme, and they rejected the policy by forty-three votes to twenty-nine at their meeting on 31 January 1967. There was now a clear split between the Borough Labour Party, who determined election policy, and the Labour group on the city council, who determined council policy; a split which Alderman Dyson did nothing to narrow when he announced that the rent rebate policy would be maintained despite the opposition of the Trades and Labour Council.[29]

The division within the Labour Party was made plain by the publication of two articles in the January edition of the official periodical of the Trades and Labour Council. One article supporting the rent rebate scheme was written by Alderman Ironmonger, and one opposing the scheme by Mr. Youle. Alderman Ironmonger announced that he would visit all the constituency Labour parties to explain the policy of the Labour group, but at least one constituency party insisted that Mr. Youle be invited at the same time to explain his opposition. Alderman Ironmonger argued in favour of the scheme for two main reasons: first, the deficit on the Housing Management account had to be met; and secondly, social justice demanded that people should not be excluded from council housing because of their inability to pay the rent. Mr. Youle agreed upon the cogency of these arguments, but not upon the details of the solution proposed. In particular he argued that the rate contribution to the scheme should be increased, and that the city council should press the government for a reduction of interest rates on housing loans. He was totally opposed to the adult occupier surcharge.

The constitutional conflict between the majority of the Labour group and the majority of the Trades and Labour Council reached a crisis at the March meeting of the Borough Labour Party when

[28] Mr. Howard, sometime member of the editorial board of the journal *International Socialism*, left the Labour Party, and consequently the Trades and Labour Council to which he was a constituency party delegate, during 1968.

[29] *Morning Telegraph*, 14 February 1967.

the manifesto for the forthcoming local elections was considered. It was clear that the majority present at the meeting were extremely hesitant about the policy of the leadership of the Labour group and of the political executive of the Trades and Labour Council. In fact the meeting opened by carrying an emergency resolution condemning the rent rebate scheme as 'contrary to the spirit and intentions of the Labour government's policy on prices and incomes.'[30]

The opposition to the scheme did not lead to the rejection of the draft manifesto. This document made the following reference to council house rents:

It has become increasingly evident that rents of many new dwellings were a burden on lower-paid workers who were unable to afford the accommodation which was their right.

Because of this, Labour will continue to approach housing as a social service, seeking to allocate housing according to need, and financing it according to ability to pay.

This can only be made effective by the introduction of a rent rebate scheme for council tenants assisted financially by the continuation of an annual rate contribution.

Such a scheme will be reviewed annually to prevent anomalies or injustices that may arise and to take into account the Labour government's proposals gradually to establish a more progressive and equitable rating system.[31]

A number of amendments were proposed to this draft manifesto, but before the vote was taken on the first of these the President of the Trades and Labour Council, who was also a city councillor, made an appeal to the delegates. He told them that if the amendments were carried he would have to resign, and that the Trades and Labour Council would find it difficult to carry on in opposition to the elected representatives. The opposition delegates backed down and the controversial amendments, including one that proposed a flat-rate rent increase of two shillings and tenpence, were not debated. After this meeting the more radical opponents of the rent rebate scheme spent less time within the Labour Party, and the tenants' associations began to grow in strength.

[30] *Morning Telegraph*, 22 March 1967.   [31] *Sheffield Forward*, May 1967.

The Conservative Party at this time were in a difficult position. In the impending local elections every member of the city council had to seek re-election, and the Conservatives had a good chance of gaining control,[32] but they were diffident about exploiting the difficulties the rent rebate scheme was causing the Labour Party. The Conservatives had always favoured income-related council rents and the abolition of the rates subsidy. Consequently they had supported the proposals made by the City Treasurer in November 1966. By May 1967, the Labour group had accepted a scheme that included a rate subsidy, and that gave improved benefits to low income tenants. The Conservatives' preference for the original scheme was not likely to commend them to the opponents of rent rebates, and their policy was gradually changed in response to electoral pressure. The Conservative dilemma was similar to the one they were to face over comprehensive education: they could only gain support in the marginal wards by adopting policies contrary to the interests of their traditional supporters. In both cases the siren call of the marginal voter was seductive enough to cause a shift in policy. By the 1968 elections they were promising to abolish the adult occupier surcharge, and to reduce the rent increases payable by tenants on the pre-war council estates where most of the agitation was centred.

The council tenants provided most of the public excitement during the 1967 local elections in Sheffield. In wards with a predominance of council housing there were boisterous election meetings attended in some instances by several hundred people— a very unusual occurrence. At the same time the Arbourthorne Tenants' Association, on the advice of the committee members who were also members of the Trades and Labour Council, was seeking to widen its support. At the end of April the Tenants' Association invited trade union branches to support their opposition to the rent rebate scheme. A number of trade union organizations responded to this appeal, and loaned about £50 to the tenants' associations to enable them to hire the City Hall for a mass meeting on 7 May—four days before polling day. The bulk of the money came from the Amalgamated Engineering Union whose local leadership contained many

---

[32] The 1967 local elections in Sheffield are discussed in Chapter 7. The results are analysed in my article, 'The Electoral Response to a Multi-vote Ballot', *Political Studies*, XVI, 2 (June 1968).

Communists. About a thousand tenants from most of the council estates in Sheffield attended the City Hall meeting. The trade union representatives were not allowed to speak; the tenants made it clear that they wished to conduct their own campaign without embarrassing political commitments. Resolutions were passed at the meeting calling upon the council to withdraw the scheme, and to allow representatives of the tenants' associations to sit on the housing committee which determined their rents. The meeting also resolved to constitute a federation of tenants' associations in Sheffield, and to encourage the establishment of associations on every estate in Sheffield. A mass petition against the scheme was to be sent to the Minister for Housing and Local Government.

The tenants' associations were not alone in seeking the aid of the minister. The Trades and Labour Council opposition had been subdued by the electoral necessity of presenting a common front with their Labour group colleagues, but they had not been inactive. The day before the election it was announced that the Housing Minister, Mr. Anthony Greenwood, had agreed to meet a deputation from the Trades and Labour Council to discuss the rent rebate scheme. The deputation was to be led by the late Mr. Richard Winterbottom, Member of Parliament for Brightside, who had been seeking such a meeting for some time, and it included Mr. Youle. The announcement, as would be expected from its timing, was not particularly critical of the Labour group, but the group leadership were nevertheless annoyed at the Trades and Labour Council for going 'over their heads' to the minister.

It was clear that once the election was over the Trades and Labour Council would not be so restrained in their criticism of the rent rebate scheme. The deputation to Mr. Greenwood urged the minister to freeze the scheme until a satisfactory alternative was produced.[33] The executive of the Trades and Labour Council still maintained that they had agreed to a rent rebate scheme in principle, and that they were concerned only about 'anomalies' in the version adopted by the city council, but many delegates were far more critical than this moderate stance would suggest.[34]

The tenants were also intensifying their campaign and associations were mushrooming on estates all over Sheffield. Shiregreen Tenants' Association, for example, which was formed at the

[33] *The Star* (Sheffield), 17 May 1967.   [34] *The Star* (Sheffield,) 24 May 1967.

beginning of May, had a membership of 1,500 by 15 May and 2,000 less than a week later.[35] The Shiregreen Association proposed to withhold the payment of all rent increases except for a nominal shilling and it was rapidly supported by other associations. In the space of three weeks the tenants' associations had become a major political force and the Labour group began to make conciliatory noises. Alderman Ironmonger announced that the scheme might be reconsidered in the light of the implications of the Government White Paper on the period following the end of severe economic restraint,[36] and on 17 May spoke of 'anomalies' that had come to light during the election campaign.[37] On 22 May it was announced that Alderman Dyson was to relinquish the chairmanship of the Housing Management Committee, and return to the chairmanship of the Transport Committee. He had recently broken his leg, but it was widely believed that his withdrawal was prompted by political rather than health reasons. The Labour group were willing to temporize.

On 31 May the deputation from the Trades and Labour Council met the parliamentary secretary—the minister was called away because of a Middle East crisis—and received a more favourable response than they could have hoped for. They 'learned that it was the Government's intention to publish its own guide lines on rent rebates at the end of June, and Mr. Mellish [the parliamentary secretary] said that he hoped Sheffield would consider these proposals before bringing into operation their own scheme. In view of the operative date of 3 July set for introduction of the city's rent rebate scheme, he felt that this might justify a deferment'.[38] Alderman Ironmonger considered that the minister had been most 'discourteous' in allowing knowledge of the impending circular to come to the city council second-hand from an unofficial deputation,[39] and he instructed the Town Clerk to write to the minister for official information. A letter from the minister arrived on the day that the Trades and Labour Council deputation met representatives of the Labour group to report on their visit to London. Later that day (5 June) the full Labour group decided to defer the introduction of the rent rebate scheme for three

---

[35] *The Star* (Sheffield), 19 May 1967.
[36] *The Star* (Sheffield), 11 May 1967.
[37] *The Star* (Sheffield), 17 May 1967.
[38] *Sheffield Forward*, July 1967.
[39] *Morning Telegraph*, 6 June 1967.

months. The deferment was confirmed at the meeting of the city council on 7 June when the Conservatives voted against the deferment of a scheme which they had previously condemned. Alderman Hebblethwaite maintained that 'whatever scheme [was] introduced there would still be anomalies. Even if it was deferred for twelve months or twenty-four months a start had to be made. . . .'[40]

The tenants' associations became increasingly vocal during the frantic political activity between the local elections and the deferment of the scheme. They lobbied most of the important meetings that took place and over 500 people were outside the Town Hall when the Trades and Labour Council deputation met the representatives of the Labour group. There was a strong contrast between the reaction of Labour leaders on this occasion: Alderman Ironmonger received a delegation of five tenants and listened to their protest; Alderman Dyson argued on the pavement and accused one of the tenants of repeating 'a Communist cliché'. Immediately after this insult fifty tenants forced their way into the Town Hall and had to be ejected by the police. The leader of the five who saw Alderman Ironmonger, on the other hand, said 'I feel a little happier now we have seen him'.[41] Mr. Maris, who made this comment, was later to support the 'democratic' tenants' federation who rejected the Communist influence in the parent body.

The most contentious part of the rent scheme was the adult occupiers' surcharge, commonly referred to as the 'lodger tax'. The surcharge was payable by adult children of the tenant and evoked great emotional opposition from tenants who interpreted the proposal as an attack on the unity of the family. This view was expressed very clearly by one of the tenants' leaders, Mr. Alex McLean, when he described the 'lodger tax' as 'the most diabolical scheme I have ever listened to in my life. My son is 21. Now all of a sudden he is not my son any more, he is a lodger'.[42]

The Conservative party at that time (July 1967) was still maintaining the validity of the adult occupier surcharge, but the Trades and Labour Council continued to press its opposition. When it became known in June that fewer people than expected

[40] *Morning Telegraph*, 8 June 1967.
[41] *Morning Telegraph*, 6 June 1967.
[42] *The Star* (Sheffield), 1 July 1967.

would qualify for a rebate,[43] Mr. Vernon Thornes, Secretary to
the Trades and Labour Council, suggested that the money saved
as a consequence should be used to reduce the 'lodger tax'. The
Conservatives described this suggestion as 'absurd', but as a
compromise it undoubtedly appealed to the Labour group.
Amendments to the surcharge were included among a number of
changes in the rent scheme announced during July.[44] The
surcharge became payable by '*bona fide* lodgers and sub-tenants'
only, unless the tenant claimed a rebate. If the parents claimed a
rebate then single children over twenty-one years of age would
pay the surcharge, or such part of it as brought the total payment
to the level of the standard rent. This meant that a concession
was being made to the better paid rather than to the lower paid
tenants, but few people considered this strange. The most vocal
opponents of the rent rebate scheme were naturally those who
would pay rent increases, not those who would benefit from a
rebate; the amendments were intended to allay criticism rather
than to develop principles. The other amendments included a
previous proposal to disregard the first two pounds of a wife's
earnings and certain other forms of income. The total cost to the
scheme of the amendments would be about £250,000.

The ministry circular was published on 30 June and it seemed
to justify the attitude of the Conservatives to the three-month
postponement of the Sheffield scheme. After elaborating the
principles which should support a rent rebate scheme, the
circular outlined a scheme similar to Sheffield's, but apparently
harsher to the tenants, especially with regard to the adult occupier
surcharge. The minister, however, proposed that the standard
rent should be based upon the gross ratable value of the property,
whereas the Sheffield scheme used a multiple of one and a third.
The ministry circular also proposed that the first two pounds of a
wife's earnings should be disregarded. This later proposal was
incorporated into the Sheffield scheme. The differences between
the Sheffield scheme and the proposals made by the minister were
not sufficient to justify any further delay, and the starting date of
the scheme, including the revisions mentioned in the previous
paragraph, remained October 1967.

[43] *Morning Telegraph*, 8 June 1967. The original over-estimate confirmed the doubts
about the accuracy of the results obtained from the questionnaires returned to the
council.
[44] *Morning Telegraph*, 11 July 1967.

T

The Labour group were not alone in seeking to placate the increasing pressure from tenants for amendment or abolition of the rent rebate scheme. At the local elections in May the Labour Party had lost a lot of support in wards affected by the scheme. The Communist candidates had trebled their vote, and the Conservatives had come within one council seat of controlling the local authority for the first time since 1932. The Conservatives were convinced that they could win in 1968, but to do so they needed to win seats in traditional Labour strongholds. At the end of July they produced an alternative rent scheme to help them in their task.[45] There were two main features of this scheme. First, there was to be no adult occupier surcharge. This represented a complete reversal of the previous policy of the Conservative group; it was less than a month since a similar proposal by Mr. Thornes had been described as 'absurd'. Secondly, a distinction would be made between pre-war and post-war houses. The standard rent of the former would be 1·1 times the gross ratable value and of the latter 1·4 times the gross ratable value. Under the Labour scheme the rents of the older, and lower rental, houses were to increase, while the rents of the newer, and higher rental, houses were to come down. The Conservatives felt this to be unjust, and their proposals produced an average increase of about five shillings a week for both types of houses. The Conservative proposals received a sympathetic response from several of the tenants' associations, which were strongest on the older estates, and one Labour councillor, Mr. George Wilson, supported them in the council chamber.[46] The Labour majority, however, ensured that the proposals were defeated.

In a period of nine months from November 1966, the Labour group had introduced amendments to the original scheme supported by Alderman Dyson that would reduce the revenue obtained by over £600,000, but the tenants' associations were still determined to get the scheme withdrawn. As the date approached for the implementation of the scheme the tenants' associations prepared to call for a 'rent strike' by their members. By withholding a part of his rent a tenant becomes liable to eviction, and the tenants' associations made extensive plans to

[45] Details of the scheme are given in *The Star* (Sheffield), 1 August 1967.
[46] *Morning Telegraph*, 3 August 1967. Two years later, after the rumpus had subsided, Councillor Wilson became deputy chairman of the Housing Committee.

prevent selective evictions that would destroy the morale of their members. The Shiregreen Tenants' Association, for example, proposed that each tenant should pay a quarter of his proposed rent increase to the association, which would use the money to pay the legal fees for the defence of any member threatened with eviction. This idea was elaborated by the Arbourthorne Tenants' Association at a meeting held a fortnight before the start of the scheme. At this meeting Mr. Nick Howard began by assuring the tenants that the corporation would not evict anyone. The reason he gave was that the council had not enough temporary accommodation to fulfil their statutory duty to house the homeless, and they would not dare add to this problem by their own action. To guard against any individual cases of victimization a steward would be appointed in every street to keep the tenants' committee in close contact with the tenants. Every tenant was urged to pay the existing rent plus one shilling of any increase demanded. The balance between the amount paid and the new rent should be saved, or handed to the association for deposit in a special account. In the event of a member being summoned a solicitor would immediately be engaged and the court appearance would be made the occasion of a demonstration of solidarity by corporation tenants from all over the city. The money held back would be available for an emergency, such as having to pay the arrears of rent. Mr. Howard concluded, however, by saying that he felt the council would have to climb down in the face of a rent strike by the majority of their tenants.[47] The detailed plans announced by Mr. Howard were not, of course, entirely consistent with his view that the corporation would not dare to evict anyone, but the object was to reassure tenants who were naturally frightened at a risk, however small, of losing their homes.

In addition to preparing for a rent strike, the tenants' associations held a series of meetings on housing estates throughout the city. Hundreds of tenants attended these meetings to listen to representatives of the two main political parties who were invited to give their views on the rent rebate scheme. Both Alderman Ironmonger and Alderman Hebblethwaite attended some of these meetings and they were given a noisy reception before the meetings voted unanimously to support the rent strike.

The rent rebate scheme came into operation on 2 October

[47] *The Star* (Sheffield), 20 September, 1967.

1967, and the rent strike began. The secretary of the Federation of Tenants' Associations expected about half the tenants of the 28,000 pre-war houses to refuse to pay the increases; many of the tenants of post-war houses, on the other hand, would find that their rent had gone down, and he expected only a few hundred, out of 35,000, to join in the protest.[48] In fact these estimates were much too high. In the first few days of the strike the tenants' associations were claiming that three-quarters of the tenants on some estates were refusing to pay, but the housing department denied these claims. After the dispute was over figures were produced, at our request, that supported the department's point of view. Initially about 2,650 of the 66,000 council tenants were withholding rent either partially or wholly. This figure dropped by about 500 each month until the end of January 1968, and became negligible within a further three months.

The city council took the rent strike very calmly. Alderman Ironmonger had warned the tenants that their action was illegal and that 'the law at the time would have to take its course',[49] but he was in no hurry to set the law in motion. The normal procedure of the housing department was to issue a notice to quit when a tenant became four weeks in arrears. For the 'rent rebels' this was interpreted as the *equivalent* of four weeks in arrears, and as most of them were withholding only a few shillings each week it was several months before they became so far in debt. When notices to quit were issued early in 1968 the tenants paid the arrears and no evictions resulted from the rent strike.

After the failure of the Federation of Tenants' Associations to stop the implementation of the rent rebate scheme their internal dissensions came into the open. There was a conflict between the Communists and others who supported 'militant tactics', and those who felt that the rent strike was the limit to which 'direct action' should go. On 17 October the Federation secretary, John Maling, resigned and joined the Labour Party. In a subsequent letter to a local newspaper he gave two main reasons for resigning: 'firstly because of the insistence of the present secretary, supported by his friends, that an extremist be invited to speak on our platform. Secondly, because I realised that the latest rent scheme (subject to any anomalies being dealt with quickly)

---

[48] *The Star* (Sheffield), 25 September 1967.
[48] *The Star* (Sheffield), 13 September 1967.

would be of benefit to old age pensioners and the less affluent'.[50]
His successor as Federation secretary, Mr. Alex McLean, also
came into conflict with the militants, and within a month he was
threatening to resign. Some of the Federation members had begun
to lobby individual councillors at their work or at their homes on
Sundays. The lobbying was of such an extreme nature in the early
part of November that Mr. McLean dissociated the Federation
from these actions. The Labour group reacted strongly against
the attempted intimidation, and Councillor Roberts, chairman
of the Housing Management Committee, was engaged in some
bitter exchanges with tenants' leaders. The majority of the Labour
group decided to attend no further tenants' meetings: the Labour
Whip complained that 'they are using us as political stooges.
We always have to speak first and then we have to sit and endure
vilification and abuse.'[51]

Two of the Labour councillors refused to accept the decision
of their group to boycott tenants' meetings. Councillors Roy
Thwaites and George Wilson continued to attend, and sought to
devise a new rent scheme to end the dispute between the city
council and the tenants.[52] Some of the tenants, including Mr.
McLean, were willing to end the rent strike to give the two councillors a chance to convince the rest of their group, but the majority
of the Federation executive voted to continue although there were
only a thousand tenants still withholding rent.

Within the Labour Party the conflict over the rent rebate
scheme continued. The evenly divided struggle—majorities of
two or three votes were usual in the Trades and Labour Council—
led to further meetings and sub-committees. Overtly these had the
task of investigating 'anomalies' in the scheme, but in reality
they were seeking to re-establish a consensus within the Labour
movement. Throughout 1967 the Trades and Labour Council
were officially opposed to the rent rebate scheme introduced by
the city council, though not opposed to rebate schemes in principle.
Their opposition was not always pushed to the point of an open
clash with the Labour group, but they were constantly taking the
initiative in pressing for revisions of the scheme. At their October
meeting delegates carried, by 26 votes to 24, a resolution calling for

[50] *The Star* (Sheffield), 23 November 1967.
[51] *The Star* (Sheffield), 14 November 1967.
[52] *The Star* (Sheffield), 4 December 1967.

the withdrawal of the rent rebate scheme despite the modifications made after their representations the previous summer. In November the city council made further changes in the scheme that would cost £120,000 a year,[53] but in December the Trades and Labour Council, still not satisfied, resolved to hold an additional political delegates' meeting on Sunday, 7 January 1968, to discuss the rent rebate scheme. Members of the Labour group were 'particularly invited to be present'.

The January meeting was intended to be exploratory and no firm decisions were taken. The chairman of the Trades and Labour Council explained the point of view of the Borough Labour Party, and he was followed by most of the leading protagonists in the dispute. Speeches were made by Aldermen Lewis and Dyson, Mr. Youle and Mr. Howard, and many other representatives of trade unions and local Labour parties, including several councillors and members of tenants' associations. In his reply to the discussion at the end of the meeting, Alderman Ironmonger promised that the rate contribution to the Housing Account would not diminish as a consequence of the rent rebate scheme. He thought also that it would be possible to look again at the details of the scheme when it came up for review in a few weeks' time. He pointed out that he had never turned away a tenants' deputation, but they must realize the difficulties caused for the city if houses were to be built at a time of high interest changes.[54]

The moderate attitude taken by Alderman Ironmonger at the meeting was typical of his approach throughout the controversy. As leader of the Labour group he was obviously concerned to reunite the various wings of his party even if certain aspects of the rebate scheme had to be changed in the process. Alderman Ironmonger was assisted in the political task of seeking an acceptable compromise by the Secretary to the Trades and Labour Council. Mr. Thornes, *ex officio*, also sat on the executive of the Labour group, and he kept communications open between the

---

[53] *Morning Telegraph*, 2 November 1967.

[54] The pound was devalued on 18 November 1967 and Bank Rate rose to 8 per cent. In December 1967, the Sheffield rent increases were referred to the Prices and Incomes Board together with those of other local authorities, but when it reported the following May, the Sheffield increases were found to be within the limits recommended. National Board for Prices and Incomes, Report No. 62, *Increases in Rents of Local Authority Housing*, Cmnd. 3604 (H.M.S.O. 1968).

two bodies even when their official policies were opposed. At one stage he even claimed to be a member of a sub-committee of the Labour group in his 'personal capacity' to avoid difficult questions of allegiance. The presence, within the leadership, of men prepared to compromise for the sake of unity with their colleagues undoubtedly helped the Labour party to avoid the worst consequences of their political schism.

The divisions within the Federation of Tenants' Associations resulted in an open split in January 1968. Mr. McLean resigned the secretaryship, complaining of 'Communist domination',[55] and led five of the thirteen tenants' associations to form a Democratic Federation that would not be run by 'anyone engaged in active party politics'.[56] He was joined by Mr. Wilfred Maris, the former chairman of the original federation, and Mrs. Mary Macdonald, the woman who had helped organize the first meeting of housewives on Arbourthorne estate. The new federation called off the rent strike as far as their members were concerned,[57] and sought a meeting with Alderman Ironmonger. Mr. McLean promised that 'this time we will listen to what the council has to say and not be obstructive'.[58] The original federation accused the breakaway leaders of becoming 'stooges and informers to the council',[59] and relations between the two groups became even more bitter as the rent strike petered out.

The policy of the Democratic Federation was to negotiate with the city council while preparing to nominate their own candidates in the local elections if the rent scheme was not altered to their satisfaction. It was the readiness to nominate their own candidates that had provided the occasion for the split with the original federation. The Communists were opposed to independent tenants' candidates, and one or two of their members who held office in tenants' associations were prospective party candidates. Mr. Wilkinson, the secretary of the local Communist party, explained that they would not 'hide behind either the tenants' movement, or any other organisation',[60] but the Democratic leaders claimed

[55] *Morning Telegraph*, 19 January 1968.
[56] *Morning Telegraph*, 22 January 1968. Later the Democratic Federation was supported by seven tenants' associations. *The Star* (Sheffield), 24 January 1968.
[57] *The Star* (Sheffield), 28 January 1968.
[58] *Morning Telegraph*, 22 January 1968.
[59] *Morning Telegraph*, 28 February 1968.
[60] *The Star* (Sheffield), 2 February 1968.

that the Communists were trying to obtain the votes of tenants who would prefer a 'non-political' candidate.[61]

The Democratic Federation was at first optimistic about the results of its policy. After the meeting with Alderman Iron-monger, Mr. Maris commented: 'It has been the best meeting that we have had. We have achieved far more than we would have done with a march or a physical demonstration.'[62] But the optimism was short-lived. On 19 February Alderman Ironmonger announced that the Labour group had decided not to change its rent rebates system; government directives associated with cuts in expenditure had made such changes impossible.[63] The tenants' associations were furious. Mr. McLean said: 'It's war all over again',[64] and announced that the Democratic Federation would definitely support their own candidates in the local elections. Mr. Howard announced that he would contest a forthcoming parliamentary by-election if council house tenants would support him.[65] Apparently the money for the deposit was not forthcoming, for no tenants' candidate intervened when the by-election took place.

At the May local elections three tenants' candidates and eleven Communist candidates were nominated in addition to those of the major parties. The most successful tenants' candidate, Mrs. Macdonald, received over 600 votes; and while the Communist vote fell from the high point of the previous year, it was still much higher than the usual vote the party could expect. The Conservatives won twenty of the twenty-seven wards, and assumed control of the city council.[66]

The failure of the Labour party was due in part to the dissatisfaction felt by the council tenants for the rent rebate scheme, and in August 1968, a new scheme was introduced by the victorious Conservatives. The standard rent for the pre-war houses was reduced, and that for the post-war houses increased. In addition, the qualification for a rebate was related to the 'principal wage-earner' in the family and not to the tenant. In most cases, of course, the two would coincide. These changes did not provoke the same

---

[61] *Morning Telegraph*, 19 January 1968.
[62] *Morning Telegraph*, 2 February 1968.
[63] *The Star* (Sheffield), 20 February 1968.
[64] Ibid.
[65] *The Star* (Sheffield), 24 February 1968.
[66] This election is discussed in more detail in Chapter 7.

outcry that had accompanied the Labour scheme. The changes in standard rent appeared favourable to the majority of the organized tenants, and the principal wage-earner clause affected only a small number of families.[67] There were protests from the new estates; a Conservative leader was abused at a tenants meeting;[68] but there were no rent strikes or mass lobbying. The controversy had exhausted itself. Labour Party members campaigned against the scheme on the newer council estates, several of which were in marginal areas, and promised to abolish the principal wage-earner clause;[69] but when they returned to power in 1969 they were understandably in no hurry to re-open the old wounds.

The interviews conducted in preparation for the present study were undertaken at the height of the rent rebate controversy in the winter of 1967–8. We are able, therefore, to give an indication of the opinions both of the electorate and of the councillors. Over three-quarters of the councillors agreed with the introduction of the scheme compared with half the electorate. Support was stronger in the Conservative group than in the Labour group, and we may suspect that several of the Labour councillors who

Table 10.1
Attitudes towards Sheffield City Council's decision to introduce rent rebate scheme

	Total		Cons. supporters		Lab. supporters	
Base	Cllrs. 108	Electors 584	Cllrs. 48	Electors 198	Cllrs. 59	Electors 300
	%	%	%	%	%	%
Very strongly agree	56	31	67	41	47	23
Quite strongly agree	23	19	21	20	25	19
Neither agree nor disagree	2	7	0	6	3	8
Quite strongly disagree	6	11	4	11	7	12
Very strongly disagree	10	30	6	21	14	36
Don't know	3	2	1	1	3	2

Note: The percentages may not add to one hundred owing to rounding.
Sources: Survey of Sheffield Electorate and Survey of Sheffield City Council.

[67] The Conservative scheme was intended to produce the same amount of rent income as the previous scheme, but in fact the total paid out in rebates was considerably reduced. In January 1969, therefore, the City Treasurer could announce an increase in net rent income over the original estimate.

[68] *The Star* (Sheffield), 13 July 1968.

[69] The specimen scheme circulated by the Labour Party Research Department in July 1967, had included a principal wage-earner clause.

'quite strongly agreed' were reluctant supporters who had been persuaded by the concessions made by their leadership in the early stages of the dispute.

Among the electorate opinions on the rent rebate scheme were evenly divided. The Conservative supporters were inclined to favour the scheme and the Labour supporters to oppose it, but both views were substantially represented in each party. Indeed the distribution of opinion among manual workers who supported the Conservative Party was almost identical to the distribution among Labour supporters. The divisions over the rent rebate scheme become much sharper, however, when the respondents are analysed by the type of property they occupy. Nearly three-quarters of the owner-occupiers were in favour of the scheme, and two-thirds of the council tenants were opposed. The private tenants were evenly divided. They were, in the main, less prosperous than the owner-occupiers, and many were waiting for council

Table 10.2

Attitudes towards Sheffield rent rebate scheme by type of accommodation

		Type of accommodation		
Base	Total 584	Own property 268	Private tenant 110	Council tenant 201
	%	%	%	%
Very strongly agree	31	47	25	12
Quite strongly agree	19	24	22	11
Neither agree nor disagree	7	6	8	7
Quite strongly disagree	11	7	13	16
Very strongly disagree	30	15	27	52
Don't know	2	1	5	1

Note: Five respondents lived in other types of accommodation. The percentages may not add to one hundred owing to rounding.
Source: Survey of Sheffield Electorate.

accommodation to become available as their existing homes were demolished. The rent rebate scheme would give the poorer of these applicants a wider choice of future accommodation.

Tenants' associations are one of the few available examples of spontaneous mass involvement in political affairs. The threat to one's home, either through eviction or through a demand for increased rent, provokes a natural and emotional response that causes normally reserved people to undertake public activities that are quite foreign to them. Frequently the temper of the tenants is so aroused that local authorities alter their policies to placate the angry electorate. Professor Frank Bealey noticed this in Newcastle-under-Lyme,[70] and in Colchester, my home town, a rent rebate scheme was withdrawn in 1955 after tenants' agitation which led to a political change of control on the town council. Tenants' associations are less effective at a national level: at the height of a local campaign they may be persuaded to lobby their Member of Parliament, or to write to the minister, but such activity is out of character. Tenants' associations are essentially parochial organizations; they are based on one estate, and send delegates to form federations with similar groups in other parts of the city. A tenants' association is the local community acting in defence of their homes, and community feeling, as we have shown, is restricted to one's immediate environment. This is why attempts by local political activists to 'widen the struggle' into an attack on their political enemies, or the 'capitalist system' in general, usually result in failure and disagreement within the tenants' movement. It also explains why the spontaneous eruption of feeling that can shake a city council is not a noticeable influence on national housing policy. Even the Rent Act, 1957, produced little response from tenants, though it was greeted by the Labour Party with great verbal fury.[71]

The tenants' movement in Sheffield in 1967–8 illustrates these general points. The early attempts of people already politically active to arouse opposition to the *possibility* of a rent rebate scheme met with only limited success. There was a flurry of protest at the council questionnaires, but the response of 58 per cent was good for a postal questionnaire, even if legitimate doubts can be held about its validity as a sample. When the details of the proposed scheme became known, however, there was an immediate attempt at organization by the housewives on Arbourthorne estate, and the tenants became more responsive to the approaches made by politically active outsiders. The protest movement began slowly, reaching one climax as the date for the implementation of the

[70] Bealey, Blondel, and McCann, *Constituency Politics*, pp. 381–2.
[71] Malcolm Joel Barnett, *The Politics of Legislation: The Rent Act of 1957*, pp. 123–6, but see also p. 242 where he suggests that a 'tenants' lobby' emerged after the Rent Act, and that it was consulted by the Milner Holland Committee in 1964.

scheme became near, dying away during the summer months after the postponement, and reaching a second, more violent climax when the scheme actually started.

There were three strands in the opposition to the rent rebate scheme in Sheffield. At times these overlapped, but the three positions were quite distinct; co-operation between people holding these different views was always a matter of tension, and never an occasion for absorption. First, there were the 'non-political tenants'. They were opposed to the rent rebate scheme root and branch, and they were willing to oppose the Labour Party or to support the Conservative Party if such tactics seemed to offer the changes they demanded. The strongest support for this position came from the estates where the rent increases were highest—even if the rents were still relatively low compared to the post-war estates—and it is difficult to escape the conclusion that much of this opposition was against the *increases* as such, rather than against the social principles upon which they were demanded. In the speeches of this group there were references to the iniquity of taking more rent from a man who had worked hard to improve his earnings either by working overtime or by obtaining a better job.[72] After the split in the Sheffield Tenants' Federation, the 'non-political tenants' organized in the Democratic Federation complained to Alderman Ironmonger about the false returns which some tenants were submitting to the council. Evasion of this kind was not regarded by the Democratic Federation as a protest against the rebate scheme, but as a dishonest attempt to place a still heavier burden on other tenants. It was this attitude that led the Communists to describe the Democratic Federation as 'informers'.

The Communists formed the second main strand in the opposition to the rent rebate scheme. Their influence was minimal at first, but gradually increased as the tenants' organizations became more formal. The Communists tried to link the Sheffield tenants' associations with the National Federation of Tenants' Associations which had strong backing from the Communist Party nationally. They also tried to show that the policy of the Sheffield City Council was a result of national policies that favoured the capital-

---

[72] The Newcastle-under-Lyme study found that the leadership of a tenants' movement to oppose council rent increases 'consisted entirely of "white-collar" workers or their wives'. Bealey, Blondel, and McCann, op. cit., p. 382.

ists and money-lenders. This meant that on occasion the Communists were ready to be more conciliatory towards the city council than the 'non-political tenants'. They proposed, for example, that a joint protest against high interest rates for housing should be made to the government, and in other ways tried to create a common front between the Labour group and the tenants. They also refused, for somewhat different reasons, to support independent tenants' candidates in the local elections.

The International Socialist group had an affinity to both the Communist and the 'non-political' opposition. They were concerned to link the tenants' movement to a general struggle against capitalism, but they stressed the importance of the spontaneous organizations developed by the tenants themselves. They opposed both Labour and Communist attempts to 'institutionalize' the tenants' movement and supported independent tenants' candidates. Although very small numerically, this group gave some important help to the tenants' organizations, particularly in the early stages of the dispute, but there is no sign that the leaders of the 'non-political tenants' responded by accepting the wider objectives of International Socialism.

Both the 'non-political tenants' and the extreme left were powerful forces within the tenants' movement itself; the third strand in the opposition to the rent rebate scheme came from within the Labour Party, and it did not have a strong influence within the tenants' associations. Indeed, spokesmen for this group were, on occasion, subject to severe barracking when they spoke at tenants' meetings. Their association with the Labour group, and even more the acceptance by most councillors of the group whip on this issue, made the tenants distrustful of those who claimed to be opposing the scheme in the inner councils of the Labour Party. The mainstream of the 'Labour opposition' believed that housing should be seen as a social service. They accepted, therefore, the arguments that a rent rebate scheme of some sort was needed to provide social justice for the poorer tenants. They disagreed, however, with the view that a rebate scheme should also be used to restrict the rate contribution to the housing revenue account, and they opposed the 'lodger tax' and some details of the scheme as implemented. They could not in logic use the emotional cry of 'means test'; although they did so on occasion. They recognized that any rebate scheme must include some assessment of means if it is to avoid the difficulties of the earlier scheme introduced to benefit retirement pensioners.

The opposition to the rent rebate scheme did not succeed in forcing the withdrawal of the scheme, but the alterations made in response to the protests indicated that the tenants' campaign was effective. Both party groups on the city council changed their policy during the course of the dispute. The Labour group made three major revisions to the scheme and these resulted in a rate contribution of over £600,000 to the housing revenue account. The Conservatives changed their mind about the 'lodger tax', and allowed for a rate contribution to the Housing Revenue account. One of their leaders told our interviewer that there were two reasons for these changes in policy. First, the continuing high interest charges made a rate contribution seem reasonable. Secondly, the Conservatives were prepared to concede that their scheme was not politically acceptable to the tenants. The dropping of the 'lodger tax' did not impose a great financial strain upon the scheme, and our informant considered that in this case 'one was prepared to sacrifice principles to political expediency if it only cost a little money. If a lot of money had been involved then it would have been different.'

The tenants produced their effect upon the rent rebate scheme by orthodox political means. The direct action advocated by the 'extreme left' opposition was not supported by a disciplined majority, or even a substantial minority, of the tenants. In these circumstances the rent strike became an inconvenience rather than a challenge to the council, and the mass lobbying of individual councillors was provocative rather than persuasive. The changes to the original scheme were secured by the indirect influence of the tenants both on the struggle within the Labour Party and on the election programme of the Conservatives. Many of the Labour councillors lived in council houses, or were closely associated either in their party or at work with council house tenants. They were under considerable social pressure to oppose a scheme that so many tenants rejected, and they were aware that re-nomination might not be forthcoming for those who continued their support. The chairman of the Housing Management Committee, Mr. Maurice Roberts, lost his council seat in this way. The group leadership complained that it was unethical for prospective candidates to promise ward selection committees that if elected they would oppose the scheme, but members of these committees continued to ask the question—and answers were given. The 'Labour opposition' were able, therefore, to quote the mass pressure of the tenants' associations in support of their demands for amendments to the scheme. In addition the Borough Labour Party, as it struggled to reach an acceptable compromise, could reproach the leadership of the Labour group for pursuing a policy that would lead the party to electoral defeat. The pressure group tactics of the tenants' associations were principally successful, therefore, through their articulation of the views of their members as electors. The political parties changed their policies not because the gardens of their councillors were trampled upon, nor because rents were unpaid, but because the tenants' votes were needed in the crucial marginal elections of 1967 and 1968.

11

The Reform of Local Government

The characteristic result of local government action is seen in such material things as schools, homes, traffic signs and refuse-bins. But the purpose of such action is invariably human happiness. And the action itself is taken by people for people.
Management of Local Government, I, Report, p. xii

LOCAL government is in such flux that no excuse is needed before we attempt to apply the experience of a study of the relationship between political structure and social community, as set out above for one large city, to some speculation about the future. Since things will change anyway, they may as well change for the better. Local government reform is concerned with the twin objectives of efficiency and democracy. The reformers, whatever their other differences, suggest that greater efficiency is unobtainable unless local authorities become larger,[1] but their recommendations have been opposed by those who believe that larger units would destroy the intimate character of local democracy. At a conference of Urban District Councils held near Sheffield, for example, the proposals of the Royal Commission on Local Government were attacked for anticipating '1984 by 1974'. One councillor maintained that the proposals for sixty-one main authorities would create a dictatorial vacuum in which local spirit and initiative would die.[2] Such sentiments were repeated in nearly every district council in the country.

The Sheffield City Council did not share the alarmist views of the smaller authorities: the city was already too large for the inhabitants to identify local authority boundaries with the

[1] The relevant findings of forty-nine government reports published since 1950—forty-three of them since 1960—are summarized in Royal Commission on Local Government in England 1966–9, III, *Research Appendices*, Appendix 9.
[2] *The Derbyshire Times*, 1 August 1969.

community feeling that towns with populations below 60,000 were striving to maintain.[3] The city council, in a statement prepared by the leaders of both parties, welcomed the Royal Commission recommendation to create unitary authorities as the main tier of local government.[4] Sheffield would become part of the largest authority in the country: Sheffield and South Yorkshire, with a population of over one million. The statement expressed a wish by the city council to examine the proposed boundaries; it was understood that a rather smaller authority, with a population around 800,000, was preferred; but in principle they agreed with the Royal Commission. The surrounding local authorities were less enthusiastic, and strongly opposed the dominant position which Sheffield would hold in the proposed authority. The city council also gave general support to the concept of provincial councils, as long as their powers were clearly limited to strategic planning in matters of regional significance, but they rejected completely the Royal Commission's proposals for local councils. We shall return to this point later.

Much of the discussion surrounding the Royal Commission's proposals assumes that the claims of efficiency and democracy are incompatible; but if we consider the purpose of local government then we may understand both objectives to be part of the larger aim of human happiness. The point is made in the quotation at the head of the chapter: we need an institution capable of fulfilling our needs efficiently. It is necessary, therefore, to distinguish three aspects of democracy in discussions about local government reform: first, the efficacy of the institution in administering the needs and wishes of the people; secondly, the degree of control exercised by elected representatives over local administration; and thirdly, the extent to which local people are able to participate in and to be heard on their own local affairs. These three aspects will be considered in turn, with illustrations drawn from the Sheffield experience. We will try to show that if the scale of the top tier needs to be larger than many can still

[3] Royal Commission on Local Government in England 1966–9, I, *Report*, para. 235. The opinion of the Royal Commission is based on their Research Study 9, *Community Attitudes Survey: England*, Table 7, see Table 5.5 above and the surrounding text. Sheffield, of course, retains some of the community characteristics of a smaller urban area. See Chapters 5 and 6.

[4] The full text of the statement, adopted at the September meeting of the city council, is given in *Sheffield Forward*, September 1969.

U

easily accept, yet the scale of the democratic underpinning, or neighbourhood councils, needs to be smaller and more varied than may have been imagined hitherto.

The use of the term 'efficacy' in this context implies rather more than the ability to carry out efficiently the tasks allocated to a local authority. Efficiency is, in any case, a difficult concept to define for an organization with the diffuse objectives of a local authority: we are not concerned solely with the 'output' achieved, but with the performance related to the political choices of the electorate. The constraints implied by the needs of democratic control may lengthen the decision-taking process, but this should not be regarded as a sign of inefficiency: democracy is one of the objectives of the system.

The research studies[5] carried out for the Royal Commission sought to measure the performance of various categories of local authorities, but the difficulties of quantifying the elusive attribute of 'quality' were fully accepted by the Commissioners. The research studies found that the performance of a local authority in some services was related to environmental characteristics, such as the density of population, or the social composition of the area; but they found little statistical relationship between the size of a local authority and its efficiency in carrying out its existing functions. These studies were concerned mainly with the services provided by the major authorities—county councils and county boroughs—but one included material from the district authorities and its results were just as inconclusive.[6] The allegation that the smaller local authorities were inefficient in the provision of the services for which they were responsible was not, therefore, supported by the statistical evidence available to the Royal Commission; but efficiency in this sense is not enough. The research studies were supplemented by the subjective impressions of the inspectors concerned with the quality of local authority education and children's services. Her Majesty's Inspectorate at the Department of Education and Science concluded that the education authorities providing the better service were those with larger

[5] The results of these studies are summarized in Royal Commission on Local Government in England, 1966–9, I, *Report*, at pp. 56–9. See also Research Studies 1, 3, 4, and 5.

[6] Royal Commission on Local Government, Research Study 3, *Economies of Scale in Local Government Services*.

populations; and the Home Office, though not so positive, reached a similar conclusion for the children's service.

For a local authority to be efficacious, rather than efficient, it must be large enough to accept such functions as enable it to meet the wishes of the local electorate. A small district authority may perform efficiently a limited number of functions, with an admirable degree of accessibility to the public, but this is not sufficient. A local authority also needs to be large enough to accept responsibility for its own actions without detailed control from central, or higher tier, authorities. When considered in this way the protestations by the small district authorities that they are large enough to be efficient become less persuasive. They may be efficient, but the limited range of functions with which they are entrusted, and the degree of control to which they are subjected, leaves only a façade of local democracy.

Sheffield County Borough is a powerful local authority, but even so over three-quarters of the council members interviewed in 1968 considered that the government put unnecessary limitations on the freedom of the council. A rather smaller majority thought that the council needed more powers than it already possessed. The Sheffield councillors[7] were more critical of their relationship to the government than were the national sample of

Table 11.1
Councillors' attitudes to existing powers of local authorities

	England and Wales			Sheffield				
				Labour				
	All Councils	County Boroughs	Total	Cttee. Chmn.	Deputies	Others	Total	Cons.
Base	1,235	134	108	20	18	21	59	48
	%	%	%	%	%	%	%	%
Central govt. puts unnecessary limitations on freedom of council	44	55	79	95	50	71	73	87
Council needs more power	43	45	56	75	61	48	61	52

Sources: Survey of Sheffield City Council; and *M.L.G.*, II, *The Local Government Councillor*, Tables 4.23 and 4.24.

[7] Aldermen are included with councillors throughout this chapter unless the context clearly demands otherwise.

councillors interviewed in 1964–5. This may be partly explained by the different years in which the two surveys were undertaken: in 1964–5 the government were still optimistic about the prospects of economic growth providing for an improvement in the social services; by 1967 the local authorities were being restrained by the demands of economic stringency. In addition, there is a feeling in a great city that its citizens are capable of running their own affairs without government interference: that they should be, as one councillor put it, 'almost autonomous' in their dealings with the central authorities.

The Conservatives were more critical of the central government —it was, of course, a Labour government—than the Labour councillors; but this distinction disappeared when the views of the committee chairmen were considered. The chairmen were all members of the Labour group, but only one did not consider that the government imposed unnecessary limitations on the freedom of the council. The committee chairmen were also more inclined than their back-bench colleagues to believe that the council needed more powers than it already possessed. Increased powers were wanted to cover most areas of local responsibility; many of the councillors referred to the petty restrictions imposed on traffic management decisions, and there were complaints about the detailed control exercised over loan sanctions. The councillors also wanted a greater degree of freedom to control land use within the city, and to implement policies to attract new industries. In short, the majority of the Sheffield City Council considered that the corporation was capable of running the affairs of the city without the restrictive influence of the *ultra vires* rule. The government, as one Labour alderman complained, 'think they are the only people with any competence'.

The councillors' wish for a greater degree of independence may be satisfied in the larger authorities which the Royal Commission propose, but these will involve a change in the councillors' attitudes towards their public responsibilities; and also the adopting of a managerial approach to executive control of broad policy decisions to replace their present obsession with administrative detail. Such a change in attitudes raises important questions for the councillors, and we asked for their opinions on two of the major recommendations of the Committee on the Management of Local Government (Maud Committee).

Table 11.2
Purposes for which Sheffield councillors consider the council needs more power

Base—councillors considering council needs more power	Total 61	Lab. 36	Cons. 25
	No. of mentions	*No. of mentions*	*No. of mentions*
Housing	12	5	7
Roads	14	3	11
Education	6	2	4
Hospitals	4	3	1
Building	3	2	1
Rating	17	11	6
To take major decisions (general)	26	18	8
Others	19	11	8

Note: Some councillors mentioned more than one purpose.
Source: Survey of Sheffield City Council.

A majority of the councillors agreed that the number of council committees should be considerably reduced: the Conservatives were overwhelmingly in favour, and a majority of the Labour

Table 11.3
Attitudes of Sheffield councillors to Maud Committee proposals

(a) *Number of council committees should be considerably reduced*

		Labour				
Base	Total 108	Cttee. Chrmn. 20	Deputies 18	Others 21	Total 59	Cons. 48
	%	%	%	%	%	%
Very strongly agree	43	30	0	5	12	79
Quite strongly agree	16	20	17	10	15	17
Neither agree nor disagree	9	20	22	10	17	0
Quite strongly disagree	13	5	28	33	22	2
Very strongly disagree	19	20	33	43	32	2
Don't know	1	5	0	0	2	0

Note: The percentages may not add to one hundred owing to rounding.
Source: Survey of Sheffield City Council.

group were opposed.[8] Once again the committee chairmen were more inclined to favour reform than their back-bench colleagues. The Labour councillors who opposed the Maud Committee

[8] The committee structure of Sheffield City Council is discussed in Ch. 3.

recommendation mentioned committees that had been replaced by sub-committees, with the result that business took even longer to conclude. They stressed that their aim was the efficient trans-action of business within the council, and that this was not necessarily related to the number of committees: it is, of course, related to the business that the councillors choose to conduct.

Table 11.4
Attitude of Sheffield councillors to Maud Committee proposals

(b) *Councillors should leave the day-to-day running of affairs in the hands of officers and confine themselves to broad policy decisions*

	Labour					Cons.
	Total	Cttee. Chrmn.	Deputies	Others	Total	
Base	108	20	18	21	59	48
	%	%	%	%	%	%
Very strongly agree	46	25	33	14	24	73
Quite strongly agree	16	30	17	5	17	15
Neither agree nor disagree	6	5	6	10	7	6
Quite strongly disagree	4	5	6	5	5	2
Very strongly disagree	27	35	33	67	46	4
Don't know	1	0	6	0	2	0

Note: The percentages may not add to one hundred owing to rounding.
Source: Survey of Sheffield City Council.

A majority of the councillors accepted that councillors should confine themselves to broad policy decisions and leave the day-to-day running of affairs in the hands of officers; the majority included nearly all the Conservative group but thirty out of the fifty-nine Labour councillors were against this proposal. A polarity of opinion within the Labour group was noticeable, and some members of the group, particularly among the senior chairmen of committees, were very strongly in agreement with the Maud proposal: 'one of the weaknesses of elected representatives,' replied one alderman, 'is their tendency to tell the park-keeper how to cut grass'. Other members of the Labour group, including a few of the leaders and most of the back-benchers, were vehem-ently opposed to the Maud proposal. One of the most experienced members of the Labour group thought that 'the Maud Committee is falling into the trap of streamlining because of a shortage of time. If you become a public servant you must find the time necessary to do the job.' He went on to suggest that 'the public representative must be concerned with day-to-day administration to keep in touch with people'.[9] Such an attitude imposes an unnecessary constraint upon the number of people who can accept nomination for council service: few people can spare two or three days a week for voluntary public service.

There was a widespread feeling within the Labour group that detailed knowledge was necessary if councillors were to control the implementation of policy; and a few councillors were critical of the ability, or willingness, of the chief officers to carry out Labour policies without constant supervision. The desire to control in detail the work of the officers is not solely a class-war phobia; it has its roots in the nature of political responsibility. A Conservative councillor, who was also critical of the Maud proposal to leave more administrative decisions in the hands of officers, considered that it was a mistake to draw analogies from industrial organizations: 'compared with industry,' he said, 'we in politics need a considerable amount of detail to find out what is going on'. There were suggestions during their year of office, 1968–9, that some Conservative chairmen found difficulty in implementing their policies. Councillor Martyn Atkinson spoke to a local newspaper of 'a tremendous amount of friction [with officers]. We were putting forward new policies and some were policies they did not agree with. In fact, some of the policies we were seeking to change had been devised by the officers.'[10] Councillor Atkinson also suffered from a conflict between the demands of his work as an accountant and his responsibilities as chairman of the Housing Committee, and during the year he gave up his job. He believed that to run the Housing Department properly the chairman would need to be there all day.[11] Councillor Atkinson was not a typical member of the Conservative group: a few months after the interview we have quoted he was complaining of the hostile attitude adopted towards him by other members of his party,[12] however, the group leader himself accused the

[9] The amount of time devoted to council work by councillors is discussed in Ch. 8.

[10] *The Star* (Sheffield), 13 May 1969. The chairman of the Sheffield branch of National and Local Government Officers 'refuted some of these sweeping statements' in a letter a few days later. *The Star* (Sheffield), 21 May 1969.

[11] *The Star* (Sheffield), 22 August 1968 and 13 May 1969.

[12] *The Star* (Sheffield), 5 September 1969. He subsequently left the Conservatives to join the Liberal Party.

Medical Officer of Health of making comments in his annual
report that reflected upon the political decisions taken by the
Conservatives during their year of office.[13]

The response of the Sheffield city councillors indicates that the
reform of local authority administration is not a straightforward
matter for management consultants (see Chapter 3). The need to
maintain the element of democratic control adds complications
to an already difficult administrative problem; and the chairmen
of committees are neither full-time, as are their counterparts in
Whitehall, nor as professional as the chairman of a business concern. Nevertheless, the views of many Labour councillors showed
a worrying confusion between personal intervention in administrative details and the duties of their representative function. The
local councillor, as we noticed in Chapter 8, fulfils a dual function:
he or she must both execute local policy and be a tribune of his or
her constituents; but many councillors do not realize that a different approach is needed as they exercise each of these responsibilities. In their role as executive members of committees, the
councillors should be concerned with debating the broad policy
choices open to the corporation; they should also examine
critically the criteria upon which the officers recommend one
course of action rather than another; there is no need for them
to choose the colour of the curtains at a children's home, and it is
often positively harmful for them to interfere with the professional
decisions of social workers.[14] In their role as representatives of
their *individual* constituents, however, the councillors must be
able to question any administrative or professional decision taken
within the local authority, and to obtain information from the
relevant department. When these two roles are confused there is a
danger that neither is fulfilled: a mass of detail on an agenda may
cloud the policy decisions that need to be taken, without providing
the greater openness in local administration that is needed in the
interests of democratic control.

Larger units of local government may, if other complementary
reforms are not considered at the same time, make it more difficult
for people to participate in local political affairs. The administrative centre of the local authority could be many miles away, and

[13] *Morning Telegraph*, 28 August 1969.
[14] Examples of the work undertaken by local authority committees are given in
M.L.G., V, *Local Government Administration in England and Wales*, Ch. 9.

each councillor might represent ten thousand constituents. For these reasons, the Royal Commission supplemented their proposals for unitary authorities with local councils whose 'most important function . . . will be the duty to voice the opinions and wishes of the local community'.[15] Local councils would also have the power to provide certain local amenities and services if the local people were willing to meet the cost.

The local councils proposed by the Royal Commission are too ambiguous to be successful: they would include councils for all the existing urban authority areas, from the smallest towns to the largest free-standing city, as well as the rural parishes. The towns and cities would retain their mayors and lord mayors, and rather more of their functions than might at first be expected.[16] The local council would provide amenities that might include theatres, museums, swimming baths, and conference halls. Other powers that might be delegated by the main authorities could include car parks, markets, sea defence works, but not 'such things as airports'.[17] It seems odd, after the discussion of the Sheffield airport controversy in Chapter 9, to be reminded that a local council without executive powers would not be responsible for a service as expensive as a local airport. Local councils could also be associated with the management, and indeed the building, of council housing; and with certain other services if they could persuade the main council to agree.

Let us consider, as an example, the position of the Lord Mayor and City Council of Sheffield—the former style and title may be retained—should the Royal Commission reforms be implemented. Within the existing city boundaries the annual expenditure on parks, cemeteries, and allotments is about one million pounds; on art galleries and museums it is about £15,000; and on baths, wash-houses, and conveniences it is about £300,000. A city of this size cannot be treated as a parish council. Any attempt to do so will hinder, rather than assist, the development of genuine local councils based upon neighbourhood units.[18]

---

[15] Royal Commission on Local Government in England 1966–9, I, *Report*, para. 381.

[16] Details are taken from the Royal Commission on Local Government in England 1966–9, I, *Report*, Ch. 9.

[17] Ibid., para. 384.

[18] Lord Redcliffe-Maud, commenting upon my earlier criticism of the Royal Commission's proposals, said that he did not find the idea of a new-style Sheffield City Council at all alarming, nor inconsistent with the unitary principle. He quoted the

Mr. Senior, in his memorandum of dissent,[19] criticized the Royal Commission's proposals for local councils and substituted the concept of a common council. He wrote: '. . . it is essential that the people represented by a common council should in fact form a real community—not just one of the functional social entities of various scales that are united only by their objective community of interest,[20] but an organic social unit whose individual members can really feel they belong to it. Such units do not exist everywhere. [But where they do, their] key function . . . must be to act as a sounding-board for community opinion—to focus the sense of the local community, whether in protest against, in agitation for, or in consultation about anything that affects its social or environmental well-being, and to bring that consensus to bear on the responsible decision-makers, whether they be members of a local authority or any other agency, public or private.'[21] That expresses it exactly; but it does not follow that the major recommendations of the Royal Commission are invalidated by these criticisms of their proposals for local councils.

The concept of a representative council at neighbourhood level is based on a secure social foundation. The respondents to the surveys discussed in Chapter 5 spoke of their home areas in neighbourhood terms, and gave them names that suggested 'villages embedded in a town':[22] the people of Sheffield continue to live in Heeley, Totley, or Handsworth; the local government

---

French communes in support of his approach. *Local Government Chronicle*, No. 5354 (11 October 1969), p. 1925. He was referring to a series of articles reprinted from that journal in a booklet edited by Geoffrey Smith, *Redcliffe-Maud's Brave New England*. In the subsequent White Paper (published while this study was in the press) the government rejected 'the [Royal] Commission's suggestion that the larger local councils should play a part in the provision of major services', but agreed 'that for overriding practical reasons local councils must be based initially on the areas of existing local authorities'. *Reform of Local Government in England*, Cmnd. 4276, paras. 49 and 53.

[19] Royal Commission on Local Government in England, 1966–9, II, *Memorandum of Dissent by Mr. D. Senior*, Ch. 4.

[20] See the discussion of community in Chapter 1.

[21] Ibid. paras. 427 and 428.

[22] This phrase was used in evidence presented to the Royal Commission on Local Government in Greater London, 1957–60, by one section of the Greater London Group at the London School of Economics. That Royal Commission rejected the proposal for 'urban parishes with limited executive and certain advisory functions' on the grounds that they would suffer from two defects that are inevitably attached to a 'body that can express views but has no responsibility for carrying them into effect': they would become irresponsible and frustrated. Cmnd. 1164, paras. 737 and 739.

units created in the past hundred years have done little to change
their allegiances. The redevelopment of the older areas of our
cities, and the greater mobility that accompanies the 'affluent
society', have led to the disintegration of many traditional
communities; but neighbourliness and interest in community
organizations have survived such upheavals, even if the basis of
community feelings is radically different.[23] The community life
of the great working-class housing estates in the Brightside constituency of Sheffield, of the neat nineteenth-century houses in
Walkley, and of the middle-class villas of Dore, varies in its social
origins and in its public manifestations; but in each case it is
conducive to an interest in local affairs.

The enhanced interest that follows from identification with a
home area may not, as we have shown in Table 5.12, extend to a
greater knowledge of the existing political institutions. Community
feeling is a social rather than a political experience; the emphasis
(both by Sheffield councillors and in government reports) upon
involvement in social administration rather than upon political
control at the community level is not misplaced. The fear that
local councillors will become 'irresponsible and frustrated' will
only become justified if local councils assume the character of the
existing district councils: they must be *new* bodies, with a *new*
conception of their functions; and if they are to be in any sense
'communities' they must, as Chapter 5 demonstrates, be on a far
far smaller scale than the Royal Commission envisages, with lines
drawn, as Senior suggests, according to local conditions, whatever
the 'anomalies', not national rules.

Community participation has been a theme in several recent
reports. The Seebohm Committee proposals embodied 'a wider
conception of social service, directed to the well-being of the
whole of the community and not only of social casualties, and
seeing the community it serves as the basis of its authority,
resources and effectiveness'.[24] The committee recognized that the
changes they were suggesting implied 'a belief in the importance of
the maximum participation of individuals and groups in the
community in the planning, organisation and provision of the

---

[23] See Peter Willmott and Michael Young, *Family and Class in a London Suburb*,
Ch. 11.
[24] *Report* of the Committee on Local Authority and Allied Personal Social Services,
Cmnd. 3703, para. 474.

social services. . . .'[25] The importance of action, as distinct from simple information or consultation, was stressed by the Skeffington Committee in their report on methods of securing the participation of the public in the making of development plans; the responsibility for securing such participation was laid on local authorities by the Town and Country Planning Act, 1968. Skeffington suggested that 'participation involves doing as well as talking and there will be full participation only where the public are able to take an active part throughout the plan-making process'.[26]

The Seebohm proposals on participation received less attention than their recommendations for unified social work departments: the struggle between the local health departments and children's departments for dominance obscured the new attitude that Seebohm sought to encourage. The Skeffington Report received a ready response from the many civic societies that had developed during the 1960s; the report might lack the means to harry a stubborn local authority, but at least it improved the standing of these pressure groups. Skeffington's warning that the public should not be thought of 'in terms of the community as it shows itself in organized groups'[27] for fear that an inarticulate majority might be overborne by a vociferous minority received less attention. An example from Sheffield, however, indicates that a mass response can be obtained from a community threatened with extinction by planning, and the sanctions needed can be provided by the electoral system.

At the end of the 1960s Sheffield corporation were considering the redevelopment of Walkley, an area mostly built in the late nineteenth century (see Diagram 2.1). The area included a mixture of properties: some had deteriorated beyond repair, while other houses were enthusiastically maintained by owner-occupiers. The corporation intended to clear and redevelop the area over a period of twenty years. In April 1969, Mr. Geoffrey Green,[28] a young research student who lived on the borders of

[25] *Report* of the Committee on Local Authority and Allied Personal Social Services, Cmnd. 3703, para. 491.

[26] *People and Planning*, Report of the Committee on Public Participation in Planning (H.M.S.O., 1969), para. 5.

[27] Ibid.

[28] Mr. Green acted as my research assistant for one year while the material for the present study was being collected. He had left the local research project before he commenced his political activities, and, naturally, none of the research material was used to assist his campaign.

Walkley, distributed duplicated leaflets asking residents to write to him if they were willing to form an organization to represent their views. He received over seventy letters in reply, and a provisional committee began gathering information and protesting at the lack of consultation between the corporation and the local inhabitants. A few weeks after the leaflets had been distributed, Mr. Green was persuaded to contest the Walkley ward as an Independent candidate in the municipal elections. He received 773 votes, and the Labour candidate unseated the Conservative councillor by the narrow majority of eighteen.[29] Mr. Green's election campaign was remarkable both for the enthusiasm of his supporters and for the responsible tone adopted: there was no demagogy, and no easy promises. His election address consisted of a 2,000-word essay, complete with a map of the area, entitled: 'For more consultation between people and planners'. His election meeting, attended by nearly 300 people, was addressed by an architect and by a town planner from the university who explained the possibilities, and the difficulties, facing the city council.

The vigorous support given to the Walkley Action Group, as Mr. Green's supporters called themselves, caused both political parties to treat it seriously. A meeting held to establish the group on a permanent basis was attended by local councillors from both parties; and the chairman of the Housing Committee, accompanied by the city architect, extended an official welcome on behalf of the city council. The group had, by that time, acquired a very active and competent local leadership, with Mr. Green undertaking the organization of research into the planning preferences of local residents. The group also gave advice to people wishing to apply for various housing grants and issued a regular newsletter. By August 1969, the Action Group were trying to encourage voluntary groups to maintain derelict sites as playgrounds or gardens.

In July 1969, the city council invited the Walkley Action Group to join a working party to help council officials prepare a plan for the area. It was made clear that the elected representatives were responsible to the electorate for the final decisions, but the working party was to discuss the possibilities before these decisions were taken. The first meeting was attended by the

[29] The result was: Labour 1,786 votes, Conservative 1,768, Independent 773, and National Front 144.

chairmen of the Housing and Town Planning Committees, the city architect, representatives of the public health, town planning, and town clerk's departments, and six representatives of the Walkley Action Group.[30] The Action Group was subsequently asked by the chairman of the Housing Committee, Alderman H. Lambert, to try to extend its membership to include representatives of all the various sections of social, commercial, religious, recreational, and service elements within the area.[31]

The Walkley Action Group provides an example of the experiments mentioned by the Skeffington Committee, and it supports their contention that 'there is an active and willing audience waiting for authorities who encourage participation, and a particularly vigorous response may be expected when local plans are being prepared'.[32] The success of the group was based upon their parochialism and the distribution of detailed information; there was no attempt, as there was in the different circumstances of the tenants' movement, to 'broaden the struggle' into a general political platform. The expectation that the general public are receptive only to the generalized slogans of mass communications was shown to be false: the people were interested because their homes and neighbourhood were directly affected, and they wanted detailed knowledge. Most of the questions at the meetings were not concerned with broad policy, but with the consequences for a particular street or group of houses.

The electoral success of the Walkley Action Group showed also that elections remain an effective method of establishing local support. Voting strength, as the opponents of the rent rebate scheme also discovered, enables representatives of a pressure group to bargain rather than simply listen. Votes can be the political teeth that the Skeffington recommendations, among others, so noticeably lack. This is why some form of elected neighbourhood council is preferable to a total reliance upon voluntary organizations. The Sheffield City Council in their rejection of the Royal Commission proposals for local councils

[30] *Morning Telegraph*, 26 July 1969.
[31] Walkley Action Group, *Newsletter*, No. 1, August 1969.
[32] *People and Planning*, Report of the Committee on Public Participation in Planning, para. 54. Mr. Green was co-author, with Professor Bernard Crick, of 'People and Planning', *New Society*, 5 September 1968. Professor Crick later gave evidence to the Skeffington Committee.

considered 'that the numerous distinctive communities within each unitary area can best "have the means of expressing their own wishes and opinions, and of commenting on the policies and proposals of the main authorities" through bodies such as political parties, local churches, voluntary social organizations, civic and amenity societies, residents' and tenants' associations, trade unions, chambers of commerce and trade, and youth and other organizations interested in the working of the community; and that unitary authorities should be under a duty to establish and maintain machinery for close consultation with such bodies, so that the opinions and wishes of the local communities are constantly made known to them'.[33] These proposals of the city council have merit; they express an attitude towards improved consultation with groups of local citizens that is to be welcomed; but they do not represent a complete alternative to the concept of local councils.

The initiative in forming the Walkley Action Group came from a student of politics and sociology who had lived in Sheffield for only eighteen months. Once the first steps were taken a local leadership quickly emerged, but the original stimulus of someone versed in the techniques of social action was necessary. Such stimulus may be readily available in some areas, but in others it will be absent and community activities will languish. Both the Seebohm Committee and the Skeffington Committee recognized that many people need encouragement before they will participate in public affairs. In their recommendations the committees suggest that local authorities should employ community development workers whose 'role . . . is that of a source of information and expertise, a stimulator, a catalyst and an encourager'.[34] Community workers are obviously more politically sensitive than other social workers employed by local authorities; their work has been described as 'part of a protest against apathy and complacency and against distant and anonymous authority. It is also part of the whole dilemma of how to reconcile the "revolution of human dissent" with the large-scale organisation and economic and social planning which seem to be inseparably interwoven with the parallel revolution of rising expectations. This boils down to the

---

[33] *Sheffield Forward*, September 1969.

[34] *Report* of the Committee on Local Authority and Allied Personal Social Services, Cmnd. 3703, para. 480. See also *People and Planning*, op. cit., paras. 80-90.

problem of how to give meaning to democracy'.[35] Community
work is only in its infancy in Britain and most of the officers
have been appointed by voluntary bodies such as the Councils
for Social Service. The Home Office, however, are sponsoring
twelve pilot projects in urban areas to test the effectiveness of
community work and some local authorities are expressing interest.[36]

The introduction of community workers could have an important effect upon local democracy and councillors will need to
reconsider traditional attitudes if the experiment is to be successful. The most obvious difficulty will arise when a community
worker stimulates a community organization which then opposes
the policy of the council. It will need an understanding councillor
to accept this as part of a welcome development in democracy;
in many cases a community worker will be expected to act as a
tranquillizer rather than a stimulant, but the electorate will not
respond to such an approach. People may welcome help in formu-
lating their opinions, but they are suspicious of attempts, from
whatever quarter, to manipulate their involvement in favour of
any political group. The responsible attitude adopted by the
community worker will need to be accompanied by a measure of
independence unusual in local authority employees, which is
why the Councils of Social Service have taken the lead; but no
social worker could have acted with the political initiative shown
by Mr. Green.

The approach favoured by Skeffington would also introduce
public discussion during the process of policy formation and
some officers, and councillors, will object to the outside pressure
this will place upon them. Councillors maintain, quite correctly,
that they are elected to determine the policy of the local authority,
and the officers have, in the past, reserved their advice for the
committees. A greater measure of consultation with the public
must involve a change in the style of work within the departments
as the dialogue between officials and councillors becomes an open

[35] *Community Work and Social Change*, the Report of a Study Group on Training set up
by the Calouste Gulbenkian Foundation (Longmans), p. 4.
[36] The Home Office pilot projects were announced in July 1969. See Ben Whitaker,
'Tentative Steps towards an Anti-Poverty Programme', *The Times*, 24 July 1969.
The concept of community action is discussed by Anne Lapping in 'Social Action',
New Society, 2 January 1969. And see Peter Hodge, 'The Future of Community Development', in W. A. Robson and Bernard Crick (eds.), *The Future of the Social Services*.

discussion. The working party established between the Sheffield City Council and the Walkley Action Group, for example, met seldom, and both sides were obviously inexperienced in using the newly created committee; but the plans were changed.

There are indications that Sheffield City Council is ready to adopt a more open approach in their dealings with the public. In the past few years there has been a considerable change from the closed system existing in the earlier years of Labour power. The discipline of the party groups—once so fierce in the Labour Party—has become flexible enough to absorb public dissent among their members during important local controversies: no Sheffield councillor has been excluded from a political group for indiscipline during the past few years, although several have defied the party whip. During local controversies the party leaders were willing, indeed eager, to meet organizations to explain their party's policy on rent rebates, education, or the local airport, even though their reception was frequently rowdy.[37] The city council have also taken more interest in the local press. Press conferences are held after closed committee meetings at which leaders of both parties explain the agenda and answer questions; the majority of the executive of the Labour group even wanted to admit the press to group meetings, but this was not accepted by the back-benchers. The Conservative group also retained their private meetings which their deputy-leader considered necessary to enable the party to discuss policy with complete frankness; the Labour executive were accused of 'political gimmickry'.[38] As a final example of the councillors' readiness to discuss their activities and opinions, *every* member of the city council was willing to be interviewed in the course of our research, and subsequent enquiries met with a ready response.

Openness in public decision-taking will need to be accompanied by a greater measure of voluntary participation in the provision of local services if the discussions of policy are to be more than formal consultation. The Seebohm Report mentions mothers caring for their own children in hospital, foster-parents helping to recruit others, and members taking part in the management of

[37] For a short time the Labour group refused to attend tenants' meetings during the rent rebate controversy, but even then two Labour councillors defied the group decision without serious consequences. One of them became deputy-chairman of the Housing Committee when Labour regained office in 1969.

[38] Interview on Radio Sheffield, 30 September 1969.

old people's clubs,[39] as well as more traditional methods of voluntary service. The Skeffington Committee 'believe strongly in participation by activities' and argued that 'the public are far more likely to make representations and feel that they have contributed if they have undertaken some of the activities involved in processes of publicity and participation'. They mention the involvement of local societies and individuals in arranging meetings and exhibitions, some survey work, and the distribution of information on a door-to-door basis.[40] The Walkley Action Group engaged in all these activities.

Community participation in the provision of local services is not a new development; many of the social services have been pioneered by voluntary organizations and some, meals-on-wheels for example, remain largely voluntary. Clubs for young people, and those suffering from physical, mental, or social handicaps are frequently organized by voluntary workers. An interesting example of voluntary effort may be taken from the pre-school playgroup movement. A national association was formed in 1962 to press for an adequate provision of nursery education by local education authorities. The duty of providing nursery schools, or classes, for children under five years of age was placed upon local authorities by the Education Act of 1944,[41] but these schools were not regarded with the same urgency as other educational facilities. In addition to acting as a pressure group the Pre-School Playgroup Association (P.P.A.) encouraged people to form playgroups on their own initiative. In Sheffield there were about seventy playgroups by May 1969, and another sixteen were being considered. As each of these groups had its own organization for fund-raising and administration, several hundred people were involved. The area organizer of the Sheffield branch of the P.P.A. was a trained nursery school teacher, and the branch sought training facilities for local playgroup organizers. Courses were organized at an Education Centre for Child Care, and in conjunction with the Workers' Educational Association. The W.E.A. course in 1968/69 was tutored by a local nursery/infant school headmistress and it was attended by over thirty people. This course continued during

[39] *Report* of the Committee on Local Authority and Allied Personal Social Services, Cmnd. 3703, para. 493.
[40] *People and Planning*, op. cit. para. 96.
[41] Education Act, 1944. 7 and 8 Geo. VI, Ch. 31. Section 2(b).

1969/70 and a second course was started for beginners, each of these courses being attended by about fifty people.

Sheffield Education Committee have supported the local branch of the P.P.A. both with advice and a grant of £500 (1968–9). This is not much money within an education budget of about £19 million, but the editor of the P.P.A.'s national magazine commented that 'Sheffield City Council has been considerably more generous than many other authorities. Sheffield is held up as an outstanding example of cooperation between the local education authority and a voluntary association'.[42] She also praised the Parks Manager for providing play spaces for the playgroups in the parks.

The pre-school playgroup movement is a link between the provision of a social service by a voluntary organization supported by the local authority, and the Seebohm suggestion that people should participate in the provision of a service from which they benefit. Some of the Sheffield playgroups are provided by social work organizations, such as the Family Service Unit, but others are run by the mothers themselves who help in the supervision of the group and in fund-raising activities. The play-groups meet in halls belonging to churches, the Labour Party, or the corporation, and serve the immediate area—the distance a mother can push a pram. About a quarter of the groups do not even belong to the P.P.A., and therefore do not qualify for a grant from the corporation. The pre-school playgroups illustrate that a neighbourhood organization for community self-help can overcome a general apathy towards local government.

The Sheffield city councillors interviewed had mixed feelings about the use of voluntary organizations in meeting new and developing needs within the community. Nine out of every ten councillors thought that there were advantages, and nearly three-quarters could name corresponding disadvantages. These proportions were both higher than those found in the national sample of councillors interviewed for the Committee on the Management of Local Government. The reason is not immediately obvious, but it is noticeable that councillors from the larger authorities in the national sample quote the advantages and disadvantages of voluntary organizations more frequently than

---

[42] Quoted in *Morning Telegraph*, 21 May 1969. Some of the other information in this account is taken from Angela Stoner's article in that issue.

Table 11.5
Councillors' attitudes to voluntary organizations
meeting new and developing needs

	England and Wales		Sheffield		
	All Councils	C.B.	Total	Lab.	Cons.
Base	1,235	134	108	59	48
	%	%	%	%	%
Advantages	80	85	91	85	98
Disadvantages	42	51	73	66	81

Sources: Survey of Sheffield City Council and *M.L.G.*, II,
The Local Government Councillor, p. 191.

those from smaller authorities.[43] Their views may simply reflect the
greater variety of voluntary organizations in large urban areas.

The Labour councillors were more hesitant than the Conservatives in their attitude towards voluntary organizations. There was
a strong feeling among one section of Labour councillors that
voluntary organizations 'undermine the principle that things are
of right rather than charity'.

A similar view led other Labour councillors to accept voluntary
organizations only as an expedient forced upon them by economic
stringency. They believed that ideally the local authority should
provide all services. Other Labour councillors held views similar
to most of the Conservative councillors and thought that the
council should help voluntary organizations to provide some
services to meet the new and developing needs of the people.

The councillors mentioned many advantages and disadvantages
arising from the use of voluntary organizations, but most can be
grouped into two categories. The first is concerned with the use
of resources; both of finance and of personnel. The financial
advantages to the city council are fairly obvious, but some councillors were not sure that the public got better value for money.
One Conservative said: 'some voluntary organizations are more
efficient than the council, [but] generally voluntary organizations
are not very efficient. They are expensive in that their cost of
collecting money is usually very high.' Some councillors spoke of
the advantages of recruiting voluntary help in areas where the
local authority workers were unable to meet the potential needs,

[43] *M.L.G.*, II, *The Local Government Councillor*, p. 191.

Table 11.6
Councillors' opinions of the best way to meet new and developing needs

	England and Wales		Sheffield		
	All Councils	C.B.	Total	Lab.	Cons.
Base	1,235	134	108	59	48
	%	%	%	%	%
Council to provide all services	20	20	22	36	6
Council to help vol. orgs. to provide some services	73	78	69	61	79
Vol. orgs. to meet most new needs	4	2	4	2	6
D.K./Q.N.A.	3	0	5	2	8

Note: The percentages may not add to one hundred owing to rounding.
Sources: Survey of Sheffield City Council and *M.L.G.*, II, *The Local Government Councillor*, Table 6.7.

but more councillors could see disadvantages in supplementing local authority resources in this way. They mentioned that untrained workers were unsuitable for many branches of social work and always difficult to organize. These disadvantages could lead to a 'lack of co-ordination and control on the part of the council'; one Conservative reminded us that 'the priorities of voluntary workers are those that interest them, and not the socially most pressing needs'.

The councillors spoke frequently of the advantages and disadvantages arising from the use of voluntary organizations in particular services. These are grouped together in Table 11.7 under the heading 'character of service'. The advantages were concerned mainly with the less formal approach of volunteers. 'An old person,' thought one Conservative councillor, 'would rather be visited by someone doing it voluntarily than coming because they are paid'. There were other councillors, however, who saw disadvantages in allowing volunteers to participate in some forms of social work. They suggested that some 'nosy parkers' might work with problem families, for example, out of morbid curiosity.

The councillors confined themselves almost entirely to the social services and youth work as services suitable for voluntary provision.[44] The services provided by the Sheffield Council of Social Service were mentioned frequently. There was no mention of voluntary maintenance of environmental amenities, or of the kind

[44] The services quoted, and the order of frequency, were very similar to the national sample response to this question. *M.L.G.*, II, *The Local Government Councillor*, Table 6.8.

Table 11.7
Sheffield councillors' opinions of advantages/disadvantages
of using voluntary organizations

	Advantages			Disadvantages		
	Total	Lab.	Cons.	Total	Lab.	Cons.
Base—cllrs. mentioning	98	50	47	79	39	39
	%	%	%	%	%	%
Use of resources	14	12	17	38	44	33
Character of service	44	30	57	46	46	44
Other/Don't know	43	58	28	23	18	28

Note: The percentages may not add to one hundred as some councillors
mentioned more than one advantage or disadvantage.
Source: Survey of Sheffield City Council.

of activities proposed in the Skeffington Report; and very little
mention of voluntary help within the education service, although
the Education Committee have—since the interviews—extended
the opportunities for people to participate in the administration
of their local schools. The existing pattern of school visitors,
drawn almost entirely from the Education Committee, has been
replaced by boards of governors for the thirty-one comprehensive
schools, and boards of managers for the 200 primary schools.
Over 2,000 places are available on these bodies.

The chairman of the Education Committee, Councillor Peter
Horton, announced that they wished 'to promote the widest
participation in the running of schools by parents, teachers, trade
unionists, people from all walks of life within the locality'.[45] In
schools where a parent-teacher association did not exist then a
general meeting of parents would be convened to appoint representatives to the board. Some primary schools in Sheffield are
also beginning to welcome parents into the classroom during
teaching hours. The council have also provided for better consultation with council house tenants. A Housing Advisory Committee
has been constituted, consisting of Housing Committee members
and representatives of Tenants' Associations, to consider matters—
repairs, amenities, etc.—relating to the management of the estates.

In answer to our interviews the councillors described existing
patterns of voluntary help, without speculating about future
possibilities; but some of these were foreshadowed by the
Labour councillor who spoke of voluntary service as 'an extension

[45] *Sheffield Forward,* July 1969.

of the democratic principle behind councils themselves. . . . It is a good thing when people voluntarily take on responsibility.'

The three aspects of democracy—efficacy, control, and participation—are all closely involved in discussions about local government reform. The possibilities are frequently obscured, however, by the tendency to use democracy in the restricted sense of a conventional, compendious, council. Such councils are defended with great energy: both against encroachments on their boundaries, and from attacks based upon their alleged inefficiency; but by trying to satisfy all three aspects of democracy through one institution there is a danger that none will be adequately fulfilled. Proposals for local government reform should start from an understanding that no local authority area large enough to be efficacious can be small enough to encourage citizen participation; democracy in its limited sense of political control is no longer associated with community feeling. There must be two sets of institutions: one concerned with devising and controlling policy; and the other involving people in local community affairs. The councillors on the main authority would control the policies carried out by local authority officers within areas large enough to be efficacious; they would naturally be subject to the democratic control of the ballot box. The community institutions could include the common councils—preferably named 'neighbourhood councils'—suggested by Mr. Senior, social and religious groups, trade unions and commercial organizations, pressure groups for particular objectives, and organizations such as pre-school playgroups. The wide variety would be an important part of the system which would consist not of two tiers sharing the functions of local government, but of a single tier supported by a network of community organizations.

The problem, as G. D. H. Cole wrote nearly thirty years ago, 'is to find democratic ways of living for little men in big societies'. He believed, as we have argued throughout this book, that 'democracy can work in the great States . . . only if each State is made up of a host of little democracies, and rests finally . . . on groups small enough to express the spirit of neighbourhood and personal acquaintance'.[46] Voluntary organizations can form some

---

[46] G. D. H. Cole, 'Democracy Face to Face with Hugeness', first published as a supplement to *The Christian Newsletter* in 1941, reprinted in *Essays in Social Theory*, pp. 94–5.

of these 'little democracies', but often they are unrepresentative and always, by their nature, insular. Common councils created on the Senior model could provide a local forum subject to popular control, and would become appropriate bodies to manage local amenities; they would also provide a useful framework for community workers.

Our units of local government need to be and can be both larger and smaller: there is no contradiction, on the contrary. A local government system based upon relatively large executive authorities, but supplemented by a mass of small and largely non-executive bodies, could provide for local democracy if the possibilities are realized. First, councillors on the main authorities must be ready to adopt less detailed methods of control in return for a wider span of policy-making; secondly, the local councils must be based upon the social communities of neighbourhood units rather than the existing district authorities. Within this system participation in local affairs should be actively encouraged: it is not sufficient simply to provide the facilities of democracy without providing the means and incentive to make use of them. Criticisms of neighbourhood councils, and other methods of participation on the grounds that they will have no power are misplaced. *Power* is never absolute—nor should it be in a democracy—and the proposals outlined would provide opportunities for more people to exercise more *influence* than at present. The neighbourhood councils would also bring local government closer to true community feeling than it has been in the larger cities.

The arguments about the Royal Commission's proposals, and the variations offered by Mr. Senior and other commentators, are sure to continue; but reform does seem to be on the way. The present study of one of the largest county boroughs comes, therefore, at the end of an era in English local government.

APPENDIX A

Sheffield Occupational Statistics

Table A.1

Proportions per 10,000 persons in employment by industry, 1961

Industrial classification	Eng. & Wales	Shef-field	Leeds	Liver-pool	Man/ster	M/d/s boro'	New-castle	Bris-tol	Nor-wich
I Agriculture, forestry and fishing	344	17	16	12	9	7	4	21	48
II Mining and quarrying	301	62	46	5	50	3	59	7	—
III Food, drink and tobacco	294	328	227	700	221	225	465	791	662
IV Chemicals and allied industries	219	55	157	298	284	81	246	153	62
V Metal manufacture	267	1,767	300	10	113	1,719	46	146	66
VI Engineering and electrical goods	886	1,083	840	670	984	834	1,173	544	761
VII Shipbuilding and marine engineering	82	—	—	130	4	20	424	59	4
VIII Vehicles	382	164	201	191	92	15	55	97	58
IX Metal goods not elsewhere specified	238	1,390	216	176	194	111	93	104	138
X Textiles	328	10	242	137	289	102	23	59	62
XI Leather, leather goods and fur	27	3	70	16	30	3	27	15	50
XII Clothing and footwear	245	30	1,373	155	647	297	98	155	1,282
XIII Bricks, pottery, glass, cement, etc.	143	107	95	63	49	39	43	44	17
XIV Timber, furniture, etc.	131	105	177	103	133	32	101	147	222
XV Paper, printing, publishing	260	117	399	259	458	99	209	758	331
XVI Other m/fing industries	131	38	40	337	196	30	63	61	34
XVII Construction	675	641	628	602	513	710	700	798	706
XVIII Electricity, gas and water	165	185	205	139	148	170	232	178	234
XIX Transport and communication	708	569	628	1,634	796	1,147	897	1,185	759
XX Distributive trades	1,360	1,373	1,672	1,759	2,161	1,875	1,954	1,810	1,721
XXI Insurance, banking, finance	251	146	288	325	455	208	294	308	452
XXII Professional and scientific services	902	820	866	887	887	1,007	948	1,081	842
XXIII Miscellaneous services	1,000	699	877	967	935	828	979	1,036	1,006
XXIV Public Admin. and Defence	617	280	396	403	325	425	835	421	473
Industry inadequately described	33	11	40	20	28	13	31	23	8

Source: Census 1961: Industry Tables, Table A and Occupation, Industry and Socio-Economic Groups, County reports, Table 4.

Table A.2
Occupations per 10,000 economically active population, 1961

Occupational classification	Eng. & Wales	Sheffield	Leeds	Liverpool	Manchester	M/d/sboro'	Newcastle	Bristol	Norwich
I Farmers, foresters and fishermen	384	54	51	52	40	43	38	65	112
II Miners and quarrymen	211	93	83	17	28	4	83	4	2
III Gas, coke and chemical makers	60	24	31	67	76	344	37	40	20
IV Glass and ceramics makers	47	31	32	18	15	3	25	15	13
V Furnace, forge, foundry and rolling mill workers	99	584	129	42	95	382	74	43	20
VI Electrical and electronic workers	225	172	182	267	240	240	233	228	198
VII Engineering and allied trades workers n.e.c.	1,110	1,890	1,040	981	1,010	1,350	1,190	1,070	779
VIII Woodworkers	186	186	186	179	154	144	218	163	265
IX Leather workers	69	15	92	25	33	10	32	59	1,180
X Textile workers	184	5	196	39	115	68	24	5	16
XI Clothing workers	206	80	994	215	585	225	134	145	158
XII Food, drink and tobacco workers	157	172	134	278	156	150	182	326	233
XIII Paper and printing workers	139	66	220	164	221	29	109	352	191
XIV Makers of other products	135	95	65	218	216	80	87	62	93
XV Construction workers	237	256	232	240	212	316	231	229	295
XVI Painters and decorators	141	129	136	151	137	127	161	168	219
XVII Drivers of stationary engines, cranes, etc.	130	265	102	134	110	425	140	105	86
XVIII Labourers n.e.c.	550	692	530	758	649	1,180	776	579	604
XIX Transport and communication workers	631	575	585	1,080	716	862	741	855	574
XX Warehousemen, storekeepers, packers, bottlers	344	409	401	548	549	220	422	485	524
XXI Clerical workers	1,310	1,200	1,240	1,370	1,440	903	1,550	1,510	1,170
XXII Sales workers	950	895	1,030	913	974	921	1,060	1,070	1,030
XXIII Service, sport and recreation workers	1,040	976	1,120	1,190	1,220	1,030	1,160	1,110	1,110
XXIV Administrators and managers	278	288	249	167	163	157	204	207	171
XXV Professional, technical workers, artists	866	740	661	654	679	706	834	933	745
XXVI Armed forces (British and foreign)	142	24	18	19	18	27	61	27	86
XXVII Inadequately described occupations	166	103	256	221	157	55	193	142	109

Note: Economically active means those people aged 15 or over who were in employment during the week before the census, and those who though intending to work, were out of employment, or sick, at the time of the census.
n.e.c.—not elsewhere counted.
Source: Census 1961: Occupation Tables, Table 1 and Ocupation, Industry and Socio-Economic Groups, County Reports, Table 1.

Table A.3

Number of Sheffield men and women employed by occupation, 1961

		Men		Women	
Occupational classification	No.	Per 10,000 economically active		No.	Per 10,000 economically active
I Farmers, foresters and fishermen	1,200	74		110	13
II Miners and quarrymen	2,280	138		—	—
III Gas, coke and chemical makers	570	34		30	4
IV Glass and ceramics makers	620	37		140	17
V Furnace, forge, foundry and rolling mill workers	13,870	838		550	67
VI Electrical and electronic workers	4,150	251		80	10
VII Engineering and allied trades workers n.e.c.	36,990	2,234		9,870	1,207
VIII Woodworkers	4,280	258		330	40
IX Leather workers	330	20		40	5
X Textile workers	10	1		100	12
XI Clothing workers	470	28		1,550	185
XII Food, drink and tobacco workers	2,550	154		1,710	209
XIII Paper and printing workers	860	52		770	94
XIV Makers of other products	1,570	95		760	93
XV Construction workers	6,320	382		10	1
XVI Painters and decorators	2,700	163		500	61
XVII Drivers of stationary engines, cranes, etc.	6,030	364		210	26
XVIII Labourers n.e.c.	15,860	958		1,230	150
XIX Transport and communication workers	12,340	745		1,810	221
XX Warehousemen, storekeepers, packers, bottlers	4,910	296		5,230	640
XXI Clerical workers	9,940	600		19,700	2,410
XXII Sales workers	11,460	692		10,650	1,303
XXIII Service, sport and recreation workers	5,760	348		18,370	2,247
XXIV Administrators and managers	6,730	406		400	49
XXV Professional, technical workers, artists	11,580	699		6,700	820
XXVI Armed forces (British and foreign)	590	36		10	1
XXVII Inadequately described occupations	1,610	97		930	114
Totals	165,600	10,000		81,750	10,000

Note: Economically active means those people aged 15 or over who were in employment during the week before the census, and those who though intending
to work, were out of employment, or sick, at the time of the census.
n.e.c.—not elsewhere counted.
Source: Census 1961: Occupation, Industry and Socio-Economic Groups, County
reports, Tables 1 and 2.

Table A.4
The structure of Sheffield industry, 1966

Industrial classification	*	5–10	11–50	51–100	101–200	201–500	501–1000	1001–2000	Over 2000	Total
				No. of manufacturing establishments employing						
I Agriculture, forestry and fishing	1	5	4	0	0	0	0	0	0	10
II Mining and quarrying	0	2	9	0	1	2	1	1	0	16
III Food, drink and tobacco	0	8	33	8	9	5	4	1	1	69
IV Chemicals and allied industries	0	4	8	6	0	0	0	1	0	19
V Metal manufacture	1	12	56	19	12	18	15	2	6	141
VI Engineering and electrical goods	2	52	119	32	24	20	6	3	3	261
VII Shipbuilding and marine engineering	0	0	0	0	0	0	0	0	0	0
VIII Vehicles	0	2	5	5	0	1	0	0	1	14
IX Metal goods not elsewhere specified	5	74	186	55	34	18	12	5	1	390
X Textiles	0	2	4	0	0	0	0	0	0	6
XI Leather, leather goods and fur	0	0	0	0	0	0	0	0	0	0
XII Clothing and footwear	0	1	3	2	1	1	0	0	0	8
XIII Bricks, pottery, glass, cement, etc.	0	5	11	7	4	6	2	1	0	37
XIV Timber, furniture, etc.	1	10	30	7	8	3	0	0	0	59
XV Paper, printing and publishing	2	11	23	6	2	2	1	0	0	47
XVI Other m/fing industries	0	5	20	2	1	0	0	0	0	28
XVII Construction	3	88	174	37	16	5	3	1	1	328
XVIII Electricity, gas and water	0	0	1	0	1	3	1	1	1	8
XIX Transport and communication	2	23	50	15	2	6	0	0	2	100
XX Distributive trades	9	270	378	44	20	13	8	3	1	746
XXI Insurance, banking, finance	3	46	87	15	5	1	0	0	0	157
XXII Professional and scientific services	1	58	102	13	7	5	2	3	3	194
XXIII Miscellaneous services	8	143	235	30	14	9	0	1	0	440
XXIV Public Admin. and Defence	12	19	21	3	3	7	3	1	0	69
Total	50	841	1,559	306	164	125	58	24	20	3,147

* Up-to-date number of employees not known or not available.

Source: This table has been derived from figures provided by the Ministry of Labour. I am indebted to Dr. Martin Howe for making these available to me. The figures are those current for the beginning of 1966.

Table A.5
Occupational characteristics of Sheffield electorate, 1967

		Sex		Socio-economic status				
Base—all informants	Total 584	Male 275	Female 309	1 & 2 60	3 156	4 139	5 144	6 83
	%	%	%	%	%	%	%	%
Does paid work†	59	83	37	77	55‡	80	67	0
Does not do paid work	41	17	63	23	45	20	33	100
Base—all paid workers	342	227	115	46	86	111	97	0
No. of people employed at place of work:	%	%	%	%	%	%	%	%
Less than 20	23	19	30	22	30	19	23	0
20–500	44	42	46	50	38	41	48	0
Over 500	33	38	23	28	31	41	29	0
D.K.	1	*	1	0	1	0	1	0
Length of time employed at present firm:								
Under 1 year	12	10	18	9	16	8	16	0
1–5 years	28	26	33	28	26	26	33	0
5–15 years	30	29	33	28	33	32	27	0
Over 15 years	28	35	15	33	24	34	24	0
D.K.	*	0	1	0	1	0	0	0
Length of time expect to remain with present firm:								
Short time§	7	7	7	9	9	6	6	0
Next few years	22	14	37	9	22	20	29	0
Until retirement	54	64	33	67	50	59	47	0
D.K.	17	15	23	15	21	15	19	0
No. of firms worked for since leaving school:								
1	16	19	10	41	12	14	9	0
2–3	41	36	50	41	49	35	40	0
4–6	30	30	31	15	26	33	38	0
More than 6	13	15	8	0	14	17	12	0
D.K.	*	0	1	0	1	0	0	0

* Less than 0·5 per cent.
† A national (England excluding London) survey conducted the same year found 60 per cent (men 80 per cent, women 41 per cent) of the sample currently undertaking some form of paid employment. The proportion for county boroughs was 63 per cent. Royal Commission on Local Government, Research Study 9, *Community Attitudes Survey: England*, p. 48 and Table 48.
‡ Socio-economic status in this study is based on last job held by the informant. Group 3 includes female clerical workers, and the lower economic activity rate for women causes the overall proportion of this group employed to be depressed.
§ Twenty-four (7 per cent) of those employed expected to leave their employment within a short time. Five gave the reason as redundancy; ten expected to move to a better job; eight gave other reasons; and one gave no reason.
Note: The percentages may not add to one hundred owing to rounding.
Source: Survey of Sheffield Electorate.

APPENDIX B

Local Election Results in Sheffield, 1919–69

		Distribution of votes†				Composition of council§			
	Wards		Turn-	Political party‡ 'Anti-				Political party‡ 'Anti-		
Year	contested *No.*	Total 000	out %	Lab. %	Lab.' %	Others %	Total *No.*	Lab. *No.*	Lab.' *No.*	Others *No.*
1918	Elections suspended						64	2	60	2
1919	14/16	172	34	15	13	5	64	12	49	3
1920	12/16	150	44	17	22	6	64	13	47	4
1921	16/17	211	53	20	24	9	68	15	43	10
1922	17/17	197	57	27	28	2	68	20	41	7
1923	16/17	190	55	23	26	6	68	22	40	6
1924	16/17	188	49	22	27	*	68	24	38	6
1925	17/17	206	55	28	26	2	68	24	39	5
1926	17/17	206	60	32	27	1	68	38	25	5
1927	17/17	211	53	25	24	5	68	39	24	5
1928	15/17	191	53	29	23	2	68	40	24	4
1929	21/24	338	41	22	16	3	96	63	31	2
1930	21/24	210	44	18	21	5	96	57	36	3
1931	23/24	233	59	22	34	3	96	49	43	4
1932	20/24	208	56	33	21	2	96	41	50	5
1933	19/24	200	49	27	20	1	96	49	43	4
1934	19/25	204	49	27	20	2	100	56	42	2
1935	18/25	195	50	29	20	1	100	57	41	2
1936	17/25	178	45	24	22	*	100	56	42	2
1937	16/25	174	45	21	22	1	100	55	43	2
1938	19/25	208	46	23	23	*	100	53	45	2
1939–1944	Elections suspended. During this period the anti-Lab. group gained one aldermanic seat from the Independents and one Labour councillor joined the Communist party.									
1945	21/25	496	43	22	20	1	100	59	39	2
1946	22/25	339	41	21	18	1	100	63	36	1
1947	24/25	360	53	26	25	1	100	67	32	1
1948	No elections held because of change in election month						100	68	31	1
1949	23/25	345	52	27	25	*	100	64	35	1
1950	23/25	338	43	22	20	1	100	64	36	—
1951	25/25	393	38	18	19	*	100	63	37	—
1952	25/25	393	40	25	14	*	100¶	68	31	—
1953	22/25	324	33	18	15	*	100	70	30	—
1954	23/25	344	30	18	12	*	100	73	27	—
1955	24/25	344	34	17	16	1	100	71	29	—
1956	22/25	321	26	13	12	1	100	71	29	—
1957	20/25	282	33	16	16	2	100	71	29	—
1958	20/25	278	32	17	13	2	100	72	28	—
1959	18/25	263	31	14	15	2	100	72	28	—
1960	22/25	318	25	11	13	1	100	67	32	1
1961	24/25	363	33	16	13	2	100	67	32	1
1962	25/25	373	31	15	11	5	100	67	32	1

Democracy and Community

| | | | | Distribution of votes† | | | Composition of Council§ | | | |
| | | | | Political party‡ | | | | Political party‡ | | |
Year	Wards contested *No.*	Total 000	Turn-out %	Lab. %	'Anti-Lab.' %	Others %	Total *No.*	Lab. *No.*	'Anti-Lab.' *No.*	Others *No.*
1963	25/25	369	31	17	10	4	100	72	28	—
1964	25/25	343	29	16	11	2	100	72	28	—
1965	25/25	369	26	13	12	2	100	71	29	—
1966	25/25	407	22	10	10	2	100	71	29	—
1967	27/27	1,110	33	13	19	2	108	59	48	1
1968	27/27	405	34	12	20	2	108	52	56	—
1969	27/27	386	33	14	17	2	108	57	51	—

* Less than 0·5 per cent.
— Nil
† The total votes available exclude the electorate in uncontested wards and include a multiple of the electorate in contested wards with more than one vacancy. The political party percentages may not add to the turn-out owing to rounding.
‡ The main opposition group to the Labour group has changed its name several times in the past fifty years and it is referred to as 'anti-Lab.' 'Others' include Independents, Liberals outside the 'anti-Lab.' coalition, Ratepayers, etc.
§ There are three councillors for each ward and one alderman to three councillors.
¶ One vacancy.
Source: The figures are taken from the *Sheffield Telegraph Year Books*, but all the percentages have been re-worked with consistent conventions and in many cases do not agree with those given in the source.

APPENDIX C

The Sample Survey and the Survey of Councillors

THE two surveys were designed together to allow comparability. The same definitions were adopted throughout. The drawing of the sample, interviewing, and analysis of the elector's survey was conducted by Research Services Ltd., under the direction of Mr. G. Levins, on the basis of instructions given by the author. The councillors were interviewed by Mrs. Patricia Chandler and Mr. G. Green, and the analysis performed on an I.C.T. Counter/Sorter 302/4.

SURVEY OF SHEFFIELD ELECTORATE

Sample design

A two-stage sampling design was employed. At the *first stage* the number of interviews to be carried out in each ward was calculated on the principle that each of the 27 wards making up Sheffield County Borough be sampled with probability proportional to its electorate. This sample design was planned to give the following proportional distribution of interviews by constituency (100% = 758 issued addresses):

Constituency	Electorate (1967)	%
Attercliffe	61,889	16·7
Brightside	53,015	14·3
Hallam	56,078	15·2
Heeley	75,345	20·4
Hillsborough	47,788	12·9
Park	47,165	12·7
Non-Sheffield*	29,022	7·8
Total	370,302	100

* Non-Sheffield indicates the parts of North-East Derbyshire and Penistone constituencies that were brought within the county borough by the boundary extensions of 1967.

Having determined the appropriate number of addresses to be allocated to each ward, two polling districts were selected within each ward with probability proportional to their electorates, and the allocation of addresses for each ward was divided equally between the two polling districts.

At the *second stage* of sampling the names and addresses of a predetermined number of electors for each polling district were selected by a systematic interval method from the 1967 Electoral Register.

In this way a sample of 758 addresses representative of the distribution of the electorate of Sheffield C.B. by ward was issued. Interviewers were permitted to elect a substitute for interview in those cases where the person selected from the Electoral Register had died or moved away permanently from that address. In such circumstances the interviewer listed all persons within the household who were aged 21 or over at the time of the compilation of the Register (October 1966), but who did not have an opportunity to be selected at that address at the original sampling stage. One of those listed persons was then selected for interview by a random procedure.

Sample response

A total of 585 fully productive interviews was achieved. A full analysis of the response is given below:

Total sample set (named individuals)	758
Ineligible informants:	
Informant dead	11
Informant moved away	55
Premises empty/demolished	21
Total eligible sample set	737 (100%)
(671 + 66 substitutes)	
Non-contact	
No reply after 3 or more calls	46
Informant away permanently	14
Informant away for duration of fieldwork	7
Informant ill	18
Other reasons for non-contact	8
Total informants not contacted	93 (12·6%)
Refusals	
Informant 'too busy'	2
Informant refused interview	56
Informant on Sheffield C.B. Council	1
Total refusals	59 (8·0%)
Total interviews achieved from issued sample	519
Total interviews achieved from substitute informants	66
Total interviews achieved and used in analysis	585 (79·4%)

Sample weighting

Because of slight variations in overall response from ward to ward, it was decided to weight the data before analysis in order to achieve the correct sample distribution by constituency. Accordingly, the following weighting factors were applied:

Constituency	Achieved sample	Factor	Weighted sample
Attercliffe	103	0·95	98
Brightside	78	1·08	84
Hallam	67	1·33	89
Heeley	120	0·99	119
Hillsborough	64	1·17	75
Park	93	0·79	73
Non-Sheffield	60	0·76	46
	585		584

Weighting was carried out on an IBM/360 Model 20 computer, as was the subsequent analysis.

DEFINITIONS

Education

Higher: full-time education past the secondary level (i.e. at technical college, teacher-training college or university).

Secondary: informants who finished their full-time education at state or private grammar-type schools, technical or commercial schools, or (in the case of older people) the old 'central' or 'intermediate' schools.

Lower: informants who finished their full-time education at secondary modern schools, the old 'elementary' schools, or other equivalent schools.

Socio-economic status of informant

Six-fold grouping	*Registrar-General's socio-economic groups*
1. Large employers and professional workers	1, 3, 4
2. Small employers and farmers	2, 13, 14
3. Intermediate non-manual workers	5, 6, 7, 12
4. Skilled manual workers	8, 9
5. Semi- and unskilled workers	10, 11, 15
6. Never employed/Q.N.A.	16, All others

This is a classification of the informant himself or herself, not a grouping by the status of the head of household. Non-working housewives and retired people are classified according to last job held.

Index of neighbourhood attachment

After consideration of the factor analysis prepared for the Royal Commission on Local Government (Research Study 9, *Community Attitudes Survey: England*), Mr. G. Levins of Research Services, Ltd.

devised the following index based upon questions that had shown high significance for community involvement (see footnote to p. 116 for a comment on the name given to the index).

	Category	Question 1 Is there an area round here ... where you feel 'at home'?	Question 7 How sorry or pleased would you be to leave (HOME AREA)	Question 8 How many people would you say you know who live in (HOME AREA)	No. in sample
High	1	Yes	Very sorry	Very many	110
	2	Yes	Very sorry	One or two A few Many (Unclassifiable)	128
	3	Yes	{ Quite sorry { Neither sorry { nor pleased	—	217
		No	Very sorry	—	
	4	Yes	{ Quite pleased { Very pleased	—	130
		No	{ Quite sorry { Neither sorry { nor pleased { Quite pleased { Very pleased		
Low		(Unclassifiable)	—		
				Total	585

List of clubs and groups (Q. 14 electors' survey)

A. *Organizations connected with your work*
   Trade union?
   Professional association?
   Club to help your workmates or colleagues (benevolent soc., sick club)?
   Business group or club (Rotary or Chamber of Commerce)?
   Social or sports club at work?
   (Anything else connected with work)?

B. *Public bodies or committees*
   (A public or statutory committee or board of governors i.e. national savings, hospital management, school governors)?

C. *Organizations connected with politics*
   A political party or association?
   (Any other political group)?

D. *Organizations connected with education and training*
Organization for further education (W.E.A., Evening Institute)?
Military training group (Territorials, Civil Defence, Cadets)?
Youth training organization (Scouts, Guides, Boys' or Girls' Brigade)?
Nursing or first aid organization (St. John Ambulance, Red Cross)?
(Anything else giving education or training)?

E. *Organizations connected with the church or other religious groups*
A church club or group (missionary society, church council)?
A social club connected with the church?
(Any other religious organization or group)?

F. *Organizations connected with welfare*
Charitable organization (Spastics Society)?
Voluntary welfare organization (W.V.S., National Council for Social Service)?
(Any other welfare group)?

G. *Civic or community groups*
Tenants' or ratepayers' associations?
A parents' association (parent/teachers')?
A resident's club or community centre?
(Any other civic group)?

H. *Any other group connected with leisure activities*
A sports team or club (darts, rifle, tennis)?
A club for games (bingo, billiards, bridge)?
A dance club?
A club for hobbies or pets (gardening, stamps, cats)?
A music, drama, jazz, or art club, or anything like that?
A motoring association, car, scooter or cycling club?
(Anything else concerned with leisure activities)?

J. *Any other social club*
A fraternal or ex-serviceman's club (Freemasons, British Legion)?
A woman's social club (Townswomen's Guild, Women's Institute)?
A working men's club?
A youth club?
A club for old people?
(Any other social club)?

K. *(Anything else not covered here)?*

The Questionnaires

Many of the questions in the questionnaires used in the research reported in this book were taken from surveys conducted for the Committee on the Management of Local Government and the Royal Commission on Local Government. We are very grateful for this co-operation which made it possible to compare the Sheffield results with appropriate national averages. Other questions, of course, were developed with our own local needs in mind. The following lists of questions will indicate the range covered by the two questionnaires, but the actual questionnaires could be made available to any research worker who intended to enter this field. Not all the questions listed were asked of every informant as some are dependent upon the answers given to previous questions.

Survey of Sheffield Electorate

Q. 1.   Is there an area round here (which would include your home address but which could be of any size or any shape), which you would say you belong to and where you feel 'at home'?

Q. 2 a.

   (i)   This area which you feel you belong to, then—is there a name you could give it?

  (ii)   Taking the area round here, where you are now living, is there a name you could give it?

   b.   How could you describe it then?—I mean, which places, districts, streets does it include?

   c.   Does the area you are thinking about make up the whole of —— (name), just part of it, or does it take in more than just —— (name)?

   d.   What part or parts of —— (name) does it take in?

   e.   What other parts does it also take in, apart from —— (name)?

Q. 3 a.   How long have you lived in —— (home area)?

   b.   Where did you live before you came to live in —— (home area)?

   c.   Would you say that is more, or less, than a ten minute walk from this address?

   d.   Would you say that is more, or less, than ten miles from this address then?

Q. 4.   Why did you *first* come to live in —— (home area)? Any other reasons?

Q. 5.   How interested are you to know what goes on in —— (home area)?

Q. 6 a.   Would you go through these local daily newspapers with me and tell me which, if any, of them you read regularly?

b. Repeat for weekly and other local newspapers.

Q. 7. Supposing, for some reason, you had to move away from —— (home area), how sorry or pleased would you be to leave?

Q. 8. How many people would you say you know who live in —— (home area)?

Q. 9 a. How many adult relatives and in-laws do you have who live within ten minutes' walk from your home?

   b. And how many adult friends do you have who live within ten minutes' walk from your home?

Q. 10 a. Do you go out to any sort of paid work at all?

   b. Whereabouts do you work?

   c. Is that in —— (home area), or outside it?

Q. 11 a. How many people in all are employed at the place where you work—and by that I mean the entire building or set of buildings?

   b. How long have you worked in your present firm?

   c. How many firms have you worked for since you left school?

   d. How long do you expect you will remain with your present firm?

   e. Why do you expect to be in your present job for only a short time?

Q. 12. Do you have to be a member of a Trade Union to work in your present job?

Q. 13 a. Has the age at which you finished your education ever stopped you from taking a job which you would have liked to do?

   b. And has the age at which you finished your education ever stopped you from going in for any other form of activity to which you were attracted?

Q. 14 a. Now I'd like to ask you one or two questions about your leisure activities, both in —— (home area) and outside it. I'm going to read out some types of clubs or groups that people might belong to and I'd like you to tell me if you belong to any of them at present?

   b. Is that in —— (home area), or outside it?

   c. Are you a committee member or official of that?

Q. 15 a. Do you attend any place of worship these days, such as a church, chapel, or synagogue, etc.?

   b. And which church or denomination is that?

Q. 16 a. Do you have any children (up to and including 18 years) having full-time education—including nursery schools (but not nurseries)?

   b. Do you have any children under school age?

Q. 17 a. And now I'd like to come on to some questions about various
          public services in the local community. Take *education and
          schools* first of all; in Sheffield do you think they are mainly
          the responsibility of the Government, the County Borough
          Council, or some other body, perhaps?
       b. Hospitals.
       c. Libraries.
       d. Social Security (National Assistance).
       e. Refuse collection and disposal.
       f. Recreation facilities—like parks, swimming pools, etc.
       g. Electricity supply.
       h. Town planning.
       i. Provision of housing.

Q. 18 a. Are there any of these services, or any others, which are
          quite well run in Sheffield? (*Show card E.*)
       b. Which ones?
       c. In what ways?

Q. 19 a. Are there any of these services, or any others, which are not
          very well run in Sheffield?
       b. Which ones?
       c. In what ways?

Q. 20 a. (*Show card F.*) Here are some of the matters with which the
          Sheffield City Council has been involved during the last year
          or two. I'd like you to tell me the three most important
          issues as they seem to you. Which would you put as the most
          important? And which second? And which third?
       b. Are there any other matters or issues, apart from those on
          this card that you think are important? (If 'yes')—Which
          are they?
       c. In which of these fields do you think that the council has
          done the most to help people or improve things during 1967?
       d. Is there one particular problem that you think will require a
          good deal of attention by the council in the next year or so?

Q. 21.   At the last local elections in Sheffield, in May this year,
          nearly three-quarters of the people did not vote, for one
          reason or another. Can I ask you—if you did not vote at that
          election—what was your reason?

Q. 22.   When you *do* vote, which party do you *usually* vote for?

Q. 23 a. Do you happen to know which political party has most seats
          on the Sheffield council at present?
       b. (If correct)—How long have they been in control on the
          Sheffield council?

   c. (Unless 'since last election')—During this time have they come close to losing control at any election? When?

   d. Do you think there is any chance of the Conservatives gaining control of the city council during the next few years?

Q. 24 a. How much do you think that members of the city council make their decisions with an eye to the next local election?

   b. And how much do you think the members of the Government at Westminster make their decisions with an eye to the next General Election?

Q. 25. Who do you think is the most important person in local affairs here in Sheffield? What position, if any, does he/she hold?

Q. 26. Here are five decisions that the Sheffield City Council have recently made. I would like you to tell me how strongly you agree or disagree with each one by selecting one of the phrases on this card.

   i. that council house tenants should pay higher rents unless they prove that their income is low enough to entitle them to receive a rebate.

   ii. that all the secondary schools in the city should become comprehensive schools.

   iii. that all manual workers who work for the council must become members of a trade union.

   iv. that the council should not go ahead with the development of an airport close to Sheffield.

   v. that Sheffield should support its own local radio station.

Q. 27 a. (*Show card E again.*) Suppose you wanted to make an inquiry or complaint about any of these services, or any others, whom would you get in touch with *first* of all?

   b. And supposing you didn't get any satisfaction with person/office mentioned (at Q. 27a), would you get in touch with any other person? (If 'yes')—With whom would you get in touch?

Q. 28 a. Would you think of getting in touch with your local councillor?

   b. Why not?

Q. 29 a. If you *did* want to get in touch with your local councillor, how would you go about it? Where would you go, write to, or telephone?

   b. Do you happen to know where he/she lives?

Q. 30 a. Have you ever been in touch with a *local councillor* over any matters—either for help, advice or to complain about anything?

  b. What did you get in touch with him about?

Q. 31 a. Have you ever been in touch with your M.P. over any matters—either for help, advice or to complain about anything?

  b. What did you get in touch with him about?

Q. 32 a. Have you ever been in touch with the council or any council department over any matters—either for help, advice or to complain about anything?

  b. (If 'yes')—What was it about?

  c. What happened as a result?

Q. 33. Now, you probably know that local councillors represent various parts of the city, called wards. Do you happen to know the name of the ward in which you live? What is it?

Q. 34 a. Do you happen to know the names of any of the councillors for this ward? (If 'yes')—Can you tell me who they are?

  b. Which political party does he/she belong to?

Q. 35. Members of Parliament each represent constituencies throughout the country. Do you happen to know the name of the constituency in which you live? (If 'yes')—What is it?

Q. 36 a. Do you happen to know the name of your M.P.? (If 'yes')— Can you tell me what it is?

  b. Which political party does he/she represent?

Q. 37 a. Have you ever been interested in taking an active part in the running of local government?
  (If 'yes')—
   i. Have you ever stood for election as a local councillor?
   ii. Have you ever seriously thought about standing for election but not gone ahead with it?
   iii. Have you ever been co-opted to a council committee?
   iv. Have you ever been asked to stand for a local council but turned it down?

Q. 38. Would you say that either of your parents is or was *actively* interested in local politics?

Q. 39 a. Could you tell me where Sheffield Town Hall is situated?—I mean the precise location?

  b. During the past twelve months, how many times have you yourself been to the Sheffield Town Hall, for any reason?

Q. 40 a. Do you happen to know what is the rate in the pound for domestic property here in Sheffield this year?

  b. Has the rate altered since last year? (If 'yes')—In which way?

  c. (If 'lower this year')—How much lower than last year's is the rate this year?

Q. 41.   Do you know when the city boundaries of Sheffield were last altered? (If 'yes')—When?

Q. 42 a.   Do you think that Sheffield Council should take over all those areas outside the city boundaries where people live who regularly shop or work in Sheffield, or should those areas stay under their present local authorities?

     b.   Why do you think that?

Survey of Sheffield City Council

Q. 1 a.   Was your family associated with council work in Sheffield or in any other area before you became a councillor?

     b.   Was your family associated with council work in the ward you now ('used to' for aldermen) represent, the ward you now live in, or with another ward or area in Sheffield?

Q. 2 a.   Before you became a councillor were any of your friends associated with council work in Sheffield or any other area?

     b.   Were your friends associated with council work in the ward you now (used to) represent, the ward you now live in, or another ward or area in Sheffield?

Q. 3 a.   What proportion of your Sheffield friends live in the ward that you (used to) represent?

     b.   (If ward represented is different from the ward lived in)— What proportion of your Sheffield friends live in the ward you live in?

Q. 4 a.   Most councillors have activities apart from council and committee work. Could you tell me if you belong to, or spend time on any of these organizations? (*Show card.*)

     b.   Did you join it before or after becoming a councillor?

     c.   Did you *officially* represent the council on it?

     d.   How much time do you spend on all these organizations in an average month?

Q. 5 a.   Was it your connection with these kinds of activities before you became a councillor which first brought you into contact with people connected with council work?

     b.   Which ones?

     c.   (To all those answering 'No' at Q. 5a and to those who did not agree to belonging to an organization—How were you brought into touch with council work?

Q. 6 a.   When you first considered standing for council, was it your own idea or were you asked to do so by some person or organization?

     b.   Who asked you to stand?

Y

Q. 7.   How old were you when you were first asked to stand (or put
          yourself forward)?

Q. 8.   When you were making up your mind to stand, what was the
          main thing that influenced your decision?

Q. 9 a.   Were you elected to the council the first time you were
          nominated?

    b.   How many years was it after your first nomination that you
          were elected?

    c.   Did you contest any other elections during this period?

Q. 10.   How would you describe the attitude of the general public to
          the work of the council in this area?

Q. 11 a. (*Show card.*) Here are some of the matters with which the city
          council has been involved during the last year or two. I'd like
          you to tell me the three most important issues as they seem to
          you. Which would you put as the most important? And which
          second? And which third?

    b.   Are there any other matters or issues apart from those on the
          card that you think are important? Which are they?

    c.   In which of these fields do you think that the council has done
          the most to help people or improve things during 1967?

    d.   Is there one particular problem that you think will require a
          good deal of attention by the council in the next year or so?

Q. 12 a. Speaking for yourself, what are the main ways you get to
          know about the needs and about the attitudes of members of
          the public in Sheffield as a whole?

    b.   (If more than one)—Of the ones you have mentioned, which
          is the main way?

Q. 13 a. (For councillors only)—What are the main ways in which you
          keep informed about the needs and attitudes of the people in
          the ward you represent?

    b.   Of the ones you have mentioned, which is the main way?

Q. 14 a. (*Show booklet of mastheads.*)—Would you go through these local
          daily newspapers with me and tell me which, if any, of them
          you read regularly?

    b.   Repeat for weekly and other local newspapers.

Q. 15 a. During the last four weeks how many of the people in
          Sheffield have spoken to you or sent letters to you as a member
          of the council. (*Show card of possible ways.*)

    b.   (Ask councillors only)—Could you tell me what proportion of
          these people were from the ward you represent? For instance
          how many of the —— (insert number) . . . that called at your
          home were from that ward you represent.

c. (If home ward is different from the ward the councillor represents)—What proportion of these people were from the ward in which you live?

Q. 16 a. Have you had any contact with your local M.P.(s) about anything arising from your work as a city councillor since you were elected last May?

b. Could you tell me what sorts of things were discussed and how many times particular subjects cropped up.

c. Could you tell me if any of the subjects under discussion arose out of a complaint by a member of the public?

d. Were there matters other than council work about which you have had contact with your M.P.?

Q. 17 a. Do you usually have letters, telephone calls, or personal calls on behalf of groups or organizations interested in particular aspects of the council work you are doing?

b. So would you say that you had this sort of contact frequently, sometimes, rarely, never?

c. Could you tell me what sort of groups you have had this sort of contact with in the last six months and what this matter was about?

Q. 18 a. Has any group or organization volunteered information which has helped you form an opinion on a particular council matter?

b. (If 'yes')—Which groups? When? What matters?

Q. 19. Is there any organization or group whose opinions you generally take into account when forming your own opinion on a council matter? Which are they?

Q. 20 a. (All except Independent)—Does your party group on the council generally take into account the opinions of any other group or organization?

b. (If 'yes')—Which groups are these?

c. (All except Independent)—Does the party group take into account the opinions of certain groups when dealing with specific issues?

d. (If 'yes')—Could you give me one or two examples?

e. (All except Independent)—Does the Labour/Conservative group generally take into account the opinions of any other group or organization?

f. (If 'yes')—Which groups are these?

Q. 21 a. *Now I would like to ask a few questions on the nature of representation in local government:* Would you say that the public knows enough to make good use of existing services?

   b. Would you say that the public knows enough to get a
      balanced picture of the way the council conducts its affairs?
   c. Would you say that the public knows enough to vote in an
      informed way at local elections?
   d. (If 'no' at a, b, or c)—Do you think that this is because the
      information is not avilable or because they are not
      interested?

Q. 22 a. (Ask councillors only. If lives in the ward he represents)—
      You, yourself, live in the ward that you represent and you
      must know quite a lot about people in your ward, but do you
      think that your main job as a councillor is to represent ward
      members (predominantly) or to govern the city as a whole?
   b. (If does not live in the ward he represents)—Although you do
      not live in the ward you represent, you must know quite a lot
      about people in it. But do you think that your main job as a
      councillor is to represent ward members (predominantly) or
      to govern the city as a whole?

Q. 23 a. (Ask councillors only)—Do you find that sometimes the
      interests of the people in the ward you represent differ from
      the interests of the people of Sheffield as a whole?
   b. (If 'yes')—In what proportion of the issues coming before the
      council do you feel that this is the case?
   c. (If 'yes' at Q. 23 a)—Could you give me any examples of
      when there was a difference between the interest of your
      ward and that of the city?

Q. 24 a. Looking back on the time you have spent so far as a coun-
      cillor/alderman, what are the things that have given you
      most satisfaction?
   b. (If more than one)—Of the things that you have mentioned
      which one did you find most rewarding?

Q. 25 a. Could you tell me what are the things that you have found
      most frustrating or unsatisfactory as a councillor/alderman?
   b. (If more than one)—Of the things you have mentioned,
      which one did you find most unsatisfactory or frustrating?

Q. 26. Which of these two aspects of council work do you prefer:
      Making the broad policy decisions or dealing with the prob-
      lems of particular individuals?

Q. 27. Could you tell me how many council committees and sub-
      committees you serve on at the moment?

Q. 28 a. Could you give me an estimate of the time you spend in a
      month on committees or preparation work for council
      meetings?

b. Could you give me an estimate of the time you spend in a month in dealing with electors' individual problems?

Q. 29 a. Does your council need more powers of any sort than it now has?

b. (If 'yes')—For what purposes?

Q. 30 a. Do you think that the central government puts unnecessary limitations on the freedom of your council to act as it wants to?

b. (If 'yes')—In what way?

c. (If 'yes' at Q. 30 a)—Has the event of a Labour government made any difference here?

Q. 31 a. When considering new and developing needs of the people, councils sometimes leave it to voluntary organizations to develop the services required or they develop the services themselves: Does it seem to you that there are any advantages for councils in using voluntary organizations to meet people's needs?

b. (If 'yes')—What are the advantages?

c. (If 'yes' at Q. 31 a)—Are there any disadvantages?

d. (If 'yes' at Q. 31 c)—What are they?

Q. 32 a. So on the whole what do you think would be the best way to meet new and developing needs of people in Sheffield? Would it be best for:

    i. The council to provide all services?

    ii. The council to help voluntary organization to provide some services?

    iii. Voluntary services to meet most new needs?

    iv. Don't know.

b. For what kinds of services are voluntary organizations most suitable?

Q. 33 a. Now for this final section I should like to ask you about a number of issues with which the city council has been concerned recently: The first of the recent issues that I should like to ask you about is that of rent rebates. First of all what is your opinion on this issue briefly?

b. (If relevant)—So, if I were to ask you how you felt about the decision that council house tenants should pay higher rents unless they prove that their income is low enough to entitle them to receive a rebate, which of the phrases on this card most closely represent how you feel about the decision?

c. Could you tell me how you came to form your opinion?

d. What part have you taken in the discussions?

e. (*Ask councillors only, not aldermen.*) Could you tell me whether or not this issue played an important part in your ward in the elections in May of last year?

f. How do you think this issue will resolve itself in the future?

Q. 34 a. The question of comprehensive schools is the next issue I would like to ask you about. What is your opinion on this issue briefly?

b. (If relevant)—So if I was to ask you about the decision that all secondary schools in the city should become comprehensive schools, which of the phrases on the card most closely represents how you feel about the decision?

   i. Very strongly agree.

   ii. Quite strongly agree.

   iii. Neither agree nor disagree.

   iv. Quite strongly disagree.

   v. Very strongly disagree.

   vi. Don't know.

c. Could you tell me how you came to form your opinion?

d. What part have you taken in the discussions?

e. (*Ask councillors only, not aldermen.*) Could you tell me whether or not this issue played an important part in your ward in the elections of May of last year?

f. How do you think this issue will resolve itself in the future?

Q. 35 a. The question of a closed shop for manual workers employed by the council is the next issue I would like to ask you about. What briefly is your opinion on this issue?

b. (If relevant)—So if I was to ask you about the decision that all manual workers who work for the council must become members of a trade union, which one of the phrases on the card mostly closely represents how you feel about the decision?

   i. Very strongly agree.

   ii. Quite strongly agree.

   iii. Neither agree nor disagree.

   iv. Quite strongly disagree.

   v. Very strongly disagree.

   vi. Don't know.

c. Could you tell me how you came to form your opinion?

d. What part have you taken in the discussions?

e. (*Ask councillors only, not aldermen.*) Could you tell me whether or not this issue played an important part in your ward in the elections of May of last year?

f. How do you think this issue will resolve itself in the future?

Q. 36 a. The question of the development of an airport close to Sheffield is the next issue I would like to ask you about. What is your opinion on this issue briefly?

b. (If relevant)—So if I was to ask you about the decision that the council should not go ahead with the development of an airport close to Sheffield, which of the phrases on the card most closely represents how you feel about the decision?
   i. Very strongly agree.
   ii. Quite strongly agree.
   iii. Neither agree nor disagree.
   iv. Quite strongly disagree.
   v. Very strongly disagree.
   vi. Don't know.

c. Could you tell me how you came to form your opinion?

d. What part have you taken in the discussions?

e. (*Ask councillors only, not aldermen.*) Could you tell me whether or not this issue played an important part in your ward in the elections of May last year?

f. How do you think this issue will resolve itself in the future?

Q. 37 a. The question of Sheffield supporting its own local radio station is the last issue I would like to ask you about. Briefly what is your opinion on this issue?

b. (If relevant)—So if I was to ask you about the decision that Sheffield should support its own local radio station, which of the phrases on the card most closely represents how you feel about the decision?
   i. Very strongly agree.
   ii. Quite strongly agree.
   iii. Neither agree nor disagree.
   iv. Quite strongly disagree.
   v. Very strongly disagree.
   vi. Don't know.

c. Could you tell me how you came to form your opinion?

d. What part have you taken in the discussions?

e. (*Ask councillors only, not aldermen.*) Could you tell me whether or not this issue played an important part in your ward in the elections of May last year?

f. How do you think this issue will be resolved in the future?

Q. 38 a. Do you agree or disagree with the Maud Committee recommendation that the number of council committees should be considerably reduced?

b. Why do you think that?

Q. 39 a. Do you agree or disagree with the Maud Committee recommendation that councillors should leave the day-to-day running of affairs in the hands of local government officers and confine themselves to (broad) policy decisions?

b. Why do you think that?

Classification questions

Both the electorate and the councillors were asked the following questions:

1. Sex
2. Age
3. Marital status
4. Household composition
5. Position of informant in household
6. Employment situation (hours worked, etc.)
7. Job description (inf., inf.'s father, and head of household)
8. Net income
9. Education
10. Qualifications
11. Type of home accommodation

APPENDIX D

Membership of Sheffield City Council, 1967–8

SHEFFIELD CITY COUNCIL, 1967–8

Lord Mayor: Ald. H. Lambert, J.P.

Deputy Lord Mayor: Ald. L. S. Farris, J.P.

Aldermen:

S. K. Arnold
E. Bingham
S. I. Dyson
L. S. Farris
G. L. Fisher
H. K. Hawson
H. Hebblethwaite
C. R. Ironmonger
P. H. Jackson

P. C. T. J. Kirkman
H. Lambert
I. Lewis
J. W. Mate
D. J. O'Neil
J. P. Peile
H. Redgate
A. E. Richardson
Mrs. F. Roebuck

G. E. Salmons
E. Scott
M. J. Sewell
Mrs. P. Sheard
J. W. Sterland
Mrs. M. Strafford
J. Thorpe
A. V. Wolstenhome
J. S. Worrall

Councillors:

Attercliffe
N. Eldred
H. Firth
W. J. Robins

Burngreave
R. Ellis
J. V. Osborne
J. Pate

Gleadless
M. Atkinson
C. F. Davison
D. I. Heslop

Beauchief
F. W. Adams
G. E. A. Beardshaw
T. E. Crewe

Castle
P. Horton
G. R. Munn
R. E. Munn

Hallam
A. G. Blake
W. G. Walker
G. Wragg

Birley
Mrs. E. Richardson
Mrs. P. Minns
L. Stones

Darnall
F. R. Hattersley
W. Owen
A. Wood

Handsworth
L. Cope
G. Hutchinson
W. S. Hyde

Brightside
A. S. Longmore
H. Sturrock
G. C. E. Wilson

Dore
W. G. Blake
T. W. Lambert
Miss P. Santhouse

Heeley
P. R. W. Earl
J. T. Garlick
M. Swain

Broomhill
G. Cheetham
R. W. Hadfield
Mrs. M. Jackson

Ecclesall
A. McT. Cook
Miss E. S. Edeson
J. Neil

Hillsborough
Mrs. C. Dodson
B. Lee
C. I. Patnick

Intake
D. Johnson
M. H. Moore
F. H. Woodger

Nether Edge
J. I. H. Harrington
C. B. MacDonald
H. Mercer

Park
J. W. Ashton
D. H. Dunn
C. W. Knowles

Firth Park
J. D. S. Levick
T. Lowe
A. J. Oxley

Nether Shire
C. J. Moseley
C. Simms
F. Staton

Sharrow
C. R. Barnsley
Mrs. V. Boyd
D. Pinder

Manor
G. Armitage
Mrs. D. Fitter
G. Machin

Netherthorpe
Mrs. E. A. Hattersley
Mrs. D. Mulhearn
Mrs. M. E. Rodgers

Southey Green
A. Crosby
Mrs. W. M. Golding
F. M. O'Shaughnessy

Mosborough
Mrs. M. Foulds
Rev. C. Neild
Mrs. D. Walton

Owlerton
H. Bright
R. Thwaites
J. Yeardley

Walkley
L. P. Hesp
M. V. Roberts
J. A. Towns

Bibliography

The following sources have been used in the course of this study. The place of publication is London unless otherwise specified.

SHEFFIELD

Buckatzsch, E. J., 'Origins of Immigrants into Sheffield 1624–1799', *Economic History Review*, Vol. 2, No. 3 (1950)

Chapman, J. J., *The Royal Commission on Local Government in England: a Study of the Proposals for South Yorkshire, North Derbyshire and North Nottinghamshire* (Department of Urban and Regional Studies, Sheffield Polytechnic, 1969)

Freeman, A., *et al.*, *The Equipment of the Workers* (Allen and Unwin, 1919)

Furniss, J. M., *Fifty Years Municipal Record, 1843—1893* (Sheffield, William Townsend and Son, 1893)

Green, G., 'The Measurement of National and Local Factors in Elections', unpublished M. A. thesis (University of Sheffield, 1969)

Hampton, W. 'The Electoral Response to a Multi-vote Ballot', *Political Studies*, Vol. XVI, No. 2 (1968)

Hawson, H. K., *Sheffield: Growth of a City, 1893–1926* (Sheffield, Northend, 1968)

Hodges, M. W., and Smith, C. S., 'The Sheffield Estate', *Neighbourhood and Community* (Liverpool, University of Liverpool Press, 1954)

Linton, D. L., *Sheffield and its Region* (Sheffield, British Association for the Advancement of Science, 1956)

Lloyd, G. I. H., *The Cutlery Trades* (Longmans, 1913)

Mendelson, J., Owen, W., Pollard, S., and Thornes, V. M., *The Sheffield Trades and Labour Council, 1858–1958* (Sheffield, Sheffield Trades and Labour Council)

Pollard, S., *A History of Labour in Sheffield* (Liverpool, University of Liverpool Press, 1959)

Stainton, J. H., *The Making of Sheffield, 1865–1914* (Sheffield, E. Weston and Sons, 1924)

Walton, Mary, *A History of the Parish of Sharrow, Sheffield* (Sheffield, privately published, 1968)

Walton, Mary, *Sheffield: Its Story and Its Achievements* (Sheffield, The Sheffield Telegraph and Star, 1948)

Wickham, E. R., *Church and People in an Industrial City* (Lutterworth Press, 1957)

Population in Sheffield, 1086–1951 (Sheffield City Library: Local History Leaflet No. 2)

Sheffield Education Committee Reports, 1955–7 and 1957–9

'A Regional Airport for Yorkshire and the North East', Yorkshire Airport Development Association (1964)

'Report to the Town Clerk of Sheffield in Support of a Request for Airstrip Facilities for the City of Sheffield', The Sheffield Chamber of Commerce (1964)

'The Commercial Prospects for an Airport for the City of Sheffield', Alan Stratford and Associates (1967)

'Report on Proposed Development of Sheffield (Todwick) Airport', Sir Frederick Snow and Partners (1967)

Housing Finance in Sheffield (Sheffield Corporation, 1966)

Report on Sheffield County Borough Council by Urwick, Orr, and Partners, Limited (1968)

Derbyshire Times

Sheffield Forward (Official journal of the Sheffield Trades and Labour Council)

Sheffield Telegraph (title changed to *Morning Telegraph*, 15 September 1965)

Sheffield Year Books (Sheffield Telegraph and Star, Ltd.)

The Star (Sheffield)

Walkley Action Group, *Newsletter*

GOVERNMENT

Commission of Inquiry into Large Towns and Populous Districts, 1844 and 1845

Sheffield Corporation Act, 1920 (10 and 11 Geo. V, c. xcii)

Education Act, 1944 (7 and 8 Geo. VI, c. 31)

Housing Subsidies Act, 1956 (4 and 5 Eliz. II, c. 33)

Ministry of Housing and Local Government Circular, 29/56 (1956)

Royal Commission on Local Government in Greater London, 1957–60, *Report*, Cmnd. 1164 (H.M.S.O. 1960)

Sheffield Police Appeal Inquiry, Cmnd. 2176 (H.M.S.O. 1963)

The Housing Programme 1965–70, Cmnd. 2838 (H.M.S.O. 1965)

Committee on the Management of Local Government (H.M.S.O. 1967)
Vol. I *Report*

Vol. II *The Local Government Councillor*
Vol. III *The Local Government Elector*
Vol. IV *Local Government Administration Abroad*
Vol. V *Local Government Administration in England and Wales*
Housing Subsidies Act, 1967 (Ch. 29)
'Rent Rebate Schemes', Ministry of Housing and Local Government
   Circular, 46/67 (1967)
Report on Children and their Primary Schools, Central Advisory Council on
   Education (England), (H.M.S.O. 1967)
Town and Country Planning Act, 1968
National Board for Prices and Incomes, Report No. 62, *Increases in Rents
   of Local Authority Housing*, Cmnd. 3604 (H.M.S.O. 1968)
Committee on Local Authority and Allied Personal Social Services,
   Report, Cmnd. 3703 (H.M.S.O. 1968)
Royal Commission on Local Government in England, 1966-9
   (H.M.S.O. 1969)
   Vol. I *Report* (Cmnd. 4040)
   Vol. II *Memorandum of Dissent by Mr. D. Senior* (Cmnd. 4040-I)
   Vol. III *Research Appendices* (Cmnd. 4040-II)
   Research Studies:
      1. *Local Government in South-East England*
      2. *The Lessons of the London Government Reforms*
      3. *Economies of Scale in Local Government Services*
      4. *Performance and Size of Local Education Authorities*
      5. *Local Authority Services and the Characteristics of Administrative Areas*
      6. *School Management and Government*
      7. *Aspects of Administration in a Large Local Authority*
      8. *The Inner London Education Authority. A Study of Divisional Adminis-
         tration*
      9. *Community Attitudes Survey: England*
     10. *Administration in a Large Local Authority. A comparison with other
         County Boroughs.*
People and Planning, Report of the Committee on Public Participation in
   Planning (H.M.S.O. 1969)
Reform of Local Government in England, Cmnd. 4276 (H.M.S.O. 1970)

GENERAL

Almond, G. A., and Verba, S., *The Civic Culture* (Princeton, New Jersey,
   Princeton University Press, 1963)
Barnett, Malcolm Joel, *The Politics of Legislation: the Rent Act of 1957*
   (Weidenfeld & Nicolson, 1969)
Bealey, F., Blondel, J., and McCann, W. P., *Constituency Politics* (Faber
   and Faber, 1965)

Benewick, R. J., Birch, A. H., Blumler, J. G., and Ewbank, Alison, 'The Floating Voter and the Liberal View of Representation', *Political Studies*, Vol. XVII, No. 2 (1969)

Benney, M., Gray, A. P., and Pear, R. H., *How People Vote* (Routledge and Kegan Paul, 1956)

Berrington, H. B., 'The General Election of 1964' (with discussion), *Journal of the Royal Statistical Society*, Vol. CXXVIII (1965)

Blalock, M., *Social Statistics* (New York, McGraw-Hill, 1960)

Birch, A. H., *The British System of Government* (Allen and Unwin, 1967)

Birch, A. H., *Small-Town Politics* (O.U.P. 1959)

Budge, I., 'Electors' Attitudes towards Local Government: A Survey of a Glasgow Constituency', *Political Studies*, Vol. XIII, No. 3 (1965)

Bulpitt, J. G., *Party Politics in English Local Government* (Longmans, 1967)

Butler, D., and King, A., *The British General Election of 1966* (Macmillan, 1966)

Butler, D., and Stokes, D., *Political Change in Britain* (Macmillan, 1969)

Cole, G. D. H., 'Democracy Face to Face with Hugeness,' reprinted in *Essays in Social Theory* (Oldbourne, 1962)

Crick, B., and Green, G., 'People and Planning', *New Society*, No. 310 (5 September 1968)

Disraeli, B., *Coningsby* (Longmans, 1844)

Dowse, R. E., 'The M.P. and His Surgery', *Political Studies*, Vol. XI, No. 3 (1963)

Frankenberg, R., *Communities in Britain* (Penguin Books, 1965)

Goldthorpe, J. H., Lockwood, D., Bechhofer, F., and Platt, Jennifer, *The Affluent Worker: Political Attitudes and Behaviour* (C.U.P. 1968)

Green, B. S. R., 'Community Decision-Making in Georgian City', unpublished Ph.D. thesis, University of Bath (1968)

Gregory, R., 'Local Elections and the "Rule of Anticipated Reactions"', *Political Studies*, Vol. XVII, No. 1 (1969)

Hampton, W., 'The County as a Political Unit', *Parliamentary Affairs*, Vol. XIX, No. 4 (1966)

Hampton, W., 'Local Government and Community', *Political Quarterly*, Vol. 40, No. 2 (April–June 1969)

Harrison, M., *The Trade Unions and the Labour Party since 1945* (Allen and Unwin, 1960)

Hayek, F. A., *The Road to Serfdom* (Routledge and Kegan Paul, 1962)

Hill, Dilys M., 'Democracy in Local Government: A Study in Participation and Communication', unpublished Ph.D. thesis, Leeds, 1966

Hobhouse, L. T., *Social Development* (Allen and Unwin, 1924)

Hodge, P., 'The Future of Community Development,' in Robson, W. A., and Crick, B. (eds.), *The Future of the Social Services* (Penguin Books for *Political Quarterly*, 1970)

Jones, G. W., *Borough Politics* (Macmillan, 1969)

King, A., 'Why All Governments Lose By-Elections', *New Society* (21 March 1968)

König, René, *The Community* (Routledge and Kegan Paul, 1968)

Lapping, Anne, 'Social Action', *New Society*, No. 327 (2 January 1969)

Lawrence, D. H., *Lady Chatterley's Lover* (Penguin Books, 1960)

Lawrence, D. H. 'Nottingham and the Mining Country', *Selected Essays* (Penguin Books, 1954)

Lawson, N., 'A New Theory of By-elections', *The Spectator* (8 November 1968)

Lee, J. M., *Social Leaders and Public Persons* (O.U.P. 1963)

Lipset, S. M., *Political Man* (Mercury Books, 1963)

MacIver, R. M., *Community: a Sociological Study* (Macmillan, 1924)

McKenzie, R., *British Political Parties* (Mercury Books, 2nd edn., 1964)

McKenzie, R., and Silver, A., *Angels in Marble* (Heinemann, 1968)

Michels, R., *Political Parties* (Collier Books, 1962)

Mill, J. S., *Representative Government* (Everyman edn., 1910)

Miller, D. C., 'Industry and Community Power Structure: A Comparative Study of an American and an English City'. *American Sociological Review*, Vol. XXIII (1958)

Morris, D. S., and Newton, K., 'Profile of a Local Political Elite: Businessmen on Birmingham Council, 1920–66', University of Birmingham, Faculty of Commerce and Social Science, Discussion Papers, Series F, No. 6 (1969)

Morris-Jones, W. H., 'In Defence of Political Apathy', *Political Studies*, Vol. II, No. 1 (1954)

Newton, K., 'City Politics in Britain and the United States', *Political Studies*, Vol. XVII, 2 (1969)

Nordlinger, E. A., *The Working Class Tories* (MacGibbon and Kee, 1967)

Parkin, F., 'Working-class Conservatives: a Theory of Political Deviance', *British Journal of Sociology*, Vol. XVIII (1967)

Pulzer, P. J., *Political Representation and Elections in Britain* (Allen and Unwin, 1967)

Rasmussen, J., 'The Disutility of the Swing Concept in British Psephology', *Parliamentary Affairs*, Vol. XVIII (1964–5)

Redlich, J., and Hirst, F. W., *Local Government in England* (Macmillan, 1903)

Rousseau, J.-J., *The Social Contract* (Penguin Books, 1968)

Runciman, W. G., *Relative Deprivation and Social Justice* (Routledge and Kegan Paul, 1966)

Senior, D., 'The City Region as an Administrative Unit', *Political Quarterly*, Vol. 36, No. 1 (1965)

Senior, D. (ed.), *The Regional City* (Longmans, 1966)

Sharpe, L. J., 'Elected Representatives in Local Government', *British Journal of Sociology*, Vol. XIII, No. 3 (1962)

Sharpe, L. J., 'Leadership and Representation in Local Government', *Political Quarterly*, Vol. XXXVII, No. 2 (1966)

Sharpe, L. J. (ed.), *Voting in Cities* (Macmillan, 1967)

Smith, G., (ed.), *The Brave New World of Redcliffe-Maud* (Charles Knight and Co., Ltd., 1969)

Stacey, Margaret, *Tradition and Change* (O.U.P. 1960)

Tocqueville, A. de, *Democracy in America* (O.U.P. World's Classics edn., 1946)

Walkland, S. A., *The Legislative Process in Great Britain* (Allen and Unwin, 1968)

Whitaker, B., 'Tentative Steps towards an Anti-Poverty Programme', *The Times* (24 July 1969)

Willmott, P., and Young, M., *Family and Class in a London Suburb* (Mentor Books, 1967)

Young, M. and Willmott, P., *Family and Kinship in East London* (Penguin Books, 1962)

Community Work and Social Change, Report of a Study Group on Training set up by the Calouste Gulbenkian Foundation (Longmans, 1968)

Labour Party Research Department, Information Paper No. 56 (1967)

Signposts for the Sixties (Labour Party, 1961)

The Times House of Commons Reports

Index

This index should be used in conjunction with the lists of tables and of diagrams. References to other studies are indexed if they occur in the text, but not if they occur in a footnote only.